Accessible. Powerful. Urgently needed. In a time marked by escalating misinformation, political attacks, and systemic harm targeting trans communities, this new edition offers a clear, evidence-based road map for clinicians, educators, advocates, and families committed to protecting and affirming trans and gender diverse youth. Grounded in the latest research and rich in clinical implications, this second edition of *Pediatric Gender Health Care* powerfully demonstrates what justice-centered, developmentally responsive, and strength-based care for trans and gender diverse youth looks like in real-world practice.

—**Roberto L. Abreu, PhD,** Associate Professor, Psychology Department, University of Florida, Gainesville

This is a critical compendium on pediatric gender health care written by many of the world's foremost experts in the area. I recommend this book to any and all clinicians and clinicians-in-training working with gender diverse youth.

—**Kristina R. Olson, PhD,** Professor of Psychology, Princeton University, Princeton, NJ

If you work with, advocate for, or care about gender diverse children and adolescents, this book belongs on your shelf. This timely and thoroughly updated edition covers empirically-grounded best practices for working with gender diverse youth, complete with rich case examples and a strong framework of cultural humility and intersectionality.

—**Diane Chen, PhD, ABPP,** Professor of Psychiatry & Behavioral Sciences, Pediatrics, and Medical Social Sciences, Ann & Robert H. Lurie Children's Hospital of Chicago/ Northwestern University Feinberg School of Medicine, Chicago, IL; Fellow of the American Psychological Association

This book masterfully blends clinical expertise, rigorous research, and community perspectives to offer an indispensable, grounded guide for clinicians supporting trans and nonbinary children and their families across diverse contexts. It will quickly become the go-to recommendation for providers at every level of experience.

—**Sebastian Barr, PhD,** licensed psychologist; coauthor of *Transness Is Our Salve: Trans People's Experiences of Healing From Parental Trauma*

Once again, these authors have compiled an ideally crafted compilation of topics covering every area of pediatric gender care. The depth and breadth of clinical information makes this book a perfect resource to use for a college course, and the contemporary relevance makes it a must-have for every professional's desktop. This is an indispensable book for all professionals who want the best science, research, and references at this important time.

—**Linda A. Hawkins, PhD, MSEd, LPC,** Director, LGBTQ+ Policy & Practice, Children's Hospital of Philadelphia, Philadelphia, PA

Authored by pioneering leaders in the field, this book offers a rigorous, evidence-based guide to supporting transgender and gender diverse youth. During a time of widespread misinformation, it is an essential resource for clinicians, researchers, and anyone wanting to better understand and support today's youth.

—**Jack Turban, MD, MHS,** author of *Free to Be: Understanding Kids & Gender Identity*

PEDIATRIC GENDER HEALTH CARE

Perspectives on Sexual Orientation and Gender Diversity

David P. Rivera, Series Editor

Affirmative Counseling and Psychological Practice With Trans and Nonbinary Clients, Second Edition
Edited by Anneliese Singh and Rafe McCullough

Affirmative Counseling and Psychological Practice With Transgender and Gender Nonconforming Clients
Edited by Anneliese Singh and lore m. dickey

Affirming LGBTQ+ Students in Higher Education
Edited by David P. Rivera, Roberto L. Abreu, and Kirsten A. Gonzalez

Dismantling Everyday Discrimination: Microaggressions Toward LGBTQ People, Second Edition
Kevin Leo Yabut Nadal

The Gender Affirmative Model: An Interdisciplinary Approach to Supporting Transgender and Gender Expansive Children
Edited by Colt Keo-Meier and Diane Ehrensaft

HIV+ Sex: The Psychological and Interpersonal Dynamics of HIV-Seropositive Gay and Bisexual Men's Relationships
Edited by Perry N. Halkitis, Cynthia A. Gómez, and Richard J. Wolitski

Lesbian and Gay Parents and Their Children: Research on the Family Life Cycle
Abbie E. Goldberg

LGBTQ Mental Health: International Perspectives and Experiences
Edited by Nadine Nakamura and Carmen H. Logie

Pediatric Gender Health Care: The Gender Affirmative Model Revisited, Second Edition
Edited by G. Nic Rider, Diane Ehrensaft, and Colt St. Amand

Supporting Gender Identity and Sexual Orientation Diversity in K–12 Schools
Edited by Megan C. Lytle and Richard A. Sprott

Teaching LGBTQ Psychology: Queering Innovative Pedagogy and Practice
Edited by Theodore R. Burnes and Jeanne L. Stanley

That's So Gay! Microaggressions and the Lesbian, Gay, Bisexual, and Transgender Community
Kevin L. Nadal

The

Gender Affirmative Model

Revisited

PEDIATRIC GENDER HEALTH CARE

Edited by

G. Nic Rider · Diane Ehrensaft · Colt St. Amand

SECOND EDITION

AMERICAN PSYCHOLOGICAL ASSOCIATION

Published by
American Psychological Association
750 First Street, NE
Washington, DC 20002
https://www.apa.org

Order Department
https://www.apa.org/pubs/books
order@apa.org

Typeset in Charter and Interstate by Circle Graphics, Inc., Reisterstown, MD

Cover Designer: Anthony Paular Design, Newbury Park, CA

Library of Congress Cataloging-in-Publication Data

Names: Rider, G. Nic, 1983- editor | Ehrensaft, Diane editor | St. Amand, Colt editor
Title: Pediatric gender health care : the gender affirmative model revisited / edited by G. Nic Rider, Diane Ehrensaft, and Colt St. Amand.

Other titles: Gender affirmative model
Description: Second edition. | Washington, DC : American Psychological Association, [2026] | Series: Perspectives on sexual orientation and gender diversity series | Includes bibliographical references and index.
Identifiers: LCCN 2026013455 (print) | LCCN 2026013456 (ebook) | ISBN 9781433844010 paperback | ISBN 9781433844027 epub | ISBN 9781433851483 pdf
Subjects: LCSH: Gender dysphoria in children | Gender dysphoria in children--Treatment | Gender dysphoria in adolescence | Gender dysphoria in adolescence--Treatment | Trans children--Mental health services | Trans youth--Mental health services | BISAC: PSYCHOLOGY / Psychotherapy / Child & Adolescent
Classification: LCC RJ506.G35 P44 2026 (print) | LCC RJ506.G35 (ebook)
LC record available at https://lccn.loc.gov/2026013455
LC ebook record available at https://lccn.loc.gov/2026013456

https://doi.org/10.1037/0000494-000

Printed in the United States of America

10 9 8 7 6 5 4 3 2 1

Contents

Contributors

Kellan Baker, PhD, MPH, MA, (he/him), Movement Advancement Project, Boulder, CO, United States; Department of Health Policy and Management, Johns Hopkins Bloomberg School of Public Health, Baltimore, MD, United States

Karisa L. Barrow, PsyD, (she/her), inMind Care, Oakland, CA, United States

Dianne Berg, PhD, (she/her), National Center for Gender Health, Eli Coleman Institute for Sexual and Gender Health, Department of Family Medicine and Community Health, University of Minnesota Medical School, Minneapolis, MN, United States

Jessica M. Bernacki, PhD, (she/her), University of California Los Angeles (UCLA) Medicine-Pediatrics, Division of General Internal Medicine & Health Services Research, Department of Medicine, David Geffen School of Medicine at UCLA, Los Angeles, CA, United States

Drew B. A. Clark, PhD, HEC-C, RCC, School of Nursing, The University of British Columbia; Ethics Service, Provincial Health Services Authority, Vancouver, BC, Canada

Jessie Rose Cohen, AM, LCSW, (they/them), Department of Pediatric Social Work, University of California San Francisco; UCSF Benioff Children's Hospital, San Francisco, CA, United States

Deb Coolhart, PhD, LMFT, (she/her), Syracuse University, Syracuse, NY, United States

Inclusion of pronouns in this list of contributors was voluntary. If pronouns are not included, they should not be assumed.

Claire Coyne, PhD, (she/her), Ann & Robert H. Lurie Children's Hospital of Chicago; Northwestern University Feinberg School of Medicine, Chicago, IL, United States

Catelyn G. Devlin, MSSW, (she/her), Texas LGBTQ+ Child Welfare Workgroup, Newton, MA, United States

Diane Ehrensaft, PhD, (she/her), Department of Pediatrics, University of California San Francisco; Child and Adolescent Gender Center, UCSF Benioff Children's Hospital, San Francisco, CA, United States

Molly Ober Fechter-Leggett, PsyD, (she/they), independent consultant and clinical psychologist, Burlington, VT, United States

Shawn V. Giammattei, PhD, (he/him/his), Gender Health Training Institute, Santa Rosa, CA, United States; Department of Pediatrics, UCSF Benioff Children's Hospital, San Francisco, CA

Elizabeth Glaeser, PhD, (she/her/hers), Transgender Youth Health Program, Gender and Sexuality Service, NYU Child Study Center; Department of Adolescent and Child Psychiatry, Hassenfeld Children's Hospital at NYU Langone, New York, NY, United States

Matthew Ethan Goldenberg, PsyD, (he/him), Seattle Children's Hospital, Adolescent Medicine, Seattle, WA, United States

Braylen Jack, BS, (he/they), New Pride Agenda and Riverside Family Medicine, New York, NY, United States

Derrick T. Jordan, LCSW, MDiv, MS, (he/him), independent psychotherapist and consultant, New York, NY, United States

Laura Kuper, PhD, ABPP, (they/them), Division of Psychiatry, University of Texas Southwestern Medical Center, Dallas, TX, United States

Jean Malpas, LMFT-D, LMHC-D, (he/him), JEM Therapy, independent practice, New York, NY, United States

Sara A. Mar, MPH, (they/them), The Institute for Health Research & Policy at Whitman-Walker, Washington, DC, United States

Mak Morin, LCAT, (they/them), supervising clinician and psychotherapist, private group practice, New York, NY, United States

AndreAs Neumann-Mascis, PhD, (he/him), The Meeting Point, Jamaica Plain, MA, United States

Aydin Olson-Kennedy, DSW, LCSW, (he/him), private practice, Los Angeles, CA, United States

Johanna Olson-Kennedy, MD, Director, Prosilio Care, Pasadena, CA, United States

Elizabeth Panetta, MSW, LICSW, (they/she), National Center for Gender Health, Eli Coleman Institute for Sexual and Gender Health, Department of Family Medicine and Community Health, University of Minnesota Medical School, Minneapolis, MN, United States

Benjamin Parchem, PhD, (he/him), Ann & Robert H. Lurie Children's Hospital of Chicago; Northwestern University Feinberg School of Medicine, Chicago, IL, United States

Jonathan Poquiz, PhD, (he/him), National Center for Gender Health, Eli Coleman Institute for Sexual and Gender Health, Department of Family Medicine and Community Health, University of Minnesota Medical School, Minneapolis, MN, United States

G. Nic Rider, PhD, LP, (they/them), National Center for Gender Health, Eli Coleman Institute for Sexual and Gender Health, Department of Family Medicine and Community Health, University of Minnesota Medical School, Minneapolis, MN, United States

Catherine Schaefer, MS, (they/she), National Center for Gender Health, Eli Coleman Institute for Sexual and Gender Health, Department of Family Medicine and Community Health, University of Minnesota Medical School, Minneapolis, MN, United States

Kayden J. Schumacher, PhD, (they/he), Coventry University, Coventry, United Kingdom

Colt St. Amand, PhD, MD, (he/they), Founder and Medicine Bearer, Riverside Family Medicine, Oneonta, NY, United States

Darlene Tando, LCSW, (she/her), Tando Therapy Team, San Diego, CA, United States

De'Shay Thomas, PhD, MSW, LGSW, (she/her), University of Minnesota Physicians, Minneapolis, MN, United States

Amy Tishelman, PhD, (she/her), Boston College, Chestnut Hill, MA, United States

PEDIATRIC GENDER HEALTH CARE

INTRODUCTION

Honoring and Not Dulling the Light of the Youngest Among Us

G. NIC RIDER, DIANE EHRENSAFT, AND COLT ST. AMAND

To say much has changed since the publication of the first edition of this book in 2018 (*The Gender Affirmative Model: An Interdisciplinary Approach to Supporting Transgender and Gender Expansive Children*; Keo-Meier & Ehrensaft, 2018) would be an understatement. There has been an unprecedented amount of interest in the topic of gender health, particularly in children and adolescents, across the globe. The gender affirmative model (GAM; Hidalgo et al., 2013; Keo-Meier & Ehrensaft, 2018) has become the leading model of care for transgender, nonbinary, and gender diverse people and has a large evidence base supporting the work of professionals who provide care in line with the theoretical bases of the GAM. Since 2018, we have seen a devastating increase in legislative attacks and harmful rhetoric toward transgender and gender diverse (TGD) youth and the weaponization of gender-affirming terminology. Major media outlets continue to cover stories featuring TGD children and adolescents, but those accounts are often riddled with misinformation and disinformation (Billard, 2024; McNamara et al., 2022).

Several professional organizations, including the American Academy of Pediatrics (Rafferty et al., 2018), the American Medical Association (2021),

https://doi.org/10.1037/0000494-001
Pediatric Gender Health Care: The Gender Affirmative Model Revisited, Second Edition, G. N. Rider, D. Ehrensaft, and C. St. Amand (Editors)

the American Psychiatric Association (2020, 2025), and the American Psychological Association (2024), have issued statements in support of TGD gender health care. At the same time, an organized political effort to deny access to gender health care has succeeded in banning or limiting access to gender health care for TGD youth in 28 U.S. states, as of July 2025 (Dawson & Kates, n.d.). Thus, the need to prepare mental health professionals and professionals from all disciplines who work with children and families has never been more dire.

The World Professional Association for Transgender Health (WPATH) recently published version 8 of the Standards of Care for the Health of Transgender and Gender Diverse People, which addresses treatment of children and adolescents (Coleman et al., 2022). The chapter on children in the latest WPATH guidelines cites the first edition of this book (Keo-Meier & Ehrensaft, 2018). Despite the proliferation of pediatric transgender health research in recent years and even in the time since the first edition of this book was published, treatment of prepubertal children continues to be a topic of great controversy. This is a particularly glaring problem because research has indicated that social support of children in their gender development is directly correlated with positive mental health outcomes for children (e.g., Durwood et al., 2021; Grossman et al., 2021; Simons et al., 2013). This edition will continue to address this concern in our field, present up-to-date scholarship on the GAM, and describe the evolution of the model, which we posit continues to be best practice for children and youth in their gender development.

With the increase in political attacks on access to gender health care for TGD youth, many outpatient clinics that specialize in working with this group of children have closed (e.g., the GENECIS Clinic at Texas Children's Hospital and the gender program at Children's Hospital Los Angeles), even though referral numbers continue to increase (Kim et al., 2025). Graduate students and practitioners alike in counseling, health, and education programs continue to report that they are not adequately prepared to meet the needs of TGD youth (Carroll, 2010; Corliss et al., 2007; Gonzalez & McNulty, 2010; Knudson et al., 2023; Obedin-Maliver et al., 2011; Rider et al., 2019). Even programs that include training for professionals who provide care to lesbian, gay, bisexual, transgender, and queer or questioning (LGBTQ+) individuals either only briefly comment on or completely exclude the topic of transgender issues. When transgender health is included, the experiences of adults who transition after puberty are typically discussed, and prepubertal children may not be mentioned at all (Carroll, 2010; Case et al., 2009). Because gender identity develops as early as age 3 years (Ehrensaft, 2016), access to information about how to work with TGD children is essential for professionals who work with young children (Gonzalez & McNulty, 2010).

A NEW EDITION

The prior edition of this book (Keo-Meier & Ehrensaft, 2018) was the first of its kind representing the expertise of several gender specialists in the field, and it served as a substantive guide to inform interdisciplinary clinical work with prepubertal children using the GAM as the predominant framework. It laid the groundwork for further dialogue on and research into incorporating and developing evidence-based practice for working with TGD children and their families.

Given the substantive developments and advancements in the care of TGD people of all ages, we posit that *gender health* is now an entire field of study and practice. Thus, the second edition incorporates this broad term, as reflected in the new title (*Pediatric Gender Health Care: The Gender Affirmative Model Revisited*), and we aim to improve pediatric gender health. At this point in time, efforts to improve gender health are inherently affirming, supporting an individual's gender development within their culture and context; in this way, we view the term *gender affirmative care* as redundant. Further, as more professionals of lived experience shape the field, the need for attention to social and structural power dynamics has become increasingly apparent.

In this edition, the GAM will be supplemented with frameworks and concepts such as intersectionality (Bowleg, 2012; Crenshaw, 1991), cultural humility (Tervalon & Murray-García, 1998), trauma-informed care (Butler et al., 2011), and gender embodiment (DuBois et al., 2022; Hastings et al., 2021). Additional chapters and content are included that focus on the ethical basis of providing pediatric gender health care, interventions to use when working with children, and advocacy given the recent restrictions on gender care. Although several authors from the first edition returned for this volume, the editors were intentional in their efforts to include more TGD authors from disciplines relevant to the field of gender health.

Whereas the first edition of this volume presented an affirming model of therapy for clinicians to use with TGD children and their families, this edition incorporates an intersectional lens to improve gender health in children and their families. We also highlight the GAM as one of the foundational frameworks to inform the field of gender health and guide interdisciplinary collaborative practice to address medical, psychosocial, educational, legal, and ethical matters pertaining to the gender health of children.

OVERVIEW OF THIS BOOK

We have had the privilege of working with an expanded group of experts from coast to coast in the United States and beyond to bring this volume together. Some of us are transgender ourselves, some have raised TGD children, some have had TGD partners, and all of us have been touched by the lives of TGD people around us. We lecture, educate, write, advocate, build a professional community, and conduct research on the lives of TGD people who have been our greatest teachers.

Each of the following chapters is designed to be its own independent learning module about psychological, social, and community issues as we get in clearer focus of the infinite variety and rapidly growing population of TGD children. Chapters 1 through 7 focus on child gender development, psychotherapy, and fostering resilience. These chapters guide a reader through what is currently understood about gender development, describe the importance of collaborative interdisciplinary care coordination, increase consciousness about intersectional issues that TGD children and their families face, emphasize resilience and empowerment in mental health care, and discuss trauma-informed practice. Chapter 8 details a strengths-based comprehensive assessment process with TGD children and their families. Chapter 9 centers on family therapy and helping family members move toward greater attunement with regard to a child's gender. Chapter 10 covers the interdisciplinary and collaborative nature of GAM providers in their pediatric gender health care. Chapter 11 focuses on the current sociopolitical climate for gender health care, particularly for children and youth, and considerations for advocacy. Chapter 12 brings the reader through ethical concepts relevant to gender health care for children and their families, ethical reasoning, and strategies for ethically navigating constraints on practice.

OUR FUTURE GENERATIONS

When we think about future generations, we often think about children as well as our children's children and perhaps their children too. We want to work toward a better world for them and continue the pathways and strength from those who came before us. When we think about children, it is not uncommon for images of movement, singing, laughter, play, curiosity, and joy to come to mind. The familiar saying, "we take care of each other," is more salient now than ever. Everyone has a role—even the youngest among us—in our collective well-being. The update and continuation of this book is an organized effort to honor and not dull the light of the youngest among us.

REFERENCES

American Medical Association. (2021). *AMA reinforces opposition to restrictions on transgender medical care*. https://www.ama-assn.org/press-center/press-releases/ama-reinforces-opposition-restrictions-transgender-medical-care

American Psychiatric Association. (2020). *Position statement on treatment of transgender (trans) and gender diverse youth*. https://img1.wsimg.com/blobby/go/07e14cc0-12d9-49d2-9d91-e13208928839/downloads/Position-Treatment-of-Transgender-Gender-Diver.pdf?ver=1774319065667

American Psychiatric Association. (2025). *Position statement on gender-affirming care for transgender youth*. https://www.psychiatry.org/getattachment/8665a2f2-0b73-4477-8f60-79015ba9f815/Position-Treatment-of-Transgender-Gender-Diverse-Youth.pdf

American Psychological Association. (2024). *APA policy statement on affirming evidence-based inclusive care for transgender, gender diverse, and nonbinary individuals, addressing misinformation, and the role of psychological practice and science*. https://www.apa.org/about/policy/transgender-nonbinary-inclusive-care

Billard, T. J. (2024). The politics of transgender health misinformation. *Political Communication*, *41*(2), 344–352. https://doi.org/10.1080/10584609.2024.2303148

Bowleg, L. (2012, July). The problem with the phrase women and minorities: Intersectionality—An important theoretical framework for public health. *American Journal of Public Health*, *102*(7), 1267–1273. https://doi.org/10.2105/AJPH.2012.300750

Butler, L. D., Critelli, F. M., & Rinfrette, E. S. (2011). Trauma-informed care and mental health. *Directions in Psychiatry*, *31*(3), 197–212.

Carroll, L. (2010). *Counseling sexual and gender minorities*. Merrill/Pearson Education.

Case, K. A., Stewart, B., & Tittsworth, J. (2009). Transgender across the curriculum: A psychology for inclusion. *Teaching of Psychology*, *36*(2), 117–121. https://doi.org/10.1080/00986280902739446

Coleman, E., Radix, A. E., Bouman, W. P., Brown, G. R., De Vries, A. L., Deutsch, M. B., Ettner, R., Fraser, L., Goodman, M., Green, J., Hancock, A. B., Johnson, T. W., Karasic, D. H., Knudson, G. A., Leibowitz, S. F., Meyer-Bahlburg, H. F. L., Monstrey, S. J., Motmans, J., Nahata, L., . . . Arcelus, J. (2022). Standards of care for the health of transgender and gender diverse people, version 8. *International Journal of Transgender Health*, *23*(Suppl. 1), S1–S259. https://doi.org/10.1080/26895269.2022.2100644

Corliss, H. L., Shankle, M. D., & Moyer, M. B. (2007). Research, curricula, and resources related to lesbian, gay, bisexual, and transgender health in U.S. schools of public health. *American Journal of Public Health*, *97*(6), 1023–1027. https://doi.org/10.2105/AJPH.2006.086157

Crenshaw, K. (1991). Mapping the margins: Intersectionality, identity politics, and violence against women of color. *Stanford Law Review*, *43*(6), 1241–1299. https://doi.org/10.2307/1229039

Dawson, L., & Kates, J. (n.d.). *Policy tracker: Youth access to gender affirming care and state policy restrictions*. KFF. https://www.kff.org/other/dashboard/gender-affirming-care-policy-tracker/

DuBois, L. Z., Puckett, J. A., & Langer, S. J. (2022). Development of the gender embodiment scale: Trans masculine spectrum. *Transgender Health, 7*(4), 287–291. https://doi.org/10.1089/trgh.2020.0088

Durwood, L., Eisner, L., Fladeboe, K., Ji, C. G., Barney, S., McLaughlin, K. A., & Olson, K. R. (2021). Social support and internalizing psychopathology in transgender youth. *Journal of Youth and Adolescence, 50*(5), 841–854. https://doi.org/10.1007/s10964-020-01391-y

Ehrensaft, D. (2016). *The gender creative child: Pathways for nurturing and supporting children who live outside gender boxes*. The Experiment.

Gonzalez, M., & McNulty, J. (2010). Achieving competency with transgender youth: School counselors as collaborative advocates. *Journal of LGBT Issues in Counseling, 4*(3–4), 176–186. https://doi.org/10.1080/15538605.2010.524841

Grossman, A. H., Park, J. Y., Frank, J. A., & Russell, S. T. (2021). Parental responses to transgender and gender nonconforming youth: Associations with parent support, parental abuse, and youths' psychological adjustment. *Journal of Homosexuality, 68*(8), 1260–1277. https://doi.org/10.1080/00918369.2019.1696103

Hastings, J., Bobb, C., Wolfe, M., Amaro Jimenez, Z., & St. Amand, C. (2021). Medical care for nonbinary youth: Individualized gender care beyond a binary framework. *Pediatric Annals, 50*(9), e384–e390. https://doi.org/10.3928/19382359-20210818-03

Hidalgo, M. A., Ehrensaft, D., Tishelman, A. C., Clark, L. F., Garofalo, R., Rosenthal, S. M., Spack, N. P., & Olson, J. (2013). The gender affirmative model: What we know and what we aim to learn. *Human Development, 56*(5), 285–290. https://doi.org/10.1159/000355235

Keo-Meier, C., & Ehrensaft, D. (Eds.). (2018). *The gender affirmative model: An interdisciplinary approach to supporting transgender and gender expansive children*. American Psychological Association. https://doi.org/10.1037/0000095-000

Kim, H.-H., Thayer, N., Bernstein, C., Cruz, R., Roby, C., & Keuroghlian, A. S. (2025). On the frontlines: Protecting and advancing gender-affirming care in a hostile sociopolitical environment. *Journal of General Internal Medicine, 40*(2), 458–461. https://doi.org/10.1007/s11606-024-09080-3

Knudson, G. A., Feldman, J., Neira, P., & Fraser, L. (2023). Closing the gap in education: Raising medical professionals' knowledge and attitudes in transgender health. *Best Practice & Research Clinical Obstetrics & Gynaecology, 89*, 102339. https://doi.org/10.1016/j.bpobgyn.2023.102339

McNamara, M., Lepore, C., Alstott, A., Kamody, R., Kuper, L., Szilagyi, N., Boulware, S., & Olezeski, C. (2022). Scientific misinformation and gender affirming care: Tools for providers on the front lines. *Journal of Adolescent Health, 71*(3), 251–253. https://doi.org/10.1016/j.jadohealth.2022.06.008

Obedin-Maliver, J., Goldsmith, E. S., Stewart, L., White, W., Tran, E., Brenman, S., Wells, M., Fetterman, D. M., Garcia, G., & Lunn, M. R. (2011). Lesbian, gay, bisexual, and transgender-related content in undergraduate medical education. *JAMA, 306*(9), 971–977. https://doi.org/10.1001/jama.2011.1255

Rafferty, J., AAP Committee on Psychosocial Aspects of Child and Family Health, AAP Committee on Adolescence, AAP Section on Lesbian, Gay, Bisexual, and Transgender Health and Wellness. (2018). Ensuring comprehensive care and support for transgender and gender-diverse children and adolescents. *Pediatrics, 142*(4), e20182162. https://doi.org/10.1542/peds.2018-2162

Rider, G. N., McMorris, B. J., Gower, A. L., Coleman, E., Brown, C., & Eisenberg, M. E. (2019). Perspectives from nurses and physicians on training needs and comfort working with transgender and gender-diverse youth. *Journal of Pediatric Health Care, 33*(4), 379–385. https://doi.org/10.1016/j.pedhc.2018.11.003

Simons, L., Schrager, S. M., Clark, L. F., Belzer, M., & Olson, J. (2013). Parental support and mental health among transgender adolescents. *Journal of Adolescent Health, 53*(6), 791–793. https://doi.org/10.1016/j.jadohealth.2013.07.019

Tervalon, M., & Murray-García, J. (1998). Cultural humility versus cultural competence: A critical distinction in defining physician training outcomes in multicultural education. *Journal of Health Care for the Poor and Underserved, 9*(2), 117–125. https://doi.org/10.1353/hpu.2010.0233

1 GENDER IDENTITY DEVELOPMENT

JOHANNA OLSON-KENNEDY, AYDIN OLSON-KENNEDY, AND DARLENE TANDO

While language used to describe transgender and nonbinary experiences has been historically limited, the world of gender and gender care provision is now seeing constant evolution in language. As we work to close these linguistic gaps, it is critical to acknowledge that some of the language used in this chapter will likely be rendered archaic in a few years. Additionally, throughout this book, the term *parent* is used inclusively to refer not only to biological or legal parents but also to other family members, guardians, caregivers, and community members who play a role in raising and supporting transgender and gender diverse (TGD) children.

WHEN DO CHILDREN KNOW AND UNDERSTAND THEIR GENDER?

Studies performed in the context of second wave feminism focused on the questions of (a) when children were able to know themselves as boys or girls and (b) when they might understand some level of certainty about

The authors of this chapter would like to acknowledge our positionality. Two of the authors identify as White, cisgender women. One of the authors identifies as a White, queer, transgender man.

https://doi.org/10.1037/0000494-002
Pediatric Gender Health Care: The Gender Affirmative Model Revisited, Second Edition, G. N. Rider, D. Ehrensaft, and C. St. Amand (Editors)

this identification (Martin & Ruble, 2010). These studies demonstrated that children were able to differentiate between male and female and designated gender labels accordingly by age 24 to 48 months (Martin & Ruble, 2010).

Earlier studies have supported the findings of Martin and Ruble (2010). Kohlberg's (1966) theory of childhood gender identity development was one of many that explored gender development, suggesting that by age 2 years, children can typically identify their gender accurately. This theory served as a foundational framework for understanding the developmental trajectory of gender identity at the time. This understanding becomes stable by age 4; by age 7, children can recognize their gender as independent of external factors (Boston, 1991). This developmental trajectory is significant, particularly in light of assertions that gender identity in TGD youth can only be consolidated during or after the completion of endogenous puberty. Notably, such claims are not commonly made regarding cisgender children.

Gender identity is a multidimensional construct encompassing self-perception, a sense of belonging to gendered categories, external pressures, and the influence of societal attitudes toward gender (Katz-Wise et al., 2017). These elements often generate conflicting discourses about gender identity development and gender role expectations (Abrams, 2003). The pervasive influence of *cisgenderism*—the systemic invalidation of TGD identities and the privileging of cisgender identities as more legitimate (Lennon & Mistler, 2014)—has resulted in a dearth of research on the experiences of TGD children. Cisgenderism also establishes the ideological foundation for *cisnormativity*, the assumption that all individuals are cisgender and that cisgender identity is natural, expected, and preferable (Serano, 2007). Furthermore, considerations of intersectionality are largely absent from existing studies.

In this context, Olson and Gülgöz's (2018) TransYouth Project, one of the largest studies to date focused on transgender children, represents a critical contribution to understanding the development and identity formation of TGD children. Transgender and cisgender children are equally capable of understanding their gender. However, before their gender is affirmed, TGD children tend to have completely different experiences of their gender in relation to how others understand them and different interactions between their gender identity and the outside world. Once their gender is affirmed, TGD prepubertal children typically exhibit clarity and consistency in their gender identity comparable to their cisgender peers, and they experience similar benefits from social acceptance (Rafferty et al., 2018).

The TransYouth Project (https://hudl.princeton.edu/research) now has 300 participants ranging in age from 3 to 12 years. It is the largest study to date seeking to understand the gender development of transgender children. The project is planned to span 20 years, with the aim of examining gender development and well-being. The study includes transgender youth, their sibling closest in age, a parent, and cisgender youth matched by age and gender to the main participants, for a total of 800 participants. The study has enrolled participants in more than 40 U.S. states and two Canadian provinces. The project to date has revealed several important findings. The first is that the basic gender development of transgender preschool children is very similar to that of other children (Fast & Olson, 2018). The second is that transgender children view themselves in terms of their expressed gender and show preferences for their expressed gender, with response patterns mirroring those of two cisgender control groups (Olson et al., 2015). Finally, and perhaps most importantly, transgender children whose gender identities are supported experience similar mental health outcomes (as related to anxiety and depression) to their siblings and the cisgender population at large (Olson et al., 2016). These findings are informative about developmental processes of transgender youth who are supported early in life.

According to the 2015 U.S. Transgender Health Survey, which queried 27,715 transgender individuals, 94% of respondents reported they started to think their gender was different from their designated sex at birth at age 20 years or younger (James et al., 2016). A full 60% reported feeling this way at age 11 years or younger. Despite the number of youths who knew this information, only 15% told anyone else they were transgender at age 15 or younger. These numbers tell a story about the difference between self-identification and disclosure of transgender identity to others (i.e., coming out). Although disclosure is often assumed to be the singular coming out event, there are many other benchmarks related to the understanding, development, integration, and disclosure of being transgender, and these benchmarks are often separated by multiple years. Turban et al. (2023) found that the realization of one's TGD identity during adolescence or later is not particularly unusual among TGD individuals in the United States, and first disclosure of one's TGD identity often occurs many years after initial identity realization.

Historically, transgender individuals have been categorized into two groups: those who had a history of child-onset gender incongruence and those who came to understand their gender to be different than their sex designated at birth in adolescence or adulthood (Sevlever & Meyer-Bahlburg, 2019). It may be helpful to consider neurodivergent TGD youth coming out in adolescence and young adulthood as a third pathway or trajectory, given the unique way autism can affect the conceptualization of both gender and gender roles, how theory of mind impacts the ability to understand the response of others, as well as how gender dysphoria is managed.

Whether these distinctions are of importance remains an unanswered question. It is possible that although the majority of transgender or nonbinary people know that something is different about their gender, the pathway for discovering one's gender identity is likely deeply influenced by both proximal and distal factors.

GENDER IDENTITY DISCLOSURE IN CHILDHOOD

As discussed in the previous section, it has long been known that children are able to know and express their gender identity by age 3 to 5 years and often younger (Boston, 1991; James et al., 2016; Martin & Ruble, 2010). Gender identity, in and of itself, is not inherently confusing; it simply exists as an integral aspect of the self. However, being told one is a gender they are not is confusing. Children typically believe the grown-ups raising them know a whole lot about not only them but the world around them as well. When these grown-ups tell a child something about the child that seems inherently wrong, it can be extremely confusing. Many times, it is a case of unintentional invalidation of the child's gender experience. Naming or categorizing the child in a way that goes against their authentic understanding of self is a troubling experience for the child, even if they do not have words for it yet.

Adults and children alike come into conscious awareness and understanding of their authentic gender identity at a wide variety of ages. This decision is not determined by the strength of one's authentic gender identity but rather by factors such as temperament, environmental context, the extent to which caretakers engage in gender policing, societal perceptions of gender nonconformity relative to one's designated sex, and other contextual influences.

There is no one trajectory of how a transgender individual comes to understand their gender identity, shares this with others, and makes changes to feel aligned in their social presentation, body, and so on. However, there are patterns that can anecdotally be observed among transgender youth as they move throughout development.

Temperament, known as the how of behavior and first evident in the earliest weeks of life, impacts how a child relates to most things, including their gender, what it feels like to be designated a gender that does not feel right, and their capacity to discuss these feelings. The individual's temperament also affects their relationship with being transgender over the course of their lifetime. A child with a shy temperament, for example, might be more hesitant to share their inner gender experiences with others compared with a child with a more extroverted, excitable temperament.

Children who tell the adults around them in early childhood about their gender often alert us to their authentic gender experience through their desires around clothing, hairstyles, name, pronouns, toys, games, and so forth. Some TGD children will undergo a social transition to live in a manner that feels representational of their experienced gender. Social transition may include wearing different clothing, trying new hairstyles, playing with different kinds of toys, using different pronouns to describe themselves, or even using a different name. Not all TGD children will undergo social transition for a variety of reasons, including the safety (or lack thereof) in their environment and support (or lack thereof) from parents or other family members—or maybe they feel fine with the way they are or are uncomfortable making any changes. Previously, families would consult professionals (medical or mental health providers) seeking information about the benefits and risks of social transition. Over the past 10 years, as transgender visibility has increased, we (the authors) have observed that more TGD children are socially transitioning on their own (with the support of their caregivers) within their private family structure before engaging in professional services related to gender.

Although some have asserted that social transition in childhood leads inevitably to medical interventions (Hall et al., 2024), it is most likely that children who socially transition in childhood are transgender and are significantly more comfortable presenting themselves to the world as they truly experience themselves rather than unauthentically. Others have argued that detransitioning following social transition may cause distress for those children, based on the report of Steensma and colleagues (2013) in a study of predictors of persistent transgender identity. In that report, the authors recounted two individuals designated female at birth who reported, at middle school age, experiencing some difficulty with detransition or reaffiliation of their gender with their sex designated at birth. Evidence suggesting that a second transition would be traumatic is limited. The concern lies in the assumption that a possible future change in a child's gender identity justifies suppressing or redirecting their current expression of identity (Temple Newhook et al., 2018).

As Giordano (2019) pointed out in her critical analysis of the ethics around social transition, "Other things being equal, one has greater reason to prefer minimizing the likelihood of imminent and certain harm than to minimize the likelihood of only future and theoretical harm" (p. 658). In other words, parents and clinicians need to balance the imminent distress associated with not allowing social transition for those who need it with the potential distress of retransition. Additionally, even if a youth were to reidentify with their sex designated at birth after transitioning, this can be a component of the continuation of gender development and exploration and does not necessarily represent anything remiss in the way the parents or clinician supported the youth.

In our experience, young transgender children (aged < 10 years) who have disclosed and been supported in their gender disclosure tend to be joyful to be recognized for who they are. There is a tendency for them to be happy to be unique, and that uniqueness is celebrated. Many times, these children are happy to find and form friendships with other children who are transgender. There is often a sense of pride in relationship to being transgender, and usually physiologic dysphoria is low. After social affirmation, these children tend to be comfortable progressing in their affirmed gender. At this stage, youth often have minimal need to discuss their gender identity, instead focusing on the joy and relief associated with authentic social recognition. The parents are usually the ones taking on the process of disclosure to family members and neighbors and contending with the logistics. For the youth, the only time being transgender comes up may be at community events or in therapy sessions.

Although the child may think their external or concrete body parts represent their actual gender identity (as many do), it is important to help the child (and everyone else) understand that gender is an internal sense of self, one that cannot be seen but can only be learned by listening to the individual themself. Therefore, for younger concrete thinkers, having one's heart and brain represent their actual gender can be quite useful. Providing a young child with language in regard to their heart and brain can be pivotal in both their own understanding of self and also knowing how to best communicate it to others. Many transgender youths can acknowledge that while others thought they were one gender at birth, they have the heart and brain of a different gender.

Based on years of combined clinical experience, the authors have noted patterns of how developmental stages affect expression regarding gender identity as well as factors that influence a child's experience of coming out to family members. The younger the child, the more likely they are to accept both their sex designated at birth and their authentic gender. Acknowledging the sex they were designated at birth does not tend to cause dysphoria the way it does for older children or adolescents. They may say something like: "When I was born, I was a boy but now I'm a girl," or "I have the heart of a boy and the brain of a girl because I'm transgender." These articulations are dependent on a social environment that is *gender literate* (i.e., the child and those around them understand that body parts are not determinants of gender).

This dualism that exists in younger children often allows them a little more fluid thinking about the self, patience with those around them adjusting to their newly asserted gender, and less distress in regard to their assumed gender based on designated sex at birth. Similarly, and perhaps relatedly, pronouns do not tend to be as important to young children. As long as those around younger children understand them and know who they are, the use or misuse of pronouns does not tend to impact them as profoundly as older children and adolescents. Many times, this flexibility in young transgender children causes parents to wonder if their child has a nonbinary gender identity rather than a binary transgender identity. Of course, it is possible that the child is nonbinary. However, if they are asserting a binary transgender identity peppered with some acceptance regarding their designated sex, this ability for the designated sex and the authentic gender to peacefully coexist may become more challenging. There may be more dysphoria associated with the designated sex, along with varying degrees of rejecting factors associated with sex designated at birth.

If social transition occurs when the child is younger than age 10 years, it can be easy to dive right into a life of authentic identification and presentation. Children who socially transition at a young age may begin to ignore their transgender history. It is important for their guardians to keep it a part of the conversation to normalize this part of the child's self and to help fold it into their identity as they get older. This may include having books on hand, discussing this unique part of their lived experience, talking about positive transgender role models, and connecting with community.

Many parents expect that transgender children hate their bodies or their genitals. Sadly, this has become part of the expected transgender narrative. Certainly not all transgender individuals hate their bodies, and it is a wonderful thing if the child does not have negative views about their body. If an individual is to experience genital dysphoria, it is likely to emerge at a later age. However, some children have genital dysphoria from the start, as primary sex characteristics can be a physical representation of not being completely aligned in body and mind. It is important at this age and stage (for those concrete thinkers) to move the focus from the genitals to the heart and brain as the body parts to represent gender. It is also important for the social environment to introduce new narratives that replace traditional ones (e.g., penis = boy and vulva = girl), because the child's self-concept is very much embedded in a feedback loop within the caregiving milieu.

If there is a supportive adult present in the child's life and if the child undergoes a social transition in childhood, they often do not begin to intentionally explore their understanding of and integration of being transgender until puberty starts or as they progress developmentally.

THE ROLE OF GENDER ESSENTIALISM IN GENDER DEVELOPMENT

The ideology of gender essentialism is alive and well across many countries in the world, and it seems to have made a significant reappearance in the past 8 years (Skewes et al., 2018). *Gender essentialism* posits that gender is binary and based solely on sex (Gülgöz et al., 2019), leaving no room for the most fundamental aspect of gender, one's innate experience of one's gender regardless of chromosomes or reproductive tract and organs. Although many would assert that one's chromosomes are what ultimately determine one's reproductive tract and genitalia, and subsequently assumed gender, many examples in humans exist for which these developmental pathways are not that clear-cut, including intersex and transgender individuals. Additionally, there are many examples of individuals who have undergone hysterectomy, orchiectomy, mastectomy, and other surgeries that remove reproductive tract and sex organs who do not subsequently become a different gender following these procedures.

Gender identity development is an experience that is largely private for transgender individuals, whereas cisgender development is the most common developmental trajectory in regard to gender and thus a more public process. Cisnormativity is deeply embedded in childhood development. This ideology fuels a multibillion-dollar industry that perpetuates gender stereotypes through products and practices such as clothing, toys, nursery decorations, gender reveal parties, and birthday themes, among others. One only has to open a catalog of children's clothing to recognize this reality. Gender development and identification are theorized to be related to the early categorization of gender and the acquisition of gender-stereotyped knowledge, a process often referred to as *gender socialization*—and, in past eras, as *sex-role socialization* (Halim et al., 2017). Therefore, the development of gender in a transgender young person is a nondominant pathway and unfolds in a different way for each person. When faced with developing gender outside of the mainstream narrative, transgender youth are deprived of clear pathways, expectations, and mirroring that can assist in the understanding of oneself. Additionally, cisnormativity often leads to shame, experienced by youth who discover that their interests, desires, and natural state of existence are considered abnormal, weird, or psychopathological by the majority of the cisgender world. How then can we expect transgender children, adolescents, and adults to celebrate their transgender identities when confronted with this unfortunate reality? As the conversation about transgender experience has catapulted its way into the sociopolitical landscape, transgender children, adolescents, and adults have faced even more discrimination, harassment, bullying, and violence (Human Rights Campaign, 2024).

PARENT AND GUARDIAN RESPONSE TO TRANSGENDER AND GENDER DIVERSE YOUTH

Parental and caregiver responses to TGD children are diverse and shaped by a range of intersecting factors, including social identities, community norms, religious beliefs, cultural frameworks, geographic location, and historical moment. These responses often span a wide emotional spectrum—from confusion, disbelief, fear, anger, or grief to support, affirmation, acceptance, and celebration (Malpas, 2011). However, much of the existing research on parental responses has centered the experiences of White parents (Abreu et al., 2020), resulting in a reductive and exclusionary narrative that reproduces and reinforces the white master narrative. A more nuanced understanding requires attention to the ways intersectional oppression—including processes such as racialization, ethnicization, and socioeconomic stratification—shape how parents and caregivers engage with a child's gender identity. Informed by their own lived experiences, some minoritized parents may arrive at affirming responses as an intentional protective strategy, anticipating the forms of oppression their child may encounter. Conversely, the compounded effects of systemic marginalization may complicate parental responses, because having a TGD child can be perceived as amplifying the family's existing vulnerabilities within oppressive social structures.

Grief has become a widely accepted, and perhaps even expected, reaction for parents of TGD youth. However, there has been limited critical examination of what parents are grieving. A variety of frameworks have been developed to help parents understand and process their grief (Abreu et al., 2019; Coolhart et al., 2018; Powell et al., 2024; Testoni & Pinducciu, 2019), and much has been written on supporting parents and caregivers through this process (Brill & Kenney, 2016; Norwood, 2012; Wahlig, 2015). Despite these efforts, centering and normalizing parental grief focused on having a TGD child risks shifting attention away from the role of cisgenderism and cisnormativity. When these assumptions are disrupted, parents often experience cognitive dissonance, requiring them to reconcile the disparity between their expectations and reality. Miseo (2022) termed this process *gender mourning,* wherein parental grief arises not from the reality of having a TGD child but from the emotional disruption of unexamined assumptions, expectations, privileges, and protections rooted in cisnormativity. This process can misdirect feelings of confusion and sadness onto the existence of having a TGD child, placing an undue and unresolvable emotional burden on TGD youth.

Rather than framing the experience of having a TGD child as a loss for parents, gender mourning shifts the focus to understanding how these feelings are rooted in societal norms and assumptions, emphasizing the need to deconstruct cisnormative frameworks to better support both parents and their children (Miseo, 2022). Parents of TGD children frequently worry about how they will be perceived if they support their child's social transition—a concern that parents of cisgender children are typically shielded from. These fears can lead to feelings of isolation, particularly regarding disclosure to extended family members or within their community (Tyler et al., 2022). Parents may also struggle with the manifestations of cisnormativity, including *transmisia*—the hatred and vitriol that is used to justify the structural discrimination and violence directed against TGD people (Serano, 2007), which creates a hostile environment for TGD individuals. Although all parents worry about their child's safety, the unique concerns surrounding a child's gender identity and expression often compound these fears.

Unexamined cisnormative disruptions can manifest as confusion, denial, fear, or anger, emotions that are commonly associated with grief. However, these emotions are often misattributed to the presence of a TGD child rather than recognized as a consequence of cisgenderism and cisnormativity. When left unexamined, such disruptions may prevent parents from exploring more nuanced understandings of their feelings, leaving them feeling untethered and distant from their child. Ironically, some TGD youth report experiencing loss and grief stemming from their parents' reactions. Catalpa and McGuire (2018) found that TGD youth whose parents expressed grief about their gender identity often struggled to make sense of these responses, leading to experiences of relational and identity loss.

Although unintentional, TGD youth who feel the emotional burden of their parents' gender mourning may restrict or modify their gender expression in an effort to reduce their parents' discomfort. While their gender identity remains intact, their relationship to their gender may be affected, potentially diminishing their sense of self. Positive identity development is a critical task for all children. Yet for TGD youth who perceive themselves as the source of their parents' grief, this process may be disrupted, increasing the risk of poor mental health outcomes and low self-esteem.

Research extensively documents poor mental health outcomes among TGD youth (Klinger et al., 2024; Wittlin et al., 2023), but the specific link between these outcomes and parental gender mourning remains underexplored. Durwood et al. (2017) found that TGD youth who received parental support and socially transitioned exhibited higher self-esteem compared to their cisgender peers. Adequate parental support allows parents to process their own gender mourning while fostering their child's positive sense of self and healthy identity development.

Parents also frequently wonder if their child is old enough to assert a gender identity that is not aligned with their designated sex at birth. Some parents may blame themselves or their partners for their child's gender identity, reflecting broader societal influences of cisgenderism and cisnormativity. However, as transgender visibility increases—particularly among children—many parents report feeling less surprised or confused when their child discloses a gender identity that differs from societal expectations. Some parents even speculate that they had anticipated such a disclosure at some future point.

The growing TGD visibility and awareness can reduce initial parental confusion, but it does not always mitigate the emotional and cognitive disruptions associated with reconciling cisnormative expectations. These disruptions often interact with broader societal pressures, including fears of discrimination, isolation, and safety concerns, which can complicate parents' responses. Without adequate support and resources to navigate these challenges, parents may unintentionally place an emotional burden on their child, further complicating the child's identity development. This underscores the importance of both professional guidance and community resources in supporting parents and their TGD children through this journey.

Professionals play a crucial role in deconstructing grief narratives. This task, however, is challenging because it risks being perceived as invalidating parents' experiences. Rather than denying grief or validating misguided grief directed at the TGD child, providers can help parents reframe their grief by identifying its true source: the falsehood of cisnormativity (Miseo, 2022). Such reframing not only offers relief to parents and reduces their distress, but it also fosters a stronger relationship with their child. Additionally, it increases opportunities for TGD youth to engage in affirming experiences, which are critical to supporting positive identity development, a strong sense of self, and healthy self-esteem.

It is essential for professionals in the field to provide psychoeducation for parents, including information related to the creation and sustainability of safer spaces for their child, information about the potential trajectories of TGD children, and encouragement for parents to seek out support from other parents of TGD youth. Parents should be informed that some TGD children may not experience gender dysphoria and may grow out of their preferences for the elements of social transition. As of now, we know that a proportion of children who are gender diverse in childhood (prepubertal) will develop into cisgender adolescents and adults over time. Studies undertaken in the 1980s, 1990s, and even early 2000s demonstrated that most gender-nonconforming children would grow out of their gender diverse expression, but these older studies have significant issues, such as generational gaps potentially creating gender pressure bias, lack of a consistent threshold for a diagnosis of gender dysphoria, and the inclusion of many children (mostly boys) who simply liked dolls and wearing dresses (Bailey & Zucker, 1995; Singh et al., 2021; Wallien & Cohen-Kettenis, 2008). The most contemporaneous studies examining the persistence of transgender identification also come out of the TransYouth Project. A 2022 study reported on outcomes 5 years after social transition, with only 2.5% of the participants endorsing a cisgender identity (Olson et al., 2022). Additionally, some studies demonstrated that once a child reaches adolescence and their gender dysphoria persists, it is unlikely that their gender dysphoria will dissipate (de Vries et al., 2014; Olson et al., 2022).

When children begin asserting a different gender at a very young age, parents often start taking note of the child's gender expression and assertions of gender identity, without a lot of focus or conversation initially. During the first consultation with a provider, parents can usually share several examples of signs that their child's authentic gender did not align with the sex designated at birth. This form of *breadcrumbing* on behalf of the child allows the parents to begin emotionally adjusting to the possibility that they may have a child of a different gender than they previously thought. Sometimes, it is the clinician's role to point out the breadcrumbs that parents may have missed.

At this stage, parents tend to feel less pressure to act immediately if the child is not yet asking for a transition. Also, the fact that there is no need for medical intervention yet when affirming a young child gives parents more space to adjust without feeling an urgent pressure to access medical interventions.

Once a parent has come to understand the asserted gender of their child and often sees them happier than ever, they begin to understand how crucial it is to address gender dysphoria as much as possible. Once a parent adjusts to the asserted gender and it feels just as natural as their child's designated gender once did, the need to prevent endogenous puberty can feel quite relevant. If their child's body begins to change as a result of impending puberty, parents may also feel an urgency for interventions before the development of secondary sex characteristics, which can worsen gender dysphoria.

Initial consultations and therapy visits with parents of young TGD children typically involve providing psychoeducation, assuaging fears and misconceptions, and providing support as parents adjust emotionally. In sessions involving the child, the task at hand is to build rapport and trust, play, create a positive association with therapy, provide language for describing gender experience, and provide developmentally appropriate explanations of gender, puberty, and so on.

ACCESS TO MEDICAL INTERVENTIONS FOR YOUTH WHO TRANSITION IN CHILDHOOD

Having disclosed their gender at a young age and had their asserted gender affirmed before puberty, TGD youth expect to have access to and likely receive early medical intervention (puberty suppression). The benefit of transitioning young and not going through one's endogenous puberty is that these youth will not have to experience the pain and panic about their body going through a puberty that does not align with their gender embodiment goals (for discussion of puberty, medical interventions, and gender embodiment goals, refer to Chapter 2, this volume) and urgently needing interventions as a crisis response. In the authors' clinical experience, some transgender individuals express the desire to have their endogenous puberty stopped in order to give them the choice of sharing their transgender status (i.e., disclosure) or not. Finally, access to puberty blockers can prevent the development of unwanted secondary sex characteristics, thereby potentially reducing or eliminating the need for future surgical interventions to alleviate gender dysphoria. It is important to note that the authors do not believe individuals need medical intervention to have a valid transgender identity; desires for medical transition are driven by the client's individual gender embodiment goals.

For youth who have come out and been affirmed early (prior to middle school), their relationship with being transgender often changes once they reach their tween (preadolescence) years. The driving force for most middle school–aged youth is conformity. Youth at this age often do not want to stand out or be different. Relationships with peers tend to become more important than relationships with parents. At this time, there is a tendency for transgender youth to be in denial about being transgender, regardless of whether they have disclosed it in their school environment. They may say things such as: "I don't really think about it" or "I don't want to talk about it." Even children who were previously very involved in the transgender community, play groups, and so forth may try to disengage from the community. This disengagement often results in their parents feeling torn, as they too have come to enjoy and appreciate the community and support from joining with other parents of transgender youth.

Because of this resistance to acknowledging this piece of identity and not wanting to talk about it in general, an established rapport with or attachment to a therapist before this stage helps. If children can remember positive associations with the therapist, they tend to be more tolerant of conversations regarding their identity and their relationship with being transgender. Often this is why it is positive to have the parents and the young child attend intermittent therapy as the child transitions (and as their parents receive support and guidance), even if the child is not demonstrating an apparent need for therapy.

Gender dysphoria, used in terms of describing one's personal experience (not necessarily a formal diagnosis), can help youth understand and embrace this unique set of feelings, experiences, discomfort, and drive for changes. Children who socially transitioned young and then continue into therapy as a part of their developmental process will sometimes have no idea what the term *dysphoria* means. It can be useful to teach them this term in the early stages so that they have the language to describe their experience and also can understand it is a collective experience felt by many transgender individuals.

For youth who have yet to disclose a gender identity that does not align with their assumed gender, the beginning of the changes associated with endogenous puberty may be the trigger of their gender dysphoria. Beginning a misaligned endogenous pubertal process can not only make their true gender identity more personally salient but also drive the need to come out to guardians more urgently. Reconciling their identity, being different while wanting to conform, and feeling intense concern that their body is about to change in ways they do not want it to make this a very intense time for transgender youth just coming to terms with their identity at this age. Dysphoria may peak at this age, and the need for interventions may be urgent.

Some TGD youth have anxiety about being behind their peers in aligned pubertal development. Because the average age of thelarche (development of breast buds) in those designated female at birth is 9.3 years (Cabrera et al., 2014) and the average age of testicular enlargement is 11.1 years (Brix et al., 2019), it is common that transgender girls feel behind their cisgender female peers in development. Transgender girls may ask about initiating hormone therapy earlier than their counterparts who transition in adolescence. They may experience negative feelings about having to do something to establish their gender that peers do not, which can lead to anxiety and stress.

THE EVOLUTION OF GENDER DYSPHORIA

If a TGD child reveals their authentic gender identity but they are not affirmed, dysphoria will likely increase over time. Extant literature examining the mental health of adolescents and young adults initiating hormone treatment for gender dysphoria who did not receive puberty blockers demonstrates high levels of depression, anxiety, nonsuicidal self-injury, and suicidality among these populations (Chen et al., 2021; Green et al., 2022; Kuper et al., 2020; Turban et al., 2020; van der Miesen et al., 2020; van Leerdam et al., 2023). As mentioned earlier, not all youth (in fact, very few) will have the benefit of early disclosure and early acceptance. However, if youth do have the opportunity to disclose an authentic gender other than that designated at birth and their gender dysphoria persists or develops with the onset of puberty, access to puberty blockers can be very beneficial. Although studies comparing a treated group versus an untreated control group are unethical (Ashley et al., 2023), there are studies highlighting the effect of puberty blockers on mental health in adolescents initiating hormones for physiologic gender transition (Chen et al., 2023; McGregor, McKenna, et al., 2024). These studies are the closest ethical mechanism to understanding the difference between those who are given puberty blockers and those who are not. McGregor, McKenna, et al. (2024) demonstrated that among youth initiating hormones, access to puberty blockers was associated with significantly lower anxiety problems, depressive problems, stress problems, and total problems. These participants were also significantly less likely to report any suicidal thoughts. Chen and colleagues (2023) demonstrated a similar finding: Youth with access to puberty blockers prior to experiencing significant changes of endogenous puberty had higher baseline and follow-up scores on measures of positive affect and life satisfaction as well as lower scores on measures of depression and anxiety.

NONBINARY CHILDREN

Many youth do not align with the perceived gender binary; they may feel like a blend of genders, genderless, or gender fluid. Many nonbinary youth will say it is liberating to realize they do not have to align with one particular, society-defined gender. Young nonbinary children often have to contend with peers telling them they cannot be genderless or a blend of genders and that they need to fit into one binary box. This experience can be both frustrating and exhausting to young nonbinary youth. Although some nonbinary youth use binary pronouns or a mix of pronouns, many use gender-neutral pronouns. A unique factor for nonbinary youth who use gender-neutral pronouns is that remaining *undisclosed* (i.e., not sharing information about their nonbinary gender with others) is often not an option; requesting the use of appropriate or neutral pronouns effectively and repeatedly discloses their gender diversity. Nonbinary youth who use gender-neutral pronouns often face a difficult choice: navigating the challenges associated with asserting their authentic pronouns or enduring the distress of being misgendered.

RELATIONSHIP TO THE COMMUNITY

Although children who disclose their gender in early childhood might have pride in being unique, their understanding and affiliation with the transgender community at large is usually sparse as they get older. These children may assert that they are essentially a cisgender boy or girl with a birth defect and that after genital surgery, they will be just like all cisgender youth. Parents will assert that their child identifies as "just a boy" or "just a girl." As mentioned earlier, this is quite common as TGD youth enter middle school, when conformity is currency. At this time, connection with the transgender community may decrease voluntarily. As TGD youth integrate their overall identity and incorporate their transgender identity as a healthy component of self, their connection with the transgender community may increase as they grow older and gain confidence in who they are. Youth who disclose later—such as after the onset of endogenous puberty—and who have not experienced the privileges of cisnormativity often afforded to TGD children affirmed at a young age tend to seek out community more actively as a source of support and coping.

DISCLOSED VERSUS UNDISCLOSED

Historically, the word "stealth" has referred to the process of being undisclosed as transgender to the outside world, thus blending in. Although being *undisclosed* means not being out as transgender, being undisclosed is not the same as being closeted: undisclosed transgender people may be living openly in a manner consistent with their authentic gender. "Passing" is another word commonly used to denote that one is perceived by others to be cisgender. The authors of this chapter choose not to use this language because it implies that something disingenuous is being imposed by transgender individuals themselves, as opposed to the goal of moving around the world in a safer and more authentic manner. Some individuals do not necessarily desire to be undisclosed, but many do (Anderson et al., 2020).

Individuals who transition early and receive puberty blockers often have the option of being disclosed or undisclosed, as opposed to the difficulty some may have if they begin their transition after experiencing endogenous puberty. For children who have socially transitioned, nondisclosure can create a scenario in which they may feel like they are carrying a secret. Parents or guardians can help by clarifying the difference between secret and private information to remove the potential for shame that some people experience around secrets. Being undisclosed in childhood may also present difficult decisions about when, how, and to whom disclosure is necessary and who gets to make the decisions. Being disclosed can lend itself to TGD youth feeling less guarded about private information being shared against their will, and it can help increase ease around other people. Conversely, some TGD youth express they feel more relaxed when they are undisclosed. Choosing whether to be disclosed or undisclosed is a deeply personal decision, influenced by factors such as age at transition, temperament, and environmental context. In the authors' clinical experience, being undisclosed or disclosed can greatly affect one's relationship with being transgender. Being around others who know and accept them can help tweens and teens accept themselves. It is important that youth are sent the message that there is no one way to be transgender, nonbinary, or any gender; therefore, it is up to them on how they both perform and share their authentic gender. Understanding that being transgender is a variation of the human condition and not something inherently negative can influence both their relationship with self and also feelings about disclosure.

SUMMARY

Disclosure of transgender identity in childhood is extremely rare. As is true with transgender identity disclosure at any age, children should be supported in their exploration of their gender and provided a safe and nurturing environment in which their gender may unfold authentically. Numerous studies have demonstrated the importance of family support in the health and well-being of this very remarkable cohort of children (McGregor, Rana, et al., 2024; Olson et al., 2016; Ryan et al., 2010). Although we have much to learn about gender development in transgender children, it remains true that all children need support and love from their parents and families.

REFERENCES

Abrams, L. S. (2003). Contextual variations in young women's gender identity negotiations. *Psychology of Women Quarterly*, *27*(1), 64–74. https://doi.org/10.1111/1471-6402.t01-2-00008

Abreu, R. L., Riggle, E. D. B., & Rostosky, S. S. (2020). Expressive writing intervention with Cuban-American and Puerto Rican parents of LGBTQ individuals. *The Counseling Psychologist*, *48*(1), 106–134. https://doi.org/10.1177/0011000019853240

Abreu, R. L., Rosenkrantz, D. E., Ryser-Oatman, J. T., Rostosky, S. S., & Riggle, E. D. B. (2019). Parental reactions to transgender and gender diverse children: A literature review. *Journal of GLBT Family Studies*, *15*(5), 461–485. https://doi.org/10.1080/1550428X.2019.1656132

Anderson, A. D., Irwin, J. A., Brown, A. M., & Grala, C. L. (2020). "Your picture looks the same as my picture": An examination of passing in transgender communities. *Gender Issues*, *37*(1), 44–60. https://doi.org/10.1007/s12147-019-09239-x

Ashley, F., Tordoff, D. M., Olson-Kennedy, J., & Restar, A. J. (2023). Randomized-controlled trials are methodologically inappropriate in adolescent transgender healthcare. *International Journal of Transgender Health*, *25*(3), 407–418. https://doi.org/10.1080/26895269.2023.2218357

Bailey, J. M., & Zucker, K. J. (1995). Childhood sex-typed behavior and sexual orientation: A conceptual analysis and quantitative review. *Developmental Psychology*, *31*(1), 43–55. https://doi.org/10.1037/0012-1649.31.1.43

Boston, M. B. (1991). Changes and differences in preschoolers' understanding of gender scripts. *Cognitive Psychology*, *6*(4), 417–432. https://doi.org/10.1016/0885-2014(91)90047-H

Brill, S. A., & Kenney, L. (2016). *The transgender teen: A handbook for parents and professionals supporting transgender and non-binary teens*. Cleis Press.

Brix, N., Ernst, A., Lauridsen, L. L. B., Parner, E., Støvring, H., Olsen, J., Henriksen, T. B., & Ramlau-Hansen, C. H. (2019). Timing of puberty in boys and girls: A population-based study. *Paediatric and Perinatal Epidemiology*, *33*(1), 70–78. https://doi.org/10.1111/ppe.12507

Cabrera, S. M., Bright, G. M., Frane, J. W., Blethen, S. L., & Lee, P. A. (2014). Age of thelarche and menarche in contemporary US females: A cross-sectional analysis. *Journal of Pediatric Endocrinology and Metabolism*, *27*(1–2), 47–51. https://doi.org/10.1515/jpem-2013-0286

Catalpa, J. M., & McGuire, J. K. (2018). Family boundary ambiguity among transgender youth. *Family Relations*, *67*(1), 88–103. https://doi.org/10.1111/fare.12304

Chen, D., Abrams, M., Clark, L., Ehrensaft, D., Tishelman, A. C., Chan, Y.-M., Garofalo, R., Olson-Kennedy, J., Rosenthal, S. M., & Hidalgo, M. A. (2021). Psychosocial characteristics of transgender youth seeking gender-affirming medical treatment: Baseline findings from the TransYouth Care Study. *Journal of Adolescent Health*, *68*(6), 1104–1111. https://doi.org/10.1016/j.jadohealth.2020.07.033

Chen, D., Berona, J., Chan, Y.-M., Ehrensaft, D., Garofalo, R., Hidalgo, M. A., Rosenthal, S. M., Tishelman, A. C., & Olson-Kennedy, J. (2023). Psychosocial functioning in transgender youth after 2 years of hormones. *New England Journal of Medicine*, *388*(3), 240–250. https://doi.org/10.1056/NEJMoa2206297

Coolhart, D., Ritenour, K., & Grodzinski, A. (2018). Experiences of ambiguous loss for parents of transgender male youth: A phenomenological exploration. *Contemporary Family Therapy*, *40*(1), 28–41. https://doi.org/10.1007/s10591-017-9426-x

de Vries, A. L. C., McGuire, J. K., Steensma, T. D., Wagenaar, E. C. F., Doreleijers, T. A. H., & Cohen-Kettenis, P. T. (2014). Young adult psychological outcome after puberty suppression and gender reassignment. *Pediatrics*, *134*(4), 696–704. https://doi.org/10.1542/peds.2013-2958

Durwood, L., McLaughlin, K. A., & Olson, K. R. (2017). Mental health and self-worth in socially transitioned transgender youth. *Journal of the American Academy of Child and Adolescent Psychiatry*, *56*(2), 116–123.e2. https://doi.org/10.1016/j.jaac.2016.10.016

Fast, A. A., & Olson, K. R. (2018). Gender development in transgender preschool children. *Child Development*, *89*(2), 620–637. https://doi.org/10.1111/cdev.12758

Giordano, S. (2019). Importance of being persistent. Should transgender children be allowed to transition socially? *Journal of Medical Ethics*, *45*(10), 654–661. https://doi.org/10.1136/medethics-2019-105428

Green, A. E., DeChants, J. P., Price, M. N., & Davis, C. K. (2022). Association of gender-affirming hormone therapy with depression, thoughts of suicide, and attempted suicide among transgender and nonbinary youth. *Journal of Adolescent Health*, *70*(4), 643–649. https://doi.org/10.1016/j.jadohealth.2021.10.036

Gülgöz, S., DeMeules, M., Gelman, S. A., & Olson, K. R. (2019). Gender essentialism in transgender and cisgender children. *PLOS One*, *14*(11), e0224321. https://doi.org/10.1371/journal.pone.0224321

Halim, M. L. D., Ruble, D. N., Tamis-LeMonda, C. S., Shrout, P. E., & Amodio, D. M. (2017). Gender attitudes in early childhood: Behavioral consequences and cognitive antecedents. *Child Development*, *88*(3), 882–899. https://doi.org/10.1111/cdev.12642

Hall, R., Taylor, J., Hewitt, C. E., Heathcote, C., Jarvis, S. W., Langton, T., & Fraser, L. (2024). Impact of social transition in relation to gender for children and adolescents: A systematic review. *Archives of Disease in Childhood*, *109*(Suppl. 2), s12–s18. https://doi.org/10.1136/archdischild-2023-326112

Human Rights Campaign. (2024). *The epidemic of violence against the transgender & gender-expansive community in the U.S.: The 2024 report*. https://reports.hrc.org/an-epidemic-of-violence-2024

James, S. E., Herman, J. L., Rankin, S., Keisling, M., Mottet, L., & Anafi, M. (2016). *The report of the 2015 U.S. transgender survey*. National Center for Transgender Equality. https://transequality.org/sites/default/files/docs/usts/USTS-Full-Report-Dec17.pdf

Katz-Wise, S. L., Budge, S. L., Fugate, E., Flanagan, K., Touloumtzis, C., Rood, B., Perez-Brumer, A., & Leibowitz, S. (2017). Transactional pathways of transgender identity development in transgender and gender-nonconforming youth and caregiver perspectives from the TransYouth Family Study. *International Journal of Transgenderism*, *18*(3), 243–263. https://doi.org/10.1080/15532739.2017.1304312

Klinger, D., Oehlke, S.-M., Riedl, S., Eschbaum, K., Zesch, H. E., Karwautz, A., Plener, P. L., & Kothgassner, O. D. (2024). Mental health of non-binary youth: A systematic review and meta-analysis. *Child and Adolescent Psychiatry and Mental Health*, *18*, 90. https://doi.org/10.1186/s13034-024-00822-z

Kohlberg, L. (1966). A cognitive-developmental analysis of children's sex-role concepts and attitudes. In E. E. Maccoby (Ed.), *The development of sex differences* (pp. 82–173). Stanford University Press.

Kuper, L. E., Stewart, S., Preston, S., Lau, M., & Lopez, X. (2020). Body dissatisfaction and mental health outcomes of youth on gender-affirming hormone therapy. *Pediatrics*, *145*(4), e20193006. https://doi.org/10.1542/peds.2019-3006

Lennon, E., & Mistler, B. J. (2014). Cisgenderism. *TSQ: Transgender Studies Quarterly, 1*(1–2), 63–64. https://doi.org/10.1215/23289252-2399623

Malpas, J. (2011). Between pink and blue: A multi-dimensional family approach to gender nonconforming children and their families. *Family Process, 50*(4), 453–470. https://doi.org/10.1111/j.1545-5300.2011.01371.x

Martin, C. L., & Ruble, D. N. (2010). Patterns of gender development. *Annual Review of Psychology, 61*, 353–381. https://doi.org/10.1146/annurev.psych.093008.100511

McGregor, K., McKenna, J. L., Williams, C. R., Barrera, E. P., & Boskey, E. R. (2024). Association of pubertal blockade at Tanner 2/3 with psychosocial benefits in transgender and gender diverse youth at hormone readiness assessment. *Journal of Adolescent Health, 74*(4), 801–807. https://doi.org/10.1016/j.jadohealth.2023.10.028

McGregor, K., Rana, V., McKenna, J. L., Williams, C. R., Vu, A., & Boskey, E. R. (2024). Understanding family support for transgender youth: Impact of support on psychosocial functioning. *Journal of Adolescent Health, 75*(2), 261–266. https://doi.org/10.1016/j.jadohealth.2024.04.006

Miseo, M. C. (2022). Grieving the transgender (assumed-cisgender) child: What gendered mourning among Midwestern parents tells us about familial cisnormativity and creating livable trans futures. *Bulletin of Applied Transgender Studies, 1*(3–4), 211–233. https://doi.org/10.57814/e4gh-9q03

Norwood, K. (2012). Transitioning meanings? Family members' communicative struggles surrounding transgender identity. *Journal of Family Communication, 12*(1), 75–92. https://doi.org/10.1080/15267431.2010.509283

Olson, K. R., Durwood, L., DeMeules, M., & McLaughlin, K. A. (2016). Mental health of transgender children who are supported in their identities. *Pediatrics, 137*(3), e20153223. https://doi.org/10.1542/peds.2015-3223

Olson, K. R., Durwood, L., Horton, R., Gallagher, N. M., & Devor, A. (2022). Gender identity 5 years after social transition. *Pediatrics, 150*(2), e2021056082. https://doi.org/10.1542/peds.2021-056082

Olson, K. R., & Gülgöz, S. (2018). Early findings from the TransYouth Project: Gender development in transgender children. *Child Development Perspectives, 12*(2), 93–97. https://doi.org/10.1111/cdep.12268

Olson, K. R., Key, A. C., & Eaton, N. R. (2015). Gender cognition in transgender children. *Psychological Science, 26*(4), 467–474. https://doi.org/10.1177/0956797614568156

Powell, Z., Angeltveit, E., Davis, C., & Dodds, L. (2024). Lived experiences of parenting transgender and gender nonconforming youth: Implications for clinical social work practice. *Clinical Social Work Journal, 53*, 89–99. https://doi.org/10.1007/s10615-024-00936-z

Rafferty, J.; Committee on Psychosocial Aspects of Child and Family Health; Committee on Adolescence; Section on Lesbian, Gay, Bisexual, and Transgender Health and Wellness; Yogman, M., Baum, R., Gambon, T. B., Lavin, A., Mattson, G., Wissow, L. S., Breuner, C., Alderman, E. M., Grubb, L. K., Powers, M. E., Upadhya, K., Wallace, S. B., Hunt, L., Gearhart, A. T., Harris, C., . . . Sherer, I. M. (2018). Ensuring comprehensive care and support for transgender and gender-diverse children and adolescents. *Pediatrics, 142*(4), e20182162. https://doi.org/10.1542/peds.2018-2162

Ryan, C., Russell, S. T., Huebner, D., Diaz, R., & Sanchez, J. (2010). Family acceptance in adolescence and the health of LGBT young adults. *Journal of Child and*

Adolescent Psychiatric Nursing, 23(4), 205–213. https://doi.org/10.1111/j.1744-6171.2010.00246.x

Serano, J. (2007). *Whipping girl: A transsexual woman on sexism and the scapegoating of femininity*. Seal Press.

Sevlever, M., & Meyer-Bahlburg, H. F. L. (2019). Late-onset transgender identity development of adolescents in psychotherapy for mood and anxiety problems: Approach to assessment and treatment. *Archives of Sexual Behavior, 48*(7), 1993–2001. https://doi.org/10.1007/s10508-018-1362-9

Singh, D., Bradley, S. J., & Zucker, K. J. (2021). A follow-up study of boys with gender identity disorder. *Frontiers in Psychiatry, 12*, 632784. https://doi.org/10.3389/fpsyt.2021.632784

Skewes, L., Fine, C., & Haslam, N. (2018). Beyond Mars and Venus: The role of gender essentialism in support for gender inequality and backlash. *PLOS One, 13*(7), e0200921. https://doi.org/10.1371/journal.pone.0200921

Steensma, T. D., McGuire, J. K., Kreukels, B. P. C., Beekman, A. J., & Cohen-Kettenis, P. T. (2013). Factors associated with desistence and persistence of childhood gender dysphoria: A quantitative follow-up study. *Journal of the American Academy of Child and Adolescent Psychiatry, 52*(6), 582–590. https://doi.org/10.1016/j.jaac.2013.03.016

Temple Newhook, J., Pyne, J., Winters, K., Feder, S., Holmes, C., Tosh, J., Sinnott, M.-L., Jamieson, A., & Pickett, S. (2018). A critical commentary on follow-up studies and "desistance" theories about transgender and gender-nonconforming children. *International Journal of Transgenderism, 19*(2), 212–224. https://doi.org/10.1080/15532739.2018.1456390

Testoni, I., & Pinducciu, M. A. (2019). Grieving those who still live: Loss experienced by parents of transgender children. *Gender Studies, 18*(1), 142–162. https://doi.org/10.2478/genst-2020-0011

Turban, J. L., Dolotina, B., Freitag, T. M., King, D., & Keuroghlian, A. S. (2023). Age of realization and disclosure of gender identity among transgender adults. *Journal of Adolescent Health, 72*(6), 852–859. https://doi.org/10.1016/j.jadohealth.2023.01.023

Turban, J. L., King, D., Carswell, J. M., & Keuroghlian, A. S. (2020). Pubertal suppression for transgender youth and risk of suicidal ideation. *Pediatrics, 145*(2), e20191725. https://doi.org/10.1542/peds.2019-1725

Tyler, T. R., Huddleston, B. S., Barton, T. N., Thornton, M. H., Calloway, E. T., Martin, K. G., Morgan, A. L., & Munoz, V. (2022). Qualitative metasummary: Parents seeking support related to their TGNC children. *International Journal of Transgender Health, 24*(2), 132–148. https://doi.org/10.1080/26895269.2022.2068724

van der Miesen, A. I. R., Steensma, T. D., de Vries, A. L. C., Bos, H., & Popma, A. (2020). Psychological functioning in transgender adolescents before and after gender-affirmative care compared with cisgender general population peers. *Journal of Adolescent Health, 66*(6), 699–704. https://doi.org/10.1016/j.jadohealth.2019.12.018

van Leerdam, T. R., Zajac, J. D., & Cheung, A. S. (2023). The effect of gender-affirming hormones on gender dysphoria, quality of life, and psychological functioning in transgender individuals: A systematic review. *Transgender Health, 8*(1), 6–21. https://doi.org/10.1089/trgh.2020.0094

Wahlig, J. L. (2015). Losing the child they thought they had: Therapeutic suggestions for an ambiguous loss perspective with parents of a transgender child. *Journal of GLBT Family Studies, 11*(4), 305–326. https://doi.org/10.1080/1550428X.2014.945676

Wallien, M. S., & Cohen-Kettenis, P. T. (2008). Psychosexual outcome of gender-dysphoric children. *Journal of the American Academy of Child & Adolescent Psychiatry, 47*(12), 1413–1423. https://doi.org/10.1097/CHI.0b013e31818956b9

Wittlin, N. M., Kuper, L. E., & Olson, K. R. (2023). Mental health of transgender and gender diverse youth. *Annual Review of Clinical Psychology, 19*, 207–232. https://doi.org/10.1146/annurev-clinpsy-072220-020326

2 COLLABORATIVE TREATMENT ACROSS DISCIPLINES

Medical and Mental Health Care Coordination

LAURA KUPER AND COLT ST. AMAND

Although no gender health medical treatment is applicable to prepubertal children, it is important for providers working with children to have a good knowledge of puberty, medical treatment options, and medical care pathways. This information allows providers to assist children and families in anticipating future changes as well as reflecting on and articulating their desires for the future. Providers can also help educate families on the logistics of seeking medical care, if needed. Being proactive in these discussions can help ensure the process is not rushed and that families will have time to navigate the health care system and potential waitlists.

When discussing puberty and medical treatment options, it is also important for providers to individualize care by considering factors such as the developmental stage of the child, the parties' degree of existing knowledge, the child's embodiment goals, parents' readiness to take in the information, and larger social and cultural factors (Coleman et al., 2022). Many gender diverse children do not seek gender-related medical care in the future; therefore, providers should avoid making assumptions regarding a child's experience of puberty and desire for future medical treatments. For example, a child who has a gender identity that differs from their sex designated at birth may

https://doi.org/10.1037/0000494-003
Pediatric Gender Health Care: The Gender Affirmative Model Revisited, Second Edition, G. N. Rider, D. Ehrensaft, and C. St. Amand (Editors)

not be inherently distressed by all endogenous pubertal changes and may not desire puberty suppression at the initial onset of puberty. Providers should also avoid conveying a message (a) that medical treatment is required to validate one's gender identity, gender expression, or both and (b) that the goal of treatment is to conform to gender stereotypes. Even when children express clearly articulated goals for future treatment, it can be helpful to provide non-directive education regarding the full spectrum of medical and nonmedical options and remain open to the possibility that these treatment-related goals may evolve over time.

EVIDENCE BASE FOR MEDICAL TREATMENT

Use of puberty suppression (e.g., gonadotropin-releasing hormone [GnRH] agonists) and hormone therapy (e.g., estrogen or testosterone) for youth experiencing gender dysphoria is supported by the World Professional Association for Transgender Health (WPATH) Standards of Care (SOC), which is the most widely used guidance for the provision of medical care for transgender and gender diverse (TGD) people. The most recent version of the WPATH SOC (SOC8; Coleman et al., 2022), available online (https://wpath.org/publications/soc8/), was based on an extensive review of the research literature combined with the expert consensus of more than 100 coauthors. Major medical and mental health associations within the United States have expressed similar support for the availability of puberty suppression and hormone therapy as a treatment option for TGD youth. However, over the past few years, misinformation surrounding the evidence base to support medical treatment has proliferated, highlighting the importance of providers remaining knowledgeable of this literature and associated critiques (McNamara et al., 2024).

A multidisciplinary clinic in the Netherlands pioneered the prescription of puberty suppression and estrogen/testosterone therapy to TGD youth in the mid-1990s. Studies of their first cohorts of youth receiving puberty suppression starting at age 12 and estrogen/testosterone between age 16 and 18 years generally demonstrated improvements in mental health and gender dysphoria an average of 3 to 6 years after starting treatment (Arnoldussen et al., 2022; Cohen-Kettenis & van Goozen, 1997; de Vries et al., 2014). Roughly a dozen cross-sectional, retrospective, and short-term follow-up (1–3 years) studies showing similar improvements in mental health and gender dysphoria have been published from community samples and clinics in the United States and several European countries (e.g., Allen et al., 2025; Chen et al., 2023; Green et al., 2022; Kuper et al., 2020; Turban et al., 2022).

However, several studies have not found short-term improvements in functioning associated with puberty suppression alone (e.g., Carmichael et al., 2021), and hormone therapy does not appear to fully resolve mental health concerns. Several systematic reviews have rated the quality of evidence from these studies to be low. However, these reviews have often relied on criteria that only consider data from randomized controlled trials to be high-quality evidence, and limitations surrounding representativeness, adherence, and dropout make randomized controlled trials impractical and likely unethical in this context (Ashley et al., 2024). Additional concerns have been raised regarding a range of biases and assumptions embedded within the reviews (e.g., Noone et al., 2024). It should be noted that the term *low-quality evidence* does not suggest poor quality or lack of evidence; rather, low-quality is the label of the best possible research that can be conducted with this population in an ethical manner.

MODELS OF MEDICAL CARE

Appropriate pediatric gender health care for TGD youth typically requires coordination between providers from various backgrounds. An interdisciplinary team approach is often recommended, ideally with providers being located within the same clinic or hospital system to optimize collaboration. Within the last 2 decades, a number of interdisciplinary clinics have been established in many medium-to-large metropolitan areas of the United States in order to provide this specialized care. Interdisciplinary teams typically include mental health providers, nurse practitioners, and physicians from various backgrounds (e.g., psychology, social work, counseling, psychiatry, pediatrics, adolescent medicine, and endocrinology). Teams may also include care navigators, nurses, fertility specialists, ethicists, and pastoral care providers (Coleman et al., 2022).

Processes vary across clinics, so providers are encouraged to inquire about the specific practices of the clinics to which they may be referring families. Some clinics require a referral letter from an outside mental health or medical provider, whereas others require a visit or series of visits with a mental health provider housed within the multidisciplinary team in addition to, or in lieu of, this referral letter. The specific requirements of the referral letter may also differ, including the scope and depth of information required. To start the process of establishing care, some clinics, hospital systems, and insurance companies require the patient's pediatrician to make a referral, whereas other clinics accept referrals from other types of providers or do not require a provider referral. For some clinics, families meet with a physician on their first visit; other clinics schedule the initial visit with a mental health provider, social worker, or care navigator. There are also clinics where the first visit includes both medical and mental health team members. The specific progression of visits, including the minimum number of visits necessary to obtain a prescription, also varies. While some clinics are able to schedule new patients quickly, others maintain waitlists of up to a year or more. Some clinics are also able to offer ongoing mental health support within the clinic (e.g., gender health assessments, parent support, therapy, psychiatric medication management, and support groups), whereas others offer more limited assessment or consultation services.

Unfortunately, a number of interdisciplinary clinics located in U.S. states with laws banning access to care for minors have been forced to close (Yurcaba, 2025). Some clinics located in states without such legislation may have also preemptively closed, modified the services they offer, or made adjustments in clinic practices due to the sociopolitical climate (Jamerson, 2025; Shanks, 2025). Even prior to the passage of legislation banning access to care for minors, barriers to accessing interdisciplinary clinics appeared commonplace (Chong et al., 2021; Gridley et al., 2016). These barriers include difficulties with locating clinics, transportation, insurance coverage and cost, meeting referral requirements, navigating the health care system, and wait times. In a large online survey of TGD youth prior to the implementation of care bans, only 9% of minors reporting a desire for hormone therapy were currently receiving it (Green et al., 2022).

Although interdisciplinary clinics are often viewed as the ideal model of care for TGD youth and families, this model may not be accessible, desired, or the best fit for any one individual youth or family. Collaboration between providers working in different settings is possible, and existing standards of care highlight the importance of this flexibility. To provide the best care possible for children and families, it is ideal for medical and mental health providers to have communication that goes beyond referral letters. Many primary care physicians and nurse practitioners, among others, are well trained and equipped to provide high-quality gender health services. Specialized training and support is available to these providers through organizations such as WPATH. As one example, in rural upstate New York, a family physician in a hospital system coordinated care for children and adolescents with a social worker in a private practice over an hour away. The family physician, the social worker, and their team members attended monthly consultation meetings to review all of their shared patients. This effort grew into the Gender Wellness Center, a multidisciplinary team that has served 3,000 transgender patients as of 2025. The previous edition of this book outlined the work of this center (Lev & Wolf-Gould, 2018). If providers are not able to form a centralized interdisciplinary team, attending annual conferences with local groups of providers can be a good way to increase collaboration and communication across providers who are not functioning as a coherent team.

As a nonmedical mental health provider collaborating with a medical provider, it can be helpful to obtain information on the medical provider's experience and training, which specific treatments they offer, what information they provide families about these treatment options, their requirements for initiating treatment, their expectations for the role of a mental health provider, and how best to communicate. In addition to sharing this information with families, mental health providers can assist families in identifying questions or topics they want to discuss with their medical provider. Historically, the WPATH SOC have recommended that both mental and physical health providers share responsibility for assessing a client's understanding of treatment options and ability to provide assent or consent (Coleman et al., 2022). However, it is important for mental health providers to be mindful of the limits of their scope of practice and help ensure that families are receiving comprehensive and detailed information on the medical aspects of treatment directly from the prescribing provider, including, for example, information about fertility and fertility preservation associated with treatment options.

BIOPSYCHOSOCIAL ASSESSMENT

The WPATH SOC8 (Coleman et al., 2022) recommends that mental health providers conduct a comprehensive biopsychosocial assessment with each TGD youth seeking medical treatment and their caregivers. Although no medical treatment is provided prior to the onset of puberty, certain clinics and providers may require this assessment in order to establish care, and the typical initial onset of puberty can occur in late childhood, as early as age 8 or 9. In addition, the WPATH SOC8 recommends an individualized and collaborative approach to assessment that seeks to gain an understanding of each youth's gender development, social development, presence of mental health and developmental concerns, and decision-making capacity. The SOC8 outlines criteria for recommending puberty suppression and hormone therapy that include a marked and sustained experience of gender diversity or incongruence, diagnosis of gender dysphoria or gender incongruence (in contexts where this is required to access care), and ability to provide informed assent or consent. Assessment should also include evaluation of level of parental support in relation to the youth's gender and desires for treatment. The criteria further note that mental health concerns that are interfering with assessment, treatment, or both should be addressed, and providers should educate

TGD youth regarding the treatment's potential impact on their fertility and fertility preservation options. In regard to puberty suppression specifically, the WPATH SOC8 notes that the expectation of several years of gender diversity or gender incongruence is less applicable, given the reversible nature of this treatment combined with the permanent changes that could occur if treatment were delayed. More broadly, the WPATH SOC8 emphasizes that "allowing irreversible puberty to progress in adolescents who experience gender incongruence is not a neutral act given that it may have immediate and lifelong harmful effects for the transgender young person" (Coleman et al., 2022, p. S48). Chapter 12 (this volume) on ethical practice provides guidance for assessing an individual's capacity to provide assent and/or consent. Lee et al. (2024) also provided guidance on how to implement the WPATH SOC8's assessment recommendations in practice.

Although assessments can be helpful to ensure that TGD youth and families are fully informed about treatment options and supported in the process of initiating care, providers should be mindful of the potential barriers to care that assessments may introduce, as well as the historical and potentially ongoing harm associated with the assessment process (Marrow, 2024). For example, emphasizing clinical diagnosis and the necessity of involving mental health providers contributes to pathologizing gender diversity. Earlier models of assessment also required TGD people's gender identity and expression to conform to binary gender stereotypes and tended to overfocus on gender identity and expression rather than physical embodiment goals. For example, TGD youth have shared that their providers kept asking if they were sure that they were a girl or a boy and what toys, activities, and clothing they preferred, largely neglecting to ask about their embodiment goals and the primary and secondary sex characteristics they wanted as well as those they did not want (Horton, 2022). The power differential between provider and clients can be particularly pronounced and potentially distressing when assessment is required to access care, and many TGD youth and families have a history of negative interactions with providers. Trauma-informed care approaches, which emphasize transparency, collaboration, empowerment, and choice, can be particularly helpful in this context (Menschner & Maul, 2016).

PUBERTY

Although no medical treatment is indicated for prepubertal TGD children, clinicians who work with families with TGD children should be familiar with the medical treatment options available across the lifespan in order to educate clients and be prepared to answer basic questions. The most recent WPATH SOC8 (Coleman et al., 2022) recommends initiation of medical treatment based on developmental stage (i.e., sexual maturity rating [SMR]) and individual embodiment goals—not the age of the patient. Although this recommendation is also consistent with our view, earlier guidelines (Hembree et al., 2009) referenced ages, and certain clinics may still follow age-based criteria, particularly for hormone therapy.

A common practice for primary care medical professionals (e.g., pediatricians, nurse practitioners, and family medicine providers) is to examine children's chests and genitals during annual well-child visits for evidence of the onset of puberty. They use an objective classification system referred to as *sexual maturity rating*, more commonly known as Tanner staging (Guidi & Sapra, 2022; see also Figures 2.1 and 2.2), to track the development of secondary sex characteristics and external genitalia during puberty.

There are five stages in the SMR classification system (Guidi & Sapra, 2022). From birth through early childhood, children are considered to be in stage 1 (prepubertal). Once an adolescent reaches stage 5, they are considered

FIGURE 2.1. Sexual Maturity Rating Stages (i.e., Tanner Stages) for Bodies With Typically Functioning Ovaries

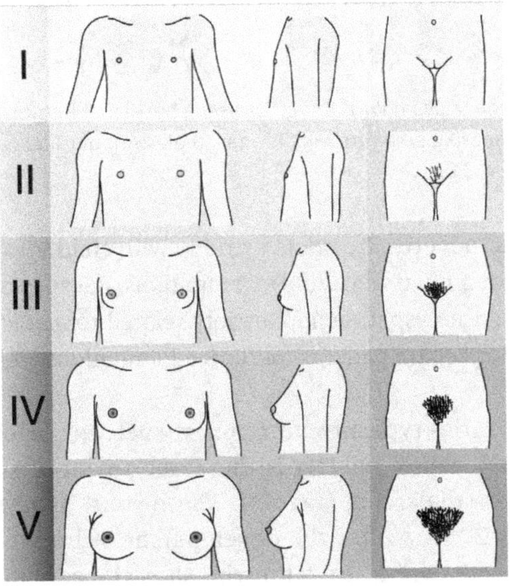

Note. From *The Tanner Scale (Also Known as the Tanner Stages/Staging)–Female*, by Michał Komorniczak, 2019b, Wikipedia (https://en.wikipedia.org/wiki/Tanner_scale#/media/File:Tanner_scale-female.svg). CC BY-SA 3.0.

FIGURE 2.2. Sexual Maturity Rating Stages (i.e., Tanner Stages) for Bodies With Typically Functioning Testicles

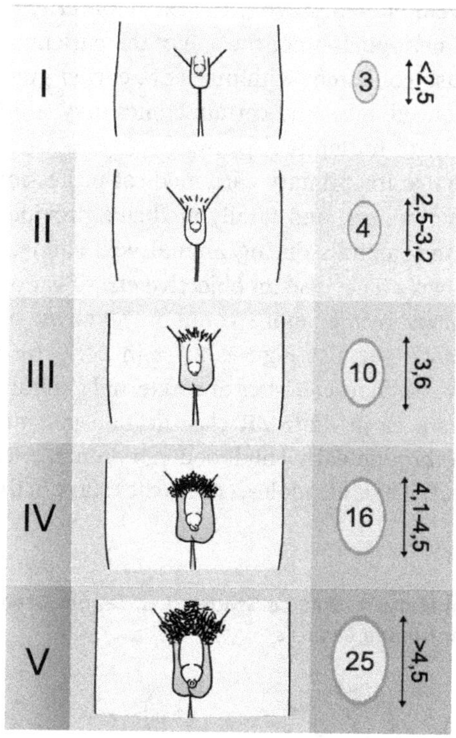

Note. From *Male Tanner Scale With Intact Foreskin*, by Michał Komorniczak, 2019a, Wikipedia (https://en.wikipedia.org/wiki/Tanner_scale#/media/File:Tanner_scale_male_intact.svg). CC BY-SA 3.0.

to have completed puberty. Providers working with children should make sure the child is seen for annual well-child examinations. Because many TGD people of all ages experience dysphoria and anxiety related to medical examinations, providers can help prepare patients for SMR examinations (see Appendices 2.1 and 2.2).

People with ovaries typically start puberty between ages 8 and 13 (Figure 2.3). The first sign of puberty is the development of small breast buds under the nipples (thelarche; stage 2). These youth typically start having menstrual cycles 2 years after the development of breast buds (stage 5). Although babies with ovaries are born with all of the eggs they will ever produce, youth are typically not assumed to be fertile (i.e., able to use these eggs to support a pregnancy) once they have reached stage 5. However, there is potential for pregnancy once stage 3 is reached, because ovulation (i.e., the

FIGURE 2.3. Range of Typical Ages for Pubertal Changes in Youth With Ovaries and Youth With Testes

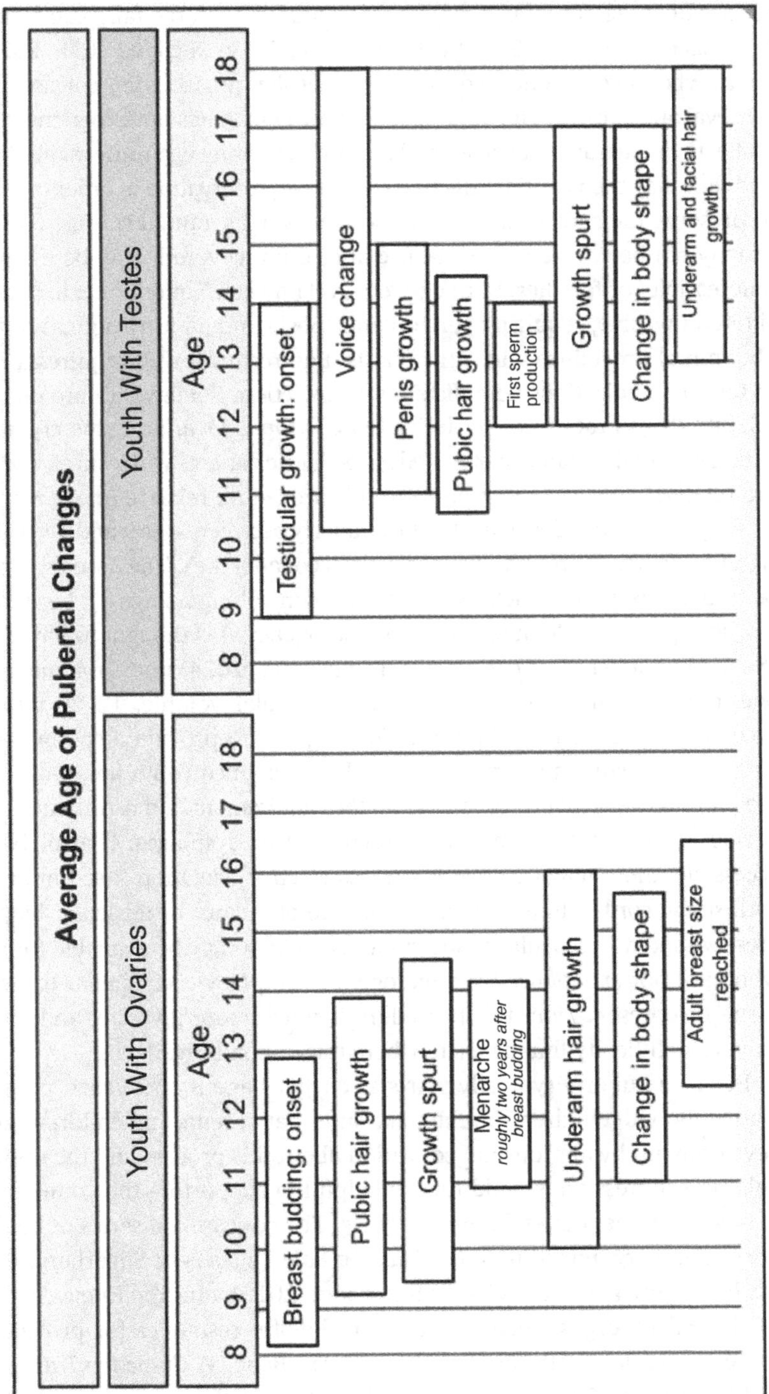

release of an egg from an ovary to the uterus through the fallopian tube) can begin as early as stage 3 or 4 (Mendle et al., 2019; Michaud et al., 2020). In youth who have experienced menarche, fertility preservation consists of egg retrieval and subsequent freezing. If a young person has not experienced menarche, their eggs are not considered mature, rendering egg retrieval ineffective, and they may then consider ovarian tissue cryopreservation in order to attempt to preserve their fertility. Either option, as well as annual storage fees, may or may not be covered by insurance and, if not covered, may be financially inaccessible for families. Both egg retrieval and subsequent freezing are considered invasive, requiring general anesthesia and an intravaginal or transabdominal procedure and ultrasounds. Egg retrieval also requires a round of fertility medications administered via injection. Some youth are unable to tolerate these procedures or decide against them. Ovarian tissue cryopreservation is most commonly performed for pediatric patients with cancer, and there are relatively few sites that perform this procedure relative to egg retrieval.

People with testicles typically start puberty between ages 9 and 14. The first sign of puberty is growth of the testicles (gonadarche). They are assumed to be fertile once their testicles grow to 12 mL in volume (stage 3), because this is when sperm development (i.e., spermatogenesis) is thought to have begun (Salas-Humara et al., 2019). Yau and colleagues (2024) noted that more than one-third of transgender girls (n = 23; testicular volume, 12–20 mL) who accepted a referral to pediatric urology agreed to provide a sperm sample, and all successfully preserved sperm. However, once youth are educated on the process of sperm preservation and the requirement of masturbation, some decide not to store sperm due to discomfort or dysphoria. If available and accessible, there may be options such as electroejaculation (used in patients with spinal cord injuries who are unable to ejaculate) or testicular biopsy to preserve sperm. Testicular tissue cryopreservation may be available for youth who have not experienced spermatogenesis yet. However, similar to ovarian tissue cryopreservation, this procedure is much more invasive, and families may have difficulty finding a site where this option is available.

Because puberty typically starts as early as age 8 or 9 years, providers who work with children should make sure that parents and children receive developmentally appropriate education about this process and the option of puberty suppression, should this be helpful in supporting the young person to reach their gender embodiment goals. The educational series of books by Cory Silverberg, including *What Makes a Baby* (ages 2–6; Silverberg, 2013), *Sex Is a Funny Word* (ages 7–10; Silverberg, 2015), and *You Know, Sex* (ages 11–12; Silverberg & Smyth, 2022), are helpful resources for providers to share and review with families. *Where's* MY *Book? A Guide for Transgender and Gender Non-Conforming Youth, Their Parents, & Everyone Else*, by Linda

Gromko (McComb, 2018), which was written for transgender children and their families, as well as *The Every Body Book* (Simon, 2020), which was written to be inclusive of lesbian, gay, bisexual, transgender, and queer or questioning people, also provide a helpful overview of puberty.

PUBERTY SUPPRESSION

Once a person enters stage 2, they are considered to have started puberty. According to international guidelines from WPATH (Coleman et al., 2022) and the Endocrine Society (2024), stage 2 is the absolute earliest that a medical intervention—puberty suppression—can be indicated. Puberty suppression is most commonly done through the use of GnRH agonists, which send a constant amount of GnRH to the brain (hypothalamic–pituitary–adrenal axis). This works because a pulsatile or intermittent pattern of increase or decrease in GnRH signals the brain to start sending hormones to the gonads (ovaries and testicles) to undergo pubertal maturation. Once the brain receives a constant signal of GnRH instead of an intermittent signal, it stops communicating with the gonads, and puberty is paused. Puberty suppression medication can be administered as a rod implanted into the arm (e.g., histrelin [Supprelin]) or regular in-office injections (e.g., leuprolide acetate [Lupron Depot]) every 3 to 6 months. Financial barriers to accessing puberty suppression can be common, particularly without insurance coverage, because it can range in cost from $6,000 to $80,000 in the United States.

Close follow-up and monitoring of laboratory results and bone density is needed for patients who are started on puberty suppression medication in order to ensure the safety of this treatment and to inform timing of further treatment decisions. Laboratory draws are commonly recommended before starting this treatment and every 3 to 6 months during treatment. A bone scan is also recommended when beginning this treatment in order to obtain a baseline measurement of bone density. Estrogen is needed for calcium to be added to the bones (Guss et al., 2022; Mayo Clinic, 2026); therefore, when a patient has their puberty paused, they are not receiving the usual amount of estrogen that they normally would and may experience thinning of the bones. Some testosterone naturally converts to estrogen (Litwack, 2022), so even patients with testicles who start puberty suppression do not get the usual amount of estrogen that would have been converted from testosterone. Thus, if patients have lower bone density, health care professionals may recommend consideration of either stopping the puberty suppression and allowing endogenous puberty to progress or starting hormone therapy to protect the patient's bone development. Health care professionals typically also recommend weight-bearing exercise and calcium and vitamin D supplementation as methods to prevent or improve lower bone mineral density. In the event that puberty suppression is discontinued without the addition of exogenous testosterone or estrogen (e.g., if embodiment goals change), endogenous pubertal changes (i.e., those associated with the individual's gonads) are expected to resume and progress typically without lasting effects on fertility.

HORMONE THERAPY

Hormone therapy for patients with functioning ovaries generally consists of testosterone therapy through weekly injections or daily gel. For those with functioning testicles, it typically consists of estradiol administered through daily pills, patches replaced every 3 to 7 days, or weekly injections as well as a medication to decrease testosterone (e.g., histrelin or leuprolide acetate, spironolactone in the United States, or cyproterone outside of the United States). Please refer to Appendixes 2.1 and 2.2 for a detailed discussion of hormone therapy options created by the chapter authors and intern Braylen Jack, BS, to educate families.

FERTILITY

Once a patient is eligible to start puberty suppression or hormone therapy (e.g., estrogen/estradiol or testosterone), it is imperative that the potential effects on fertility are discussed and understood. If a patient is started on puberty suppression before they are thought to be fertile (e.g., testicle volume < 10 mL or no further than stage 2 breast development) and later started on hormone therapy without ever pausing puberty suppression to allow their body to progress further in their endogenous puberty, they may not ever be able to use their gametes (e.g., eggs or sperm) for reproduction. If an adolescent patient has not undergone puberty suppression and their testicular volume is greater than 12 mL, or if they have had at least one menstrual cycle and then they are started on hormone therapy (i.e., estrogen or testosterone), they are likely to retain fertility. Studies have demonstrated that egg retrieval has been possible for patients who have had at least one menstrual cycle even if patients continue with testosterone therapy, and spermatogenesis in patients whose testicles developed to at least 12 mL can resume after a period of 3 to 6 months off of antiandrogen and estrogen therapy (Ausavarungnirun & Orwig, 2024; Borrás et al., 2024; De Roo et al., 2025; Ralph et al., 2025; White et al., 2023). As is done with many pediatric patients with cancer, gonadal tissue cryopreservation is now being investigated for use with pediatric gender patients (Ausavarungnirun & Orwig, 2024).

Refer to the capacity evaluation described in Chapter 12 (this volume) to review how clinicians can ensure youth and their parents are supported in making their own medical decisions as well as the WPATH SOC8 (Coleman et al., 2022) and Endocrine Society (2024) guidelines for criteria for treatment.

SURGICAL TREATMENTS

A detailed discussion of available gender embodiment surgeries (Amaro Jimenez & St. Amand, 2023) is beyond the scope of this book. As Amaro Jimenez and St. Amand discussed, several terms have been used to refer to surgical procedures that help transgender patients to achieve their physical embodiment goals. Terms such as sex change operation, sex reassignment surgery, gender reassignment surgery, and gender confirmation surgery are widely considered to be outdated, endocisnormative (Hastings et al., 2021), and even offensive. *Endocisnormativity* is a set of assumptions that everyone is or should be *endosex* (i.e., not intersex) and *cisgender* (i.e., not transgender). It is suggested to use the medical term for the specific surgery and use *gender embodiment surgery* to discuss the class of surgeries.

Available surgery options can be organized into categories of face, voice, chest/breast, internal genitalia, external genitalia, and body contouring. Face surgeries are performed by specialized surgeons, may include chondrolaryngoplasty (i.e., tracheal shave) to decrease the size of the laryngeal prominence (i.e., Adam's apple), and are typically not desired if patients do not undergo facial changes from their endogenous puberty. Voice surgeries can be helpful to adult patients who have worked for more than a year with a specialized speech-language therapist or vocal coach and have not been able to attain their goals. Similar to face surgery, voice surgery is performed by a subspecialist surgeon. Chest/breast surgery options are mastectomy and breast augmentation. Internal genital surgery includes orchiectomy (removal of the testicles), hysterectomy (removal of the uterus), salpingo-opherectomy (removal of the fallopian tubes and ovaries), and vaginectomy (removal of the vagina). The prostate is not removed in gender embodiment surgeries, and patients with a prostate should be educated on the need for eventual prostate cancer screening. External genital surgery options include metoidioplasty, phalloplasty, vulvoplasty, and vulvovaginoplasty. These surgeries are considered to be the most medically complex and are commonly performed by a team of subspecialists. Body contouring surgeries can include liposuction, implants, or fat grafting to make certain areas of the body (e.g., the buttocks) more or less pronounced.

It is exceedingly rare for patients younger than age 18 to undergo gender embodiment surgeries. Of the surgeries available, double mastectomy with chest reconstruction (i.e., breast removal with or without nipple grafting) has been offered to patients younger than 18 who developed breast tissue (Kuper et al., 2021). Initial studies of youth who received this surgery have reported positive outcomes, consistent with findings from studies of adults (Ascha et al., 2022; Mehringer et al., 2021; Tang et al., 2022; Yokoo, 2022).

CONCLUSION

Similar to the authors of the first edition of this chapter (Lev & Wolf-Gould, 2018), we believe best practices are a collaborative approach. These best practices include the following: (a) nurturing the emerging gender identity, expression, and embodiment goals of children and youth; (b) developing protective strategies to support children and youth who are living in hostile environments; (c) supporting families and social institutions to become more accepting, so that TGD children are integrated within their families and communities; (d) supporting parents and institutions who are already advocating for their children; and (e) supporting and educating children and families about the risks and benefits of medical interventions, which could include puberty suppression, hormone therapy, and surgical procedures, and assisting families in choosing appropriate treatments.

APPENDIX 2.1: EFFECTS OF ESTROGEN-BASED HORMONE THERAPY

BRAYLEN JACK, LAURA KUPER, AND COLT ST. AMAND

Estrogen-based hormone therapy may involve one or more medications, depending on the person's embodiment goals and health status. Typical regimens may include any of the following: estrogen, androgen/testosterone-lowering agents, and/or progesterone. Testosterone-lowering medications are not needed for individuals who do not have testicles (e.g., have undergone orchiectomy). There is debate and conflicting reports as to whether adding progesterone hormone therapy is helpful.

Most of the physical changes associated with estrogen-based hormone therapy occur over the course of approximately 2 to 5 years (Table 2A.1).

TABLE 2A.1. Effects of Estrogen-Based Hormone Therapy and Expected Time Course

Effect	Expected onset	Maximum effect	Reversible?	Comments
Breast growth	3–6 months	2–3 years	No, although atrophy of breast tissue may occur	Breast buds develop beneath the nipple, which may cause some pain or discomfort Unevenness in right and left breast size may occur and can be normal Fully developed breast size varies and can depend on genetics
Body fat redistribution	3–6 months	2–5 years	Yes	Less abdominal fat More fat in hips, thighs, and buttocks May notice softer facial features
Decreased muscle mass or strength	3–6 months	1–2 years	Yes	Depends on amount of exercise (staying active is recommended)
Skin softening	3–6 months	Unknown	Yes	Skin becomes a bit softer and thinner; may experience changes in touch perception (touch and temperature) Pores will become smaller and skin will also become less oily; may have less strong body odor Over the years, may become more prone to bruising and cuts
Face and body hair changes	6–12 months	Unknown	Yes	Hair follicles will continue to produce hair, yet hair may grow more slowly and be thinner Scalp balding caused by testosterone (i.e., so-called male pattern baldness) may stop or slow down, but most of the hair that was already lost will not grow back
Emotional changes	1–3 months	Unknown	Yes	Can vary from person to person; most people report improved mood May experience a broader range of emotions Changes in interests or tastes can occur

(continues)

TABLE 2A.1. Effects of Estrogen-Based Hormone Therapy and Expected Time Course *(Continued)*

Effect	Expected onset	Maximum effect	Reversible?	Comments
Decreased sex drive	1–3 months	1–2 years	Yes	Fewer spontaneous/morning erections Erections may take longer to obtain and may not be as firm Erotic sensation and the ability to orgasm are still present. Sexual arousal may be drawn out more by all over body touching and may require less genital touching. Orgasms may last longer and be more of a whole-body experience Ejaculation can change with less fluid and/or more clear fluid
Decreased testicular size	3–6 months	2–3 years	Maybe	Testicles may shrink to approximately half of the initial size, depending on when hormone therapy is initiated
Fertility	Varies	Unknown	Likely, although prolonged use may decrease fertility	If a person has already completed testosterone-based puberty and has made mature sperm, it may be possible for them to maintain their fertility. However, when deciding whether to start hormone therapy, it is generally best to assume that there may be a permanent effect on their fertility (the possibility of becoming sterile) and consider fertility preservation before starting treatment Ongoing birth control is still recommended

However, the amount of change and the exact timeline of effects can be highly variable. Factors that influence the amount and timeline of changes include inheritance (genetic influences passed down from biological parents), age, health status, lifestyle, and dosage (amount, frequency, and route of administration).

Genetics, age, health status, lifestyle, and estrogen dosage (amount, frequency, route of administration [Table 2A.2], and adherence) also impact the likelihood of experiencing risks associated with hormone therapy. To provide more specific recommendations, the youth's health care provider will collect information regarding their medical history and biological family history prior to starting hormone therapy. Regular follow-up appointments, exercise, adequate nutritional intake, and cessation or reduction of smoking and alcohol consumption are critical for youth receiving estrogen-based therapy to maintain their health and reduce risk over time (Table 2A.3).

TABLE 2A.2. Methods of Estrogen (i.e., Estradiol) Administration

Estrogen administration method	Comments
Pill	Low cost; convenient May be prescribed for administration one or two times per day Can offer slower or more gradual changes over time May not be recommended for those who smoke, have cardiovascular health risks, or are over the age of 40
Injection	Generally given weekly or every other week May provide quicker effects, and patients may not need to also take a testosterone-lowering medication Muscle soreness or pain may occur after injection Intramuscular injections are usually administered in the thighs or buttocks
Patch	Must be worn continuously; may need to wear multiple patches at the same time May need to changes patches during the week May be more expensive, depending on insurance Applied daily for a steady stream dose of medication Can cause slower or more gradual changes over time May cause skin irritation

TABLE 2A.3. Risks and Side Effects Associated With Estrogen-Based Hormone Therapy

Type	Description	Comments
Common side effects	Weight gain	Similar to changes associated with puberty
Slight increase in risk for disease	Hypertension (high blood pressure)	Hypertension increases the risk of heart attack or stroke Medications may be needed to manage blood pressure
	Cardiovascular disease (heart disease)	Monitored by blood pressure and blood tests
	Type 2 diabetes	Monitored by blood tests
Rare side effects	Elevated liver enzyme levels	Monitored by blood tests
	Gallstones	May not cause symptoms
	Hypertriglyceridemia (elevation of triglycerides in the blood)	Monitored by blood tests Very high levels can increase the risk of acute pancreatitis
	Hyperprolactinemia (elevated prolactin in the blood) or prolactinoma (noncancerous pituitary gland tumor)	Risk appears limited to the first year of treatment
	Venous thromboembolic disease (blood clots)	A blood clot that forms in the veins of the arm or leg may cause swelling, warmth, or tenderness. A blood clot that travels to the lungs can be dangerous (symptoms can include shortness of breath and chest pain). Seek medical attention immediately if concern is present

Note. Information adapted from the World Professional Association for Transgender Health Standards of Care versions 7 and 8 (https://www.wpath.org), the Endocrine Society Clinical Practice Guideline for Endocrine Treatment of Transsexual Persons (https://www.endocrine.org), QueerDoc Hormone Therapy Education (https://www.queerdoc.com), the UCSF Guidelines for the Primary and Gender-Affirming Care of Transgender and Gender Nonbinary People (https://transcare.ucsf.edu/guidelines), "Signs and Symptoms of a Blood Clot: Transgender Health and Blood Clots" (https://thrombosis.org/patients/patient-articles/signs-and-symptoms-of-a-blood-clot-transgender-health-and-blood-clots), and the Family Tree Clinic Patient Information (https://www.familytreeclinic.org/).

APPENDIX 2.2: EFFECTS OF TESTOSTERONE-BASED HORMONE THERAPY

BRAYLEN JACK, LAURA KUPER, AND COLT ST. AMAND

Many changes associated with testosterone-based therapy occur over the course of approximately 2 years and take at least 3 months to notice (Table 2A.4). However, both the amount and timeline of changes are different for different people, and some changes (e.g., body hair growth) can continue

TABLE 2A.4. Effects and Expected Time Course of Testosterone Therapy

Effect	Expected onset	Maximum effect	Reversible?	Comments
Voice deepening	3–12 months	1–2 years	No	Working with a speech-language therapist may help achieve voice goals
Body fat redistribution	3–6 months	2–5 years	Yes	More abdominal fat Less fat in hips, thighs, and buttocks The chest does not typically change
Increased muscle mass/strength	6–12 months	2–5 years	Yes	Very dependent on exercise
Skin changes	3–12 months	1–2 years	Yes	Skin will become thicker; may experience changes in touch perception (touch and temperature) Pores will become larger and produce more oil; may notice more body odor May develop acne, which should be treated
Facial/body hair growth	3–12 months	3–5 years	No, although hair might grow slower	Gradual growth of mustache/beard Thicker/coarser hair on the abdomen, chest, back, arms, buttocks, and legs
Emotional changes	3–6 months	Unknown	Yes	Most report improved mood May experience a narrower range of emotions May become irritable, frustrated, or angry more quickly. This typically improves over time, and switching from injections every other week to injections weekly may help

(continues)

TABLE 2A.4. Effects and Expected Time Course of Testosterone Therapy (*Continued*)

Effect	Expected onset	Maximum effect	Reversible?	Comments
Increased sex drive	1-3 months	Unknown	Yes	May be much more aware of sexual arousal and sexual interest Erotic sensation and the ability to orgasm are still present. May focus more on genital stimulation. Orgasms may not take as long to occur and can be shorter with more of a peak intensity May involve other changes in sexuality (e.g., changes in the types of people you find attractive), yet this is typically not related to testosterone itself but rather to the social impact of transition
Growth of glans clitoris	3-6 months	1-2 years	No	Typical growth is 1-3 cm Can be very sensitive while growing
Thinning/drying of vagina	3-6 months	1-2 years	Possible	Estrogen is necessary to maintain moisture and elasticity of vaginal tissue. Testosterone therapy lowers estrogen, which leads to vaginal dryness and can result in penetration being uncomfortable or more difficult (lubrication products and vaginal estrogen cream or tablets can help)
Menstruation and fertility	1-6 months for periods to stop	Varies	Periods likely resume, possible decrease in fertility over time	Periods may become lighter, be shorter, or arrive later Pregnancy may still be possible without regular periods. Test for pregnancy regularly if at risk, and stop taking testosterone if you believe you may be pregnant. Ongoing birth control is still recommended If a person has already completed estrogen-based puberty and has made mature eggs, it may be possible for them to maintain their fertility. However, when deciding whether to start hormone therapy, it is generally best to assume that there may be a permanent effect on their fertility (the possibility of becoming sterile), and consider fertility preservation before starting treatment

TABLE 2A.5. Methods of Testosterone Administration

Testosterone administration method	Comments
Injection	Low cost, effective Usually given once a week Subcutaneous injection uses a shorter and thinner needle that is given in fatty tissue (most commonly the abdomen) Intramuscular injections are administered in the buttocks or thigh
Gel	Applied to the upper arms or shoulder (but other areas can be discussed with the health care provider) Applied daily for a steady dose of medication Best to wait 2 or more hours before showering or swimming Can be transferred to others through skin contact, so it is important to be cautious of interactions

for many years. Factors that influence the amount and speed of changes include genetics, age, health status, lifestyle, and dosage (amount, frequency, route of administration, and adherence).

Genetics, age, health status, lifestyle, and testosterone dosage (amount, frequency, route of administration [Table 2A.5], and adherence) also impact the likelihood of experiencing side effects and risks associated with hormone therapy. To provide more specific recommendations, the youth's health care provider will collect information regarding their medical history and biological family history prior to starting hormone therapy. Regular follow-up appointments, exercise, adequate nutritional intake, and cessation or reduction of smoking and alcohol consumption are critical for youth receiving testosterone-based therapy to maintain their health and reduce risk over time (Table 2A.6).

TABLE 2A.6. Risks and Side Effects Associated With Testosterone Therapy

Type	Description	Comments
Common side effects	Weight gain	Similar to puberty
	Skin oiliness or acne	Similar to testosterone puberty Untreated acne may cause permanent scars
	Scalp balding	Dependent on age and genetics Medications may help
	Erythrocytosis (increase in red blood cell concentration)	Donating blood and staying well hydrated can reduce the risk

(*continues*)

TABLE 2A.6. Risks and Side Effects Associated With Testosterone Therapy (*Continued*)

Type	Description	Comments
Slight increase in risk of disease	Hypertension (high blood pressure)	Hypertension increases the risk of heart attack or stroke Medications can help manage blood pressure
	Cardiovascular disease (heart disease)	
	Hyperlipidemia (high cholesterol)	
	Type 2 diabetes	
	Sleep apnea (sleep disorder where breathing stops and starts)	Dependent on genetics and neck size Treatments are available to help manage symptoms
Rare side effect	Elevated liver enzymes	Monitored by blood tests

Note. Information adapted from the World Professional Association for Transgender Health Standards of Care versions 7 and 8 (https://www.wpath.org), the Endocrine Society Clinical Practice Guideline for Endocrine Treatment of Transsexual Persons (https://www.endocrine.org), QueerDoc Hormone Therapy Education (https://www.queerdoc.com), the UCSF Guidelines for the Primary and Gender-Affirming Care of Transgender and Gender Nonbinary People (https://transcare.ucsf.edu/guidelines), and the Family Tree Clinic Patient Information (https://www.familytreeclinic.org/).

REFERENCES

Allen, L. R., Dodd, C. G., Moser, C. N., & Knoll, M. M. (2025). Changes in suicidality among transgender adolescents following hormone therapy: An extended study. *Journal of Pediatrics*, 114883. Advance online publication. https://doi.org/10.1016/j.jpeds.2025.114883

Amaro Jimenez, Z., & St. Amand, C. (2023). Gender embodiment surgery. In R. J. Marek & A. R. Block (Eds.), *Psychological assessment of surgical candidates: Evidence-based procedures and practices* (pp. 101–122). American Psychological Association. https://doi.org/10.1037/0000346-007

Arnoldussen, M., van der Miesen, A. I. R., Elzinga, W. S., Alberse, A. E., Popma, A., Steensma, T. D., & de Vries, A. L. C. (2022). Self-perception of transgender adolescents after gender-affirming treatment: A follow-up study into young adulthood. *LGBT Health*, *9*(4), 238–246. https://doi.org/10.1089/lgbt.2020.0494

Ascha, M., Sasson, D. C., Sood, R., Cornelius, J. W., Schauer, J. M., Runge, A., Muldoon, A. L., Gangopadhyay, N., Simons, L., Chen, D., Corcoran, J. F., & Jordan, S. W. (2022). Top surgery and chest dysphoria among transmasculine and nonbinary adolescents and young adults. *JAMA Pediatrics*, *176*(11), 1115–1122. https://doi.org/10.1001/jamapediatrics.2022.3424

Ashley, F., Tordoff, D. M., Olson-Kennedy, J., & Restar, A. J. (2024). Randomized-controlled trials are methodologically inappropriate in adolescent transgender healthcare. *International Journal of Transgender Health*, *25*(3), 407–418. https://doi.org/10.1080/26895269.2023.2218357

Ausavarungnirun, C., & Orwig, K. E. (2024). Reproductive health in trans and gender-diverse patients: Gonadal tissue cryopreservation in transgender and gender-diverse people. *Reproduction*, *168*(6), e240253. https://doi.org/10.1530/REP-24-0253

Borrás, A., Casals, G., Méndez, M., & Manau, D. (2024). Report of fertility preservation procedure in a transmasculine person assigned female at birth on testosterone therapy. *EGO European Gynecology and Obstetrics, 2024*(1), 020–023. https://doi.org/10.53260/EGO.246015

Carmichael, P., Butler, G., Masic, U., Cole, T. J., De Stavola, B. L., Davidson, S., Skageberg, E. M., Khadr, S., & Viner, R. M. (2021). Short-term outcomes of pubertal suppression in a selected cohort of 12 to 15 year old young people with persistent gender dysphoria in the UK. *PLOS One*, *16*(2), e0243894. https://doi.org/10.1371/journal.pone.0243894

Chen, D., Berona, J., Chan, Y. M., Ehrensaft, D., Garofalo, R., Hidalgo, M. A., Rosenthal, S. M., Tishelman, A. C., & Olson-Kennedy, J. (2023). Psychosocial functioning in transgender youth after 2 years of hormones. *New England Journal of Medicine*, *388*(3), 240–250. https://doi.org/10.1056/NEJMoa2206297

Chong, L. S. H., Kerklaan, J., Clarke, S., Kohn, M., Baumgart, A., Guha, C., Tunnicliffe, D. J., Hanson, C. S., Craig, J. C., & Tong, A. (2021). Experiences and perspectives of transgender youths in accessing health care: A systematic review. *JAMA Pediatrics*, *175*(11), 1159–1173. https://doi.org/10.1001/jamapediatrics.2021.2061

Cohen-Kettenis, P. T., & van Goozen, S. H. (1997). Sex reassignment of adolescent transsexuals: A follow-up study. *Journal of the American Academy of Child & Adolescent Psychiatry*, *36*(2), 263–271. https://doi.org/10.1097/00004583-199702000-00017

Coleman, E., Radix, A. E., Bouman, W. P., Brown, G. R., De Vries, A. L., Deutsch, M. B., Ettner, R., Fraser, L., Goodman, M., Green, J., Hancock, A. B., Johnson, T. W., Karasic, D. H., Knudson, G. A., Leibowitz, S. F., Meyer-Bahlburg, H. F. L., Monstrey, S. J., Motmans, J., Nahata, L., . . . Arcelus, J. (2022). Standards of care for the health of transgender and gender diverse people, version 8. *International Journal of Transgender Health*, *23*(Suppl. 1), S1–S259. https://doi.org/10.1080/26895269.2022.2100644

De Roo, C., Schneider, F., Stolk, T. H. R., van Vugt, W. L. J., Stoop, D., & van Mello, N. M. (2025). Fertility in transgender and gender diverse people: Systematic review of the effects of gender-affirming hormones on reproductive organs and fertility. *Human Reproduction Update*, *31*(3), 183–217. https://doi.org/10.1093/humupd/dmae036

de Vries, A. L., McGuire, J. K., Steensma, T. D., Wagenaar, E. C., Doreleijers, T. A., & Cohen-Kettenis, P. T. (2014). Young adult psychological outcome after puberty suppression and gender reassignment. *Pediatrics*, *134*(4), 696–704. https://doi.org/10.1542/peds.2013-2958

Endocrine Society. (2024, October 25). *Gender dysphoria/gender incongruence guideline resources*. https://www.endocrine.org/clinical-practice-guidelines/gender-dysphoria-gender-incongruence

Green, A. E., DeChants, J. P., Price, M. N., & Davis, C. K. (2022). Association of gender-affirming hormone therapy with depression, thoughts of suicide, and attempted suicide among transgender and nonbinary youth. *Journal of Adolescent Health*, *70*(4), 643–649. https://doi.org/10.1016/j.jadohealth.2021.10.036

Gridley, S. J., Crouch, J. M., Evans, Y., Eng, W., Antoon, E., Lyapustina, M., Schimmel-Bristow, A., Woodward, J., Dundon, K., Schaff, R., McCarty, C., Ahrens, K., & Breland, D. J. (2016). Youth and caregiver perspectives on barriers to gender-affirming health care for transgender youth. *Journal of Adolescent Health, 59*(3), 254–261. https://doi.org/10.1016/j.jadohealth.2016.03.017

Guidi, J. C. A., & Sapra, A. (2022). *Physiology, sexual maturity rating*. StatPearls Publishing. https://www.ncbi.nlm.nih.gov/books/NBK551691/

Guss, C. E., Eiduson, R., Vajapeyam, S., Ecklund, K., Mulkern, R., Dahlberg, S. E., & Gordon, C. M. (2022). Bone density and bone marrow composition in transgender girls prior to pubertal blockade: A case series. *Bone, 162*, 116454. https://doi.org/10.1016/j.bone.2022.116454

Hastings, J., Bobb, C., Wolfe, M., Amaro Jimenez, Z., & Amand, C. S. (2021). Medical care for nonbinary youth: Individualized gender care beyond a binary framework. *Pediatric Annals, 50*(9), e384–e390. https://doi.org/10.3928/19382359-20210818-03

Hembree, W. C., Cohen-Kettenis, P., Delemarre-van de Waal, H. A., Gooren, L. J., Meyer, W. J., III, Spack, N. P., Tangpricha, V., Montori, V. M., & Endocrine Society. (2009). Endocrine treatment of transsexual persons: An Endocrine Society clinical practice guideline. *Journal of Clinical Endocrinology and Metabolism, 94*(9), 3132–3154. https://doi.org/10.1210/jc.2009-0345

Horton, C. (2022). "Of course, I'm intimidated by them. They could take my human rights away": Trans children's experiences with UK gender clinics. *Bulletin of Applied Transgender Studies, 1*(1–2), 47–70. https://doi.org/10.57814/20hf-7n94

Jamerson, M. (2025, July 22). *Clinic for trans youth in LA closes, leaving some families struggling to find care*. NPR. https://www.npr.org/2025/07/22/nx-s1-5470244/clinic-for-trans-youth-in-la-closes-leaving-some-families-struggling-to-find-care

Komorniczak, M. (2019a). *Male Tanner scale with intact foreskin* [Figure]. Wikipedia. https://en.wikipedia.org/wiki/Tanner_scale#/media/File:Tanner_scale_male_intact.svg

Komorniczak, M. (2019b). *The Tanner scale (also known as the Tanner stages/staging)—Female* [Figure]. Wikipedia. https://en.wikipedia.org/wiki/Tanner_scale#/media/File:Tanner_scale-female.svg

Kuper, L. E., Rider, G. N., & St. Amand, C. M. (2021). Recognizing the importance of chest surgery for transmasculine youth. *Pediatrics, 147*(3), e2020029710. https://doi.org/10.1542/peds.2020-029710

Kuper, L. E., Stewart, S., Preston, S., Lau, M., & Lopez, X. (2020). Body dissatisfaction and mental health outcomes of youth on gender-affirming hormone therapy. *Pediatrics, 145*(4), e20193006. https://doi.org/10.1542/peds.2019-3006

Lee, J., Kim, H.-H., & Budge, S. L. (2024). Psychological assessment for gender-affirming care in transgender and nonbinary youth: The companionship model. *Harvard Review of Psychiatry, 32*(5), 183–192. https://doi.org/10.1097/HRP.0000000000000404

Lev, A. I., & Wolf-Gould, C. (2018). Collaborative treatment across disciplines: Physician and mental health counselor coordinating competent care. In C. St. Amand & D. Ehrensaft (Eds.), *The gender affirmative model: An interdisciplinary approach to supporting transgender and gender expansive children* (pp. 189–207). American Psychological Association. https://doi.org/10.1037/0000095-012

Litwack, G. (2022). *Hormones* (4th ed.). Academic Press.

Marrow, E. (2024). "I hope that as our selection becomes more accurate, the number . . . will be very few": The creation of assessment criteria for gender-affirming care,

1960s–1980s. *Psychology of Sexual Orientation and Gender Diversity, 11*(2), 183–201. https://doi.org/10.1037/sgd0000633

Mayo Clinic. (2026, January 21). *Puberty blockers for transgender and gender-diverse youth*. https://www.mayoclinic.org/diseases-conditions/gender-dysphoria/in-depth/pubertal-blockers/art-20459075

McComb, J. (2018). *Where's* my *book? A guide for transgender and gender non-conforming youth, their parents, & everyone else* [Review of the book by L. Gromko]. *Journal of Sex & Marital Therapy, 44*(3), 316–317. https://doi.org/10.1080/0092623X.2017.1384166

McNamara, M., McLamore, Q., Meade, N., Olgun, M., Robinson, H., & Alstott, A. (2024). A thematic analysis of disinformation in gender-affirming healthcare bans in the United States. *Social Science & Medicine, 351*, 116943. https://doi.org/10.1016/j.socscimed.2024.116943

Mehringer, J. E., Harrison, J. B., Quain, K. M., Shea, J. A., Hawkins, L. A., & Dowshen, N. L. (2021). Experience of chest dysphoria and masculinizing chest surgery in transmasculine youth. *Pediatrics, 147*(3), e2020013300. https://doi.org/10.1542/peds.2020-013300

Mendle, J., Beltz, A. M., Carter, R., & Dorn, L. D. (2019). Understanding puberty and its measurement: Ideas for research in a new generation. *Journal of Research on Adolescence, 29*(1), 82–95. https://doi.org/10.1111/jora.12371

Menschner, C., & Maul, A. (2016). *Key ingredients for successful trauma-informed care implementation*. Substance Abuse and Mental Health Services Administration. https://www.samhsa.gov/sites/default/files/programs_campaigns/childrens_mental_health/atc-whitepaper-040616.pdf

Michaud, P.-A., Diezi, M., Guihard, L., Jacot-Guillarmod, M., Kleist, P., Sprumont, D., & Wenger, P. (2020). Including adolescents of childbearing potential in clinical trials with possible exposure to teratogenic medication: A challenge for paediatricians and researchers. *Swiss Medical Weekly, 150*(3940), w20333. https://doi.org/10.4414/smw.2020.20333

Noone, C., Southgate, A., Ashman, A., Quinn, É., Comer, D., Shrewsbury, D., Ashley, F., Hartland, J., Paschedag, J., Gilmore, J., Kennedy, N., Woolley, T. E., Heath, R., Goulding, R., Simpson, V., Kiely, E., Coll, S., White, M., Grijseels, D. M., Ouafik, M., & McLamore, Q. (2024). Critically appraising the Cass report: Methodological flaws and unsupported claims. *BMC Medical Research Methodology, 25*(1), 128. https://doi.org/10.1186/s12874-025-02581-7

Ralph, P., Mahoud, M., Schlager, D., Lee, W. G., Wafa, R., Williamson, E., Butler, G., Ralph, D., & Sangster, P. (2025). United Kingdom data collection of semen quality in transgender adolescent females seeking fertility preservation. *Fertility and Sterility, 123*(2), 313–321. https://doi.org/10.1016/j.fertnstert.2024.09.006

Salas-Humara, C., Sequeira, G. M., Rossi, W., & Dhar, C. P. (2019). Gender affirming medical care of transgender youth. *Current Problems in Pediatric and Adolescent Health Care, 49*(9), 100683. https://doi.org/10.1016/j.cppeds.2019.100683

Shanks, J. (2025, October 15). *Sharing an update about our care for trans health patients under 19 years of age*. Fenway Health. https://fenwayhealth.org/sharing-an-update-about-our-care-for-trans-health-patients-under-19-years-of-age/

Silverberg, C. (2013). *What makes a baby*. Seven Stories Press.

Silverberg, C. (2015). *Sex is a funny word: A book about bodies, feelings, and YOU*. Seven Stories Press.

Silverberg, C., & Smyth, F. (2022). *You know, sex: Bodies, gender, puberty, and other things*. Seven Stories Press.

Simon, R. (2020). *The every body book: The LGBTQ+ inclusive guide for kids about sex, gender, bodies, and families*. Jessica Kingsley Publishers.

Tang, A., Hojilla, J. C., Jackson, J. E., Rothenberg, K. A., Gologorsky, R. C., Stram, D. A., Mooney, C. M., Hernandez, S. L., & Yokoo, K. M. (2022). Gender-affirming mastectomy trends and surgical outcomes in adolescents. *Annals of Plastic Surgery, 88*(4 Suppl.), S325–S331. https://doi.org/10.1097/SAP.0000000000003135

Turban, J. L., King, D., Kobe, J., Reisner, S. L., & Keuroghlian, A. S. (2022). Access to gender-affirming hormones during adolescence and mental health outcomes among transgender adults. *PLOS One, 17*(1), e0261039. https://doi.org/10.1371/journal.pone.0261039

White, J., Jackson, A., Druce, I., & Gale, J. (2023). Oocyte cryopreservation and reciprocal in vitro fertilization in a transgender man on long term testosterone gender-affirming hormone therapy: A case report. *F&S Reports, 5*(1), 111–113. https://doi.org/10.1016/j.xfre.2023.11.004

Yau, M., Malhotra, N. R., Steever, J., Baldisserotto, E., Lin, C., Fader, R., Oransky, M., & Safer, J. D. (2024). Pubertal status at the time of fertility preservation in transgender girls. *Endocrine Practice, 30*(4), 356–359. https://doi.org/10.1016/j.eprac.2024.01.008

Yokoo, K. M. (2022). Gender-affirming mastectomy trends and surgical outcomes in adolescents. *Annals of Plastic Surgery, 88*(4), S325–S331. https://doi.org/10.1097/SAP.0000000000003135

Yurcaba, J. (2025, August 14). *At least 21 hospitals have ended or restricted trans care for minors since January*. NBC News. https://www.nbcnews.com/nbc-out/out-news/least-21-hospitals-ended-restricted-trans-care-minors-january-rcna226640

3 SUPPORTING TRANSGENDER AND GENDER DIVERSE CHILDREN OF COLOR AND THEIR FAMILIES IN CLINICAL CARE

ELIZABETH PANETTA, DE'SHAY THOMAS,
AND JONATHAN POQUIZ

Casey,[1] a biracial (Black and Osage) 10-year-old who was designated male at birth, lives in Missouri with their maternal grandmother. Six months ago, Casey started to socially transition and explore their gender by using they/them pronouns, growing out their hair, and wearing dresses and skirts around the house. While Casey's grandmother, Tammy, a Black 63-year-old cisgender woman, wants to help Casey feel comfortable in exploring their identity, she is concerned about the recent legislation banning gender health care for minors. Tammy stated, "I love that Casey feels safe with me, but I'm terrified for them. Kids at the school have bullied Casey. Even their social worker and school therapist have been weird about Casey's gender. What if I get reported and they take away Casey?" Tammy decided to bring Casey to a gender clinic in Illinois, a nearby state that continues to offer gender care to minors and their families.

Like many caregivers of color who support transgender and gender diverse (TGD) youth, Tammy is faced with a decision to seek gender health care

[1]Throughout this chapter, we as authors utilize a composite narrative from our own professional and personal experiences. All names and identifying information have been disguised to preserve client confidentiality.

https://doi.org/10.1037/0000494-004
Pediatric Gender Health Care: The Gender Affirmative Model Revisited, Second Edition, G. N. Rider, D. Ehrensaft, and C. St. Amand (Editors)

across state lines. In this chapter, we provide a multilevel overview of communities of color and their historical perspectives on gender, systemic inequalities in health care and social service systems in the United States, and healing and wellness frameworks to inform gender health care and supportive services with TGD children of color and their families. Throughout this chapter, we revisit Casey's story to demonstrate the application of clinical care in practice with prepubertal and peripubertal children and their families (e.g., biological parents, adoptive parents, guardians, elders, or other adults). Jax, a White, queer, nonbinary therapist, will guide readers in the clinical care process, demonstrating effective strategies to support TGD children of color and their families.

GENDER IDENTITY AND PRESENTATION IN COMMUNITIES OF COLOR

Gender expansiveness has historically been affirmed in many communities of color. There are more than 150 different precolonial Indigenous tribes native to the Americas that recognize a third gender, such as the Dilbaa, Lhamana, and Winkte in North America and the Zapotec and Muxe in Central America (Lang, 2016). The Māhū in the Kanaka Maoli Indigenous Hawaiian society are individuals whose gender is both between and encompassing the masculine and feminine (Associated Press, 2022). Across Africa, the Mudoko Dako of the Langi in northern Uganda, the Mwami of the Ila people in Zambia, the Chibados of Angola, and the Okule and Agule of the Lugbara are often spiritual leaders within their respective societies due to their dualistic gender identity (Elnaiem, 2021; Roxburgh, 2023). In Asia, there is also an extensive history of culturally specific terms for diverse gender identities and expressions, such as *kathoey* in Thailand, *hijra* in India, *kua xing bie* in China, and *waria* in Indonesia (Asia Pacific Transgender Network, 2021). These identities are loosely defined as people that were designated male at birth but identify as a woman or a third gender, but one must remember to hold the limits of linguistic translation upon cultural nuance.

Colonialism, eurocentrism, and white supremacy heavily impacted precolonial gender identities by using violent methods to identify and eliminate Indigenous ways of life. Perspectives that were seen as deviating from Christian dominance were demonized, leading to the banning of Indigenous languages and social practices, forcible removal of children from their families, and enslavement (Elnaiem, 2021). In this context, gender expansiveness was seen as a threat to binary gender roles, and colonizing forces were fearful of European society embracing gender exploration (Roxburgh, 2023). This led to conversion campaigns, in which transgressive gender performances became heavily targeted, leading to discrimination and persecution. Although many TGD communities of color survived, their existence is still seen as a threat to white cisheteronormativity. As of this writing, there are at least 67 countries with laws criminalizing same-sex relationships between consenting adults, and there are at least 9 countries with laws criminalizing nonconforming forms of gender expression (Human Rights Watch, 2019). As clinicians, it is essential to learn about culturally specific gender expansive identities to understand the historical impacts of colonization and white supremacy, while also centering resilience in the face of oppression.

Jax (therapist) met with Casey (10-year-old client) and Tammy (grandmother) for an initial diagnostic assessment to gather more information on Casey's gender goals. When Jax was with Casey alone, Casey informed Jax that they are two-spirit "not trans or nonbinary" and "don't want to have to explain all of that to a White person." Casey also told Jax that they have not talked to their grandmother about their identity because their grandmother "doesn't really know what two-spirit even means and will just think it means the same as nonbinary or trans or something." Jax explained to Casey that Jax understands their concerns and that their goal for Casey is to feel safe in trusting Jax as their therapist, not for Casey to be their teacher. Jax also discussed confidentiality with Casey, and they both created a plan around what information Casey would like to keep private and what information Casey would like to have shared with their grandmother. After meeting with Casey, Jax prioritized time to learn more about two-spirit identity in connection to the Osage Nation, especially from people who identify as both two-spirit and Osage. Jax also researched more about the impact of white supremacy upon Black and Osage communities.

SYSTEMIC IMPACTS UPON CLINICAL CARE ACCESS FOR TRANSGENDER AND GENDER DIVERSE CHILDREN OF COLOR AND FAMILIES

In providing clinical care to TGD children of color, it is important to acknowledge historical and ongoing systemic oppression such as racism, adultism (bias and discrimination against young people), and cisgenderism (bias and discrimination against gender diverse individuals), and their interconnecting impacts on access to care. Within the United States and its territories, health care institutions and practitioners have violent histories rooted in white supremacy. These have ranged from false beliefs about biological differences between racial groups (Hoffman et al., 2016; White, 2020) to coercion into unethical and involuntary medical procedures (Nuriddin et al., 2020; Stern, 2005). TGD individuals have also historically experienced discrimination by the medical care system, such as verbal harassment and refusal of treatment by medical providers, or they have had to teach health care providers about transgender people to receive appropriate care (James et al., 2016). Many TGD people of color experience transphobia and racism simultaneously in health care settings, resulting in inferior medical care (Howard et al., 2019). Medical insurance barriers, such as lack of access, also increase for TGD people of color (James et al., 2016). Experiences of harm within the medical system and lack of affordability for medical care at the intersection of racism and cisgenderism heavily affect the level of clinical care provided to TGD children of color and their families.

Another system that impacts access to clinical care for TGD children of color is the child welfare system. The United States has an extensive history of white supremacist systems erasing people of color's communal and intergenerational parenting practices by removing children of color from their families through slavery, government-enforced boarding schools, and child guidance clinics based on xenophobic beliefs (Legha & Gordon-Achebe, 2022). Daniel Patrick Moynihan's 1965 report, *The Negro Family: The Case for National Action*, reduced Black families, specifically those led by single mothers, to caricatures through white conceptions of what family connection and support should look like, resulting in pathologization of Black parenting (for discussion of the Moynihan report, see Robinson, 2016). Today, much of this history is embedded within Child Protective Services reports, with documented racial discrepancies toward Black and American Indian or Alaska Native children (Yi et al., 2023). TGD youth are also heavily overrepresented in public child welfare systems, at nearly three times the rate of cisgender youth (Fish et al., 2019). There have also been increasing threats to remove TGD children from their families if parents are supporting gender identity exploration, with some lawmakers labeling this as "child abuse" (Gordon, 2022). Because of this systemic racism and cisgenderism, TGD children of color are often removed from their immediate or extended family of origin or cultural community and placed into care with workers and caregivers who do not understand their identities.

Although policies such as the Indian Child Welfare Act (1978) have worked to maintain cultural connection during adoptive placement, several statutes prevent TGD children of color from requesting to be adopted by guardians who share their racial identity, framing this as a form of discrimination (Curtis, 1996). Youth of color who are placed into White homes often report discomfort over appearance related to race, minimal knowledge or space to explore their cultural heritages, and lack of support from guardians in navigating racism (Lee, 2003). Many child welfare workers and guardians are also unaware of TGD childhood development and fearful that acknowledging TGD identity development will be seen as encouraging TGD identities (Mallon et al., 2021). The medical and child welfare systems are just two of many systems that have caused harm to TGD children of color, and both TGD children of color and their families may be understandably hesitant in trusting clinicians.

Tammy (grandmother) mentioned to Jax (therapist) during the diagnostic assessment that Casey (10-year-old client) has a school therapist and a social worker, so Jax decided to learn more from both Tammy and Casey about their experiences with systems of care. Tammy explained to Jax that Casey had negative experiences with social workers and mental health clinicians in the past related to Child Protective Services. Tammy stated that clinicians have often made harmful assumptions about Casey's adoption by their grandmother and that these providers "always seem uncomfortable" talking about Casey's biracial identity, to the point where their identity is not acknowledged. For Casey, they often felt "so annoyed" because they had to "explain literally everything" to clinicians who "don't even want to listen or care at all." Jax, Casey, and Tammy discussed and processed together what safety can look like for Casey and Tammy in a therapeutic relationship and ways for Jax to uphold this safety as a White clinician.

CHALLENGING WHITE SAVIORISM IN CLINICAL PRACTICE THROUGH CULTURAL HUMILITY AND LIBERATORY CONSCIOUSNESS

In providing clinical care to TGD children of color and families, one must recognize and hold differences in culture that are present in the therapy room. Often clinicians are recommended to practice from a culturally competent framework, as in recognizing cultural differences and awareness and applying this knowledge to diverse clients (Huey et al., 2014). However, the concept of cultural competency can lead to the notion of a discrete end point in cultural learning that only takes a limited amount of work to easily master (Tervalon & Murray-García, 1998). In that context, practicing from a cultural competency–based lens runs the risk of maintaining practices centering on white cisheteronormativity if a practitioner believes that they have learned all that they need to learn in regard to cultural differences.

Dr. Melanie Tervalon and Dr. Jann Murray-García (1998) recognized these pitfalls associated with cultural competency and introduced the term *cultural humility*. Cultural humility encompasses the "lifelong commitment to self-evaluation and critique, to redressing the power imbalances in the patient-physician dynamic, and to developing mutually beneficial and nonpaternalistic clinical and advocacy partnerships with communities on behalf of individuals and defined populations" (Tervalon & Murray-García, 1998, p. 117). The evolution of this term recognizes the importance of learning centered on cultural competency while also holding that one cannot rely on training in a classroom alone in clinical practice. As clinicians, it is vital to recognize that one's knowledge will never be complete concerning different cultures and that one must always be willing to learn more to fully decenter white cisheteronormativity in clinical practice.

The *liberatory consciousness* model can also help clinicians in both confronting privilege and committing to change. Liberatory consciousness enables one to both recognize the effects of oppressive systems upon learned behavior while also intentionally challenging these same systems (Love, 2010). This model contains four major elements: awareness (developing the capacity to notice oppression in the world), analysis (theorizing about the presenting oppressive systems and what change is required), action (committing to and engaging in each of the steps required for change), and accountability and allyship (taking responsibility for one's own internalized oppressive behaviors, along with listening and sharing perspectives with others). Love (2010) described each of these elements as "reminders" to be practiced daily, as "liberatory consciousness is neither mysterious nor difficult, static nor fixed, or something that some people have and others do not" (p. 600, para. 2).

Basing one's practice on cultural humility and liberatory consciousness can also help challenge clinical care rooted in the white savior industrial complex. *White saviorism* is the concept that white intervention and rescue are necessary for individuals of color without acknowledging one's support in creating and maintaining systems of oppression (Cole, 2012). This form of intervention is created solely for rewarding whiteness, rather than actual aid, and can be perpetrated by individuals from any racial or ethnic background. White saviorism itself is rooted in colonization; historically, White Christians viewed themselves as "saving" communities of color from themselves. Teju Cole, a Nigerian American writer, combined *White savior* with *industrial complex* to describe the connections between systemic powers and individual actions that maintain the centering of whiteness through a false lens of rescue.

There are several ways that the white savior industrial complex can present in the clinical space when working with TGD children of color, such as solely using Westernized language around gender identity and not accepting other terms (Coleman et al., 2022). Practicing from lenses grounded in cultural humility and liberatory consciousness directs clinicians to ask TGD children of color what language they use to describe their gender identity and experiences, rather than assuming and automatically using language that may be familiar to the provider, such as *transgender* or *cisgender*. As shown both by Casey's experience and in exploring historical communities of color's gender identities, the specific terms for identity are often sacred and cannot be reduced through translation. Some TGD children of color also may not experience dysphoria around certain parts of their body and will not see certain surgical interventions as necessary for their embodiment goals later in life, especially in connection to certain cultural gender identities. As a clinician practicing cultural humility and liberatory consciousness, one would accept these embodiment goals that present, while exploring with TGD children of color how these embodiment goals connect to their own cultural gender identity, rather than assuming that the client does not truly experience gender dysphoria.

In working with Casey (10-year-old client), Jax (therapist) realized that they historically were taught to provide therapy from culturally competent and white saviorism frameworks. Jax decided to spend time outside of sessions journaling about how these frameworks were taught to Jax, how they have caused harm to clients and their families, and how they continue to present in their therapy practice. Rather than centering feelings of guilt, Jax embraced this time and committed themself to learning and decentering whiteness. They prioritized curating the therapy space so that it could be used by both Casey and Tammy (grandmother) to talk openly about their experiences of harm by White clinicians without Jax becoming defensive of their own identity. Jax also connected with other therapists that wanted to center cultural humility, liberatory consciousness, and care access from an intersectionality lens. Jax created a consulting group to openly discuss and challenge the ways the white savior industrial complex presents in clinical care while holding each other accountable for practicing cultural humility and liberatory consciousness.

CENTERING COMMUNITIES OF COLOR'S HEALING FRAMEWORKS INSIDE AND OUTSIDE OF CLINICAL SPACES

Recognizing healing frameworks of communities of color such as intersectionality, decolonization, and healing justice can help center cultural humility and liberatory consciousness. *Intersectionality* as a concept is grounded in the work of Black feminist activists and scholars, such as Sojourner Truth, the Combahee River Collective, Angela Davis, and Patricia Hill Collins, each of whom described the interdependence of systems of inequality and the importance of coalition work to dismantle systems of power (Moradi & Grzanka, 2017). The term intersectionality itself was coined by Kimberlé Crenshaw (2013) to address the exclusion and violence toward Black women by treating race and sex discrimination as separate matters both in activist spaces and in U.S. law (Civil Rights Act, 1991). This framework is grounded in several central tenets that should be held when working with TGD children of color and families. First, practicing from an intersectionality framework means recognizing the impact of power on interlocking identities (Bowleg, 2012). Because identities like race and gender do not exist in a vacuum, they are constantly interacting with sociostructural factors such as poverty, racism, and transphobia. These macrolevel factors impact resource accessibility through privilege and oppression, which then shape individual lived experiences. As a clinician, one may have identities that seem similar to the children and families that one is supporting, or they may have clients that seem to have similar identities. However, sharing a specific identity does not equal sharing or even being able to relate to histories or present experiences. Keeping intersectionality in mind means recognizing that identity is not a monolithic entity and that each person needs individualized care that is comprehensive of oppression and power.

When exploring healing practices outside of the Western lens, healing frameworks of communities of color also emphasize decolonization. *Colonization* is the "promotion of the dominant group's ideologies, beliefs, and cultural practices to maintain centered positions of cultural, social, and economic capital" (McDowell & Hernández, 2010, p. 95). Within the history of colonization, this act has mainly been performed by White Europeans and Americans, resulting in intergenerational wealth inequality and systems, such as schools and government, that continue to maintain colonial agendas (McDowell & Hernández, 2010). Scholars such as Frantz Fanon et al. (2008), Ngũgĩ wa Thiong'o (1986), Marie Battiste (2000), and Gerald Vizenor (1994) have explored the impact of colonization upon people of color and how their histories, experiences, and knowledge have consistently been disqualified.

Decolonization theory recognizes this violent impact upon communities of color, both in historical and current contexts, by critiquing dominant Western narratives and consciously privileging the wisdom of communities of color before colonization (Lewis et al., 2018). As a framework, decolonization is not solely meant to be practiced by those who have been explicitly colonized, but especially by individuals whose ancestors held power in colonization through "unsettling" or giving up power, privilege, or land (Tuck & Yang, 2012, p. 28). For example, utilizing a decolonization framework in the clinical space does not mean solely recognizing that the medical system and conceptualization of mental health as a whole are Western creations. *Decolonization* means actively abolishing practices that perpetuate colonization, beginning with choosing to notice and actively challenge racist practices grounded in white supremacy, such as mandated reporting rules. These current ethical guidelines are grounded in racist and xenophobic ideals of what constitutes appropriate parenting and family rearing styles. Practicing from a decolonization framework looks like reflecting on whether one is holding families of color to equitable care standards and exploring new ways to curate safety for TGD children of color outside of the mandated reporting system. It can also take the form of redistributing earned wealth by providing free therapy sessions for TGD children of color. Rather than viewing these systems as the norm, they must be challenged and taken down to truly center care for TGD children of color.

Finally, a healing justice framework can help clinicians in decolonizing clinical practice. *Healing justice* was designed in 2005 as a political strategy to "intervene and respond on generational trauma and systemic oppression, and build community/survivor-led response rooted in Southern traditions of resiliency" (Kindred Southern Healing Justice Collective, 2007, para. 1). This takes the form of non-Western individual and collective healing practices that reclaim the right to heal on one's terms (Hassan, 2022). Healing justice also recognizes the harmful impact of past and current systems of oppression upon people of color, and it challenges both the roots of the Western medical system and its current limiting views of wellness and health.

TGD children of color may utilize specific healing practices within their families and communities that are often ignored by clinicians. These can range from altar-building and collective art to protest and uplifting rights, such as accessing healing care outside of a hospital (Hassan, 2022). Clinicians must explore what health and healing practices mean to TGD children of color and support incorporating these forms of healing into clinical care plans. If clinicians are not familiar with specific healing practices, it is their responsibility to learn with an open mind about healing outside of the Western lens. TGD children of color and their families may even request that clinicians engage in cultural healing practices with clients such as including a spiritual or community leader in sessions, having intergenerational sessions with multiple family members, or attending a community dance or drum circle (all of which are not seen as therapeutic in the Western clinical framework). However, it is important that clinicians be mindful of their role when engaging in healing justice frameworks. Curating culturally specific practices outside of the clinician's identities may cause more harm through cultural appropriation. Instead, one should build community relationships with experienced healers who share these identities for referrals and continued support. Centering healing justice, decolonization, and intersectionality as frameworks within one's practice will also center one's clinical care in cultural humility and liberatory consciousness.

Jax (therapist) and Casey (10-year-old client) discussed and agreed to create intersectional identity maps (Siliman & Kearns, 2020) both for Jax and Casey, and they reflected on these maps together (see Appendix 3.1). Rather than solely focusing on similarities, Jax and Casey talked about differences in identities and how this was a space for Casey to challenge Jax's perspective, as practicing from cultural humility and liberatory consciousness meant recognizing that clinical knowledge will never be all-encompassing. In utilizing a decolonization framework, Jax had an open conversation with Tammy (grandmother) and Casey about mandated reporting, acknowledging both its history as a racist practice and how Jax will not participate in this system of violence. Jax explained to Tammy and Casey that Jax will commit to having conversations with Tammy and Casey when concerns about harm emerge, and Jax will work with them both in identifying alternatives that center community-based processes first in order to ensure choice and autonomy. Jax also stated that they will only report both when there are clear and known harms within the state's requirements, and they will do so with Tammy and Casey's involvement and awareness beforehand. Jax then supported Casey in talking with their grandmother about what being two-spirit means to Casey. Utilizing a healing justice framework, Jax researched two-spirit groups both in the Missouri area and online for Casey and Tammy to connect with and build intergenerational healing connections. Casey became more confident in communicating with Jax and Tammy, and they worked together on Casey's gender care goals as a team.

ACCESSIBILITY AND ADVOCACY FOR CLINICAL CARE FOR TRANSGENDER AND GENDER DIVERSE CHILDREN OF COLOR

When working with TGD children of color, clinical care should not solely be viewed through an individualistic lens but rather one that recognizes structural impacts on children and families both inside and outside of the clinical space. This can take the form of decentralizing White practices in clinical care and recognizing the impact of race and racism. However, there is no consistent standard of education on race and racism across clinical practices, and there are no precise ways to ensure that clinicians are practicing from a cultural humility and liberatory conscious perspective. A structural change to promote more accessibility within clinical spaces would be to have critical race theory taught within clinical curricula for gender care and held as a standard of care within clinical practice. The purpose of *critical race theory* is to "illuminate and combat root causes of structural racism" (see Box 1 in Legha & Gordon-Achebe, 2022, p. 697) by recognizing the connection between race, racism, and power. Advocating for critical race theory to be an essential component of clinical education will help create more clinicians who understand the importance of accessibility for TGD children of color and families.

Accessibility and advocacy also mean that clinicians must work to protect access to gender-affirming care for TGD children of color. In the United States, gender-affirming care bans are occurring in states with some of the highest diversity indexes, such as Texas, Georgia, Virginia, and Florida (Jensen et al., 2021). These same states have also had the highest percentage of TGD children of color and their families leave due to state laws (James et al., 2024). Gender-affirming clinics have been forced to close, with parents having to bring their children across state lines to access care, which also impacts the ability of TGD children of color and their families to work with providers with shared identities (Kidd et al., 2021). In the face of these threats, clinicians must advocate for the protection of gender-affirming care for children. There are many types of strategies for clinicians to engage in advocacy, such as providing testimony in state legislatures, amplifying feedback from TGD children of color and families regarding care needs, and keeping track of and actively challenging discriminatory policies (Kuper et al., 2022). Many TGD children of color and their families also consistently engage in self-advocacy in a variety of settings, such as building community through social media, supporting self-definitions of intersecting identities, and validating self-advocacy efforts in community settings (Singh, 2013). Mental health practitioners and clinicians who work with TGD children of color and families see how essential this care is, and these perspectives must be shared and understood by governing bodies.

As Jax continued their therapy practice both with Casey and others, they saw how structures of power harm access to care. Rather than sitting back, Jax decided to take on an advocate role both in Jax's clinic and outside of their workplace. Jax established regular trainings on critical race theory, cultural humility, and liberatory consciousness for their clinic from local trainers who identify as people of color to ensure consistent care for TGD children of color. Jax brainstormed with their clinic director about ways to make therapy more accessible for TGD children of color, such as challenging mandated reporting policies and creating free and sliding scale payment options. Jax also discussed ways to combat structural harm with their cultural humility and liberatory consciousness consultation group. As a collective, they decided to practice accountability with each other by attending protests and providing testimony to the state legislature together, while ensuring the centering of the voices of TGD children of color.

CONCLUSION

This chapter is a response to the need for cultural humility and liberatory consciousness in clinical care with TGD children of color and their families. To cultivate accessible and humble care, clinicians are instructed to create the space in their practice to intentionally (a) recognize Western colonial histories and their effect on clinical care; (b) acknowledge the separation of communities of color from their healing practices; (c) acknowledge the impact of internalized oppression on communities of color and TGD communities; (d) decenter Whiteness in their clinical approaches while recentering current people of color and TGD healing-centered frameworks; and (e) prioritize advocating for gender health care rooted in cultural humility and liberatory consciousness across multiple sectors of social welfare practice, including research, education, policy, and clinical care. Clinicians who implement these strategies are engaged in a more robust and comprehensive response to their clinical practice, creating accessible healing-centered environments for TGD children of color and their families.

To deepen the application of the concepts presented in this chapter, use the following questions to aid in a self-reflective practice:

- Take a moment to reflect on the emotions presenting to you after reading this chapter, and reflect on your personal experiences and approaches to clinical care. Were there parts that you found challenging, affirming, or both? What are ways that you can tend to these emotions while also upholding lenses of cultural humility and liberatory consciousness?
- Clinical care and supportive services often work to support children and families, yet they are known to harm communities of color and gender diverse communities. Identify the stated or unstated harms as depicted in Casey's story. What are possible solutions to mitigate or repair these types of harm?
- For therapists who identify as people of color, TGD, or both, Audre Lorde (2017) stated the following: "Caring for myself is not self-indulgence, it is self-preservation, and that is an act of political warfare" (p. 97). What are ways that you can center self-care as a political act in your practice?
- For therapists who do not share these identities, what are commitments that you can make to uplift and center the voices of TGD children of color? How do you plan to practice accountability to these commitments? For further reflection, the authors also recommend the following texts: *So You Want to Talk About Race* by Ijeoma Oluo (2018), *Me and White Supremacy* by Layla Saad (2020), *Healing Justice Lineages* by Cara Page and Erica Woodland (2023), and *Saving Our Own Lives* by Shira Hassan (2022).

APPENDIX 3.1: INTERSECTIONAL IDENTITY MAPPING EXERCISE AND EXAMPLES FROM THE CHAPTER CASE STUDY

1. At the beginning of the session, Jax asked Casey about what their knowledge is of intersectionality to make sure their awareness is aligned and provided more psychoeducation as needed.
2. On a piece of paper, Jax drew a wheel with three intersecting spokes (Figure 3.1). Jax wrote a positionality quality on each spoke, with Casey's help in naming and defining different types of positionality.
3. Jax then drew two more wheels with three intersecting spokes each on a blank piece of paper. Jax suggested to Casey that the duo could either create their own intersectional identity maps together to learn more about each other, or they could create intersectional identity maps about two different celebrities to talk more about intersecting identities. Casey requested to create personal maps.
4. After taking some time to create their own maps, Jax asked if Casey would like to share their maps with each other and Casey agreed. As a model, Jax first shared their map with Casey, and Jax named and defined each positionality quality on Jax's map (Figure 3.2). Jax engaged Casey by asking Casey how they defined each of Jax's positionality qualities.
5. Casey then shared their own map with Jax (Figure 3.3). Jax asked if Casey would be comfortable defining their own positionality qualities so that Jax could understand them from Casey's own perspective.

FIGURE 3.1. Intersectional Identity Map Template

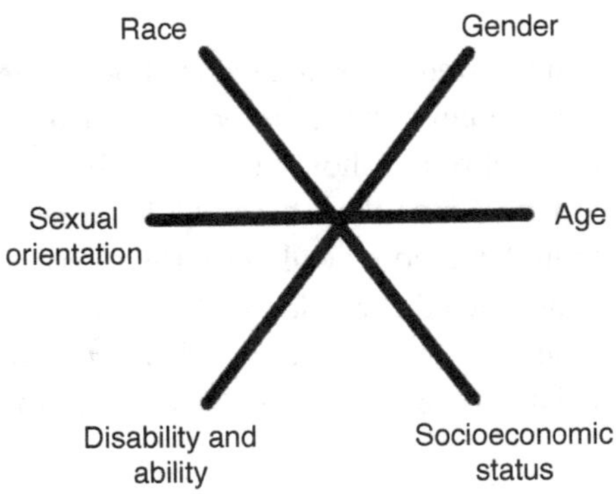

Note. These are just six examples of positionality that can be included on the map, and many more can be incorporated. This template was adapted for use from "Intersectional Approaches to Teaching About Privileges," by S. Siliman and K. Kearns, 2020, *Radical Teacher*, *116*, p. 50 (https://doi.org/10.5195/rt.2020.695). CC-BY.

FIGURE 3.2. Example of Jax's Intersectional Identity Map

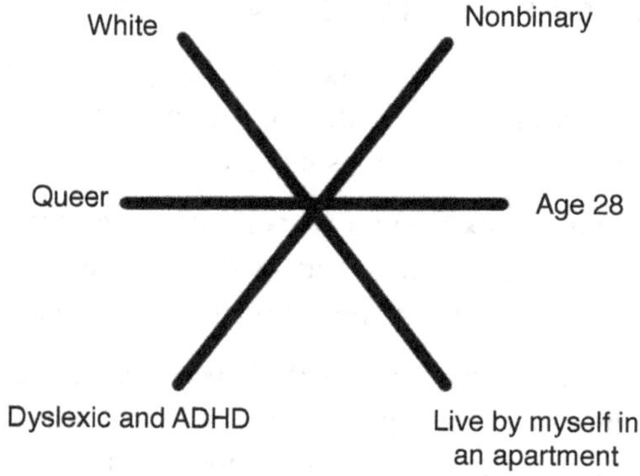

FIGURE 3.3. Example of Casey's Intersectional Identity Map

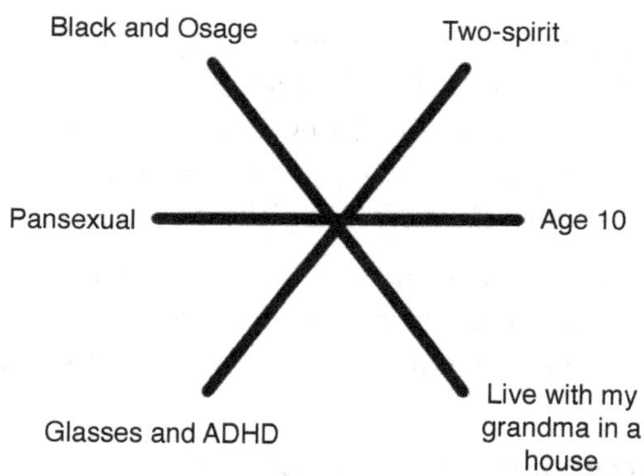

6. With consent, Jax supported Casey in talking about what differences Casey sees between the two maps. Jax returned to their psychoeducation with Casey on intersectionality and how power can be seen in both of their maps. Jax shared with Casey that there will be areas of Casey's identity that Jax does not understand or will get wrong because of both of their lived experiences, and that Jax would like Casey to feel empowered to tell Jax when this is the case. Together Jax and Casey brainstormed ways to support Casey in challenging Jax's perspective when they are incorrect.

REFERENCES

Asia Pacific Transgender Network. (2021, June 23). *Towards transformative healthcare: Asia Pacific Trans Health and Rights Module*. https://weareaptn.org/special_project/tthm/

Associated Press. (2022, July 8). *Hawaii museum revisits history of gender-fluid healers*. NBC News. https://www.nbcnews.com/news/asian-america/hawaii-museum-revisits-history-gender-fluid-healers-rcna37284

Battiste, M. A. (2000). *Reclaiming Indigenous voice and vision*. UBC Press.

Bowleg, L. (2012, July). The problem with the phrase *women and minorities*: Intersectionality—An important theoretical framework for public health. *American Journal of Public Health, 102*(7), 1267–1273. https://doi.org/10.2105/AJPH.2012.300750

Civil Rights Act of 1991, Pub. L. No. 102-166, 105 Stat. 1071 (1991). https://www.congress.gov/bill/102nd-congress/senate-bill/1745/text

Cole, T. (2012, March 21). The white-savior industrial complex. *The Atlantic*. https://www.theatlantic.com/international/archive/2012/03/the-white-savior-industrial-complex/254843/

Coleman, E., Radix, A. E., Bouman, W. P., Brown, G. R., de Vries, A. L. C., Deutsch, M. B., Ettner, R., Fraser, L., Goodman, M., Green, J., Hancock, A. B., Johnson, T. W., Karasic, D. H., Knudson, G. A., Leibowitz, S. F., Meyer-Bahlburg, H. F. L., Monstrey, S. J., Motmans, J., Nahata, L., . . . Arcelus, J. (2022). Standards of care for the health of transgender and gender diverse people, version 8. *International Journal of Transgender Health, 23*(Suppl. 1), S1–S259. https://doi.org/10.1080/26895269.2022.2100644

Crenshaw, K. W. (2013). Mapping the margins: Intersectionality, identity politics, and violence against women of color. In M. A. Fineman (Ed.), *The public nature of private violence: Women and the discovery of abuse* (pp. 93–118). Routledge.

Curtis, C. M. (1996). The adoption of African American children by Whites: A renewed conflict. *Families in Society, 77*(3), 156–165. https://doi.org/10.1606/1044-3894.890

Elnaiem, M. (2021, April 29). The "deviant" African genders that colonialism condemned. *JSTOR Daily*. https://daily.jstor.org/the-deviant-african-genders-that-colonialism-condemned/

Fanon, F., Markmann, C. L., Sardar, Z., & Bhabha, H. K. (2008). *Black skin, white masks* (New ed.). Pluto.

Fish, J. N., Baams, L., Wojciak, A. S., & Russell, S. T. (2019). Are sexual minority youth overrepresented in foster care, child welfare, and out-of-home placement? Findings from nationally representative data. *Child Abuse & Neglect, 89*, 203–211. https://doi.org/10.1016/j.chiabu.2019.01.005

Gordon, C. M. (2022). Caught in the middle: The care of transgender youth in Texas. *Pediatrics, 149*(6), e2022057475. https://doi.org/10.1542/peds.2022-057475

Hassan, S. (2022). *Saving our own lives: A liberatory practice of harm reduction*. Haymarket Books.

Hoffman, K. M., Trawalter, S., Axt, J. R., & Oliver, M. N. (2016). Racial bias in pain assessment and treatment recommendations, and false beliefs about biological differences between Blacks and Whites. *Proceedings of the National Academy of Sciences of the United States of America, 113*(16), 4296–4301. https://doi.org/10.1073/pnas.1516047113

Howard, S. D., Lee, K. L., Nathan, A. G., Wenger, H. C., Chin, M. H., & Cook, S. C. (2019). Healthcare experiences of transgender people of color. *Journal of General Internal Medicine, 34*(10), 2068–2074. https://doi.org/10.1007/s11606-019-05179-0

Huey, S. J., Jr., Tilley, J. L., Jones, E. O., & Smith, C. A. (2014). The contribution of cultural competence to evidence-based care for ethnically diverse populations. *Annual Review of Clinical Psychology, 10*(1), 305–338. https://doi.org/10.1146/annurev-clinpsy-032813-153729

Human Rights Watch. (2019). *#outlawed "The love that dare not speak its name."* https://www.hrw.org/video-photos/interactive/2019/06/26/outlawed-love-dare-not-speak-its-name

Indian Child Welfare Act of 1978, Public Law 95-608, 92 Stat. 3069 (1978). https://www.govinfo.gov/app/details/STATUTE-92/STATUTE-92-Pg3069

James, S. E., Herman, J. L., Durso, L. E., & Heng-Lehtinen, R. (2024, February). *Early insights: A report of the U.S. transgender survey.* 2022 U.S. Trans Survey. https://ustranssurvey.org/

James, S. E., Herman, J. L., Rankin, S., Keisling, M., Mottet, L., & Anafi, M. (2016). *The report of the 2015 U.S. transgender survey*. National Center for Transgender Equality. https://transequality.org/sites/default/files/docs/usts/USTS-Full-Report-Dec17.pdf

Jensen, E., Jones, N., Rabe, M., Pratt, B., Medina, L., Orozco, K., & Spell, L. (2021, August 12). *2020 U.S. population more racially and ethnically diverse than measured in 2010.* United States Census Bureau. https://www.census.gov/library/stories/2021/08/2020-united-states-population-more-racially-ethnically-diverse-than-2010.html

Kidd, K. M., Sequeira, G. M., Paglisotti, T., Katz-Wise, S. L., Kazmerski, T. M., Hillier, A., Miller, E., & Dowshen, N. (2021). "This could mean death for my child": Parent perspectives on laws banning gender-affirming care for transgender adolescents. *Journal of Adolescent Health, 68*(6), 1082–1088. https://doi.org/10.1016/j.jadohealth.2020.09.010

Kindred Southern Healing Justice Collective. (2007). *The need.* https://kindredsouthernhjcollective.org/wp-content/uploads/2020/07/Kindred-Healing-Justice-Collective-Needs-Statement-1-1.pdf

Kuper, L. E., Cooper, M. B., & Mooney, M. A. (2022). Supporting and advocating for transgender and gender diverse youth and their families within the sociopolitical context of widespread discriminatory legislation and policies. *Clinical Practice in Pediatric Psychology, 10*(3), 336–345. https://doi.org/10.1037/cpp0000456

Lang, S. (2016). Native American men-women, lesbians, two-spirits: Contemporary and historical perspectives. *Journal of Lesbian Studies, 20*(3–4), 299–323. https://doi.org/10.1080/10894160.2016.1148966

Lee, R. M. (2003). The transracial adoption paradox: History, research, and counseling implications of cultural socialization. *The Counseling Psychologist, 31*(6), 711–744. https://doi.org/10.1177/0011000003258087

Legha, R. K., & Gordon-Achebe, K. (2022). The color of child protection in America: Antiracism and abolition in child mental health. *Child and Adolescent Psychiatric Clinics of North America, 31*(4), 693–718. https://doi.org/10.1016/j.chc.2022.05.004

Lewis, M. E., Hartwell, E. E., & Myhra, L. L. (2018). Decolonizing mental health services for Indigenous clients: A training program for mental health professionals. *American Journal of Community Psychology, 62*(3-4), 330–339. https://doi.org/10.1002/ajcp.12288

Lorde, A. (2017). *A burst of light: And other essays*. Dover Publications.

Love, B. J. (2010). Developing a liberatory consciousness. In M. Adams, W. J. Blumenfeld, C. R. Casteneda, H. W. Hackman, M. L. Peters, & X. Zuniga (Eds.), *Readings for diversity and social justice* (pp. 533–540). Routledge.

Mallon, G. P., Karnoski, R., Stabbe, O., Waller, L., & Sierra, V. (2021). Social work practice with trans and gender expansive youth in child welfare systems. In J. Shelton &

G. P. Mallon (Eds.), *Social work practice with transgender and gender expansive youth* (3rd ed., pp. 210–227). Routledge. https://doi.org/10.4324/9780429297687-16

McDowell, T., & Hernández, P. (2010). Decolonizing academia: Intersectionality, participation, and accountability in family therapy and counseling. *Journal of Feminist Family Therapy, 22*(2), 93–111. https://doi.org/10.1080/08952831003787834

Moradi, B., & Grzanka, P. R. (2017). Using intersectionality responsibly: Toward critical epistemology, structural analysis, and social justice activism. *Journal of Counseling Psychology, 64*(5), 500–513. https://doi.org/10.1037/cou0000203

Moynihan, D. P. (1965, March). *The Negro family: The case for national action.* U.S. Department of Labor. Retrieved April 3, 2026, from https://www.dol.gov/general/aboutdol/history/webid-moynihan

Nuriddin, A., Mooney, G., & White, A. I. R. (2020). Reckoning with histories of medical racism and violence in the USA. *The Lancet, 396*(10256), 949–951. https://doi.org/10.1016/S0140-6736(20)32032-8

Oluo, I. (2018). *So you want to talk about race.* Seal Press.

Page, C., & Woodland, E. (2023). *Healing justice lineages: Dreaming at the crossroads of liberation, collective care, and safety.* North Atlantic Books.

Robinson, R. L. (2016). *A dark secret too scandalous to confront: Did the Moynihan report imply that poor Black caregivers' parenting styles and childhood cruelties were strongly correlated with self-perpetuating pathologies?* (Howard Law Research Paper No. 16-7). SSRN. https://doi.org/10.2139/ssrn.2756844

Roxburgh, C. (2023, June 2). *"Gender hegemony": How colonialism distorted African perspectives of trans identity.* Minority Africa. https://minorityafrica.org/colonialism-gender-trans-identity-africa/

Saad, L. (2020). *Me and White supremacy: Combat racism, change the world, and become a good ancestor.* Sourcebooks.

Siliman, S., & Kearns, K. (2020). Intersectional approaches to teaching about privileges. *Radical Teacher, 116*, 47–54. https://doi.org/10.5195/rt.2020.695

Singh, A. A. (2013). Transgender youth of color and resilience: Negotiating oppression and finding support. *Sex Roles, 68*(11–12), 690–702. https://doi.org/10.1007/s11199-012-0149-z

Stern, A. M. (2005). Sterilized in the name of public health: Race, immigration, and reproductive control in modern California. *American Journal of Public Health, 95*(7), 1128–1138. https://doi.org/10.2105/ajph.2004.041608

Tervalon, M., & Murray-García, J. (1998). Cultural humility versus cultural competence: A critical distinction in defining physician training outcomes in multicultural education. *Journal of Health Care for the Poor and Underserved, 9*(2), 117–125. https://doi.org/10.1353/hpu.2010.0233

Tuck, E., & Yang, K. W. (2012). Decolonization is not a metaphor. *Decolonization: Indigeneity, Education & Society, 1*(1), 1–40. https://clas.osu.edu/sites/clas.osu.edu/files/Tuck%20and%20Yang%202012%20Decolonization%20is%20not%20a%20metaphor.pdf

Vizenor, G. R. (1994). *Manifest manners: Postindian warriors of survivance.* University Press of New England.

wa Thiong'o, N. (1986). *Decolonising the mind: The politics of language in African literature.* J. Currey.

White, A. I. R. (2020). Historical linkages: Epidemic threat, economic risk, and xenophobia. *The Lancet*, *395*(10232), 1250–1251. https://doi.org/10.1016/S0140-6736(20)30737-6

Yi, Y., Edwards, F., Emanuel, N., Lee, H., Leventhal, J. M., Waldfogel, J., & Wildeman, C. (2023). State-level variation in the cumulative prevalence of child welfare system contact, 2015–2019. *Children and Youth Services Review*, *147*, 106832. https://doi.org/10.1016/j.childyouth.2023.106832

4 BUILDING RESILIENCE IN TRANSGENDER AND GENDER DIVERSE CHILDREN, FAMILIES, AND COMMUNITIES

A Multidimensional Family Approach

JEAN MALPAS, ELIZABETH GLAESER, SHAWN V. GIAMMATTEI, AND DERRICK T. JORDAN

When working with prepubertal transgender and gender diverse (TGD) children, the point of entry into care is most often led by their caregivers or sometimes social services referring or mandating the caregivers to care. As service providers, we are in a unique position to work with the young person, their caregivers, and often the whole community on a journey toward support and acceptance. A similar goal can be adopted regarding *building resilience*, defined as the ability for TGD youth, their families, and communities not only to overcome or survive adversity but also to grow and become stronger through the experience (Walsh, 2013).

This chapter outlines interventions to cultivate resilience in TGD children, families, and communities through the *multidimensional family approach* (MDFA; Malpas, 2011). The MDFA was developed at the Ackerman Institute for the Family's Gender & Family Project and emerged from the need for gender affirmative services for families of TGD youth in New York City (Glaeser, 2021; Malpas, 2011, 2016). We will explore the premises of the MDFA utilizing a case example of a family encompassing varying degrees of acceptance of gender diversity, establishing levels of interventions and clinical choice points for cultivating individual, family, and community acceptance

https://doi.org/10.1037/0000494-005
Pediatric Gender Health Care: The Gender Affirmative Model Revisited, Second Edition, G. N. Rider, D. Ehrensaft, and C. St. Amand (Editors)

and resilience. Special attention will be paid to interweaving gender affirmative care with culturally attuned clinical work, including intersectionality (Crenshaw, 2013), as a critical element in clinical considerations around resilience building (Zhou et al., 2023).

BUILDING INDIVIDUAL, FAMILY, AND COMMUNITY RESILIENCE

TGD youth and adults report significant levels of minority stress due to stigma, prejudice, and discrimination across the lifespan (James et al., 2016). Even in the most affirming families, minority stress will have an impact on TGD youth, and their families are likely to experience adversity that will create significant stressors (Kosciw et al., 2022). At the same time, it is possible for these children and their families not only to successfully navigate these challenges but also to use their individual and collective identities, both marginalized and privileged, to grow through the process. The ability to cultivate resilience to bounce back from and grow through the adversity in one's life has been linked with overall success and happiness (Allan & Ungar, 2014). TGD youth and their families are likely to face significant adversity in many areas of their lives, including discrimination, social stigma, bullying, lack of acceptance from peers or family, mental health struggles, limited access to gender-affirming care, and systemic barriers that affect their well-being and opportunities; thus, the ability to foster resilience is an important component to successful outcomes. Given that family resilience has been shown to positively impact the individual members, and their growth, which in turn positively affects the family (Katz-Wise et al., 2018, 2024), the importance of building family resilience for TGD youth cannot be underestimated.

Resilience factors are shaped by individual and collective intersecting identities. Seven resilience factors that individual, family, and community interventions can be designed to address are (a) access to material resources; (b) supportive relationships with significant others; (c) a sense of identity that fuels a sense of satisfaction or pride and purpose; (d) experiences of power and control; (e) cultural adherence, which fosters a connection to community; (f) social justice, or a sense that things are fair and equitable; and (g) a sense of social cohesion, which is often found through a connection to higher purpose or spirituality (Allan & Ungar, 2014).

Religion and spirituality have been a source of resilience for many families of color. As such, the role of religion and spirituality should be strongly considered, by the culturally sensitive and aware clinician, as a protective factor when working with TGD youth and families of color (Caldwell & Senter, 2012; Currin et al., 2022). Although pursuing access to material resources for TGD youth and their families may be outside the scope of our practice, we know it would be difficult for families to engage if their basic needs are not met.

Individual-level resilience-building interventions for TGD youth and their family members should focus on increasing self-efficacy and coping skills for dealing with stress and increasing health-promoting behaviors, social skills training, and social support networks; improving academic skills; and engaging in extracurricular and community activities (Fritz et al., 2018). One particularly important aspect of resilience building for TGD youth includes the ability to define and describe their own identities (Singh et al., 2014). Family-based resilience-building interventions should be focused on creating positive parent–child attachment and parental warmth, family cohesion and care, a close relationship with a caring adult, as well as encouragement and assistance (Allan & Ungar, 2014; Katz-Wise et al., 2018).

Given that most children spend the majority of their time at school, most community interventions are centered there. However, such interventions could translate just as well to places of worship, athletic groups, and other spaces offering experiences that connect with and make room for the child's intersecting identities (social, cultural, etc.) that are meaningful to them. The community-focused resilience-building interventions for TGD youth and their families focus on increasing supportive peer relationships, promoting positive teacher influences, and enhancing opportunities for success (Johns et al., 2021; Leonard, 2022).

The MDFA creates a process that can foster resilience by encompassing many of the individual, family, and community resilience-building interventions. In this approach, TGD youth and their families are helped to overcome adversity through exposure to gender-affirming practices, such as the normalizing of gender diversity and externalizing of negative cultural reactions. In other words, pathology is situated in the environment rather than in the child and family, freeing the family to develop their own self-confidence and strength in the face of such adversity. The ability of these families to not only nurture their TGD child but also grow through the process of acceptance and celebration of gender diversity can be healing for TGD youth, their families, and the communities in which they live (Malpas, 2017).

MULTIDIMENSIONAL FAMILY APPROACH: PREMISES AND LEVELS OF INTERVENTION

Although many mental health programs have focused on individual support for transgender adolescents and young adults, they rarely have included services for younger children, nor have they used a family-inclusive approach to involve caregivers, siblings, extended family, and community in care. The MDFA can be considered a multisystemic clinical application of the gender affirmative model (GAM) theoretical framework (Hidalgo et al., 2013) to TGD youth, their families, and social contexts. The MDFA is based on the GAM's premise that gender variations are not considered disorders, but rather that mental health vulnerabilities in TGD youth are most often secondary to their experiences of transphobia, cisnormativity, family and community rejection, and so forth.

The MDFA comprehends gender as culturally bound, not limited to a binary, with the potential to be fluid, and comprising a complex combination of biological, developmental, social, and cultural influences. Core clinical objectives of the MDFA include a primary focus on creating a nurturing, accepting environment where the child can freely articulate their experience of themself and where their genuine gender identities and expressions can develop and be affirmed internally and in their life contexts. The MDFA considers both the experiences and reactions of the child's ecological environments (e.g., family, school, culture, and community) that inform the child's sense of self and the child's ability to actualize general mental, physical, social, and gender health. Finally, this approach offers support to both the child and the caregivers as well as significant players involved in the family's life.

The MDFA operates with a set of sequentially ordered yet flexible modalities and levels of interventions that will be illustrated through a case example. We have identified three groups of families, ranging from exhibiting most to least accepting behaviors: accepting, ambivalent, and rejecting (Glaeser, 2021; Malpas & Janssen, 2015; Malpas et al., 2022). Ambivalent caregivers can show supportive and accepting behaviors such as attending support groups and affirmative primary care, but at the same time, they continue to display ambivalence or protectiveness by forbidding more open social transition or disclosure in the extended family and community. Fostering resilience and acceptance in each group requires different approaches and modalities. We have created a fictional case example from the rejecting group that is often the most challenging.

Winston is a 10-year-old biracial girl who was designated male at birth. She presented with her mother and father at the Gender & Family Project. Bill, an African American cisgender businessman in his 50s, and Monique, a White cisgender music teacher in her 40s, have been divorced for 5 years for reasons independent from Winston's gender identity. Following an initial intake with each parent separately, a meeting with them together, and preliminary meetings with Winston, it became abundantly clear that Winston had been experiencing a high level of distress about her designated gender since at least first grade. She said she was 80% sure she was a girl, but she did not know whether the remaining

20% of doubt was because of her parents' refusal to believe her or because she simply was not sure yet. Both Bill and Monique were progressive in their thinking and values and connected to the gay community in New York City. Yet despite Winston's ongoing articulations that she was not a gay boy but a straight girl, her parents were adamant in refusing to allow a social transition until after puberty, expressing "everyone thinks they are trans now." Winston excelled at sports and had a promising future in basketball. By the time the family came in for services, Winston presented with clinically significant depression and suicidal ideation, which had increased in recent months. Monique started to wonder whether they were taking the right path. But Bill was certain that puberty suppression, a potential next step given Winston's gender assertions, would only influence his "son" in the worst way. For example, Bill exclaimed many times that "if he isn't really transgender, these medications will convince him he is" and "these medicines aren't safe or well-studied."

Initial Interview With the Caregivers and Child Separately

The initial meeting with caregivers alone presents several advantages. First, it enables the clinician to establish an alliance with the family decision-makers. Second, it provides privacy to explore parents' and family members' genuine experiences and reactions to their child's gender, while shielding the child from any of the family's reported feelings that might prove harmful to the child. Clinicians can gather an in-depth history of the child's psychological, social, and gender development and can assess the family's request for support and resources. Focusing specifically on gender development and history, the interview aims to identify (a) the presence of discomfort with designated sex, (b) any signs that puberty has begun (voice deepening, facial hair, morning erections, etc.) and the child's response to these, and (c) features relevant to the young person's gender expression versus gender identity versus gender embodiment goals versus emerging sexual orientation. Third and most important, the initial caregiver visit is also a crucial time when family and individual protective and risk factors can be identified and considered for potential supportive recommendations.

Using a dialectical perspective on resilience in which both individual family members and family system resilience can modulate and potentiate each other, it is important to collect information on each family member's internal, interpersonal, and contextual resources and vulnerabilities. In families composed of multiple households, each parent or subgroup of parents brings to the table a different life history and set of contexts, along with their respective temperament, personalities, interpersonal styles, belief systems, cultures, and social locations. Using a family tree (*genogram*) as an organizing tool can quickly provide a map of other key family members involved in the life of the child, and this allows the clinician to inquire whether these players present a source of challenge or affirmation or, most often, both.

The separate intake processes outlined earlier allowed for the collection of experiences from both Winston and her caregivers. It also highlighted core beliefs related to the family's race, ethnicity, and social class that would be explored in family therapy and parental coaching, allowing for focus on each parent's respective lived experience.

Another section of the initial interview with caregivers focuses on the life context of the child, their school experience, and the areas of social support that might be needed. It is important to inquire with caregivers directly about their perception of their child's safety, acceptance, and integration in school, after-school programs, or other educational, sports, and extracurricular activities. Given the high rates of school bullying incidents reported by TGD youth (Kosciw et al., 2022), obtaining a third-party direct perspective, such as a teacher's or educator's observations, is often recommended as well.

The initial meeting with the child uses a developmentally appropriate format. If the child is particularly young, it is often necessary to spend time together with caregivers until the child feels comfortable being alone with the provider. The level of transparency about the nature of the meeting varies from one family to another. In general, it is recommended to make it clear that the focus of the meetings will be to help the child be supported for who they are—including gender identity and gender expression. The subsequent meetings with the child focus on engaging the child in an authentic conversation about self-perception, gender development, and any distress created by the reactions of their family, school, or friends. Methods used toward these goals vary depending on the child's age. A combination of interactive, play, observational, and structured interviewing methods tends to be optimal (Glaeser, 2016; Kaufman, 2016a; Malpas et al., 2018). It is unfortunate that empirically validated measures for preteens measuring gender identity and dysphoria are lacking and often not inclusive (see Chapter 8, this volume). Information gathered with the child helps clarify whether the child's assertions are primarily about gender expression, identity, embodiment, or perhaps something else entirely. On the basis of that information, caregivers are given feedback on appropriate next steps and recommendations (Glaeser, 2021; Malpas, 2011, 2016; Malpas & Janssen, 2015; Malpas et al., 2022).

Evaluation

The clinical choice point at the end of the set of first interviews often coalesces around several questions: whether the child would benefit from further assessment or perhaps a formal biopsychosocial assessment; whether the child and family need therapy, community participation, or both; and the type and level of gender health support that the child's school and communities would most benefit from. With prepubertal children, caregivers are the cornerstones of all support modalities and are integral to their child's resilience. Their genuine engagement, collaboration, and participation will have great influence on whether the young person will have access to needed medical, legal, or educational support.

In-depth psychological evaluations are often particularly useful in situations in which (a) the child, the family, and the therapist are uncertain as to whether the child is gender expansive/nonbinary or binary transgender identified, or both or (b) a finer differentiation needs to be made in terms of gender expression, gender identity, gender embodiment, or all of these. Also, with youth entering puberty or beyond, pediatric gender clinics typically require a more formal psychological workup before prescribing puberty suppression or hormone therapy. Some investigators have found that assessments such as these may be most helpful for parents grappling with the changes in their child's gender identity and to support family acceptance (Allen et al., 2021). In all cases, these evaluations remain systemic, integrating all caregivers' perspectives (Allen et al., 2021; Kaufman, 2016b). Gender health evaluations can play a pivotal role in fostering resilience among children, adolescents, and their families. These evaluations are essential, particularly when uncertainty surrounds the child's gender identity or expression or embodiment, as they provide clarity and guide supportive pathways forward. This process is invaluable for families facing anxiety or ambivalence about their child's transition, offering a structured approach that transforms apprehension into understanding and acceptance. Comprehensive feedback sessions serve as powerful psychoeducational interventions, enhancing the family's engagement in higher levels of care and community participation. These sessions also help reinforce a unified support system by integrating all caregivers' perspectives, which strengthens the emotional fabric of the family and fosters collective resilience. For parents who may doubt their child's TGD identity, the detailed evaluation often offers reasons to trust and validate their child, fostering empathy and acceptance. Similarly, children who may be hesitant to discuss their gender often find the process to be an opportunity for open, supportive conversations with their families, building trust and emotional safety—key elements of resilience needed to face future challenges confidently.

With Winston's family, the recommendation for gender health care (medical care, social transition, and individual and family therapy) had to be carefully crafted. Monique was moving from rejecting to ambivalent, but Bill was not ready to believe nor affirm his child. Neither parent was open to participating in a caregiver or family group. Bill kept asking for arguments to be convinced that Winston's gender assertions and expressions were not a call for attention or a product of the negative influence of living in "crazy NYC where it's cool to be trans these days." The team decided that a family-centered evaluation would provide everyone the chance to tell their side of the story, and that a comprehensive psychological workup might be useful to Bill's assessment of the legitimacy of his child's experience. The recommendation of moving forward with the evaluation was a way of showing Winston that everyone took her distress and desire to transition seriously. Because puberty was nearing fast, the evaluation could also be used to support medical care if needed. After several meetings, the lengthy process of evaluation confirmed Winston's experiences of gender dysphoria and revealed that the relationship between Winston and her father had worsened in the past year. Fights escalated often, and her father became verbally abusive whenever discussions focused on supporting Winston's gender identity.

Individual Therapy, Family Therapy, and Caregiver Coaching

Individual therapy, family therapy, caregiver coaching, or a combination of these is sometimes necessary when the child's distress has affected the child's emotional, relational, social, or educational development or when the family's response to gender diversity has eroded or complicated family relationships and greatly increased the risk factors that impair resilience. Working with the family is helpful when the tension triggered by the child's gender and the caregivers' reactions has disrupted family relationships, communication, and attachment; such work can also provide support to the family as they navigate their internal and external developmental tasks. When caregivers are particularly resistant to gender diversity, we have found that meeting with them alone and taking the time to understand their dilemmas has been effective. Rather than driving a gender-inclusive agenda that might alienate the caregiver and ultimately jeopardize the child's access to a gender affirmative team, the provider can focus on meeting caregivers where they are and developing a compassionate understanding of the individual, cultural, or relational factors affecting the parent's adjustment to the child's emerging gender identity, gender expression, or both (Malpas et al., 2022; Sheinberg & Brewster, 2014). Establishing a therapeutic relationship with the client is particularly important at the onset of treatment, where the client and therapists' social locations are often contributing factors to the clients' sense of safety and willingness toward vulnerability. Specifically, implicit and explicit awareness of shared and intersecting identities between clients and therapists can provide benefits to treatment, while reinforcing a helpful therapeutic connection with the client.

While working with caregivers, it is important to not underestimate the young person's distress and need for individual support (Testa et al., 2015) independent from the level of family support or community access that they are receiving. Fostering individual resilience, although strongly connected to family and community support, sometimes requires a therapeutic space in which the young person can express the hardship of living in a cisnormative and transphobic world or with a family that falls short of acceptance, and this can absorb extrafamilial supports in fortifying their resilience and well-being. Although support from parents is fundamental to a child's well-being, parents might struggle to understand and validate the experiences of challenging gender stereotypes and expectations. Internal or external referrals to individual therapists with extensive experience with gender diversity may be recommended.

Additionally, it is vital to give caregivers the opportunity to discuss additional stressors, such as racism, systems of oppression, and other forms of marginalization based on the family's social location, within the context of services for TGD youth. An inability to name differences in experience of various social identities, can alienate caregivers who might then be more likely not to return for services (Sue et al., 2022).

Family therapy was strongly recommended to Winston's family, who accepted the recommendation. The family therapy modality was used flexibly—sometimes mother and daughter were seen, sometimes father and daughter, sometimes each parent alone, and other times the divorced coparents together only when necessary. Over time, the treatment helped Monique identify the transphobic sources of her ambivalence. She feared for Winston's future but also felt guilty and ashamed. Monique was disconnected from her own parents, and she felt that having a transgender child would prove to her friends and extended family that she had failed as a parent and that she was more wounded than she thought. Differentiating her own narrative from her child's experience facilitated her wanting to join the parent support group. Bill, on the other hand, struggled to perceive the risks of his approach, agreeing to disagree with the information provided by the therapist. He was prepared to protect Winston's safety at all costs, yet he also did not want to lose his relationship with his child. The family therapist, who also identified as African American, was able to involve Bill's new wife and join him in understanding the challenges of raising Winston as a transgender girl who he thought needed to be a "strong Black man." Having a Black therapist, Bill felt more at ease discussing the impact of race, a conversation that would eventually open up to his wife with the hope of better understanding the fears and challenges Bill felt Winston may face as a Black transgender girl. Bill and his wife gradually opened up about the potential challenges of integrating an accepted and supported transgender daughter into their own communities.

Despite our belief that all parents love and want the best for their children, research results and clinical evidence show that many parents of TGD youth have parenting behaviors that can be described as rejecting and ambivalent (Malpas, 2011; Ryan et al., 2009). We have found it helpful for clinical intervention to keep in mind the parenting mandates that become conflicted in situations of unexpected identity differences in the family (Malpas, 2011). Indeed, in a Western context, parental tasks include nurturance and acceptance while also expecting parents to be primarily responsible for transmission of family beliefs, behaviors, language, and interpersonal habits as well as properly socializing their children around the cultural and social norms of the group to which they intend their child to affiliate (Solomon, 2012). In families where caregivers and children share cisgender gender modalities and a predilection toward conventional binary expressions, gender operates as a platform for positive interpersonal experiences where nurturance, acceptance, transmission, and socialization can all happen at once and without conflict. Reviewing each of these parental functions reveals that any one of them can become conflicted when caregivers' and children's experiences of gender do not fit within the same models and create unforeseen differences between parents and TGD children (Glaeser, 2021; Malpas, 2011; Malpas et al., 2022).

Winston's gender identity did not align with her designated sex at birth, and her gender expressions often deviated from the gender norms in place in the community of both her mother and father. Developing interventions with parents who are experiencing such parenting and cultural conflicts is important to help parents understand which beliefs might be underlying their rejecting behaviors. For instance, the stance "I will not let my child wear a dress in public because he might be rejected by his peers or our community," while coming from a loving and protective place, is a result of the conflict between the tasks of acceptance and the pull to conform to social norms and expectations. In building resilience, parents need the space and the tools to explore conflicts they experience in the execution of their parental tasks and consider the potentially negative effects on their child.

Multifamily Groups

Multifamily groups offer a unique and essential sense of belonging to a community of peers where children get to meet other TGD children and grow older together and where caregivers find a community of loving parents. These groups offer a resilience-building intervention by fostering social support, a sense of identity, cultural adherence, and an opening for learning new coping skills. Groups can be configured based on the child's age and include caregiver spaces, children spaces, teenager spaces, and sibling spaces and, at times, grandparents and extended family members. Additionally, groups can be configured with consideration of native language as well as other shared experiences and intersecting identities (Glaeser, 2021).

Caregivers' community groups focus on making room for a range of experiences from shock, fear, ambivalence, confusion, and grief to hope, joy, empowerment, and mutual support. The group emphasizes caregivers' own social location and intersectionality of race, ethnicity, class, gender, sexual orientation, physical disability, and religion (Glaeser, 2021; Malpas et al., 2016, 2022). It encourages caregivers' genuine expression of their journey while processing parenting experiences, dilemmas, and solutions. The themes that have emerged in the caregivers' community groups show that cisgender parents have a variety of reactions to their TGD youth. These experiences are contextualized by their own life history, the gendered expectations they had for their child, the larger cultural systems, and the communities with which they affiliate. Families rarely have homogenous experiences, despite shared identities and cultural experiences; and different caregivers or members of the same family might hold different voices, with some expressing unconditional love more easily and others articulating fear, grief, or denial.

The caregivers' groups also support members in their own coming out process. They must grapple with their social status and intersecting identities as they incorporate a family member who is affiliated with an often-stigmatized group, especially if they have had no experience themselves with being part of such a group. Parents may feel their own fears of shame, stigma, failure, or disconnect because their identity is different from that of their child and now that of their own family and community. Parents must figure out how to come out to their extended family and community and how to reaffiliate themselves with their child while simultaneously figuring out their own identities in the process (Giammattei, 2015; Glaeser, 2021; Hidalgo & Chen, 2019). Questions of gender identity in children can cause complications in parental and marital relationships. Relational ruptures in the coparenting or family systems are typical. Navigating the various difficulties, cultural beliefs, uncertainties, and conflicts is part of the pathway toward acceptance of their child's gender identity and may require relationship counseling with the parents (Malpas, 2017).

As a Black man, Bill feared for his child's safety and worried that he was the only person who truly understood the harsh reality of being a Black transgender woman. He found it difficult to discuss this concern openly with a coparent of a different cultural or ethnic background. Although Bill never accepted joining a parent support group, he accepted education and sought information from physicians about puberty suppression. In addition, he reached out to friends in his community and found support as a father of a transgender child.

Training and Community Consulting

Finally, in building resilience, the MDFA considers the multiple systems in which the child and family are involved. For instance, providers and community groups inquire about the multidisciplinary needs of the child and family and facilitate referrals to medical and legal services when needed or appropriate. In addition, one of the premises of the MDFA is that the support each family needs should be individually tailored to that family. Some will be best supported by individual and family therapy, whereas others will benefit most from training and community interventions (school training, groups, etc.). The direct community around the caregivers and child is of utmost importance in fostering resilience. Affirming the child's gender and improving their mental health necessitates considering any instance of oppression, danger, and marginalization they might be experiencing in a systematic or daily way. These interventions are especially important for TGD youth because they are disproportionately victims of bullying and harassment in school (Kosciw et al., 2022; Ryan et al., 2009). In the MDFA intake process, the provider asks the caregivers and the child about academic performance and school climate. Direct inquiry with teachers is made with permission from the family. In our experience, most children experience a degree of discomfort or harassment based on their gender expression, identity, and level of disclosure or social transition in school. Even in schools in which the child is accepted and affirmed, most educators and administrators often feel underequipped to optimally support the child and their family or integrate gender diversity as a core component of the school's educational program and social climate. The collaboration between the clinician and the school trainers offers the family the chance to have a coordinated effect on their larger systems and builds individual, family, and community resilience.

Winston's family therapist collaborated with her teachers to assess her safety at school and assign her to a more affirming classroom. The family also attended multiple informational meetings with a gender affirmative medical clinic and debriefed reactions separately and together in therapy. After 2 years of a slow and thoughtful process, Winston socially transitioned and started puberty blockers. She joined the tween group at the clinic and started meeting other transgender youth "in real life, not just online," as she said excitedly. In this case, the clinical approach toward gender resilience had combined slow and flexible engagement with parents, affirming feedback with the child, and subtle but clear messaging with the father about the potential risk of a rejecting stance toward his child. The treatment was layered with an in-depth exploration of each caregiver's experience and belief system, enabling the provider to have a more intimate understanding of their struggle and compassionate delivery of psycho- and socioeducation.

CONCLUSION

The MDFA is an affirming, resilience-building, multimodal intervention for working with TGD youth, their families, and communities. This model is an application of pediatric gender health care at a multisystemic level. The approach is comprehensive, meeting families where they are and offering the interventions needed to support and advocate for their child. The clinical approach emphasizes considering the multiple perspectives and varying degrees of comfort with gender diversity that exist in the family. A crucial aspect of the stance is its flexibility with sequence and modalities of interventions. Different youth and families require different points of entry and catalysts for change depending on their social location, access to resources, gender identity development, belief systems, and larger cultural contexts.

The MDFA addresses key factors of individual, relational, and family resilience. In addition to pointing families and communities in the direction of resources and support, the MDFA engages all of the relevant individuals in the TGD youth's life to develop a more coherent, empowering, and culturally attuned narrative of the family's relationship with gender diversity. The model lessens restraining forces and conflicts for caregivers, enabling them to find their way back to their functions of positive socialization, nurturance, and acceptance. By involving all family members and relevant members of the community, the MDFA gives youth and families a sense of agency and belonging, as well as a connection to a greater sense of purpose. Optimally, gender diversity is then no longer divisive but instead becomes the source of bonding and pride.

REFERENCES

Allan, R., & Ungar, M. (2014). Resilience-building interventions with children, adolescents, and their families. In S. Prince-Embury & D. Saklofske (Eds.), *Resilience interventions for youth in diverse populations* (pp. 447–462). Springer. https://doi.org/10.1007/978-1-4939-0542-3_20

Allen, L. R., Dodd, C. G., & Moser, C. N. (2021). Gender-affirming psychological assessment with youth and families: A mixed-methods examination. *Practice Innovations*, *6*(3), 159–170. https://doi.org/10.1037/pri0000148

Caldwell, K., & Senter, K. (2012). Strengthening family resilience through spiritual and religious resources. In D. Becvar (Ed.), *Handbook of family resilience* (pp. 441–455). Springer. https://doi.org/10.1007/978-1-4614-3917-2_25

Crenshaw, K. W. (2013). Mapping the margins: Intersectionality, identity politics, and violence against women of color. In M. A. Fineman (Ed.), *The public nature of private violence: Women and the discovery of abuse* (pp. 93–118). Routledge.

Currin, J. M., Knutson, D., Federici, D. J., Koch, J. M., & Ingram, P. B. (2022). Resiliency patterns suggest spirituality supports lower distress in undergraduate students who identify as an LGBTQ+ person of color. *Journal of Gay & Lesbian Social Services*, *34*(3), 302–324. https://doi.org/10.1080/10538720.2021.1958401

Fritz, J., de Graaff, A. M., Caisley, H., van Harmelen, A.-L., & Wilkinson, P. O. (2018). A systematic review of amenable resilience factors that moderate and/or mediate the relationship between childhood adversity and mental health in young people. *Frontiers in Psychiatry*, *9*, 230. https://doi.org/10.3389/fpsyt.2018.00230

Giammattei, S. V. (2015). Beyond the binary: Trans-negotiations in couple and family therapy. *Family Process*, *54*(3), 418–434. https://doi.org/10.1111/famp.12167

Glaeser, E. (2016, June). *What does it mean to socially transition: A pilot measure* [Symposium presentation]. World Professional Association of Transgender Health Conference, Amsterdam, The Netherlands.

Glaeser, E. (2021). *The impact of multifamily group services on the parents of transgender and gender expansive youth* (Publication No. 28767853) [Doctoral dissertation, Columbia University]. Columbia University Academic Commons. https://doi.org/10.7916/d8-xxnh-ww14

Hidalgo, M. A., & Chen, D. (2019). Experiences of gender minority stress in cisgender parents of transgender/gender-expansive prepubertal children: A qualitative study. *Journal of Family Issues*, *40*(7), 865–886. https://doi.org/10.1177/0192513X19829502

Hidalgo, M. A., Ehrensaft, D., Tishelman, A. C., Clark, L. F., Garofalo, R., Rosenthal, S. M., Spack, N. P., & Olson, J. (2013). The gender affirmative model: What we know and what we aim to learn. *Human Development*, *56*(5), 285–290. https://doi.org/10.1159/000355235

James, S. E., Herman, J. L., Rankin, S., Keisling, M., Mottet, L., & Anafi, M. (2016). *The report of the 2015 U.S. Transgender Survey*. National Center for Transgender Equality. https://transequality.org/sites/default/files/docs/usts/USTS-Full-Report-Dec17.pdf

Johns, M. M., Zamantakis, A., Andrzejewski, J., Boyce, L., Rasberry, C. N., & Jayne, P. E. (2021). Minority stress, coping, and transgender youth in schools: Results from the Resilience and Transgender Youth Study. *Journal of School Health*, *91*(11), 883–893. https://doi.org/10.1111/josh.13086

Katz-Wise, S. L., Ehrensaft, D., Vetters, R., Forcier, M., & Austin, S. B. (2018). Family functioning and mental health of transgender and gender-nonconforming youth in the Trans Teen and Family Narratives Project. *The Journal of Sex Research*, *55*(4–5), 582–590. https://doi.org/10.1080/00224499.2017.1415291

Katz-Wise, S. L., Sarda, V., Line, E. C., Marchwinski, B., Budge, S. L., Godwin, E. G., Moore, L. M., Ehrensaft, D., Rosal, M. C., & Thomson, K. A. (2024). Longitudinal family functioning and mental health in transgender and nonbinary youth and their families. *Journal of Child and Family Studies*, *33*, 1321–1335. https://doi.org/10.1007/s10826-023-02738-2

Kaufman, R. (2016a, June). *Social transition: Pre-pubertal TGNC children* [Symposium presentation]. World Professional Association of Transgender Health Conference, Amsterdam, The Netherlands.

Kaufman, R. (2016b, June). *Trauma and gender* [Symposium presentation]. World Professional Association of Transgender Health Conference, Amsterdam, The Netherlands.

Kosciw, J. G., Clark, C. M., & Menard, L. (2022). *The 2021 National School Climate Survey: The experiences of LGBTQ+ youth in our nation's schools—A report from GLSEN*. Gay, Lesbian and Straight Education Network (GLSEN). https://www.glsen.org/sites/default/files/2022-10/NSCS-2021-Full-Report.pdf

Leonard, M. (2022). 'It was probably one of the best moments of being trans*, honestly!': Exploring the positive school experiences of transgender children and young people. *Educational and Child Psychology*, *39*(1), 44–59. https://doi.org/10.53841/bpsecp.2022.39.1.44

Malpas, J. (2011). Between pink and blue: A multi-dimensional family approach to gender nonconforming children and their families. *Family Process*, *50*(4), 453–470. https://doi.org/10.1111/j.1545-5300.2011.01371.x

Malpas, J. (2016, March/April). The transgender journey: What role should therapists play? *The Psychotherapy Networker*. https://www.psychotherapynetworker.org/article/transgender-journey/

Malpas, J. (2017, August 1). *The gift of gender authenticity* [Video]. TEDx Talks. https://www.youtube.com/watch?v=TCQEcR7pi_Q

Malpas, J., Davis, B., Colon-Otero, S., & Raad, M. (2016, June). *The ethics of intersectionality and allyship in clinical work: Power analysis of racial and gender locations in mental health and community work with transgender clients* [Paper presentation]. World Professional Association for Transgender Health, Amsterdam, The Netherlands.

Malpas, J., Glaeser, E., & Giammattei, S. V. (2018). Building resilience in transgender and gender expansive children, families, and communities: A multidimensional family approach. In C. St. Amand & D. Ehrensaft (Eds.), *The gender affirmative model: An interdisciplinary approach to supporting transgender and gender expansive children* (pp. 141–156). American Psychological Association. https://doi.org/10.1037/0000095-009

Malpas, J., & Janssen, A. (2015, November). *Between pink & blue: Combining affirmative and evidence-based approaches to transgender & gender nonconforming youth & their families* [Presentation/training]. Ackerman Institute for the Family, New York, NY, United States.

Malpas, J., Pellicane, M. J., & Glaeser, E. (2022). Family-based interventions with transgender and gender expansive youth: Systematic review and best practice recommendations. *Transgender Health*, *7*(1), 7–29. https://doi.org/10.1089/trgh.2020.0165

Ryan, C., Huebner, D., Diaz, R. M., & Sanchez, J. (2009). Family rejection as a predictor of negative health outcomes in White and Latino lesbian, gay, and bisexual young adults. *Pediatrics*, *123*(1), 346–352. https://doi.org/10.1542/peds.2007-3524

Sheinberg, M., & Brewster, M. K. (2014). Thinking and working relationally: Interviewing and constructing hypotheses to create compassionate understanding. *Family Process*, *53*(4), 618–639. https://doi.org/10.1111/famp.12081

Singh, A. A., Meng, S. E., & Hansen, A. W. (2014). "I am my own gender": Resilience strategies of trans youth. *Journal of Counseling & Development*, *92*(2), 208–218. https://doi.org/10.1002/j.1556-6676.2014.00150.x

Solomon, A. (2012). *Far from the tree: Parents, children and the search for identity*. Scribner.

Sue, D. W., Sue, D., Neville, H. A., & Smith, L. (2022). *Counseling the culturally diverse: Theory and practice*. John Wiley & Sons.

Testa, R. J., Habarth, J., Peta, J., Balsam, K., & Bockting, W. (2015). Development of the gender minority stress and resilience measure. *Psychology of Sexual Orientation and Gender Diversity, 2*(1), 65–77. https://doi.org/10.1037/sgd0000081

Walsh, F. (2013). Community-based practice applications of a family resilience framework. In D. S. Becvar (Ed.), *Handbook of family resilience* (pp. 65–82). Springer. https://doi.org/10.1007/978-1-4614-3917-2_5

Zhou, A. N., Huang, K. J., & Howard, T. L. (2023). Beyond race, sex, and gender: Mental health considerations of transgender youth of color, intersex youth, and nonbinary youth. *Child and Adolescent Psychiatric Clinics of North America, 32*(4), 683–705. https://doi.org/10.1016/j.chc.2023.04.002

5 SUPPORTING THE MENTAL HEALTH OF TRANSGENDER AND GENDER DIVERSE CHILDREN

MATTHEW ETHAN GOLDENBERG AND KARISA L. BARROW

Gender diverse children may face a unique set of challenges that can create vulnerability to developing mental health concerns. The objective of this chapter is to examine mental health challenges that may be common among transgender and gender diverse (TGD) children. It is important to note that there is no credible research to suggest that severe mental health challenges are an inherent aspect of growing up as a TGD child; hence, much of this chapter will focus on which mental health conditions are likely to have a higher prevalence in TGD children and what clinicians can encourage in their work to help foster positive mental health outcomes for TGD children. Additionally, we will examine health conditions associated with TGD adolescents because throughout the research the categorical use of the word "youth" may refer to both prepubertal and postpubertal individuals; thus, study conclusions may be applicable across age groups.

GENDER EXPRESSION

Gender expression is essentially a culturally driven, creative task in which humans attempt to tell a story about who we are from a gendered lens. For

https://doi.org/10.1037/0000494-006
Pediatric Gender Health Care: The Gender Affirmative Model Revisited, Second Edition, G. N. Rider, D. Ehrensaft, and C. St. Amand (Editors)

instance, gender expression can include a person's hairstyle, use of accessories, a chosen name, chosen pronouns, clothing, and body language, which provide visual cues to describe gender identity. Gender expression can be a way to externally interact with our gender identity, but one can also conform one's gender expression to cultural norms for the benefits of social inclusion or safety.

Because the environments children live in are usually controlled by adults, children often have more limited choice of gender expression resources compared to what might be available for adults. Considering that social transition can progress a child's ability to articulate their own gender preferences and interests (Ashley, 2019; Sherer, 2016), we posit that supporting a child in a social transition is a milestone in gender development. When choosing clothing, toys, and activities becomes developmentally possible for the child, caregivers begin to embark on the exciting journey to see who their child is, separate from the caregiver. The slow evolution to understanding who the child is drawn to in terms of peers or characters in stories, evidence of confidence when given the opportunity to express themself with certain clothing or hairstyles and activities they find the most delight in, is called *individuation* (Brookes, 1991) and can be an exciting development for both parent and child. Caregivers who can show genuine interest and care for the preferences and interests of their child provide attunement. *Attunement* refers to our emotional, social, and behavioral ability to recognize a child's needs and respond within a range of appropriate responses (Coolhart, 2018; Field, 2014). For instance, when a child shows fear by hiding behind the parent as they are faced with meeting a stranger, an attuned response from the parent may be to gently put an arm around the child and remind the child that it can be scary to meet new people. In this example, the child is not being pushed physically or socially to interact with the stranger, but the caregiver notices the child's discomfort and externalizes the discomfort by naming it. The child may then experience relief, a sense of being seen, and being responded to in a noncoercive manner, which is the foundation of attunement.

Attuning to a child's needs (as well as the child's temperament) is a critical factor in a child feeling safe and secure. The attunement not only benefits the relationship between the child and their caregiver, but it also becomes central to how easily and consistently a child can gain healthy attachments to others in their life, such as friends, teachers, partners, and family members. We consider a caregiver's ability to attune to the child's gender identity and gender expressions (and allowing for gender expression that does not seek to hinder a child's identity development) a significant factor to promote the child's mental wellness.

Healthy attunement between a caregiver and a child can become challenged when the child is not permitted to express their own interests, needs, and wants, including those pertaining to gender. This does not mean that a parent must have the perfect response; again, attunement refers to a range of responses that are rooted in noticing the child and providing emotional capacity for the child to understand and experience validation of their needs. A parent having emotional capacity for their child suggests that the parent has regulated their own emotions, such as managing anger or fear, and is able to reduce distractions and focus on the child. In many cases, the parent's emotional availability leads to the parent successfully mirroring back or accurately reflecting the child's emotions. In this way, the child feels that the parent has witnessed who they are and what they need. Thus, parents affirming their TGD child is based on the parents' ability to attune to the child's individual expressions and needs.

Social transition refers to an expression of one's authentic gender now shared with others in the social environment (Keo-Meier & Ehrensaft, 2018). Social transition does not occur one time in a person's life, nor does it occur at a consistent age across TGD individuals. It is more helpful to conceptualize social transition as dynamic and reliant on interactional factors between oneself and the environments and contexts in which the person exists. Further, social transition is a subjective and culturally driven experience because there is no one global or constant expectation of gender expression.

Typically, gender-conforming youth are permitted to enjoy clothing, hairstyles, accessories, and activities that align with their gender identity even when there is variation over the lifetime. For instance, cisgender girls may choose masculine athletic shorts when they are younger but prefer skirts as a teenager. We think it is important to note that the natural variation in how one expresses themself over the lifetime does not predict a determination or an inconsistency of one's gender identity. Yet when TGD children show gender expressions not in cultural concordance with their affirmed gender identity, they may be suspected to be incoherent in regard to identity development, such as when a transgender boy dons one of his old dresses or a transgender girl pulls out her trucks.

TGD children benefit from caregivers attuning to gender development, allowing both for the creative and evolving style and interests of the young person, while not assuming that changing or hybrid preferences represent a total or complete shift in identity. As with cisgender children, based on our clinical experience, we recommend encouraging children to meet a diverse group of playmates and friends as well as exposing children to multiple activities that can stimulate their intellectual, social, and physical growth.

TGD youth who socially transition are expressing their gender identity in much the same way that cisgender youth are presumed to develop their gender (as congruent with their gender identity), with the distinction being that

TGD youth may experience additional stress because of negative judgment from others based on their minoritized status. Studies have found that socially transitioned children who receive positive support experience minimal elevations in anxiety and normative levels of depression compared with cisgender, same-age peers (Olson et al., 2016). For youth who adopt a name that is different from the name given at birth, data confirm that youth whose chosen name is used in various settings are at reduced risk for suicidal ideation and suicide attempts (Durwood et al., 2024; Russell et al., 2018).

DETERMINANTS OF REDUCED MENTAL HEALTH SAFEGUARDS FOR TRANSGENDER AND GENDER DIVERSE CHILDREN

Factors that may increase the risk of experiencing negative mental health outcomes for TGD youth include stigma, social isolation, and low self-esteem (Tankersley et al., 2021). Additionally, although the age when a person identifies that they are TGD varies, whether providers consider to inquire about gender identity is also a factor affecting when an individual discloses their gender identity (Rossman et al., 2017). We recommend that clinicians working with all children show curiosity about children's developing gender identities and expressions and normalize exploration of self-identity. Early exposure to positive gender diverse role models may also affect healthy self-esteem development. For instance, when a young person discloses their gender identity and they are accustomed to seeing models of healthy and thriving TGD adults, a sense of both normalcy and optimism for the future may develop. Thus, families should consider that early exposure to diverse persons is of benefit for tweens and teens (Kearns et al., 2021) as well as younger children.

Given that TGD youth may elect a variety of ways to express themselves, it is important to remove heteronormative and cisnormative expectations from youth regarding gender expression and gender roles. Thus, caregivers who successfully attune to their TGD children must confront their own biases and assumptions regarding gender and increase their capacity for a grounded emotional connection between caregiver and child. In addition to attunement as fundamental for a healthy blueprint of relationships for all children over their lifetime, healthy attunement can also serve as the predictor for the caregiver to notice and respond to mental health concerns of a child, should they arise. Youth with higher levels of internalized transphobia (e.g., negative impressions of the self that stem from negative societal attitudes and messages about TGD people) may be particularly likely to develop depression or other negative mental health outcomes (Chodzen et al., 2019); hence, we consider that exposure to positive role models, positive messages about TGD people, and immediate and clear interventions to bullying are likely to benefit TGD children.

In a systematic review of 44 peer-reviewed studies, Tankersley et al. (2021) found that parent connectedness is associated with greater resilience among TGD teens and young adults. Parent connectedness was measured on a six-item scale, including perceived safety for young people to confide in guardians as well as how well cared for young people feel. Another study of the perspectives of transgender youth found that parental support could be characterized into multiple dimensions (Andrzejewski et al., 2020). *Emotional support*, characterized by positive emotional support for coming out as gender diverse, as well as *instrumental support*, characterized by access to gender-affirming health care and support for legal and social transition, were both valuable aspects of parental support. Furthermore, *appraisal support*, characterized by usage of the chosen name and pronouns, as well as *information support*, characterized by useful advice and problem-solving with the child, are also indications of parental support, as described by TGD youth. A study published by de Bres (2022) suggested that in some families, the child coming out as transgender was a positive step forward in the parent better understanding the child's internal world and feeling clearer about tools or resources to seek out to support the child.

MENTAL HEALTH OF TRANSGENDER AND GENDER DIVERSE YOUTH FROM CHILDHOOD INTO ADOLESCENCE

The objective of this chapter is to focus on common mental health challenges for TGD children and describe how vulnerabilities of TGD children may manifest as they grow into adolescence. Using the minority stress model (Brooks, 1981; Hendricks & Testa, 2012; Meyer, 2003, 2010) to study the experiences of TGD adolescents, Jardas and colleagues (2023) found significant support in the understanding of how gender-based stressors were systematically associated with internalizing symptoms and a heightened general risk for psychopathology. The results of their study strongly suggested that TGD youth could be more vulnerable to mental health symptoms because they experience more gender-based discrimination than cisgender youth. Thus, TGD adolescents are more likely to experience depression and anxiety than their cisgender peers. More than half of TGD youth in the study met diagnostic criteria for a depressive disorder, and 37% to 48% of TGD youth met criteria for an anxiety disorder. Application of the minority stress model suggested that disparities among sexual and gender diverse individuals are related to persistent stressors associated with a marginalized identity, which are associated with an increase in psychopathology.

There has been limited research to suggest that TGD children may experience a high prevalence of emotional and behavioral challenges (Cohen-Kettenis et al., 2011). However, one study of children aged 3 to 9 years concluded that there appears to be a higher prevalence of symptoms of attention-deficit/hyperactivity disorder (ADHD) as well as a higher prevalence of anxiety among transgender and gender-nonconforming youth compared with cisgender peers (Becerra-Culqui et al., 2018).

AUTISM SPECTRUM DISORDER AND NEUROATYPICAL EXPERIENCES OF TRANSGENDER AND GENDER DIVERSE YOUTH

In the fifth edition of the *Diagnostic and Statistical Manual of Mental Disorders* (*DSM-5*; American Psychiatric Association, 2013), previous autism-related diagnoses were revised to a single diagnosis: autism spectrum disorder (ASD). ASD is a neurodevelopmental condition that is often evident in a child's impaired ability in the social and communication realms of functioning, as well as with exhibiting repetitive behavior patterns (e.g., motor movements and engagement with restricted interests and activities). According to the U.S. Centers for Disease Control and Prevention (2025), nearly 1 in 31 children aged 8 years were diagnosed with ASD in 2022. Notably, those who are misdiagnosed, undiagnosed, designated female at birth, people of color, and/or of low socioeconomic status remain underrepresented in studies on ASD. Another factor that adds complexity to the clinical conundrum is that many children have learned to *mask*, an adaptive defense that can be a conscious or unconscious effort to conform or present as nonautistic in neurotypical environments. A common misconception about autistic individuals is that they have a tendency to lack empathy. In fact, children with ASD show quite the opposite—a hypersensitivity to others' emotions and moods (Price, 2022).

Of youth between the ages of 13 and 17 in the U.S., 3.3% are estimated to identify as transgender (Herman & Flores, 2025). There is not an official census that can accurately report the number of TGD youth in the United States; however, when analyzing results of studies that ask TGD people about their identities, there seems to be a very diverse spectrum within the community. For example, the National Center for Transgender Equality Early Insights report of the 2022 U.S. Transgender Survey, which had a sample size of more than 92,000 individuals, indicated that 35% of participants identified as transgender women, 30% as nonbinary and designated female at birth, 25% as transgender men, and 8% as nonbinary and designated male at birth (James et al., 2024). It is possible our youth are not simply rejecting outdated, simplistic, and narrow expectations of gender but rather are steadfastly a part of a gender revolution who self-determine their personal meaning of gender and how they do it. Gender dysphoric symptoms stem from an incongruence between one's assumed gender at birth and one's internal experience of gender (American Psychiatric Association, 2013) and the conflict expected from their environment (e.g., family and peers). These symptoms can best be understood by the rejection of and from designated gender scripts and social roles that are founded deep within a heteronormative and binary frame of expectation.

Youth with ASD or neurodivergent disorders report diverse gender identities at a much higher rate than their neurotypical counterparts. In fact, for well over the last decade, gender health care clinicians have witnessed a significant overlap of youth who meet the criteria for both ASD or ASD traits and gender dysphoria or gender incongruence (de Vries et al., 2010; Strang et al., 2018). As interest in the study of both autism and gender development has increased substantially, we are now beginning to see these children who are gender minoritized and autistic represented empirically in our research findings. Warrier et al. (2020) found that individuals who do not identify with their sex designated at birth are three times as likely to be autistic as cisgender individuals, and TGD individuals are also more likely to demonstrate autistic traits.

In a more recent attempt to capture the accumulation of this research, Kallitsounaki and Williams (2022) conducted a literature review and meta-analysis and found that individuals with ASD were 11 times as likely to report gender dysphoric distress. Parents with children with ASD or neurodivergent traits also reported high levels of gender nonconforming behaviors. In addition, Kallitsounaki and Williams found that individuals diagnosed with ASD were four times as likely to have gender dysphoria or gender incongruence, and 15% of individuals diagnosed with ASD identified as nonbinary. Furthermore, the authors concluded that TGD youth have a 3% to 21% likelihood of a high degree of ASD diagnosis or traits among the TGD population. Compared with the adult transgender population, Kallitsounaki and Williams found that 4.8% to 7.8% individuals with gender dysphoria or gender incongruence have an ASD diagnosis and traits. Notably, this prevalence range may be an underestimate, because many adults to date have not been formally diagnosed. Children on the autism spectrum sometimes struggle to understand how to convey their internal experience (i.e., thoughts and emotions) and, in more severe circumstances, may experience co-occurring alexithymia (i.e., difficulties in identifying and naming how one feels; Kozlowski et al., 2012). As a result, it is possible that some individuals with ASD may also tend to miscommunicate social cues that represent their gender identity or may be less motivated or skilled at adapting to social norms, including gendered social norms.

In our experience, a clinical task is to assist individuals in finding the words, or nonverbal expression such as through text, to convey their internal state of what it means to be a particular gender identity. Verbal and nonverbal social behaviors may present differently. We do not find it useful to be consumed with causation, such as trying to identify why a person expresses themselves in a specific way; rather, we encourage providers to unpack what the presenting problem or area of need is. We make this recommendation to avoid acting in a role of gatekeeping (i.e., keeping children from social transition because the provider feels it may be a fixation or part of their special interest) and pathologizing human diversity. Reconsidering how children with ASD exhibit their gender expressions and the means by which they communicate their gender identity may decrease symptoms stemming from conditions related to anxiety and depression. More harrowing statistics conclude that symptoms of ASD (e.g., executive functioning impairments and cognitive rigidity [i.e., black-and-white thinking]), coupled with communication and social deficits, impair one's ability to fully adapt, develop, and utilize independent living skills (Strang et al., 2018). Despite these challenges, if TGD youth are evaluated by a gender-affirming and neuroaffirming informed provider, some challenging mental health outcomes may be prevented if the youth are supported through their social transition. In particular, adults who support TGD youth should be aware that gender expression may not be binary in nature, although that does not negate the authenticity or the stability or potential longevity of the young person's gender identity.

ASD is most often diagnosed during childhood; however, transgender youth do not always experience gender dysphoria or have a diagnosis of gender dysphoria (Olson-Kennedy et al., 2016). Cognitive and developmental psychologists tend to believe that one's gender constancy is typically established between ages 5 and 7 (prelatency stage) and is permanent (Ruble et al., 2007). Yet we find that one's gender identity—an innate sense of self—can continue to evolve over time and is influenced by biopsychosocial factors, and one's sense of self can be revisited during adolescence when one is going through puberty. We are now learning that stages and phases of gender development are not necessarily linear; for example, gender identity may expand as more language becomes accessible. ASD and gender dysphoria or gender incongruence are often present in childhood and have no agreed-upon origin; however, the scientific community converges in their understanding that both are likely to develop from multifactorial etiology (Erickson-Schroth, 2013), which includes genetic predisposition, exposure to intrauterine hormones, social environment, and the impact of other psychological phenomena. In this way, we encourage clinicians to focus less on cause and more on developing and sustaining gender-affirming and neuroaffirming practices.

Conceptual challenges exist in understanding the process of gender identity formation in individuals with ASD, which inevitably affects treatment planning and intervention. If gender identity evolution is characterized as a normal developmental stage in childhood, wherein gender roles may challenge gender stability and constancy, then individuals with ASD atypical patterns of social development are likely to travel down a differential developmental trajectory with respect to gender identity formation (Mukaddes, 2002). Accounting for these disparate developmental paths adds to the already difficult task of accurately assessing gender-related concerns in children and adolescents with ASD. Accordingly, de Vries et al. (2010) emphasized the importance of discriminating to what degree symptoms of gender dysphoria stem from the difference in being a neuroatypical individual or the difference associated with being gender diverse.

Gender identity has been defined as "the developed ability of a child to categorize themselves either as a boy or girl and the ability to recognize other children as being boys or girls" (Abelson, 1981, p. 347). From his original study, Abelson concluded that gender identity development was reliant upon cognition and developed in conjunction with mental age. He further hypothesized some autistic children may not be picking up relevant cues and qualities that would support their ability to differentiate between boys and girls. We, however, contend that perhaps youth with ASD refuse to be restricted by the so-called social rules of gender and are perhaps granted to be more carefree. It is also possible that some youth with ASD do not feel the need to internalize others' projections and expectations with regard to gender.

Because of the lack of professional training and newly found understanding of the complexities of both gender and autism traits and experiences, providers are called upon to become trained to identify and assess the co-occurrence and make clinically informed decisions for TGD children or youth with ASD who may be in need of social interventions or other supports. It is rare that gender therapists are adequately trained in the area of autism; likewise, autism specialists are rarely informed of gender as an internal experience externally demonstrated by their clients. Thus, the onus falls upon clinicians to improve our understanding of the child's ability to communicate their experiences; create therapeutic environments where children can be seen, heard, and met with unconditional care; and reconsider how one supports neurotypical children. It is imperative when working with TGD youth who show signs of autism traits that clinicians screen for such impairments and behaviors from a neuroaffirming perspective. For children with ASD, conceptualization of their experience and distress due to external invalidation (i.e., neurotypical doubt), or their limited capacity to verbally communicate their internal sense of self and how it relates to their gender journey (e.g., presenting, communicating, accessing care, or all), needs to be taken into account. Children with ASD and TGD youth are often misunderstood, which possibly can be attributed to their exacerbating mental health symptoms due to their sensory processing (perception), communication, and executive functioning issues. These experiences may lead to pathological demand avoidance or severe forms of anxiety. The provider must reflect on the meaning of gender and its manifestations for the child in the consulting room and how the provider is able to communicate this to them. In our clinical experience, TGD children are more likely to experience marginalization and isolation, more so than children with a singular diagnosis of gender dysphoria or ASD. Therefore, anxiety and depression are likely to be a part of the child's mental health needs for care. It may serve the child best to provide psychoeducation to the parents with regard to the complexities of gender, yet encourage their child's lead without hesitation, doubt, or scrutiny. Properly utilizing and interpreting assessment measures, accompanied with thorough and thoughtful developmental biopsychosocial interview questions, can lead to accurate diagnosis and treatment planning, especially for children and youth who are on the autism spectrum.

In our opinion, children with ASD have a right to gender care; however, one must take into account the child's impairments and complexity of needs. All children, regardless of neurotypicality, deserve resources, role models, and affirming social environments that are authentic to their own gender identity and gender expression. Given the alarming prevalence of mental health risks (e.g., depression, anxiety, or self-harm), we must foster healthy self-concept development, which includes gender diverse representations. Only by leaning into our learning curve, reconsidering our case conceptualizations, and modifying our interventions can we adequately address the needs of our clients. In doing so, we may not only save lives, decreasing if not preventing co-occurring conditions such as depression and anxiety, but we also may improve clients' overall quality of life. Finally, a formal diagnosis from a neuropsychologist who specializes in TGD children with ASD might be the best course of action to clinically address the co-occurring symptoms prevalent in a society that is often not autism friendly.

A specific condition that may be more likely to occur among neurodiverse and TGD children (but is not always secondary to either ASD or ADHD) is avoidant/restrictive food intake disorder (ARFID). ARFID is an eating and feeding disorder recognized in the *DSM-5* (American Psychiatric Association, 2013), which is categorized as inadequate nutritional intake and associated with decreased energy, weight loss, and effects on overall psychosocial functioning. ARFID is a newer diagnosis that can mirror a restrictive eating disorder (e.g., anorexia nervosa), limiting the foods a person is willing to eat due to concerns about texture, taste, smell, color, or fear of an adverse consequence from eating such as vomiting or choking. Although the diagnostic criteria for ARFID do not include specific fears of body weight or shape nor a negative emotional experience after eating (e.g., guilt), emerging studies suggest that a person may struggle both with symptoms of ARFID and body image–related concerns (Sharpe, 2024). Children with ADHD, ASD, or anxiety may be more likely to have indications of ARFID. This disorder goes beyond selective eating that is common in early childhood, and it is diagnosed only when there is a clear nutritional deficiency that cannot be explained by other medical conditions (American Psychiatric Association, 2013).

For caregivers of selective eaters, it may be difficult to distinguish between (a) when their child is a selective eater or anxious to try new foods in a way that is developmentally typical and (b) when the child may need additional support to decrease worries and to achieve a more dynamic food intake. Regularly scheduled checkups with a trusted primary care physician are recommended to ensure the child's growth is adequate, as well as to have live consultation on the child's nutritional needs. We do not recommend forcing a child to eat by threatening to take away the child's preferred activities (e.g., "If you do not eat this, you cannot play video games"), nor do we recommend forcing a child to sit in front of the plate until all the food is consumed. Increasing a child's anxiety of eating due to fear of punishment exacerbates the symptoms of the condition and degrades the child's growing autonomy. Whenever possible, children may fare better when choice over the food they eat is presented.

Some children diagnosed with ARFID may benefit from cognitive behavior therapy, specifically treatment seeking to honor their food preferences while offering slight modifications to the food that may increase nutritional value without overwhelming the young person. A focus on relaxation and mindfulness may be particularly helpful for children who experience fear of vomiting, choking, or gagging. In addition to cognitive behavior therapy, clients likely benefit from care with a dietitian, who can guide them through actionable steps to increase a child's nourishment and help the child begin to enjoy more diverse foods or more suitable portions. Occupational therapy can also be useful, especially for children who can benefit from learning how to physically relax themselves prior to and throughout a meal.

Although these recommendations are not specific to TGD children, it is important that providers who support TGD children with feeding or eating concerns are gender affirming. It is the right of health care consumers (and their caregivers) to ask how familiar practitioners are with TGD children's needs and what the clinic policies are in regard to equitable access to care. Clear practitioner bias, such as refusing to use a child's pronouns or assuming the feeding disorder is a result of the child being TGD, leads to difficulty trusting and following the guidance of the practitioner. Further, a TGD child is in need of a health care team that does not overly focus on their gender in such a way that their other needs are neglected. Using the gender-affirming framework, ensuring a child's nourishment needs are met and the child has choice in their food is important. Whenever possible, and potentially prior to diagnosis, a child who is suspected to be on the autism spectrum and has nourishment challenges due to food selectivity, poor appetite, or food restriction may benefit from services with a dietitian. Introducing a dietitian early may promote positive support and cooperation from the client and can help introduce the idea of how to work effectively with a dietitian (Pham et al., 2021).

Second, careful monitoring by a primary care physician throughout the child's development is recommended because children with eating or feeding disturbances are at significant risk for medical conditions or symptoms, especially gastrointestinal distress. Some evidence also shows that children with eating or feeding challenges are more likely to struggle with anxiety than those without such challenges; hence, engaging with a primary care physician to provide guidance and resources to the family is beneficial (Fisher et al., 2014).

TGD children may be at higher risk for developing mental health concerns, which correlate with increased experiences of stress. TGD children may also be likely to have two intersecting identities, such as being gender diverse and autistic. Providers who serve TGD children benefit from ongoing training and consultation to ensure that clients' needs are cared for in clinically sound and culturally relevant ways. Although any provider is vulnerable to expression of bias in their work, we encourage providers who do not have lived experience as a TGD person to be especially cognizant of attitudes and beliefs they bring into the discipline. Further, we encourage providers to be invested in the prevention of mental health concerns that may develop in adolescence by participating in advocacy, education, and outreach to all marginalized youth and their families.

To summarize the factors that affect the mental health of TGD children, consider the experiences of 9-year-old Audrey as described in the following case.[1]

Audrey, age 9, presented to an outpatient therapist because her parents had become concerned that she was seemingly more irritable at home and had begun to experience social challenges at school, which she had not experienced previously. For example, Audrey's teachers had noticed that she was increasingly playing by herself rather than with peers at recess time, and Audrey's parents were provided that feedback. Similarly, Audrey's parents had observed that she seemed less engaged in family activity times. On one occasion while playing a board game she typically enjoys playing with her family, Audrey became inconsolable when she thought she may lose the game, and she decided not to continue playing. Audrey's parents felt this new behavior was concerning, given that Audrey had no history of previous social or mental health issues.

In her first therapy session, Audrey shared that at school, she felt "everyone hates me." She denied any specific conflicts with others, but said she was often not invited to play with peers who had previously been open to playing with her. When asked what activities she would like to do with her friends, Audrey identified kickball, soccer, or costume play. She noted that her female peers had begun to show interests in activities Audrey considered "boring," such as dancing to popular music and playing with dolls. Additionally, Audrey explained that her male peers were often "mean" to her, excluding her from activities that she would like to participate in and taunting her that their games "were only for boys."

Over the course of treatment, it became clearer to the therapist that Audrey, who was designated female at birth, had diverse interests and was struggling to conform to traditional gender norms of preadolescent girls. With positive encouragement from her therapist, Audrey explored her interests and was able to find gender-inclusive spaces such as an after-school group where she could find children of multiple genders to spend time with. In that space, her being designated as female did not limit the activities or interests that she could enjoy. At age 9, Audrey did not verbally state that she was a specific gender, but she did show interest in many activities. She also was starting to notice that as she and her peers were approaching the onset of puberty, children were beginning to express a clearer gender identity of male and female. Audrey did not have a sense of her gender identity as being clearly male or female, and there was a growing difference between how her peers perceived themselves and how Audrey perceived herself. Thus, she had some increase in both social rejection

[1]The name of the patient as well as potentially identifying details have been changed to protect her identity.

and anxiety that she was not fitting in with peers due to her gender expression. Audrey's inclusion with new friends who were less concerned with fitting themselves into a gender binary relieved her growing anxiety and social isolation.

Audrey's case highlights that all children, regardless of whether they grow to express gender diverse identities, may benefit from gender-inclusive spaces.

CONCLUSION

In summary, TGD children do not have an increased risk for mental health challenges on the basis that they are gender diverse. Rather, TGD children are more likely to be subject to rejecting environments, which increases the risk of anxiety and depression. Further, just as cisgender children can be expected to thrive within environments that affirm their identities, needs, and interests, TGD children appear to fare better when regularly integrated into affirming spaces. As explored in this chapter, TGD children do seem to be more likely to also be neurodiverse compared with cisgender peers. The likelihood of being neurodiverse may increase the risk of developing commonly co-occurring conditions such as anxiety and ARFID. Regardless of neurotype, TGD children should be encouraged to explore their interests and have their needs met in ways that are equitable to cisgender children.

REFERENCES

Abelson, A. G. (1981). The development of gender identity in the autistic child. *Child: Care, Health and Development*, *7*(6), 347–356. https://doi.org/10.1111/j.1365-2214.1981.tb00851.x

American Psychiatric Association. (2013). *Diagnostic and statistical manual of mental disorders* (5th ed.). https://doi.org/10.1176/appi.books.9780890425596

Andrzejewski, J., Pampati, S., Steiner, R. J., Boyce, L., & Johns, M. M. (2020). Perspectives of transgender youth on parental support: Qualitative findings from the resilience and transgender youth study. *Health Education & Behavior*, *48*(1), 74–81. https://doi.org/10.1177/1090198120965504

Ashley, F. (2019). Thinking an ethics of gender exploration: Against delaying transition for transgender and gender creative youth. *Clinical Child Psychology and Psychiatry*, *24*(2), 223–236. https://doi.org/10.1177/1359104519836462

Becerra-Culqui, T. A., Liu, Y., Nash, R., Cromwell, L., Flanders, W. D., Getahun, D., Giammattei, S. V., Hunkeler, E. M., Lash, T. L., Millman, A., Quinn, V. P., Robinson, B., Roblin, D., Sandberg, D. E., Silverberg, M. J., Tangpricha, V., & Goodman, M. (2018). Mental health of transgender and gender nonconforming youth compared with their peers. *Pediatrics*, *141*(5), e20173845. https://doi.org/10.1542/peds.2017-3845

Brookes, C. E. (1991). Jung's concept of individuation. *Journal of the American Academy of Psychoanalysis*, *19*(2), 307–315. https://doi.org/10.1521/jaap.1.1991.19.2.307

Brooks, V. R. (1981). *Minority stress and lesbian women*. Lexington Books.

Chodzen, G., Hidalgo, M. A., Chen, D., & Garofalo, R. (2019). Minority stress factors associated with depression and anxiety among transgender and gender-nonconforming youth. *Journal of Adolescent Health, 64*(4), 467–471. https://doi.org/10.1016/j.jadohealth.2018.07.006

Cohen-Kettenis, P. T., Steensma, T. D., & de Vries, A. L. C. (2011). Treatment of adolescents with gender dysphoria in the Netherlands. *Child and Adolescent Psychiatric Clinics of North America, 20*(4), 689–700. https://doi.org/10.1016/j.chc.2011.08.001

Coolhart, D. (2018). Helping families move from distress to attunement. In C. Keo-Meier & D. Ehrensaft (Eds.), *The gender affirmative model: An interdisciplinary approach to supporting transgender and gender expansive children* (pp. 125–140). American Psychological Association. https://doi.org/10.1037/0000095-008

de Bres, J. (2022). Research on parents of gender-diverse children: From pathologization to affirmation. *LGBTQ+ Family: An Interdisciplinary Journal, 18*(2), 135–150. https://doi.org/10.1080/27703371.2022.2058669

de Vries, A. L. C., Noens, I. L. J., Cohen-Kettenis, P. T., van Berckelaer-Onnes, I. A., & Doreleijers, T. A. (2010). Autism spectrum disorders in gender dysphoric children and adolescents. *Journal of Autism and Developmental Disorders, 40*(8), 930–936. https://doi.org/10.1007/s10803-010-0935-9

Durwood, L., Gallagher, N. M., Sifre, R., & Olson, K. R. (2024). A study of parent-reported internalizing symptoms in transgender youth before and after childhood social transitions. *Clinical Psychological Science, 12*(5), 984–996. https://doi.org/10.1177/21677026231208086

Erickson-Schroth, L. (2013). Update on the biology of transgender identity. *Journal of Gay & Lesbian Mental Health, 17*(2), 150–174. https://doi.org/10.1080/19359705.2013.753393

Field, T. M. (2014). Psychobiological attunement in close relationships. In D. L. Featherman, R. M. Lerner, & M. Perlmutter (Eds.), *Life-span development and behavior* (pp. 1–25). Psychology Press.

Fisher, M. M., Rosen, D. S., Ornstein, R. M., Mammel, K. A., Katzman, D. K., Rome, E. S., Callahan, S. T., Malizio, J., Kearney, S., & Walsh, B. T. (2014). Characteristics of avoidant/restrictive food intake disorder in children and adolescents: A "new disorder" in *DSM-5*. *Journal of Adolescent Health, 55*(1), 49–52. https://doi.org/10.1016/j.jadohealth.2013.11.013

Hendricks, M. L., & Testa, R. J. (2012). A conceptual framework for clinical work with transgender and gender nonconforming clients: An adaptation of the minority stress model. *Professional Psychology: Research and Practice, 43*(5), 460–467. https://doi.org/10.1037/a0029597

Herman, J. L., & Flores, A. R. (2025, August). *How many adults and youth identify as transgender in the United States?* The Williams Institute, UCLA School of Law. https://williamsinstitute.law.ucla.edu/wp-content/uploads/Trans-Pop-Update-Aug-2025.pdf

James, S. E., Herman, J. L., Durso, L. E., & Heng-Lehtinen, R. (2024, February). *Early insights: A report of the 2022 U.S. Transgender Survey*. National Center for Transgender Equality. https://transequality.org/sites/default/files/2024-02/2022%20USTS%20Early%20Insights%20Report_FINAL.pdf

Jardas, E. J., Ladd, B. A., Maheux, A. J., Choukas-Bradley, S., Salk, R. H., & Thoma, B. C. (2023). Testing the minority stress model across gender identity, race, and ethnicity among U.S. gender minority adolescents. *Journal of Psychopathology and Clinical Science, 132*(5), 542–554. https://doi.org/10.1037/abn0000834

Kallitsounaki, A., & Williams, D. M. (2022). Autism spectrum disorder and gender dysphoria/incongruence: A systematic literature review and meta-analysis. *Journal of Autism and Developmental Disorders, 53*(8), 3103–3117. https://doi.org/10.1007/s10803-022-05517-y

Kearns, S., Kroll, T., O'Shea, D., & Neff, K. (2021). Experiences of transgender and non-binary youth accessing gender-affirming care: A systematic review and meta-ethnography. *PLOS One, 16*(9), e0257194. https://doi.org/10.1371/journal.pone.0257194

Keo-Meier, C., & Ehrensaft, D. (Eds.). (2018). *The gender affirmative model: An interdisciplinary approach to supporting transgender and gender expansive children.* American Psychological Association. https://doi.org/10.1037/0000095-000

Kozlowski, A. M., Matson, J. L., & Belva, B. C. (2012). Social skills differences between the autism spectrum disorders. *Journal of Developmental and Physical Disabilities, 24*(2), 125–134. https://doi.org/10.1007/s10882-011-9260-2

Meyer, I. H. (2003). Prejudice, social stress, and mental health in lesbian, gay, and bisexual populations: Conceptual issues and research evidence. *Psychological Bulletin, 129*(5), 674–697. https://doi.org/10.1037/0033-2909.129.5.674

Meyer, I. H. (2010). Identity, stress, and resilience in lesbians, gay men, and bisexuals of color. *The Counseling Psychologist, 38*(3), 442–454. https://doi.org/10.1177/0011000009351601

Mukaddes, N. M. (2002). Gender identity problems in autistic children. *Child: Care, Health and Development, 28*(6), 529–532. https://doi.org/10.1046/j.1365-2214.2002.00301.x

Olson, K. R., Durwood, L., DeMeules, M., & McLaughlin, K. A. (2016). Mental health of transgender children who are supported in their identities. *Pediatrics, 137*(3), e20153223. https://doi.org/10.1542/peds.2015-3223

Olson-Kennedy, J., Cohen-Kettenis, P. T., Kreukels, B. P., Meyer-Bahlburg, H. F., Garofalo, R., Meyer, W., & Rosenthal, S. M. (2016). Research priorities for gender nonconforming/transgender youth: Gender identity development and biopsychosocial outcomes. *Current Opinion in Endocrinology, Diabetes, and Obesity, 23*(2), 172–179. https://doi.org/10.1097/MED.0000000000000236

Pham, A., Kasenic, A., Hayden, L., Inwards-Breland, D. J., Sumerwell, C., Twible, H., Ahrens, K. R., & Orlich, F. (2021). A case series on disordered eating among transgender youth with autism spectrum disorder. *Journal of Adolescent Health, 68*(6), 1215–1219. https://doi.org/10.1016/j.jadohealth.2020.12.143

Price, D. (2022). *Unmasking autism: Discovering the new faces of neurodiversity.* Harmony Books.

Rossman, K., Salamanca, P., & Macapagal, K. (2017). A qualitative study examining young adults' experiences of disclosure and nondisclosure of LGBTQ identity to health care providers. *Journal of Homosexuality, 64*(10), 1390–1410. https://doi.org/10.1080/00918369.2017.1321379

Ruble, D. N., Taylor, L. J., Cyphers, L., Greulich, F. K., Lurye, L. E., & Shrout, P. E. (2007). The role of gender constancy in early gender development. *Child Development, 78*(4), 1121–1136. https://doi.org/10.1111/j.1467-8624.2007.01056.x

Russell, S. T., Pollitt, A. M., Li, G., & Grossman, A. H. (2018). Chosen name use is linked to reduced depressive symptoms, suicidal ideation, and suicidal behavior among transgender youth. *Journal of Adolescent Health, 63*(4), 503–505. https://doi.org/10.1016/j.jadohealth.2018.02.003

Sharpe, S. L. (2024). A living experience proposal for the co-occurring diagnosis of avoidant/restrictive food intake disorder and other eating disorders. *Journal of Eating Disorders, 12*, 110. https://doi.org/10.1186/s40337-024-01073-1

Sherer, I. (2016). Social transition: Supporting our youngest transgender children. *Pediatrics, 137*(3), e20154358. https://doi.org/10.1542/peds.2015-4358

Strang, J. F., Janssen, A., Tishelman, A., Leibowitz, S. F., Kenworthy, L., McGuire, J. K., Edwards-Leeper, L., Mazefsky, C. A., Rofey, D., Bascom, J., Caplan, R., Gomez-Lobo, V., Berg, D., Zaks, Z., Wallace, G. L., Wimms, H., Pine-Twaddell, E., Shumer, D., Register-Brown, K., Sadikova, E., . . . Anthony, L. G. (2018). Revisiting the link: Evidence of the rates of autism in studies of gender diverse individuals. *Journal of the American Academy of Child and Adolescent Psychiatry, 57*(11), 885–887. https://doi.org/10.1016/j.jaac.2018.04.023

Tankersley, A. P., Grafsky, E. L., Dike, J., & Jones, R. T. (2021). Risk and resilience factors for mental health among transgender and gender nonconforming (TGNC) youth: A systematic review. *Clinical Child and Family Psychology Review, 24*(2), 183–206. https://doi.org/10.1007/s10567-021-00344-6

U.S. Centers for Disease Control and Prevention. (2025). *2025 community report on autism*. https://www.cdc.gov/autism/media/pdfs/2025/04/ADDM-Community-Report-SY2022.pdf

Warrier, V., Greenberg, D. M., Weir, E., Buckingham, C., Smith, P., Lai, M.-C., Allison, C., & Baron-Cohen, S. (2020). Elevated rates of autism, other neurodevelopmental and psychiatric diagnoses, and autistic traits in transgender and gender-diverse individuals. *Nature Communications, 11*(1), 3959. https://doi.org/10.1038/s41467-020-17794-1

6 GENDER-RELATED TRAUMA

AMY TISHELMAN, AYDIN OLSON-KENNEDY,
AND ANDREAS NEUMANN-MASCIS

Alex (he pronouns) is 22 years old, White, and genderqueer. In session, Alex described having been gender expansive from a very early age. Alex also described memories that began in kindergarten of being verbally abused and bullied, physically threatened and assaulted, rejected by family, and isolated from peers, only finding a supportive community when he was old enough to move away from home. Two aspects of his trauma experiences are striking: First, the traumas came from peers and adults alike, and they occurred across contexts and developmental phases. These traumas included passive observers who did nothing to stop the aggressions, identifying the problem as Alex's general gender nonconforming presentation. Second, when the intake materials asked if there had ever been abuse, Alex responded "no." When asked about this later, Alex said simply, "So that was just because of how I look, how I am," absorbing and accepting the transphobic trope that "he asked for it."

Alice is a 35-year-old African American transgender woman coming to therapy to deal with symptoms of anxiety and depression that emerged after she lost her job as a programmer. Some facts indicated that the layoff was discriminatory.

Throughout this chapter, all case examples are fictional.

https://doi.org/10.1037/0000494-007
Pediatric Gender Health Care: The Gender Affirmative Model Revisited, Second Edition, G. N. Rider, D. Ehrensaft, and C. St. Amand (Editors)

Alice had received positive performance reviews while presenting as male. After transition, she received feedback that she was "unprofessional."

Eventually, Alice also acknowledged experiencing transphobic sexual harassment at work, but she minimized both the impact on her and the culpability of her colleagues. During treatment, Alice also described having been beaten regularly by one or both parents. This history emerged only after she made a joke about a wooden spoon having been broken on her back as an adolescent. When asked about the abuse, Alice shrugged and said, "They just really, really did not want a faggot."

PERSPECTIVES ON CHILD AND ADOLESCENT TRAUMA

Although both of the individuals described in the opening case examples are adults, their childhood histories illustrate the complex, often chronic, singularly profound adversities experienced by many transgender and gender diverse (TGD) youth. TGD youth are often raised in a milieu of rejection, psychological abuse, and isolation, all because of an aspect of self: gender diversity, including gender presentation and gender expression. Research, self-report, developmental psychopathology investigation, and common sense contribute to the conclusion that TGD youth may experience chronically traumatizing conditions, with the high risk of trauma being underrecognized and untreated. Studies indicate that TGD youth suffer elevated rates of depression, anxiety, self-harm, and suicide attempts, but these psychiatric issues are rarely interpreted through a trauma lens (e.g., Reisner et al., 2015, 2016).

Thus far, studies directly examining adverse childhood experiences (ACEs) in TGD youth consistently indicate a high risk of significant adversities. Not only do youth struggle with passive indifference from others, but they also often experience deliberately inflicted interpersonal violence and trauma (Feil et al., 2023; Schnarrs et al., 2019; Thoma et al., 2021). For instance, research has demonstrated that TGD youth are exposed to a higher level of child maltreatment (emotional abuse and neglect, physical abuse, etc.) than cisgender, gay, lesbian, and bisexual youth, and these adversities are associated with poorer mental health in TGD youth communities (Schnarrs et al., 2019). Similarly, researchers found significantly higher rates of psychological, physical, and sexual abuse in transgender adolescents ages 14 to 18 compared with their same-age cisgender heterosexual peers (Thoma et al., 2021). Another study replicated these findings by examining the history of childhood adversities in adult cisgender and TGD psychiatric outpatients (Feil et al., 2023). Findings from Feil and colleagues revealed that TGD adults had a significantly higher number of total ACEs than the cisgender group. The two groups differed specifically on the parental emotional abuse and peer abuse items, with TGD clients having a significantly higher level of inflicted abuse.

Childhood adversities in TGD children are often underrecognized and represent the difficult reality that not only does being TGD present challenges and risks independently, but these are also compounded for TGD communities by the extreme and detrimental forms of child maltreatment that TGD children commonly endure. The mental health sequelae of these traumatizing experiences can last a lifetime unless acknowledged and addressed with sensitivity and care.

Potentially traumatizing experiences for TGD youth of every age are pervasive and influenced by institutionalized, interpersonal, and internalized transphobia. Traumatic adversity in childhood is often chronic, occurs across important settings (e.g., home, school, and community), and risks impacting all essential areas of functioning; yet, it can be misidentified as a host of other conditions, including attentional and oppositional/disruptive disorders, learning disabilities, and an array of other syndromes and diagnoses.

At this juncture in history, a critical accumulation of developmental literature strongly indicates the extreme costs of certain forms of stress on children's development and adaptation. Shonkoff et al. (2012) discussed the relevance of data from myriad disciplines, including "neuroscience, molecular biology, genomics, developmental psychology, epidemiology, sociology, and economics" (p. e232), in understanding development. Their biodevelopmental framework illustrates the profound effects that early adversities can have on a child's development, at times shattering a young person's well-being and creating a circumstance of continuing stress, associated with many later-life morbidities and sometimes early mortality. This framework highlights the potentially long-lasting and toxic influence of extreme stress in early life, noting that many "adult diseases should be viewed as developmental disorders that begin early in life and that persistent health disparities associated with poverty, discrimination, or maltreatment could be reduced by the alleviation of toxic stress in childhood" (Shonkoff et al., 2012, p. e232).

A series of influential studies illuminates the profound long-term risks associated with traumatic adversities occurring during critical periods of early development (e.g., Centers for Disease Control and Prevention, n.d.; Felitti et al., 1998), concluding that as childhood adversities increase, risks for endangering behaviors, medical disease, and mental health challenges become significantly greater. In other words, not only is the immediate quality of life diminished for TGD youth, but also their childhood suffering is associated with risks of stress and challenges in numerous areas across the lifespan, with a higher possibility of earlier mortality than same-age peers. Children exposed to extreme adversities do not always experience traumatic reactions. However, the potential for trauma is highly escalated when this exposure is present.

Trauma emanating from childhood adversities often differs from traumatic experiences first encountered as an adult. Potential pervasive effects of chronic toxic stress on children may affect many domains of important functioning (Cook et al., 2005; Tishelman et al., 2010), and this is sometimes referred to as *complex trauma*. Any trauma is unfortunate and holds extreme risks. However, individuals who first experience trauma as adults often have had the opportunity to develop secure relationships, positive self-esteem, academic and professional skills, and trust. Perhaps most importantly, they may have a vision of what life can be like in the absence of trauma, as well as the cognitive capacities and confidence often associated with effective coping and resilience. Trauma in childhood, on the other hand, often starts in the family, violating a basic sense of trust, and can go on to be pervasive and chronic. As a result, the world is never experienced from the vantage point of safety, self-value, hope, and love, with the opportunity for sensitive adult guidance. Cook et al. (2005) identified seven areas of risk for children who experience complex trauma: impairments in attachment, physiology (e.g., neurobiological effects hindering emotion regulation in response to stress), affect regulation, dissociation, behavioral regulation, cognition, and self-concept. Similarly, four interacting and overlapping domains of functioning often impacted by traumatic responses at school have been identified and described, including self-regulation, physical function, relationships, and academics (Tishelman et al., 2010). These domains can be extrapolated to all settings in a child's life.

Notably, in childhood, many trauma manifestations can be misconstrued as falling under the domain of another diagnosis. As an example, a dissociating child may be perceived as inattentive and be evaluated for attention-deficit/hyperactivity disorder (ADHD), without sensitivity to the underlying distress that child may be enduring. This can potentially lead to mismanagement and improper administration of medication for ADHD, while the trauma is left unidentified, profound, and untreated. As another example, to avoid an untenable and inhospitable bullying environment, a child may act out in school and be placed outside of the classroom, be put in detention, or be suspended or expelled. Without a closer understanding of the child's deep unhappiness and associated causes, the child may be labeled with oppositional defiant disorder (ODD). TGD children are strong candidates for falling into any of these categories of overlooked trauma and subsequent misdiagnoses and mismanagement.

Consider the case of Leslie (they), a 12-year-old who identifies as both male and female and was designated male at birth. Leslie has flowing long hair and is consistently teased at school, called in a taunting way a "he/she" and pushed and shoved while teachers are not looking. Leslie had no history of aggression in school before this year but recently threw all the papers and other materials off several classmates' desks, an act that seemed unprovoked to Leslie's teacher. Leslie also recently started to resist going to gym class, arguing with teachers, sitting on the floor, and refusing to move. Although Leslie is a strong student intellectually, Leslie has been falling behind classmates academically, with frequent absences. The teacher reports that Leslie seems to have attention issues, completing worksheets only partially and spending much of class staring out the window. The teacher reported to Leslie's parents at a recent conference that Leslie needs an evaluation for ADHD and possible co-occurring ODD.

If a school-based evaluation focuses primarily on Leslie's school behaviors, in the absence of the context of Leslie's gender-related victimization, it is possible that interventions will be inadequate and even inappropriate, such as using behavior management reward techniques for attending to class work and compliance, paired with medication for ADHD. Instead, a trauma-informed focus would understand Leslie's behavioral and emotional responses as reactions to the toxic stress of bullying and rejection and would provide a different treatment plan. This treatment would first differ conceptually from one that assumes that mental illness (e.g., ADHD or ODD) stemming from within Leslie is creating havoc at school and detrimentally impacting classmates and adults. Instead, an initial reframing from a trauma perspective would recognize the direction of the problem, originating in a destructive environment impinging upon Leslie's well-being and creating an expectable distress reaction, given the circumstances of threat to Leslie's welfare. Any treatment would need to start with creating safety across environments. This would entail developing a trauma- and gender-sensitive milieu at Leslie's school, with zero tolerance for bullying. If that is not possible, alternatives would need to be explored, including changing schools or, in the unfortunate circumstance of no other options, homeschooling Leslie. Fortunately, school-related experiences like Leslie's have not gone unnoticed by gender-affirming practitioners. Groups have been working with schools to reduce or eliminate trauma and strengthen supportive environments for TGD youth.

The ultimate implication of a developmental model of trauma is that TGD youth, who are likely targets of abusive behaviors, are at risk for long-term mental health and physical health struggles enduring through adulthood (Reisner et al., 2016). These challenges are not due to gender identity per se but to the extreme stress youth endure because of attachment disruptions, isolation, and persecution within a transphobic cultural context. Masten and Cicchetti (2010) invoked the phrase *developmental cascades* to refer to the cumulative effects of these experiences on a child's life. In such a framework, development is shaped and sometimes constrained by prior experience. In addition, adversity often begets adversity. As an example, child maltreatment is associated with significantly aberrant parent–child attachment, or disorganized attachment, which then predicts a host of other childhood vulnerabilities, including peer relationship disruption and poor social skills. For a child already at risk for social ostracism because of gender differences, the lack of opportunity to develop adequate social skills exponentially increases risks. Poor peer relationships, in turn, predict school absence and school dropout, regardless of cognitive ability.

But negative mental health outcomes for TGD youth are far from inevitable. In a positive environmental context, TGD youth have the potential to be resilient, to be comfortable with themselves, and to enjoy healthy relationships. Research indicates that both family and peer acceptance are critical factors related to resilience in TGD youth, facilitating positive mental health (e.g., de Vries et al., 2016). Olson and colleagues (2016) demonstrated that TGD youth who have socially transitioned to living as their affirmed gender, with family support, are often perceived by their parents as well-adjusted and without the mental health struggles that have been demonstrated in many TGD youth in the past. Research also reflects the concept that *outness*, or living in the world as one's asserted identity, can mitigate the negative effects of a minoritized identity for lesbian, gay, bisexual, transgender, queer, and questioning (LGBTQ) youth and foster resilience, although substituting disclosure for secrecy also precipitates an increased risk for victimization (e.g., Kosciw et al., 2015).

ECOLOGICAL FRAMEWORK

On an institutionalized, community, and interpersonal level, gender nonconformity has been met with what is too often a form of sanctioned "correction" (Toomey et al., 2014). For TGD people, this has been vividly true within medical and mental health communities (Grant et al., 2011).

The beginning of a change within mental health paradigms can be credited in no small part to Harry Benjamin (1969), a German physician and sexologist. As early as the 1950s, Benjamin began to revolutionize the field by positing that care for transgender people was available if mental health professionals validated and responded to these individuals' felt sense of self. Benjamin believed that the etiology of gender variance was physiological and not psychological in nature and was therefore not impacted by a psychiatric intervention. Treating mental health symptoms may be futile if a young person's gender is not recognized.

The acknowledgment of TGD as a valid identity has only in recent years, and only haltingly, facilitated access to the framework of trauma through which transgender individuals can understand and name experiences. The ability to name an experience as traumatic and not poor behavior or a failure of character is one important aspect of healing. It properly externalizes the roots of a child's negative experiences while providing a protective barrier against internalizing a sense of oneself as deficient. It is imperative for adults across settings to recognize and be sensitive to the trauma of their children, students, or clients and thus be able to interpret a child's behavior through a trauma lens and with empathy rather than dismissal (Tishelman et al., 2010).

According to ecological and developmental frameworks (e.g., Coleman et al., 2022; Kaufman & Tishelman, 2018), children are influenced by biological, autobiographical, and historical factors, as well as family, school, culture, and community spheres that touch their lives. Environments can vary regarding safety, with some experiences replicating and/or amplifying traumatizing circumstances and other factors buffering children from harm. The child chapter in version 8 of the World Professional Association of Transgender Health Standards of Care for the Health of Transgender and Gender Diverse People emphasizes an ecological and developmental framework to best understand the needs of TGD prepubescent children (Coleman et al., 2022; see also Tishelman & Rider, 2023). This model implies that when children are manifesting symptoms of mental health distress, it is important to consider environmental factors that might be impacting them and advocate for safety in each environment in which a child functions (Tishelman & Rider, 2023). This framework also indicates that a child who is well-supported and has positive relationships in childhood will more likely traverse adolescence and adulthood with strong relationships and social skills, a positive sense of self, and abilities to both adapt and effectively self-advocate. Those with untreated and possibly protracted traumatic experiences may be vulnerable to flailing in these areas over time. Thus, the early roots of the depression, anxiety, suicidality and other mental health distress so often observed in TGD adolescents and young adults may be planted in young children through the obvious and subtle ways in which they might be burdened by early chronic traumatic stress.

INTERSECTIONALITY, MACROAGGRESSIONS, AND MICROAGGRESSIONS

The term *intersectionality* refers to a framework that explains how complex and compounding forms of oppression and marginalization are based on a person's multiple social identities (e.g., racism, cisgenderism, or ableism; Cho et al., 2013; Collins & Bilge, 2020; Crenshaw, 1991, 1998). It underscores that oppression and marginalization are not single-axis issues, as individuals do not experience these solely based on one aspect of their identity. For instance, viewed through the combined lenses of ecological systems theory and intersectionality, TGD youth may experience trauma related to the identity-based marginalization, such as ableism and racialization, operating across interrelated systems (Gower et al., 2023; MacMullin et al., 2024).

One form of oppression and discrimination faced by TGD communities is often framed as *transphobia,* a term commonly understood as fear or hatred of transgender people. However, transphobia tends to reduce this oppression to individual, personal issues (e.g., phobias), thereby minimizing the systemic and institutional forces that perpetuate the marginalization of TGD communities. In contrast, the term *cisgenderism* more accurately reflects these broader structures of oppression.

Cisgenderism is a systemic ideology that denies, denigrates, or pathologizes self-identified gender identities that do not align with an individual's sex/gender designated at birth (Lennon & Mistler, 2014). This ideology promotes and perpetuates the belief that cisgender identities and expressions hold greater value than TGD identities and expressions, thereby creating an inherent system of power and privilege. Unlike transphobia, cisgenderism acknowledges that the oppression of TGD communities stems from systemic power and structural bias rather than solely individual fear or hatred. It shifts the focus away from personal issues and toward the institutional and cultural systems that marginalize TGD communities. Research has found mental health impacts of gender-based bullying on youth younger than age 11 (Fish et al., 2023), and working to increase the psychological strengths without removing or at least lessening the sources of toxic stress is not sufficient to address the psychological impact of bias-based bullying in sexual and gender minority youth (O'Malley et al., 2022). Moreover, transphobia's emphasis on individual beliefs and behaviors often fails to account for the intersectional oppression faced by racialized, marginalized, and otherized TGD communities, further obscuring the broader mechanisms of systemic inequity. For example, TGD youth may face marginalization due to gender identity or expression while also being marginalized based on their racial and ethnic identities. Similarly, a TGD young person with limited socioeconomic resources might experience marginalization based on their gender identity or presentation, compounded by classism and restricted access to educational opportunities. These intersecting sources of oppression and marginalization lead to compounded experiences of exclusion and isolation for TGD youth, substantially elevating their risk of psychological distress.

The term *macroaggression* refers to the deliberate systemic and institutional oppression or exclusion of minoritized groups, enacted through sociopolitical institutions (e.g., government policies, legal frameworks, and educational systems; Adamakos, 2021; Gorski, 2014; Osanloo et al., 2016). Sociopolitical macroaggressions targeting TGD individuals are rooted in cisgenderist beliefs that validate cisgender identities as superior to and more legitimate than TGD identities.

Although TGD youth experience elevated levels of psychological distress, credible research refutes the notion that this population has an inherent predisposition to psychopathology (Ramos et al., 2023). Instead, heightened rates of depression, anxiety, nonsuicidal self-injury, and suicidality among TGD youth are linked with chronic stress, including the stress of sociopolitical exclusion and stigma (Flaskerud & Lesser, 2018; Ramos et al., 2023). Despite growing awareness of TGD youth, recent shifts in the sociopolitical landscape have imposed restrictive policies. These include bans on gender-affirming medical care, prohibitions on sports team participation based on gender identity, limitations on access to gender-affirming facilities, and refusals to recognize accurate pronouns in educational settings (American Civil Liberties Union, 2025; Human Rights Watch, 2025; UCLA School of Law Williams Institute, 2024). These legislative measures institutionalize identity invalidation, risking significant harm to the well-being of TGD youth.

Recent research has indicated that a degrading political climate and restrictive legislative efforts focused on TGD communities have had detrimental effects on young people (e.g., Dhanani & Totton, 2023). In addition, states with more restrictive trans care policies fall short on access to mental health care for these adolescents (Hollinsaid et al., 2024). Few studies, if any, have examined effects on young, prepubescent children. Speculatively, it is likely that they are also negatively affected—directly, through limits on gender-affirming climates, including in schools (e.g., restricted bathroom and pronoun use), and indirectly, through the anxieties expressed by families and others with whom they are close. Furthermore, although unexplored, it is possible that parents and guardians are adopting a more cautious approach to acceptance and support for their TGD children, given the hostilities that may be encountered if they did support them, ranging from interpersonal rejection to overt antagonism and even possible accusations of child abuse or criminalization of their parenting. This could be particularly difficult for TGD children, who thrive when nurtured and supported, although much of this research is conducted with TGD adolescents (e.g., Pariseau et al., 2019).

The term *microaggressions* refers to ubiquitous, subtle, verbal, behavioral, or environmental indignities, whether intentional or unintentional, that communicate hostile, derogatory, or negative slights and insults, targeting individuals due to their marginalized social identities (Sue et al., 2007). Microaggressions accumulate over time. As Nadal and colleagues (2011) described, this phenomenon is akin to "death by a thousand cuts" (p. 234) and has been found to cause psychological harm comparable to that caused by more extreme forms of victimization (Gartner & Sterzing, 2016, 2018). Microaggressions can manifest in three forms: *microassaults*, or intentional verbal assaults aimed at harming the person they target (e.g., name-calling); *microinsults*, or unintentional remarks that undermine a person's identity; and *microinvalidations*, or statements or actions that negate or diminish the reality of a person's experiences or feelings (Sue et al., 2007).

Microaggressions have been linked to psychological distress in TGD youth, including depression, sadness, low self-esteem, hopelessness, anger, and suicidal thoughts (Gartner & Sterzing, 2016; Kimber et al., 2024). In summary, many TGD youth respond to microaggressions as traumatizing experiences (Kimber et al., 2024).

The *gender minority stress framework* (Hendricks & Testa, 2012) refers to the chronic stress of navigating a transphobic, cisnormative environment, including (a) anticipating a transphobic response, (b) experiencing a traumatic event, (c) confronting barriers to resources, and (d) internalizing transphobia into a negative self-assessment. This framework emphasizes that the last of these, a negative self-assessment, can have a devastating impact on one's life. Internalizing a phobic response to one's own self significantly affects a young person's ability to mitigate the impact of corrosive external stressors.

It is essential to consider intersectionality when addressing microaggressions with TGD clients. TGD youth who hold multiple marginalized social identities are at heightened risk of experiencing intersecting and compounding forms of microaggressions. For instance, racialized TGD youth may encounter gendered racial microaggressions, whereas TGD youth with disabilities may face ableist and gender-related microaggressions. Macroaggressions may beget microaggressions, including bullying and other hostilities, as individuals adopt biases communicated through their friends, families, and others.

TRAUMA TREATMENT

We are only beginning to understand the needs and challenges of treatment that is knowledgeable about both gender and trauma as well as developmentally sensitive. Few studies have highlighted treatment of TGD youth while integrating a trauma perspective into the complexities of mental health care. Minshew (2015) presented a case study of a transgender adolescent treated from a trauma perspective, with sensitivity to this youth's gender and associated stressors. However, trauma treatment models for younger children often diverge in significant ways from treatments of adolescents and adults. Young children reside within ecological contexts with little control or choice regarding fundamental aspects of their world, such as culture, community, and school.

A unique experience of TGD children of color is that although they typically share their racial minoritized identity with their parents, they generally do not also have gender minoritized identity in common with them. Thus, TGD children of color who experience rejection from their parents may face a unique form of trauma. Joanna Fields (personal communication, November 2006), a Black transgender woman who has since passed away, shared memories of her childhood on the playground at school during her keynote presentation at a Transgender Day of Remembrance gathering in Texas. She recalled that if any of the kids called her a racial slur, she knew she could tell her parents and receive understanding, support, encouragement, and racial empowerment: "They told me that they had been called that same thing before, told me it wasn't my fault, and that my Blackness is beautiful. They went to my school to talk to the teacher and principal." However, she stated that if those same kids called her names and slurs for being perceived to be "too effeminate," their response would not be the same: "They told me that maybe I should not act that way anymore and the kids would stop calling me that," effectively blaming her for the other children's cruelty. Effective models of care for traumatized youth may need to integrate these contexts into treatment and work with families to recognize their own biases and increase their gender literacy as they relate to their child.

Creating safety across environments is a critical step for any effective approach to treating traumatized youth, which may involve school-based advocacy. However, this latter step becomes more difficult or nearly impossible when legislative efforts and local policies enshrine TGD nonacceptance. Choices, therefore, may diminish for children who strive for safety, including seeking out safe schools; instead, children and families may need to resort to homeschooling or move to states that are more protective of TGD young people.

Some newer initiatives are specifically developed to acknowledge and treat trauma in TGD youth communities, typically focused on adolescents. The National Child Traumatic Stress Network (n.d.) published a list of empirically supported and promising approaches to treating youth trauma. They also published trauma-informed considerations for clinical care with LGBTQ young people, including a helpful discussion of risk factors specific to mental health vulnerabilities in these communities (McCormick et al., 2018).

Perhaps the approach to youth trauma treatment that is most empirically validated involves trauma-focused cognitive behavior therapy (TF-CBT; Medical University of South Carolina, 2017). This intervention employs skills training, psychoeducation, and a trauma narrative and includes parents and caregivers in treatment. In a promising initiative, the Family Acceptance Project has studied adaptations of TF-CBT for LGBTQ young people (through a collaboration with the National Child Traumatic Stress Network) and published a manual describing their approach (Cohen et al., 2018; Ryan et al., 2023). Another encouraging framework for care has been developed, called Transforming Connections, which engages caregivers of TGD adolescents in a group trauma and attachment-based care approach. Ideally, this model of mental health care can be adapted for the needs of TGD prepubescent children (Dangaltcheva et al., 2021).

In recent years, some researchers and clinicians have developed therapeutic approaches meant to be specifically sensitive to the needs of TGD young people, although not trauma-focused specifically. This includes the *gender affirmative lifespan approach* (GALA; Rider et al., 2019; Spencer et al., 2021). GALA, unlike many other approaches, is meant to address the needs of both prepubescent and adolescent youth, as well as younger and older adults. Its therapeutic approach includes five target areas, as follows: (a) gender literacy; (b) building resilience; (c) moving beyond the binary; (d) exploring pleasure-oriented positive sexuality; and (e) making connections to medical interventions, if appropriate and desired. Although GALA is an exciting innovation that can be adapted for young children and is specifically geared to TGD youth, research is lacking in terms of its efficacy and effectiveness. Additionally, GALA is not geared specifically toward treating traumatized children but instead provides a more general mental health framework.

Another ongoing initiative is *gender-affirming psychotherapy* (GAP; Price et al., 2024). This approach recognizes that insensitivity, and sometimes discrimination and victimization encountered within the health care milieu, is an obstacle to accessing mental health care for TGD youth and families. Thus, GAP may indirectly be geared toward lessening traumatic experiences, through an intervention intended to diminish microaggressions. The GAP framework, developed with input from key stakeholders (mental health providers, parents, and youth) and a scoping literature review, is based on a human-centered model. This resulted in a flexible model of care, incorporating 10 domains. GAP, unlike many other existing care frameworks for TGD youth, represents empirically and community-informed mental health care specifically meant to address the unique needs of TGD youth. Nevertheless, GAP is limited for transgender children because (a) it was developed primarily to be useful with TGD adolescents, and (b) it does not focus specifically on adapting trauma-specific clinical treatments for use with TGD youth.

Importantly, no mental health treatment should assume trauma in TGD youth, but at the same time, treatment should consider the possibility that trauma is there. Approaches to care should address the specific needs of the youth and family requesting intervention and should therefore include a careful assessment integrating a screening for trauma. As with any young person, care should be taken to ensure safety for TGD youth across settings and to advocate and advise as appropriate to create safety. In the most unfortunate situations, child protection agencies may need to be contacted when maltreatment is occurring, with the caveat that filing a mandated report of abuse suspicion does not always immediately create safety for a child and may engender another set of stressors. Placement in an unsupportive foster home, which sometimes follows a report to child protection, can compound trauma rather than be ameliorative.

CASE STUDY

Chris (she) is an 11-year-old Latine transgender girl who was recently removed from an urban public school following chronic taunting and physical aggression and placed in a therapeutic day school environment for LGBTQ youth. She currently resides in a therapeutic foster care placement after she ran away from home a year ago in response to physical and verbal abuse from her biological parents. Chris was raised as a boy but for many years asserted a female identity to the dismay of her parents, for whom it was profoundly important to have a son and inconceivable that their child could repudiate their maleness.

Starting at a young age, Chris gravitated toward "girly" activities, such as playing with dolls and dressing up in princess clothes, often preferring her sister's toys and clothes, even after redirection and punishment from her parents. Chris presented as a boy when she started kindergarten, where she excelled academically and displayed an outgoing and fun-loving personality. However, Chris soon started to be perceived as "different" by classmates, as she played with girls and displayed other "female" choices. For instance, when asked to bring favorite toys to school, Chris brought her sister's portable pink princess house with dolls and was widely ridiculed. By the end of first grade, Chris's demeanor had become more withdrawn and somber. Notably, although not all classmates and teachers were overtly hostile, many were confused by Chris, and peers often asked her whether she was a boy or a girl, whereas teachers would make statements such as "Why are you reading that book? That's a girl's book!" Chris was relentlessly ridiculed by her father at home for being a "sissy"—soon the ridicule escalated to beatings for wearing items such as her sister's underwear. Although Chris's mother was not physically abusive, she regularly admonished Chris and forbade her to "act like a girl."

By third grade, Chris stopped completing homework and often stared listlessly into space when she was asked to engage in academic work at school. On a number of occasions, Chris lashed out at classmates and had crying meltdowns at school, from her teachers' perspective seemingly without provocation. Often Chris would ask to go to the nurse's office, complaining of headaches or stomachaches. Doctor visits suggested no biological cause for these symptoms, and Chris was thought to be feigning illness to get out of class. Her teachers called her parents several times suggesting that mental health treatment might be helpful for Chris, without response. At school, Chris attended a social skills group and visited with the school social worker once a week, where she was typically subdued and guarded. By the time Chris ran away from home at age 10, she was considered a disturbed and difficult child, in need of academic remediation despite considerable intellectual potential.

Chris was placed with foster parents whose family structure included a biological transgender son and who were supportive of Chris. Residing with an accepting family and attending school in a community of acceptance for TGD youth was the first exposure that Chris had to enduring safety. It was a thankful novelty for Chris to have contact with people who embraced her gender presentation, as opposed to being considered a "sickness" that should be thwarted or punished or at its least be perceived as a stigmatized oddity. Following placement, Chris showed positive changes almost immediately: Her aggression diminished, and she demonstrated interest in attending school without her long-standing dread of recess, gym, and lunch. However, weekly visits with her parents in a supervised setting triggered reminders of her complex and chronic traumatic experiences under their care, paired with a sense of loss and attachment disruption. These visits often concluded with Chris becoming more withdrawn and refusing to eat. She also experienced frequent vivid nightmares, yelling out and crying in her sleep; she avoided going to sleep for this reason and was frequently fatigued. In addition, Chris continued to balk at using school bathrooms, as she associated bathrooms with extreme forms of bullying and would sometimes become physically sick if she needed to use the bathroom at school, even within her current context of safety. The teacher would notice Chris staring into space often, as if she were not even in the room; it was very difficult to get her to refocus her attention during these episodes. These represented periods of dissociation, common in traumatized children. Chris often refused to go on school trips and avoided unfamiliar settings, people, and contexts, exhibiting emotional dysregulation if teachers or peers tried to persuade her to participate. She was slow to trust others; upon initially meeting new people, she would often look down and refuse eye contact. At times, new acquaintances presumed that Chris was on the autism spectrum (i.e., a child who met diagnostic criteria for autism spectrum disorder level 1), although this was untrue.

As described, Chris's symptoms appeared to be consistent with a traumatic reaction to a life of chronic adversity, relationship disruption, and gender confusion as her self-identity was repeatedly negated by others. Although Chris was in a safe network at present, she had experienced the world as dismissive and dangerous until that point. From a trauma lens, she was exhibiting symptoms of fear and avoidance, re-experiencing (nightmares), and mood extremes from which she had difficulty emerging. Her lapses at school were related to episodes of dissociation, when either her own cognitions or environmental traumatic reminders became overwhelming. Chris also had a long history of experiencing people and contexts as unsafe, and she had never experienced a secure attachment or sensitive and loving caregiving before moving to her current placement. Before she ran away, she frequently made statements such as "I hate myself" or other remarks suggesting self-loathing. Such overt verbalizations diminished over time; although upon questioning, Chris would admit she did not like herself and felt unlovable.

A trauma-informed approach to mental health treatment should help Chris understand her reactions in light of her life history, develop positive coping skills, engage in a process of self-acceptance, and include her caregivers so that they can advocate for Chris across environments. Without the newly created network of school and home safety, a trauma-sensitive approach to care would be unlikely to succeed. However, in the context of support, and most likely through a gradual process, Chris should be able to develop a relationship of trust with a therapist and eventually with her peers and foster family. She will need an intervention that acknowledges and helps her explore issues of gender with acceptance and without judgment, including her desire for possible gender health care interventions (e.g., puberty blockers) as she approaches puberty. Chris can be helped to develop a perspective on the unwarranted physical and emotional victimization and the microaggressions she endured, as well as her emotional, behavioral, and cognitive responses to these experiences, including self-defeating negative self-beliefs. Therapy should help her develop positive stress management and coping skills that will engender confidence in her ability to navigate future challenges and help her learn to challenge herself to face feared situations (e.g., school bathrooms). Her foster family can be helped to acquire a perspective that promotes an understanding of Chris through a lens of empathy. If possible, Chris's biological parents can work toward an empathetic understanding of their daughter as well and toward building a positive alliance, involving a recognition of their detrimental contribution to Chris's unhappiness and current mental health struggles. Their history suggests that relationship repair may be fraught and difficult.

CONCLUSION

All mental health assessments and interventions for TGD youth should incorporate developmentally and ecologically sensitive as well as trauma-informed care approaches. Additionally, clinicians who evaluate and treat TGD children and adolescents can proactively develop competencies in child trauma and reach out for training and supervision as necessary. As described in this chapter, more recent research has demonstrated that misery and gender diversity are not necessarily partners. TGD young people can be happy and well-adjusted. Psychological perspectives from many frameworks can be brought to the service of creating gratifying and hopeful lives for TGD youth, who need the same love, compassion, acceptance, and support as any child.

Aspirationally, over time, gender will be just one aspect of a child, to be explored rather than pathologized—an exploration that will be free from trauma. For prepubescent TGD children, the only accessible treatments are in the mental health realm (medical gender health care interventions are not available for young TGD prepubescent children; refer to Chapter 2, this volume). Thus, it is imperative that those who care about the well-being of these young children focus on developing empirically supported approaches to care that recognize the unique needs of TGD youth, including trauma vulnerabilities, and intervene early and effectively to support the hopes, talents, abilities, and confidence of each child.

REFERENCES

Adamakos, F. (2021). What are gender micro- and macroaggressions in medicine and what are the solutions? *AEM Education and Training*, *5*(4), e10615. https://doi.org/10.1002/aet2.10615

American Civil Liberties Union. (2025). *Mapping attacks on LGBTQ rights in U.S. state legislatures*. https://www.aclu.org/legislative-attacks-on-lgbtq-rights-2025

Benjamin, H. (1969). Newer aspects of the transsexual phenomenon. *Journal of Sex Research*, *5*(2), 135–141. https://doi.org/10.1080/00224496909550610

Centers for Disease Control and Prevention. (n.d.). *Adverse childhood experiences*. https://www.cdc.gov/violenceprevention/acestudy/

Cho, S., Crenshaw, K. W., & McCall, L. (2013). Toward a field of intersectionality studies: Theory, applications, and praxis. *Signs: Journal of Women in Culture and Society*, *38*(4), 785–810. https://doi.org/10.1086/669608

Cohen, J. A., Mannarino, A. P., Wilson, K., & Zinny, A. (2018). *Trauma-focused cognitive behavioral therapy LGBTQ implementation manual*. Allegheny Health Network.

Coleman, E., Radix, A. E., Bouman, W. P., Brown, G. R., de Vries, A. L. C., Deutsch, M. B., Ettner, R., Fraser, L., Goodman, M., Green, J., Hancock, A. B., Johnson, T. W., Karasic, D. H., Knudson, G. A., Leibowitz, S. F., Meyer-Bahlburg, H. F. L., Monstrey, S. J., Motmans, J., Nahata, L., . . . Arcelus, J. (2022). Standards of care for the health of transgender and gender diverse people, version 8. *International Journal of Transgender Health, 23*(Suppl. 1), S1–S259. https://doi.org/10.1080/26895269.2022.2100644

Collins, P. H., & Bilge, S. (2020). *Intersectionality* (2nd ed.). Polity Press.

Cook, A., Spinazzola, J., Ford, J., Lanktree, C., Blaustein, M., Cloitre, M., DeRosa, R., Hubbard, R., Kagan, R., Liautaud, J., Mallah, K., Olafson, E., & van der Kolk, B. (2005). Complex trauma in children and adolescents. *Psychiatric Annals, 35*(5), 390–398. https://doi.org/10.3928/00485713-20050501-05

Crenshaw, K. (1991). Mapping the margins: Intersectionality, identity politics, and violence against women of color. *Stanford Law Review, 43*(6), 1241–1299. https://doi.org/10.2307/1229039

Crenshaw, K. (1998). Demarginalizing the intersection of race and sex: A Black feminist critique of antidiscrimination doctrine, feminist theory, and antiracist politics. In A. Phillips (Ed.), *Feminism and politics* (pp. 314–343). Oxford Academic. https://doi.org/10.1093/oso/9780198782063.003.0016

Dangaltcheva, A., Booth, C., & Moretti, M. M. (2021). Transforming connections: A trauma-informed and attachment-based program to promote sensitive parenting of trans and gender non-conforming youth. *Frontiers in Psychology, 12*, 643823. https://doi.org/10.3389/fpsyg.2021.643823

de Vries, A. L. C., Steensma, T. D., Cohen-Kettenis, P. T., VanderLaan, D. P., & Zucker, K. J. (2016). Poor peer relations predict parent- and self-reported behavioral and emotional problems of adolescents with gender dysphoria: A cross-national, cross-clinic comparative analysis. *European Child and Adolescent Psychiatry, 25*(6), 579–588. https://doi.org/10.1007/s00787-015-0764-7

Dhanani, L. Y., & Totton, R. R. (2023). Have you heard the news? The effects of exposure to news about recent transgender legislation on transgender youth and young adults. *Sexuality Research and Social Policy, 20*, 1345–1359. https://doi.org/10.1007/s13178-023-00810-6

Feil, K., Riedl, D., Böttcher, B., Fuchs, M., Kapelari, K., Gräßer, S., Toth, B., & Lampe, A. (2023). Higher prevalence of adverse childhood experiences in transgender than in cisgender individuals: Results from a single-center observational study. *Journal of Clinical Medicine, 12*(13), 4501. https://doi.org/10.3390/jcm12134501

Felitti, V. J., Anda, R. F., Nordenberg, D., Williamson, D. F., Spitz, M., Edwards, V., Koss, M. P., & Marks, J. S. (1998). Relationship of childhood abuse and household dysfunction to many of the leading causes of death in adults: The Adverse Childhood Experiences (ACE) Study. *American Journal of Preventive Medicine, 14*(4), 245–258. https://doi.org/10.1016/S0749-3797(98)00017-8

Fish, J. N., Bishop, M. D., & Russell, S. T. (2023). Age trends in bias-based bullying and mental health by sexual orientation and gender identity. *Prevention Science, 24*(6), 1142–1151. https://doi.org/10.1007/s11121-023-01530-4

Flaskerud, J. H., & Lesser, J. (2018). The current socio-political climate and psychological distress among transgender people. *Issues in Mental Health Nursing, 39*(1), 93–96. https://doi.org/10.1080/01612840.2017.1368751

Gartner, R. E., & Sterzing, P. R. (2016). Gender microaggressions as a gateway to sexual harassment and sexual assault. *Affilia, 31*(4), 491–503. https://doi.org/10.1177/0886109916654732

Gartner, R. E., & Sterzing, P. R. (2018). Social ecological correlates of family-level interpersonal and environmental microaggressions toward sexual and gender minority adolescents. *Journal of Family Violence, 33*(1), 1–16. https://doi.org/10.1007/s10896-017-9937-0

Gorski, P. C. (2014). Consumerism as racial and economic injustice: The macroaggressions that make me, and maybe you, a hypocrite. *Understanding and Dismantling Privilege, 4*(1), 13097. https://wpcjournal.com/article/view/13097

Gower, A. L., Rider, G. N., Del Río-González, A. M., Erickson, P. J., Thomas, D., Russell, S. T., Watson, R. J., & Eisenberg, M. E. (2023). Application of an intersectional lens to bias-based bullying among LGBTQ+ youth of color in the United States. *Stigma and Health, 8*(3), 363–371. https://doi.org/10.1037/sah0000415

Grant, J. M., Mottet, L. A., Tanis, J., Harrison, J., Herman, J. L., & Keisling, M. (2011). *Injustice at every turn: A report of the National Transgender Discrimination Survey*. National Center for Transgender Equality and National Gay and Lesbian Task Force. https://www.thetaskforce.org/static_html/downloads/reports/reports/ntds_full.pdf

Hendricks, M. L., & Testa, R. J. (2012). A conceptual framework for clinical work with transgender and gender nonconforming clients: An adaptation of the minority stress model. *Professional Psychology: Research and Practice, 43*(5), 460–467. https://doi.org/10.1037/a0029597

Hollinsaid, N. L., Price, M. A., & Hatzenbuehler, M. L. (2024). Transgender-specific adolescent mental health provider availability is substantially lower in states with more restrictive policies. *Journal of Clinical Child & Adolescent Psychology, 53*(5), 828–839. https://doi.org/10.1080/15374416.2022.2140433

Human Rights Watch. (2025, June 3). *"They're ruining people's lives": Bans on gender-affirming care for transgender youth in the U.S.* https://www.hrw.org/news/2025/06/03/us-bans-gender-affirming-care-harm-trans-youth

Kaufman, R., & Tishelman, A. (2018). Creating a network of professionals. In C. Keo-Meier & D. Ehrensaft (Eds.), *The gender affirmative model: An interdisciplinary approach to supporting transgender and gender expansive children* (pp. 173–188). American Psychological Association. https://doi.org/10.1037/0000095-011

Kimber, B., Oxlad, M., & Twyford, L. (2024). The impact of microaggressions on the mental health of trans and gender-diverse people: A scoping review. *International Journal of Transgender Health, 25*, 1–21. https://doi.org/10.1080/26895269.2024.2380903

Kosciw, J. G., Palmer, N. A., & Kull, R. M. (2015). Reflecting resiliency: Openness about sexual orientation and/or gender identity and its relationship to well-being and educational outcomes for LGBT students. *American Journal of Community Psychology, 55*(1–2), 167–178. https://doi.org/10.1007/s10464-014-9642-6

Lennon, E., & Mistler, B. J. (2014). Cisgenderism. *TSQ: Transgender Studies Quarterly, 1*(1–2), 63–64. https://doi.org/10.1215/23289252-2399623

MacMullin, L., Mvunga, J., & VanderLaan, D. (2024). Risk and resilience among BIPOC trans youth: An interpretative phenomenological study. *Bulletin of Applied Transgender Studies, 3*(3–4), 177–203. https://doi.org/10.57814/j5s8-tj45

Masten, A. S., & Cicchetti, D. (2010). Developmental cascades. *Development and Psychopathology, 22*(3), 491–495. https://doi.org/10.1017/S0954579410000222

McCormick, A., Scheyd, K., & Terrazas, S. (2018). Trauma-informed care and LGBTQ youth: Considerations for advancing practice with youth with trauma experiences. *Families in Society, 99*(2), 160–169. https://doi.org/10.1177/1044389418768550

Medical University of South Carolina. (2017). *TF-CBT Web 2.0: A course for trauma-focused cognitive behavioral therapy*. https://tfcbt.musc.edu/en

Minshew, R. (2015). Lost in place: An adolescent case of gender fluidity and secondary trauma. *Journal of Gay & Lesbian Mental Health, 19*(2), 201–208. https://doi.org/10.1080/19359705.2014.997910

Nadal, K. L., Issa, M.-A., Leon, J., Meterko, V., Wideman, M., & Wong, Y. (2011). Sexual orientation microaggressions: "Death by a thousand cuts" for lesbian, gay, and bisexual youth. *Journal of LGBT Youth, 8*(3), 234–259. https://doi.org/10.1080/19361653.2011.584204

National Child Traumatic Stress Network. (n.d.). *National Child Traumatic Stress Network empirically supported treatments and promising practices*. http://nctsn.org/training-guidelines

Olson, K. R., Durwood, L., DeMeules, M., & McLaughlin, K. A. (2016). Mental health of transgender children who are supported in their identities. *Pediatrics, 137*(3), e20153223. https://doi.org/10.1542/peds.2015-3223

O'Malley, M. D., Cerna, R., Romero, L., Zhang, G., & Furlong, M. J. (2022). Reducing the impact of bias-based bullying on suicidal thoughts among sexual and gender minority youth: Are psychological strengths enough? *School Mental Health, 14*(3), 655–671. https://doi.org/10.1007/s12310-021-09490-2

Osanloo, A. F., Boske, C., & Newcomb, W. S. (2016). Deconstructing macroaggressions, microaggressions, and structural racism in education: Developing a conceptual model for the intersection of social justice practice and intercultural education. *International Journal of Organizational Theory and Development, 4*(1), 1–18.

Pariseau, E. M., Chevalier, L., Long, K. A., Clapham, R., Edwards-Leeper, L., & Tishelman, A. C. (2019). The relationship between family acceptance-rejection and transgender youth psychosocial functioning. *Clinical Practice in Pediatric Psychology, 7*(3), 267–277. https://doi.org/10.1037/cpp0000291

Price, M. A., Rakhilin, M., Johansen, K., Collins, L., Pachankis, J. E., Lyon, A. R., & Allen, M. (2024). Gender-affirming psychotherapy (GAP): Core principles and skills to reduce the mental health care "GAP" for transgender youths. *Psychiatric Services, 75*(11), 1075–1083. https://doi.org/10.1176/appi.ps.20230460

Ramos, N., Burgess, A., & Ollen, E. (2023). The current status of sociopolitical and legal issues faced by lesbian, gay, bisexual, transgender, queer, and questioning youth. *Adolescent Psychiatry, 12*(3), 180–195. https://doi.org/10.2174/2210676611666211105120645

Reisner, S. L., Vetters, R., Leclerc, M., Zaslow, S., Wolfrum, S., Shumer, D., & Mimiaga, M. J. (2015). Mental health of transgender youth in care at an adolescent urban community health center: A matched retrospective cohort study. *Journal of Adolescent Health, 56*(3), 274–279. https://doi.org/10.1016/j.jadohealth.2014.10.264

Reisner, S. L., White Hughto, J. M., Gamarel, K. E., Keuroghlian, A. S., Mizock, L., & Pachankis, J. E. (2016). Discriminatory experiences associated with posttraumatic stress disorder symptoms among transgender adults. *Journal of Counseling Psychology, 63*(5), 509–519. https://doi.org/10.1037/cou0000143

Rider, G. N., Vencill, J. A., Berg, D. R., Becker-Warner, R., Candelario-Pérez, L., & Spencer, K. G. (2019). The gender affirmative lifespan approach (GALA): A framework for competent clinical care with nonbinary clients. *International Journal of Transgenderism, 20*(2–3), 275–288. https://doi.org/10.1080/15532739.2018.1485069

Ryan, C., Barba, A., & Cohen, J. A. (2023). Family-based psychosocial care for transgender and gender-diverse children and youth. *Child and Adolescent Psychiatric Clinics of North America, 32*(4), 775–788. https://doi.org/10.1016/j.chc.2023.03.002

Schnarrs, P. W., Stone, A. L., Salcido, R., Jr., Baldwin, A., Georgiou, C., & Nemeroff, C. B. (2019). Differences in adverse childhood experiences (ACEs) and quality of physical and mental health between transgender and cisgender sexual minorities. *Journal of Psychiatric Research, 119*, 1–6. https://doi.org/10.1016/j.jpsychires.2019.09.001

Shonkoff, J. P., Garner, A. S., Committee on Psychosocial Aspects of Child and Family Health, Committee on Early Childhood, Adoption, and Dependent Care, & Section on Developmental and Behavioral Pediatrics, Siegel, B. S., Dobbins, M. I., Earls, M. F., Garner, A. S., McGuinn, L., Pascoe, J., & Wood, D. L. (2012). The lifelong effects of early childhood adversity and toxic stress. *Pediatrics, 129*(1), e232–e246. https://doi.org/10.1542/peds.2011-2663

Spencer, K. G., Berg, D. R., Bradford, N. J., Vencill, J. A., Tellawi, G., & Rider, G. N. (2021). The gender-affirmative life span approach: A developmental model for clinical work with transgender and gender-diverse children, adolescents, and adults. *Psychotherapy, 58*(1), 37–49. https://doi.org/10.1037/pst0000363

Sue, D. W., Capodilupo, C. M., Torino, G. C., Bucceri, J. M., Holder, A. M. B., Nadal, K. L., & Esquilin, M. (2007). Racial microaggressions in everyday life: Implications for clinical practice. *American Psychologist, 62*(4), 271–286. https://doi.org/10.1037/0003-066x.62.4.271

Thoma, B. C., Rezeppa, T. L., Choukas-Bradley, S., Salk, R. H., & Marshal, M. P. (2021). Disparities in childhood abuse between transgender and cisgender adolescents. *Pediatrics, 148*(2), e2020016907. https://doi.org/10.1542/peds.2020-016907

Tishelman, A., & Rider, G. N. (2023). Assessment of gender diverse children: Incorporating the Standard of Care 8th edition. *Child and Adolescent Psychiatric Clinics of North America, 32*(4), 719–730. https://doi.org/10.1016/j.chc.2023.05.008

Tishelman, A. C., Haney, P., O'Brien, J. G., & Blaustein, M. (2010). A framework for school-based psychological evaluations: Utilizing a 'trauma lens.' *Journal of Child and Adolescent Trauma, 3*(4), 279–302. https://doi.org/10.1080/19361521.2010.523062

Toomey, R. B., Card, N. A., & Casper, D. M. (2014). Peers' perceptions of gender nonconformity: Associations with overt and relational peer victimization and aggression in early adolescence. *The Journal of Early Adolescence, 34*(4), 463–485.

UCLA School of Law Williams Institute. (2024). *The impact of transgender sports bans*. https://williamsinstitute.law.ucla.edu/publications/impact-trans-sports-ban-eo/

7 THE SPACE TO TRY

Creative Arts Approaches to Identity Exploration With Children

MAK MORIN

Transgender and gender diverse (TGD) youth discover and experience their gender identity at different times and in different ways. Transition, also referred to as embodiment (Dubois et al., 2022; Hastings et al., 2021), is individualized to each person. Many factors are incorporated into the development of healthy growth, including acceptance from family and from community, exposure to gender diverse people, acceptance or rejection of gender identification or cross-gender behaviors, comfort with the body, personal safety, and experiences of microaggressions, discrimination, and oppression (Brill & Pepper, 2008; Erickson-Schroth & Davis, 2021; Olson et al., 2016; Singh et al., 2011).

During early development, it is normal for children to have gender expansive behaviors as they explore, question, and craft their understanding of gender as it applies to themselves, their families, peers, and the world (Brill & Pepper, 2008; Erickson-Schroth & Davis, 2021; Langer, 2019). All children establish a sense of physical autonomy and gender identity between age 18 to 24 months (Erikson, 1963), but the ways in which this is incorporated into self-image, self-confidence, and personal identity can vary for children who are transgender or gender diverse (Darke & Scott-Miller, 2021). As children investigate preferences and affinities in early childhood, affirming support such as

https://doi.org/10.1037/0000494-008
Pediatric Gender Health Care: The Gender Affirmative Model Revisited, Second Edition, G. N. Rider, D. Ehrensaft, and C. St. Amand (Editors)

psychotherapy can help strengthen their resilience and self-image (Berberian, 2020; Erickson-Schroth & Davis, 2021).

CREATIVE ARTS THERAPY AND TGD CHILDREN

As a licensed creative arts therapist, specifically a drama therapist, I believe in the power of creativity to support persons across the lifespan in attuning to self and integrating a resilient sense of identity and expression (Epp, 2007; Fancourt & Finn, 2019; Jackman, 2022; Orkibi et al., 2025; Rosenfeld Halverson, 2010). Creative arts therapies (CATs) encompass music therapy, art therapy, drama therapy, dance movement therapy, and integrated expressive arts approaches. These modalities are demonstrably beneficial for therapeutic change across populations, mental health concerns, and lifespans (de Witte et al., 2021; Fancourt & Finn, 2019; Orkibi et al., 2025). My specific modality, drama therapy, focuses on integrating cognitive, verbal, and embodied processes, using play, embodiment, projection, role, story, metaphor, empathy, distancing, witnessing, performance, and improvisation to help people make meaningful change (Jones, 2007; Landy, 1996, 2008; Orkibi et al., 2025). CATs and modalities like drama therapy can also be especially impactful with young children for whom symbolic language and play are powerful and developmentally appropriate forms of processing and communication (Berberian, 2020; Winnicott, 1971). These approaches are well-suited to provide TGD individuals with a space to practice a variety of ways of being and expressing that align with their autonomous identity, especially when verbal methods alone cannot always capture the nuance of gender shaping and development (Beauregard & Long, 2019; Jackman, 2022).

CATs are inherently integrative and interdisciplinary, drawing from diverse therapeutic, artistic, and cultural frameworks to meet the unique needs of TGD youth. With this interdisciplinary benefit in mind, this chapter seeks to demonstrate how integration of arts-based interventions in an individual therapy setting can benefit TGD children in their identity exploration. In my work, I find the tenets of mirroring and attunement within the therapeutic alliance to be of particular salience with TGD youth, and I will endeavor to illustrate how these can be facilitated through, and complemented by, creative arts processes.

Mirroring

According to Winnicott (1971), developmental mirroring includes how the infant is spoken to, played with, and comforted, and adequate mirroring early in life leads to better self-awareness, resilience, and emotional self-regulation. Children deprived of this good-enough mirroring may develop what Winnicott (1971) called the false self, which Langer (2019) saw as a product of the TGD child's effort to conform to the gender designated at birth, leaving space between what the caregiver offers and what the child actually needs. From a psychodynamic perspective, *mirroring* is commonly defined as a therapist repeating elements of a client's phrase in order to indirectly prompt further elaboration. This repetition can also allow clients to listen to their own words and consider their meaning and impact more carefully, often prompting greater integration of insight and self-knowing (Ferrara, 1994; Jones, 2007). In a CAT space, mirroring can be as simple as validating the client's gender identity and using their correct name and pronouns regularly so they can hear them and attune to how it feels to be known and recognized as such. It may also look like using reflective listening and narrative summary, intentionally enacting the client's body language or gestures, augmenting major themes in their life through play and art, celebrating and encouraging new forms of self-expression, or joining them in embodied or symbolic exploration.

Attunement

Attunement in the therapeutic encounter is more of an affective state that asks the therapist to enter into the intimate world of the client and stay in alignment. This becomes especially important for a population that has often experienced relational trauma and may experience distrust or disconnect from their somatic self. *Misattunement*, in the context of therapeutic rapport, presents the opportunity for modeling accountability, repair, and secure attachment, while continuing to work toward attuned connections that can emerge into a flow or playful state that is permissive and validating of identity exploration (Beauregard & Long, 2019; Winnicott, 1971). This kind of mutual resonance is often experienced by the client as connectivity, understanding, support, and empathy that can contribute greatly to creating a sense of psychological healing (Kossak, 2009). In CATs, the artmaking itself can be viewed as a vehicle to create and modulate attunement. This may look like acknowledging and expanding on a client's words or gestures by turning them into full movement and sound. It may also be turning a clay sculpture into a dance, a passing comment into a song, or a drawing into a theatrical scene. Whatever the modality, attunement is a fundamental tool for forging a strong therapeutic alliance, and arts-based interventions serve to increase the opportunity and means for these connective attunements to emerge (Beauregard & Long, 2019; Kossak, 2009; Pendzik, 2006).

Therapeutic Process

de Witte et al. (2021) highlighted three factors of therapeutic change that are jointly utilized across CAT disciplines: embodiment, concretization, and symbolism. *Embodiment* is the expression and physicalization of emotions, thoughts, ideas, reactions, impulses, and inner experiences (Armstrong et al., 2015; de Witte et al., 2021; Jones, 2007). (*Note:* Because the term embodiment is also used in the context of gender development, for the purposes of this writing I will delineate it as *personal embodiment* and *therapeutic embodiment*.) *Concretization* refers to changing an abstract content or statement into a tangible form that can be physically perceived, experienced, and related to (de Witte et al., 2021). *Symbolism* involves the projection of internal and often unconscious material into visual, narrative, musical, and enacted forms (de Witte et al., 2021; Jones, 2007). In practice, these factors may look like creating and exploring a gender spectrum with preexisting or self-created images; rehearsing for difficult conversations via roleplay, comic strips, or story writing; fostering mind–body connection and expression via dance, music, or acting exercises; understanding emotions and related needs by creating music playlists or original music or exploring a fairytale rich in relevant imagery to clients; or exploring self-expression, parts of self, and archetypes in toys, self-portrait, or sculpture.

Throughout this chapter, I will offer composite case vignettes focused on gender exploration work within the therapeutic dyad to illustrate ongoing attunement and mirroring through CAT interventions. These are composite cases pulled from my work in private practice with children seeking to explore and articulate (i.e., develop) their gender identity. Any specific or identifying information has been changed or editorialized to serve this writing. Other elements of this work can unfortunately not be as thoroughly explored in this writing, but it is integral to remember that there are many layers to working with TGD children, especially in consideration of intersecting identities (e.g., race, ethnicity, socioeconomic status, disability, sexuality, national origin, and religion), as well as collaborating with a child's caretakers and important communities. Holding all of these factors is essential to ensuring that therapeutic approaches honor the full complexity of each individual's lived experience (Berberian, 2020; Brill & Pepper, 2008; Erickson-Schroth & Davis, 2021).

With this holistic approach in mind, my clients and I embark on a collaborative journey with several overarching treatment goals, which are as follows:

1. Guide clients in developing a deeper understanding of how they feel internally about themselves, and determine if and how they wish to share this with others.

2. Explore the presence and impact of experiences of gender dysphoria and negative body image, as well as strategies for alleviation of this distress (i.e., potential embodiment goals).
3. Process the impact of social and cultural introjection (i.e., internalization of external messages) on sense of self, and create opportunities for more expansive connection.

Because even if it is too difficult for clients to see themselves yet, we must allow them the space to try.

GENDER IDENTITY AND EXPRESSION

The first treatment goal—to support clients in developing a deeper understanding of internal knowledge, and determine how to share this with others—is grounded in guiding clients through navigation of the intrinsic relationship between gender identity and expression. Ultimately, this relationship may be described as "gender expression is a complex series of actions that serve to prompt those around us to better understand who we are inside [gender identity]" (Erickson-Schroth & Davis, 2021, p. 6). It is from this understanding that I explore with young clients who they are inside and how they want to share that with others. Concurrently, we explore how they feel they are perceived by others and what of this is resonant or dissonant to their internal sense of self. As children start to develop a sense of being a separate person, they may begin to trust others' perceptions more than their own, and the misattuned influence of adults around them can override a child's burgeoning sense of self, leading them to mistrust their own internal awareness and knowing (Langer, 2019). Thus, clinicians can and should mirror the language clients use, and they should work with parents and families around education, as increasing affirming support is vital. Changes in communication, such as using different name or pronouns, may reduce psychological strain; similarly, shifts in gender expression, including dress or presentation, can ease the dissonance of misgendering and mistrust, allowing for greater comfort in one's body, mind, and environment (Brill & Pepper, 2008; Langer, 2019; Olson et al., 2016).

In my work, I gear this mirroring toward the literal and the symbolic, and I strive for an embodied attunement that can cross modalities to affirm clients. This process will often include exploring gender roles, current language, and expectations they are already absorbing and making sense of, as well as providing widened or alternative perspectives on the range of gender diversity in humanity. Additionally, using arts-based interventions with this exploration can encourage acceptance of gender expansive play, dress, and images, while also empowering the child towards free expression and building a resilient self-image (Berberian, 2020; Darke & Scott-Miller, 2021).

Case Vignette: From the Inside Out

Ari, 8 years old, came to treatment struggling with expressing and articulating a nonbinary identity while coping with burgeoning anxiety. Ari came from a separated family. Their mother was openly affirming; their father was conflicted and often rejecting. I was aware throughout treatment of tension between familial beliefs and Ari's gender expression, which was sometimes embraced but just as often met with chronic judgment given Ari's affinities towards feminine behaviors, activities, and clothing. This split between households was confusing and disarming for Ari. Part of helping them feel confident in advocating for self-determination and respect in a strained family dynamic was helping Ari understand and articulate themself more clearly, with the knowledge that people are allowed to change and grow. I also met with Ari's parents separately to discuss challenges with support and solutions for greater family harmony.

Ari loved artmaking, particularly drawing and coloring, and they found the structure of a direct prompt to be enabling and reassuring. I gave Ari an empty sketch of a simple human outline (which often looks like a gingerbread figure) and guided them through a body scan focused on questions like "How do I feel in my body right now? What sensations are coming up, and where do I feel them?" Then I encouraged Ari to represent these visually inside the human outline, giving feelings and sensations colors, shapes, textures, and symbols. We then explored what other inner knowing they could add, including personal identifiers and labels, primary emotions and where they live in the body, and where different aspects of their identity (including gender) live. For Ari, gender was in and around the heart, beating a steady rhythm of "not a boy, not a boy," to encourage and remind them of this truth, even as the external world may deny it.

A few sessions later, Ari and I returned to these human containers, and we added a layer of complexity. I presented Ari with a blank mask of a human face and delineated that the outside was representative of the External Self ("what I think others see, what I want them to see"), and the inside was representative of the Internal Self ("what others don't see, what I feel inside"). These could be represented using colors, images, words, shapes, and symbols. For the external-facing part of the mask, Ari focused on others' perceptions and known identity factors related to the previous project, as well as adjectives commonly used to describe them by others. For the inside, Ari recreated that steady beating heart and some additional private emotions and physical sensations. We reflected on the mask as a whole: "Are the inside and outside different? Why? Is there something inside that you wish was on the outside or vice versa?" Ari was able to consider internal traits and experiences they would like to bring to the outside, as well as external perceptions they wished they could "erase from people's minds"—some related to gender, some not.

Later still, Ari and I brought out the masks again, this time to wear. Using Ari's creation and a blank mask for myself, we explored and physically enacted in sound, movement, and gesture Ari's frustration and confusion with the many ways they had experienced gender stereotypes. I would repeat and mirror Ari's expressions, and I also invited them to direct me as an actor in several short scenes where they had the opportunity to make new choices when reflecting on and re-enacting microaggressions from the far and recent past. This session was a triumph and a challenge for Ari, who feared perception and craved affirmation. To have me "get it wrong" when portraying them or playing back an important moment from their memory, while also listening to their feedback and adjusting faithfully, gave them the opportunity to tolerate uncertainty and the empowerment to speak for their own truth. Ari was also able to directly acknowledge experiences of gender incongruence and discomfort to me, noting frustration and alienation from "people telling me what to do, or how to be myself." Ari said, "I don't mind if people mess up my pronouns sometimes, but when people call me 'little man' or say my clothes are girly, I get really mad. It's not true. They're just mine. I'm just me."

For clients like Ari, whose sense of internal mistrust can be more directly connected to gender harm and conflict, there is immense power in the arts to support young people "with identity development and coping when spoken words are not always accessible enough" (Darke & Scott-Miller, 2021, p. 130). By starting with an opportunity to tune into their inner sensations and felt knowledge and to express them in a visual medium that allowed for simultaneous abstraction and concretizing, Ari was able to slowly build the mind–body connection and move toward greater self-attunement. This also sets a foundation for therapeutic embodiment, which may overwhelm clients for whom the body is a source of distress, particularly because it can increase emotional arousal (Armstrong et al., 2015). Moderating the focus on the body through different levels of therapeutic embodiment requires careful attunement on the therapist's part and intentional modulation to allow the client to stay grounded (Armstrong et al., 2015; Jones, 2007). The mask intervention, for example, creates opportunity for therapeutic embodiment, in which the therapist can attune to and reflect the client's choices and play with the body narratives and expressions of gender (Darke & Scott-Miller, 2021; Jackman, 2022) while providing an aesthetic and physical layer of protection from a potentially overwhelming or vulnerable focus on the physical self (Landy, 2008). As Landy (1996) put it, "the transformational quality of therapeutic mask dramas is centered in the paradox of masking as a means of unmasking" (p. 64). Meaning, Ari felt freer to embody both outside expectations and their own authenticity by hiding their actual face. With time, Ari was able to tolerate and even enjoy therapeutic embodiment without masks, embracing another layer of comfort in self-expression and presence in the body. As Ari grows, this comfort will support them in understanding and communicating about their gender embodiment needs and bring themself and others into closer alignment with their inner knowing. For TGD children, having this foundation for self-attunement and therapeutic embodiment becomes increasingly beneficial as gender and expression begin to merge into the world of puberty and expectations of physical changes.

DYSPHORIA AND FUTURE ORIENTATION

The second guiding treatment goal in this work is to explore with clients the presence and impact of gender dysphoria and negative body image, as well as strategies for alleviation of this distress. It is important to understand that the term *gender dysphoria* is used by both mental health professionals and by transgender community members, although sometimes in different ways. Colloquially, the term gender dysphoria is used "to refer to emotional difficulty related to living in bodies or societal roles that do not fit" (Erickson-Schroth & Davis, 2021, p. 73). Dysphoria is always a unique experience and most often tolerated, resolved, or carried best with support networks and internalized strength (Singh et al., 2011). However, it is vital for clinicians who wish to attune to the individual needs of each client to understand that the distress a TGD person has or could experience should not be "misunderstood as the etiology of their trans identity or gender expression" (Langer, 2019, p. 184; see also Olson et al., 2016). Pathologizing gender diversity in this way can hinder the therapeutic alliance and dampen honest and safe exploration of a client's gender or any associated experiences.

Although not all TGD persons experience dysphoria, the looming presence of puberty can cause a number of questions, concerns, or fears for young people regardless of gender identity, and to be growing into an incongruent body can cause another layer of distress (Brill & Pepper, 2008; Langer, 2019). This anticipation of incongruent development can create feelings of anxiety and shame, and it may diminish hope for a future that can still hold the joy and strength the client had already been cultivating in their own body and sense of self. Sharing relevant resources, reinforcing the presence of emotional and medical support, and laying a foundation for open communication with children, families, and caregivers about evolving needs can provide much needed relief (Erickson-Schroth & Davis, 2021; Hastings et al., 2021; Singh et al., 2011), especially for children who, understandably, are not yet sure what they want or what is possible.

In support of this, CAT modalities can employ a space of dramatic or aesthetic reality encompassed in the therapeutic mechanism of symbolism, which can help children face daunting and distressful material in playful, empathetic, and flexibly distanced ways (Landy, 2008). Ultimately, because the content of each person's imagination is relevant to the landscape of their internal and external influences, use of CATs can benefit the continued shaping of the present self and the future self via the relationship between imagination and identity as well as the co-created dramatic reality that allows for intensified attunement and expansive mirroring (Pendzik, 2006). Essentially, if a child is having trouble imagining a positive future, they can create one.

Case Vignette: Imagining the Possibilities

Hugh, age 9, came to treatment, with the family's primary concern being social support. However, Hugh had a history of prominent genital dysphoria. Work with Hugh focused on navigation of social transition, particularly in interpersonal dynamics with school peers. At the time, Hugh used the neo-pronouns xe/xem/xyr, adaptive personal pronouns that exist outside of standard language. Classmates and staff found these pronouns challenging to use correctly, causing frequent feelings of alienation and dysphoria for Hugh. Hugh and I worked on strategies for self-advocacy and for self-affirmation, while Hugh's parents and I worked to help the school feel equipped to support xem and xyr classmates.

Hugh then began puberty earlier than anticipated, and xyr parents were concerned that the genital dysphoria, which had been debilitating, would re-emerge. The parents began the consultation process with Hugh's physicians to have Hugh started on pubertal suppression treatment. I engaged in my informed consent assessment process with Hugh and family; and for the first time in my months of working with xem, I saw a glimpse of Hugh's younger self. Usually, Hugh had an energized presence, bursting with creativity. Now Hugh was quiet and nearly laconic, and xe had developed a nervous tick involving the hands and shoulders. Hugh's parents and I monitored xem; as soon as Hugh was approved and received xyr first pubertal suppression injection, Hugh returned to xyr former affect, bouncing back almost literally—dashing into my office and throwing dance scarves and plush toys all around. Knowing puberty blockers are not an indefinite medication, I adjusted treatment toward further exploration of puberty and the role of hormones in growth, fertility, and development to help acclimate Hugh to impending medical discussions and to give time and space for xem to process this information and apply it toward xyr self-image.

One day, I had Hugh create an imaginary creature as a form of assessment as well as to explore xyr current feelings and needs. I prompted xem with questions like these: "What can this creature do? What environment do they live in?" "What does the creature need? How do they feel?" "How similar or different is the creature to yourself—their desires, needs, and feelings?" Hugh created a bipedal jack-o-lantern, and from it a diorama of a Halloween-themed, undergarment department store was built. This space included the originating jack-o-lantern mascot, a genderless robot shop assistant, and several shoppers of varying gender expressions and gender identities. We explored in this world what it would be like to have a truly affirming—dare we say, fun—experience shopping for an item that was once supremely triggering for Hugh. This land of underwear was a beacon of celebration for all bodies, and those who came in holding fear or shame were quickly held in love and celebration by staff and patrons alike.

I would often ask Hugh what xe thought xyr own experience would be if xe could enter this place as xyr current self. Hugh would smile and say, "I'd steal all the underwear and throw it on the streets for everyone to have!" I also saw parts of Hugh in the tiny nonbinary child in the diorama with three sets of pronouns (she/they/it), which the robot shop assistant faithfully interchanged. I saw Hugh's fear and experiences of rejection in the lonely child with no pronouns and no caretaker to buy the underwear they wanted (the jack-o-lantern gave it to them as a gift, of course). I even saw Hugh in an adult character, a nonbinary mother who Hugh insisted had "realized who they really are when her kid came out. They helped each other figure it out." I hoped Hugh might also see some of xyr own future in this affirmed, gender diverse adult.

By incorporating the symbolism of story and metaphor, as well as flexible and tolerable layers of therapeutic embodiment via enactment, play, sculpting, and projective devices (e.g., toys, sand trays, images, story), Hugh was able to enter a "less psychological, less personal plane" and see the many parts of self "reflected in these archetypes," as well as explore "how these images have shaped" the conception of self (Landy, 1996, p. 51). Therapeutic use of play and projective devices also relies on a theory of distancing inspired by both aesthetic movements in the arts and Winnicott's (1971) *transitional space*, defined as a psychological gap that stands between one stage of development and another and between inner experience and the outside world. Winnicott (1971) theorized play as a bridge between the inner experience of the child and the external reality, creating a transitional space "that allows the child to repeat and process misattuned or damaging experience in the play, but also resolves it through imaginative, symbolic action" (Landy, 2008, p. 45). In Hugh's case, xe was able to concurrently play with gender and physicality on the projective bodies of the dolls xe created and xyr own exploration of body and identity (Darke & Scott-Miller, 2021). For children still building and testing their knowledge about themselves and the world, integrating symbolic play and the power of imagination into treatment can allow greater freedom for them to express their thoughts, feelings, and desires and resolve inner tensions and misattunements (Jones, 2007; Pendzik, 2006).

SOCIAL AND CULTURAL (DIS)CONNECTION

The third treatment goal—process the impact of social and cultural introjection on a client's sense of self, and create opportunities for more expansive connection—necessitates an understanding of gender development. Between ages 1 and 3 years, children begin investigating the boundaries of gender congruent and incongruent behavior (Erickson-Schroth & Davis, 2021). Most scholars believe some of our understanding of gender is socially constructed: not objective reality, but gender expectations we agree to perceive as real. This social learning theory posits that "children learn about how gender functions in the world through modeling of gender behaviors, experiencing rewards and punishments for their own gendered behaviors, and directly being taught ideas" (Erickson-Schroth & Davis, 2021, p. 69). The gender schema theory shows how children initially pay closer attention to the schemas and social scripts that apply to their designated gender, likely because they are trying to learn as much as possible about how they are expected to interact with the world (Bem, 1981). As children grow, they will begin to gather and "test new information against these schemas to determine whether they should change their schemas or make exceptions" (Erickson-Schroth & Davis, 2021, p. 71).

As children start to develop a sense of being a separate person, the misattuned influence of adults around them can override a child's burgeoning sense of self, leading them to mistrust their own internal cues and personal embodiment in favor of that which more closely aligns with the expectations and perception of those around them (Langer, 2019). In early development, the processing of social messages becomes integral to identity development long term, because those who are targeted by and subjected to oppressive narratives and belief systems often internalize them as negative beliefs that can take a lifetime to untangle (Nadal, 2013; Rosenfeld Halverson, 2010). Although gender theory and terminology continues to evolve, language is still more limited than an individual's experience itself, and CATs offer forms of verbal and nonverbal concretization, symbolism, and embodiment that allow for intuitive navigation of an individual's experiences and influences on identity. It is my intention to guide clients in navigating these shifting layers and cultural schemas, toward fostering their ability to translate and communicate their inner knowing and forge attuned connections throughout life.

Case Vignette: Telling Your Story Through Another

Ellie, 12, was brought to therapy for gender health support and exploration of posttraumatic stress disorder symptoms with a history of trauma in the foster care system. Notably, Ellie was processing a recent rejection from a biological parent after she bravely chose to disclose her identity as a trans girl, with the support of her adoptive family. Fear of continued rejection, exacerbated by the rise of antitrans rhetoric and political awareness, was heavy on Ellie's mind.

Typically, Ellie and I would engage in improvised dramatic play, driven by Ellie and subtly shaped by me. Ellie, homeschooled by her affirming parents, often played out scenes in a traditional school setting, with imagined cruel teachers and neglectful adults. My efforts to include supportive adults were almost always rejected. Additionally, Ellie found it challenging at first to engage with any offering of peer characters, preferring to act out power struggles and interpersonal harm from adults. Often, she would critique that I wasn't "mean or scary enough," and she would have to play the powerful adult character and I the meek, terrified child in order to faithfully render the story. It took time for Ellie to work through these repetitions and allow new images, relationships, and outcomes to enter into her consideration.

Parallel to our play, Ellie was also becoming a more confident reader, often wanting to play out scenes of characters from books she was interested in, all of them featuring TGD children resolving challenges, loving themselves, and finding strength in adversity. One day, she announced to me, "I want to do that! Let's write a book!" And so our improvisational storytelling became concrete, and we spent several months writing, editing, making art and music for, and recording an audiobook version of Ellie's original tale of a trans girl's experience. It was not directly a story about Ellie herself, but about a young trans girl whose parents decide to move to a state with a trans care ban, prompting this young girl to come out to her parents before she is ready in order to avoid a dangerous situation.

Similar to our improvisation play, Ellie found it difficult to imagine or include supportive adult figures. Yet, I noticed a few key differences, including a prominent presence of supportive peers for Ellie's main character, as well as Ellie's willingness to include at least one supportive extended family member, who she had teamed up with the main character to change the parents' minds about trans people. Through her main character's resilience, Ellie was also able to face some of her own fears of the world around her, harsh parental rejection, and the cultural repudiation she was seeing as well.

Ellie and I often reflected on the story we were writing, and I would model making connections to the events and characters in the narrative—similarities and differences. Ellie was eventually able to do the same and decided to draw the main character on the cover "to look a little like me." Ellie was also able to "use some of [her] own emotions" to create several short musical refrains expressing the ebb and flow of the main character's moods throughout the tale, which were included in the recording process. When the project was done, Ellie's mother turned the recording into an audiobook so she could listen to it whenever she wanted, her own creation equal alongside those from her favorite authors.

TGD youth can often experience misattunement and relational traumas within their family of origin, as well as from the larger world around them, that are replicated and played out in their lives (Beauregard & Long, 2019). The therapeutic dyad can become a place for repairing some of this harm by developing interpersonal attunement and secure attachments and mitigating the impact of trauma on TGD youth (Langer, 2019). Additionally, CATs can provide symbolic spaces for clients to explore how these experiences in culture, family of origin, and social systems have influenced their sense of self and expression. When using storytelling in session, therapists can guide client-driven stories toward relevant themes, or they can allow for a story entirely self-generated by the client. Ellie's love for fiction and dramatic play, particularly with stories where she saw herself and her community reflected, allowed her to discover narrative mirrors and cultivate hope for the future (Rosenfeld Halverson, 2010; Singh et al., 2011). In making her own story, she was able to create a symbolic, concretizing environment that became a safe, controlled container upon which she could project fantasies, wishes, expectations, fears, pain, and anxieties (Landy, 1996). To stay attuned to Ellie, I focused on encouraging her ideas while also directly facilitating new perspectives, and I allowed Ellie to react to, relate to, or reject them as she needed in the moment. Over time, I saw growth in Ellie's ability to make self-to-story connections and to integrate new perspectives into her own schemas as well (Jones, 2007; Rosenfeld Halverson, 2010). Through her use of embodied imagination and symbolic play as well as narrative concretization, Ellie demonstrated how our sense of self is largely built relationally and now also through medialike books—in those places where we do or do not see ourselves mirrored, where we are or are not seen. I want my clients to know that all choices in gender are available, although they are not all received or treated the same by others. Ellie was clearly navigating this reality for her characters and herself. CATs can support this process by helping children identify and express their psychological and environmental realities, allowing for integration of their emotions, experiences, and inner worlds into their identity and self-concept (Epp, 2007; Jones, 2007).

CONCLUSION

It is an integral task in these early, blossoming years of personal and worldly awareness to model safe self-discovery, exploration, and identification for children as they begin to embark on what is, for most humans, our lifelong journey of self-actualization and, for those intentionally navigating the world of gender, a journey of liberation with notable adversity. As Langer (2019) said, "the full spectrum of one's gender and body and behavior continue to take shape over the lifespan" (p. 115). Thus, it is imperative in this work to provide young people with a framework for self-reflection and self-advocacy, as well as the resilience it will take not only to be fully themselves but also to ask others to embrace them there. We are all making sense of the world we have emerged into, and encouraging freedom of exploration, expression, connection to and celebration of the body, and confident communication lays a strong foundation for TGD children to continue their journeys with robust internal and external guidance.

CATs can aid in this pursuit by facilitating therapeutic transformation as well as freeing the imagination toward resilient future orientation and expression. Self-expression—to bring our internal sense of self to fruition and to transform stories and metaphors into a resilient and enduring narrative of ourself and our place in the world around us—is an act that hinges on our inherent creative muscles, ones all humans possess but which can atrophy under duress (Berberian, 2020; Winnicott, 1971). Thus, I encourage clinicians to access and employ their creativity, to encourage young people to lead with their own, and when possible, to find continuing education on arts-based modalities or seek trained creative arts practitioners to join their clinical team. Gender, after all, is an act of creation.

REFERENCES

Armstrong, C. R., Tanaka, S., Reoch, L., Bronstein, L., Honce, J., Rozenberg, M., & Powell, M. A. (2015). Emotional arousal in two drama therapy core processes: Dramatic embodiment and dramatic projection. *Drama Therapy Review, 1*(2), 147–160. https://doi.org/10.1386/dtr.1.2.147_1

Beauregard, M., & Long, K. (2019). Attuning to the needs of LGBTQ youth. In B. MacWilliam, B. T. Harris, D. G. Trottier, & K. Long (Eds.), *Creative arts therapies and the LGBTQ community: Theory and practice* (pp. 119–137). Jessica Kinglsey Publishers.

Bem, S. L. (1981). Gender schema theory: A cognitive account of sex typing. *Psychological Review, 88*(4), 354–364. https://doi.org/10.1037/0033-295x.88.4.354

Berberian, M. (2020). Creative problem solving in art therapy. In M. Berberian & B. Davis (Eds.), *Art therapy practices for resilient youth: A strengths-based approach to at-promise children and adolescents* (pp. 13–32). Routledge.

Brill, S., & Pepper, R. (2008). *The transgender child: A handbook for families and professionals*. Cleis Press.

Darke, K., & Scott-Miller, S. (2021). *Art therapy with transgender and gender-expansive children and teenagers*. Jessica Kingsley Publishers.

de Witte, M., Orkibi, H., Zarate, R., Karkou, V., Sajnani, N., Malhotra, B., Ho, R. T. H., Kaimal, G., Baker, F. A., & Koch, S. C. (2021). From therapeutic factors to mechanisms of change in the creative arts therapies: A scoping review. *Frontiers in Psychology, 12*, 678397. https://doi.org/10.3389/fpsyg.2021.678397

DuBois, L. Z., Puckett, J. A., & Langer, S. J. (2022). Development of the gender embodiment scale: Trans masculine spectrum. *Transgender Health, 7*(4), 287–291. https://doi.org/10.1089/trgh.2020.0088

Epp, E. (2007). Locating the autonomous voice: Self-expression in music-centered music therapy. *Voices: A World Forum for Music Therapy, 7*(1), 463. https://doi.org/10.15845/voices.v7i1.463

Erickson-Schroth, L., & Davis, B. (2021). *Gender: What everyone needs to know*. Oxford University Press.

Erikson, E. H. (1963). *Childhood and society*. Norton.

Fancourt, D., & Finn, S. (2019). *What is the evidence on the role of the arts in improving health and well-being? A scoping review*. World Health Organization. https://www.ncbi.nlm.nih.gov/books/NBK553773/

Ferrara, K. W. (1994). *Therapeutic ways with words*. Oxford University Press. https://doi.org/10.1093/oso/9780195083378.001.0001

Hastings, J., Bobb, C., Wolfe, M., Amaro Jimenez, Z., & Amand, C. S. (2021). Medical care for nonbinary youth: Individualized gender care beyond a binary framework. *Pediatric Annals, 50*(9), e384–e390. https://doi.org/10.3928/19382359-20210818-03

Jackman, K. B. (2022). Theoretical basis for dance movement therapy with transgender and nonbinary people. *The Arts in Psychotherapy, 80*, 101910. https://doi.org/10.1016/j.aip.2022.101910

Jones, P. (2007). *Drama as therapy: Theory practice and research* (2nd ed.). Routledge.

Kossak, M. S. (2009). Therapeutic attunement: A transpersonal view of expressive arts therapy. *The Arts in Psychotherapy, 36*(1), 13–18. https://doi.org/10.1016/j.aip.2008.09.003

Landy, R. (1996). *Essays in drama therapy: The double life*. Jessica Kingsley Publishers.

Landy, R. (2008). *The couch and the stage: Integrating words and action in psychotherapy*. Jason Aronson.

Langer, S. J. (2019). *Theorizing transgender identity for clinical practice: A new model for understanding gender*. Jessica Kingsley Publishers.

Nadal, K. L. (2013). *That's so gay! Microaggressions and the lesbian, gay, bisexual, and transgender community*. American Psychological Association. https://doi.org/10.1037/14093-000

Olson, K. R., Durwood, L., DeMeules, M., & McLaughlin, K. A. (2016). Mental health of transgender children who are supported in their identities. *Pediatrics, 137*(3), e20153223. https://doi.org/10.1542/peds.2015-3223

Orkibi, H., Keisari, S., Sajnani, N. L., & de Witte, M. (2025). Effectiveness of drama-based therapies on mental health outcomes: A systematic review and meta-analysis of controlled studies. *Psychology of Aesthetics, Creativity, and the Arts, 19*(4), 878–895. https://doi.org/10.1037/aca0000582

Pendzik, S. (2006). On dramatic reality and its therapeutic function in drama therapy. *The Arts in Psychotherapy, 33*(4), 271–280. https://doi.org/10.1016/j.aip.2006.03.001

Rosenfeld Halverson, E. (2010). The dramaturgical process as a mechanism for identity development of LGBTQ youth and its relationship to detypification. *Journal of Adolescent Research, 25*(5), 635–668. https://doi.org/10.1177/0743558409357237

Singh, A. A., Hays, D. G., & Watson, L. S. (2011). Strength in the face of adversity: Resilience strategies of transgender individuals. *Journal of Counseling and Development, 89*(1), 20–27. https://doi.org/10.1002/j.1556-6678.2011.tb00057.x

Winnicott, D. W. (1971). *Playing and reality*. Routledge.

8 CHILD AND FAMILY ASSESSMENT

BENJAMIN PARCHEM, DIANNE BERG, CATHERINE SCHAEFER, AND G. NIC RIDER

The word *assessment* has no ubiquitous meaning across professional disciplines. Even in the field of psychology, there are several interpretations of what an assessment looks like in clinical care. Most importantly, the term assessment in the field of gender health has become quite loaded. As a collective of gender health providers who work with transgender and gender diverse (TGD) children, some of us identifying within the TGD community ourselves, this chapter's authors recognize the range of experiences, thoughts, perspectives, and feelings that TGD community members and gender health clinicians have about the history of assessment in gender health, the purpose and utility of assessment, and what and who should be included in the assessment process. Some of the authors can attest to overhearing audience members at professional gatherings critiquing talks focused on assessment with TGD youth from both the perspective of thinking certain approaches are too liberal or uncritical and others thinking approaches are too intrusive or regulatory (Kuper et al., 2022; Leibowitz et al., 2016; St. Amand et al.,

---

Benjamin Parchem and Dianne Berg are co–first authors of this chapter.

https://doi.org/10.1037/0000494-009
Pediatric Gender Health Care: The Gender Affirmative Model Revisited, Second Edition, G. N. Rider, D. Ehrensaft, and C. St. Amand (Editors)

2023). Although many of these controversies primarily concern adolescents in the context of readiness for medical interventions, the rhetoric around assessment trickles down to children as well, even though gender health medical treatments are not indicated for prepubescent children.

Many people have strong feelings and opinions about assessment with TGD children. In a society that often synonymizes childhood with naivete, it can be difficult for people to believe that TGD children have the capacity to think about multifaceted ideas, like gender, and make decisions about who they are and what is important to them. Others believe that if gender diversity is natural diversity in the human experience, then TGD children do not need any type of assessment or mental health support because nothing is wrong with them. Although there is a lack of shared meaning surrounding assessment in the gender health field, particularly for prepubescent children who are transgender, gender diverse, gender expansive or exploring some aspect of their gender identity, embodiment, or both, we use the term assessment in this chapter due to its commonality in the field and for readers' utility in locating information about this topic. We are focusing on what is most important in learning about a child and coconstructing a gender health plan, with the superordinate goal of empowering TGD children to live fulfilling, healthy lives.

No matter what we call it, assessment is happening all the time in different contexts of a TGD child's life, such as a clinician asking questions about one's gender story, a caregiver learning what types of clothes and costumes their child gravitates toward, or a teacher observing peer interactions. We see the assessment phase as a space to organize all of this information. With children in clinical settings, we have found it more helpful to frame assessment as the *getting-to-know-you process* or "taking time to learn about your strengths and needs," as we would with any child. However, because of the stigma related to gender diversity, understanding someone's gender-specific strengths and needs may require more focus and support with TGD children. We are distinguishing the assessment/getting-to-know-you process from psychological evaluations, which typically use formal evaluation testing tools and are designed to answer a specific set of questions in order to come up with a diagnosis and recommendations (e.g., for attention-deficit/hyperactivity disorder [ADHD], autism spectrum disorder, or learning disorders).

Before we dive into this chapter, we want to acknowledge that the current sociopolitical climate affects how we wrote about the topic of assessment and will likely have an impact on how you receive the topic. In a time when misinformation and disinformation is fueling legislative efforts to delegitimize the existence of transness, we want to be explicitly clear that we believe TGD children, we uplift the autonomy of TGD children, and we center TGD children and their families as collaborators and advocates in their care.

In the coming pages, we will elaborate on the history of assessment with TGD children to provide context for the strengths-based and sensitive approach we are taking in this chapter. We will then describe theoretical approaches to assessment with TGD children, followed by a practical discussion of what information is (and is not) important, and how to gather such information in the assessment process with TGD children. We then conclude with a sample getting-to-know-you process protocol with TGD children and families.

THE PATHOLOGIZING HISTORY OF ASSESSMENT WITH TGD CHILDREN

The current polarizing state of assessment with TGD children is the aftermath of the history of decades of pathologizing approaches (Riggs et al., 2019). Some examples include conversion attempts to curb gender expansive behaviors by encouraging children to "live in their own skin" (meaning their sex/gender designated at birth) or assessing unnecessary aspects of functioning, such as IQ testing (Berg & Edwards-Leeper, 2018). These approaches are considered inhumane and have caused significant harm to TGD children and their families, in addition to fracturing the relationship between TGD communities and gender health clinicians.

We, as part of the field of gender health, must acknowledge this history, allow ourselves to have whatever feelings we might have about it, process those feelings in ways that do not compromise our capacity to deliver high-quality care to TGD children, and channel those feelings into self-growth and repairing trust with TGD communities. This will require centering the lived experience of those community members.

Because many existing assessment tools were developed in this pathologizing context, these tools frame gender as binary and ground differences in gender in Western stereotypes (e.g., hairstyles, clothing, colors, toys, and peer groups). For example, in Western cultures, long hair is typically considered feminine; in many Indigenous cultures, long hair is less indicative of gender and more ingrained in cultural practices. Gender health clinicians should be particularly aware of these underlying culture-bound assumptions embedded in assessment tools. Aspects of the assessment process are inherently influential based on the language, questions, and reactions that a gender health clinician offers in their interactions with TGD children and families, including when using these assessment tools. When used with TGD children without awareness that these tools are imperfect and that societal stereotypes are not facts, assessment runs the risk of harm through perpetuating colonizing and pathologizing messaging about gender.

Historically, one can argue that the purpose of assessment with TGD children was to determine whether a diagnosis of gender dysphoria existed. Because the presence of gender dysphoria was seen as synonymous with a TGD identity (even though the previous diagnostic criteria of what is now called gender dysphoria heavily conflated gender identity with gender expression; American Psychiatric Association, 2022), the assessment process was also focused on understanding how a TGD identity developed from the perspective of what "went wrong." In this historical context, the introduction of the gender affirmative model (Hidalgo et al., 2013; Steensma et al., 2013) aimed to challenge this pathologization of TGD children and introduced the language of "insistent, persistent, and consistent" (Hidalgo et al., 2013, p. 286). This paradigm de-emphasized diagnosis with an eye to the experience of the child while also emphasizing that TGD children do exist and deserve to be affirmed rather than pathologized. At the same time, while not the original intent, this model has been misused with predictive aims: If a child advocates for a specific gender identity with certainty (insistent: "I'm a girl") in the face of others questioning or challenging them (persistent: "I'm really a girl") and if the child does not experience any shifts in their gender identity over time (consistent: "I'm still really a girl"), then we could better predict their gender trajectory into adulthood. This overemphasis on prediction has shaped child gender health assessment and resulting treatment recommendations for over a decade. In some circumstances, it was used to try and change the trajectory of someone's gender journey (e.g., the "living in your own skin" approach) or avoid regret; and for others, it was used more purely to inform what supports would be most useful to the child.

As our understanding of gender has evolved, we see the foray into predictive trajectories as a wrong turn that was not useful nor evidence based (Temple Newhook et al., 2018) and likely contributed to potentially harmful practices (e.g., asking unnecessary and intrusive questions to try to get any potentially useful information, or consciously or unconsciously pushing children toward a binary, endocisnormative identity). Thus, the child chapter of version 8 of the World Professional Association for Transgender Health (WPATH) Standards of Care for the Health of Transgender and Gender Diverse People (SOC8) intentionally stated that "there are no reliable means of predicting an individual child's gender evolution, and the gender-related needs for a particular child may vary over the course of their childhood" (Coleman et al., 2022, p. S68). How can something so layered, multifaceted, internal, dynamic, learned, oppressed, and human as gender be predicted? In our assessment approach, we advocate for uplifting the dynamic nature of gender, focusing on lived experience rather than diagnosis or identity, improving our ability to embrace ambiguity—the not knowing, centering cultural humility, integrating decolonized understandings and conceptualizations of gender, and being planful toward supporting shifts in gender identity and embodiment goals over time, should they arise.

U.S.-based health care systems and health insurance companies that mandate a diagnosis for billable services further pathologize TGD people. Broadly, the framing of gender dysphoria as a mental disorder is problematic, but many TGD children whose gender was (or is) embraced and supported by their immediate environment do not meet the criteria for a gender dysphoria diagnosis, particularly the distress clause, as outlined in the *Diagnostic and Statistical Manual of Mental Disorders, Fifth Edition, Text Revision* (*DSM-5-TR*; American Psychiatric Association, 2022). Some of these children who do not meet criteria may still find benefit in a variety of individual, group, and family-based gender health interventions for holistic well-being. Requiring a diagnosis (which assumes inherent pathology of gender diversity) to access these interventions places gender health clinicians in an uncomfortable and ethically compromising position. To insurance companies, a diagnosis provides some degree of certainty and predictability that ultimately gives peace of mind and a sense of protection against fears of litigation. While we operate within systems (and continue to advocate for change), as part of the assessment process, we should explain to TGD children and families if and why a gender dysphoria diagnosis is being considered and how symptoms of distress are often a function of stigma and oppression. There have been some movements in health care systems to use the term *gender incongruence* rather than gender dysphoria to reduce the pathologizing language of the diagnosis. However, although gender incongruence is now categorized as a sexual health diagnosis instead of a mental health diagnosis, it still maps to the same *International Classification of Diseases 11th Revision* code (World Health Organization, 2019).

GUIDING PRINCIPLES OF ASSESSMENT

Theoretically, there are a few guiding principles that frame the getting-to-know-you process with TGD children. The process should be (1) gender affirmative, (2) multidisciplinary, and (3) family based. Each principle is described next.

Gender Affirmation

Two authors of this chapter were part of a collective that developed the gender affirmative lifespan approach (GALA; Rider, Vencill, et al., 2019; Spencer &

Vencill, 2017; Spencer, Berg, et al., 2021), a therapeutic framework that speaks to the components of what is included in a pediatric gender health approach. These components include the following:

- cultivating gender literacy (understanding distinctions and interconnections between gender identity, gender embodiment, and sex designated at birth as well as the societal norms underlying so-called gender rules),
- increasing resilience (learning how stigma and oppression shape thoughts, feelings, and behaviors and cultivating adaptive strategies and supportive networks for action-oriented change),
- expanding beyond the limits of the gender binary (embracing all possibilities of gender experiences),
- promoting pleasure-oriented positive sexuality (helping children understand the many ways bodies can look and that body parts are distinct from gender identity), and
- facilitating connections to medical care (identifying pediatric gender health care providers and, when appropriate, educating on options for gender health medical interventions in the future).

In the context of assessment, these principles drive an affirming information-gathering process by informing what types of questions to ask or activities to do together with the TGD child in order to obtain a baseline understanding of their gender experience. Underlying the components of the GALA model are the central values of affirmation, transparency, intersectionality, a lifespan approach, interdisciplinary collaboration, and empiricism. These values underscore how the getting-to-know-you process should be conducted by gender health clinicians to create an optimal experience for TGD children and their families.

Multidisciplinary Collaboration

A common approach in pediatric settings is to collaborate with multiple disciplines on a TGD child's health care team, particularly mental/behavioral health providers and medical providers (see Chapter 2, this volume; Chen et al., 2016). Multidisciplinary approaches are often assumed to be exclusive to supporting goals for medical interventions (e.g., puberty blockers or hormones), but they can be useful for any TGD child with gender-related needs. Although it is not necessarily a part of the initial assessment, a multidisciplinary approach also might include liaising with social workers (to address psychosocial needs, insurance navigation, and referrals), speech-language therapists (to support social communication in the context of neurodiversity), occupational therapists (to support gender embodiment in activities of daily living or emotion regulation), school personnel (to implement a gender support plan), community resources (e.g., faith-based communities, child-care systems, and youth recreational programming), and legal professionals (to support navigating oppressive sociopolitical climates and patient rights). The underlying premise of a multidisciplinary approach is that each TGD child's individualized needs and goals can be best supported by a team of providers who collaborate with the TGD child and family, and that collaboration starts with an assessment.

Family-Based Approach

Gender is inherently relational, and family members directly affect children's gender development; as such, these assessments need to involve the family and not just the child. A TGD child's immediate environment is a focal point of the getting-to-know-you process because so much of what a child has access to in terms of information, ideas, and resources is dependent on their caregivers. As such, taking a family-based approach is a central principle to assessment with TGD children. Importantly, who is considered family is individualized to each TGD child and includes biological relatives as well as chosen family. Siblings tend to be an overlooked but important component of the family environment for a TGD child, and they should be asked about during the assessment process and integrated into treatment, as clinically indicated. The *multidimensional family approach* (MDFA) offers a guiding model for how to integrate families into the care of TGD children to support positive socialization, nurturance, and acceptance (Malpas et al., 2018). The MDFA recommends meeting with caregivers individually during the initial interview process to build rapport and trust and to allow for adequate privacy to express their genuine experiences. For more about the MDFA, see Chapter 4, this volume.

WHAT TO CONSIDER IN THE ASSESSMENT

Although the getting-to-know-you process with TGD children is often focused on one's gender journey, the child's gender experience is just a fraction of who they are. The purpose of a gender health assessment is to better understand the TGD child holistically, with an attention to gender, and inform a plan of care to meet the child's gender-related and social–emotional needs. The plan of care may include ongoing supportive therapy, connections to community resources, psychoeducation for caregivers, or periodic check-ins as requested by the family should there be no clear need for ongoing treatment. All of the features of a typical psychosocial history are important (e.g., developmental history, medical history, mental health history, trauma history, family history, school history, social determinants of health, and access to resources). It is also critical to think beyond the individual and explore the ways in which aspects of a child's psychosocial environment and individual experience are shaped by overlapping power relations, including how stigma, discrimination, chronic minority stress, legislative bans, and oppression are embedded in multiple levels of systems in the child's life (e.g., extended family, school boards and policies, faith-based communities, neighborhood resources, law enforcement, and social services; Bronfenbrenner, 1996; Crenshaw, 1991). Additionally, because of the field of psychology's deficit framing tendency, the entire psychosocial history should use a strengths-based approach that emphasizes resilience and coping skills (Srinath et al., 2019). For this chapter, we will not detail components of a psychosocial history and instead will focus on the gender-related aspects of the assessment with TGD children (see Table 8.1).

Gender Literacy

As discussed in the GALA model (Rider, Vencill, et al., 2019; Spencer, Berg, et al., 2021), *gender literacy* is the extent to which children and caregivers understand differences between gendered concepts, and it also encompasses the child and caregivers' awareness of stereotypes about gender in their culture and how these do or do not fit with their own gendered experience. For example, one aspect of this is to what extent the TGD child associates genitals with gender identity, as this is often taught to children as a defining characteristic of gender by society and has the potential to contribute to body-related distress if not addressed in treatment. Relatedly, the family's awareness of how gender diversity is oppressed and stigmatized or celebrated (past or present) within their culture is also useful information. Related to the GALA gender evolution across the lifespan, expectations of someone's gender (and gender literacy) can change as they move through different developmental stages, which do not always correspond with chronological age (Rider, Vencill, et al., 2019; Spencer, Berg, et al., 2021). We center both the child and their family when assessing gender literacy because the extent to which a child has been able to think critically about gender-related concepts is often gatekept by adults in the child's life (either unintentionally due to lack of understanding or intentionally due to beliefs about gender diversity).

TABLE 8.1. Assessment With Prepubescent Transgender and Gender Diverse Children: What to Consider and How to Consider It

Assessment component	What it is	How to measure it
Gender literacy	The extent to which one understands the options for and differences between sex designated at birth, gender identity, gender embodiment, and sexual orientation, as well as the ways they can be interconnected	DAP-GS GDS-Child PGP GIIC-GS GPI-GS MGDs
Gender embodiment	How gender is internalized into the body in the way one behaves, thinks, moves, speaks, and interacts with others. Embodiment can also include a spiritual aspect for some individuals	DAP-GS GDS-Child PGP GPI-GS MGDs
Gender distress/ dysphoria	Social dysphoria includes experiences of stress or discomfort navigating gender in social environments. Body dysphoria encompasses discomfort or negative feelings toward one's body or body parts due their gendered meanings	DAP-GS GDS-Child GPI-GS MGDs
Gender joy/ euphoria/ contentment	Positive emotions and experiences or pride with regard to gender identity or embodiment	GPI-GS MGDs
Puberty literacy	The extent to which one understands what physical changes will occur to their body during puberty	DAP-GS GDS-Child MGDs
Ability to adjust to shifts in gender identity and/or embodiment over time	One's capacity to cope with changes in their gender journey through flexibility skills and social support	GDS-Child PAGES-P BRIEF
Ability to advocate	One's ability to ask for what they need or want, as well as the family unit's ability to support these needs or wants	PAGES-P BRIEF (to measure components necessary for self-advocating, such as being planful, organizing thoughts, regulating emotions, impulse control, etc.)

(continues)

TABLE 8.1. Assessment With Prepubescent Transgender and Gender Diverse Children: What to Consider and How to Consider It (*Continued*)

Assessment component	What it is	How to measure it
Family environment/ attitudes	How a family thinks or feels about or behaves toward gender diversity	PAGES-P
School environment/ attitudes	How a school system thinks or feels about or behaves toward gender diversity	Questions about school safety, gender-based bullying, and student-teacher relations SCS
Neurodiversity	Differences in how one's brain processes the world that can result in differences in thinking and communication styles	BRIEF SCQ BASC-3

Note. BASC-3 = Behavior Assessment System for Children, Third Edition (Reynolds & Kamphaus, 2015); BRIEF = Behavior Rating Inventory of Executive Function (Gioia et al., 2000); DAP-GS = Draw-A-Person-Gender Spectrum (Berg, Becker-Warner, Connor, & Rider, 2019); GDS-Child = Gender Development Scale-Child Report (Strang, Harrop, et al., 2023); GIIC-GS = Gender Identity Interview for Children-Gender Spectrum (Berg, Becker-Warner, Connor, LeClair, et al., 2019a); GPI-GS = Gender Preference Interview-Gender Spectrum (Berg, Becker-Warner, Connor, LeClair, et al., 2019b); MGD = MyGender Doll (Berg et al., 2024, 2025; Parchem et al., 2024); PAGES-P = Parental Attitudes of Gender Expansiveness Scale for Parents (Reguitti et al., 2022); PGP = Perth Gender Picture (Moore et al., 2021); SCQ = Social Communication Questionnaire (Rutter et al., 2003); SCS = School Climate Scale (Schueler et al., 2014).

Gender Embodiment

Gender embodiment is how gender is internalized into the body in the way someone behaves, thinks, moves, speaks, and interacts with others (Hastings et al., 2021; Langer, 2019). This embodiment may include physical qualities such as hairstyle, clothing, voice, gestures, and desires for particular primary and secondary sex characteristics, as well as internal experiences (e.g., emotions), roles in relationships and within community, thinking styles, spirituality, and so on. Because so many of these physical qualities and experiences are informed by gendered stereotypes, it is important to ask the child questions that will uncover motivations for gender embodiment in a way that accommodates the child's vocabulary. To be clear, there is nothing wrong, for instance, with a trans boy wanting short hair, but it is important to understand why the child thinks particular ways about hair, which may inform their gendered self (e.g., social stereotypes such as "boys have short hair," or peer socialization such as "I wish my hair could be longer, but the other boys would make fun of me"), as this will, in turn, inform gender literacy growth areas. Part of gender embodiment is how a child wants to feel connected to their gender in their body (sometimes referred to as *body embodiment*)—to be at home in their body—and another part is how the child wants to be perceived by others; both have value and are worth exploring. The conversation around gender embodiment as an experience shifts to gender-related needs to inquire about the ways the child would like to move closer to their gender embodiment goals and the barriers that get in the way. It is also important to explore whether caregivers have specific desires for their child's gender embodiment and why those desires are present, because messaging from caregivers can trickle down to the child (e.g., encouraging the child to pass as a cisgender boy or girl based on binary stereotypes of clothing or toys to avoid gender-related bullying).

Gender Distress/Dysphoria

For TGD children, it is often helpful to distinguish between social and body dysphoria. *Social dysphoria* includes experiences of stress or discomfort navigating gender in social environments such as schools, bathrooms, sports teams, and so on. *Body dysphoria* encompasses discomfort or negative feelings toward one's body or body parts due to their gendered implications. Both types of dysphoria have the capacity to be socially induced because of oppressive societal messaging related to gendered stereotypes (e.g., "Girls have vulvas; therefore, if I do not have a vulva, I am not a 'real' girl"). Some TGD children have experiences that give rise to gender dysphoria, such as being misgendered (i.e., referred to with the incorrect name, pronoun, relational terms, nickname, or term of endearment), being excluded from gendered social activities, feeling pressure related to navigating bathrooms or avoiding public bathrooms altogether, disliking genitals, internalizing binary stereotypes about gender roles or genitals, or experiencing anticipatory anxiety about the development of secondary sex characteristics. Others do not experience much or any stress or discomfort related to their gender experience. The extent to which a TGD child experiences gender dysphoria is often related to the degree of affirmation they feel in their environments and the degree of openness they are given to form their own ideas about gender—an aspect of gender literacy. Often, if a child is surrounded by caregivers, siblings, peers, teachers, and others who are affirming of their gender identity and/or embodiment and do not enforce binary gendered stereotypes, they do not regularly experience the chronic minority stressors of social exclusion or internalization of stigma that tend to cultivate dysphoria (Malpas et al., 2018; Olson et al., 2016). Because these experiences often contribute to mental health challenges, it is important to explore to what extent a child's anxiety or depression intersects with gender dysphoria and how the anxiety, depression, and/or gender dysphoria might be distinct in order to inform interventions. Caregivers can also be helpful informants because they may observe children displaying behaviors that may be related to dysphoria, such as avoidance of activities (e.g., swimming) or using public restrooms. Caregivers' expectations may also be one source of dysphoria, and there is benefit in exploring the extent to which caregivers understand the full scope of their child's experiences of dysphoria.

Gender Joy/Euphoria/Contentment

In the field of psychology that historically has focused on risk, disparities, and pathology, asking about euphoria, joy, or positive emotions and experiences that a TGD child has with regard to their gender is crucial. *Gender joy* might include the child feeling excitement from being perceived as their gender identity by a stranger, or a family member starting to be more consistent with using their pronouns correctly, or feeling pride in the way their body looks in their clothes; as one child recently said, "I like everything about my body. I'm a girl with a penis." Some youth have requested refraining from the term euphoria, as they experience the term as an overblown valence of positive emotion, preferring the phrase *gender contentment*.

If a child is not able to identify salient positive gendered experiences, however phrased, this is not necessarily a cause for concern, but it can later be a point of intervention in treatment. A TGD child who has been comfortably living in their affirmed gender for an extended period of time may experience primarily neutral feelings toward their gender, seeing it as just another thing about them (not the most important or salient). Additionally, pride in one's gender history or transness can take some time to develop in TGD children because social conformity is often highly valued in childhood, and outwardly expressing pride in their gender history may be seen as increasing vulnerability to victimization. For TGD children, it can be important to assess whether the child wants their gender diversity to be private or rather a secret, as the latter carries more shame and suggests an area to support (Rider & St. Amand, 2022). Similar to gender dysphoria, caregivers can be helpful informants for experiences of gender joy because children often have an obvious shift in mood, facial expression, or body language when they have a positive experience related to their gender.

Puberty Literacy

Curiosities often emerge about how bodies change as children get closer to puberty; for some TGD children, there is an additional layer of feelings about these changes in the context of their gender identity. Gauging a TGD child's *puberty literacy*, or the extent to which they understand both physical changes that occur in bodies in general and which of those changes will occur to their own body during endogenous puberty, can be challenging to assess. Puberty is generally awkward for children—and many adults—to talk about, and there can be even more discomfort with the topic for TGD children. As such, often the child knows more about puberty than they are willing to talk about until more rapport is established. We encourage revisiting conversations about puberty over the course of the getting-to-know-you process as more comfort is built with the child and family. Some key information we look for TGD children with ovaries to understand about puberty includes the following: (a) chest/breast size increases, (b) body shape becomes curvier around hips, and (c) the menstrual period starts. We look for TGD children with testicles to understand the following: (a) testicle and penis size increases, (b) facial hair develops, and (c) the voice deepens. We intentionally talk about these changes with respect to the gonads someone has and do not attribute any changes to a specific gender because this perpetuates the false conflation of body and gender (e.g., avoiding language such as "male puberty"). It is important to be specific and inclusive about one's language when discussing puberty to be sensitive to differences of sex development. Using correct anatomical language also helps minimize shame, is associated with decreased vulnerability to sexual abuse (i.e., speaking openly about body parts opens up conversations about consent to help a child understand what is and what is not appropriate), and increases the chance of help-seeking, including health/medical related, if needed (Nienow, 2024). Similar to gender literacy, it is important to inquire about ways caregivers are talking about puberty with their child or sexual education programs the child will be receiving to prevent the child's exposure to limiting or pathologizing information about puberty. A few resources that discuss development and puberty in a gender-neutral way include *What Makes a Baby* and *Sex Is a Funny Word* by Cory Silverberg (2013, 2015) and *The Every Body Book* by Rachel E. Simon (2020).

Ability to Adjust to Shifts in Gender Over Time

As the field of gender health moves away from trying to predict a TGD child's gender journey, it will be important to assess the extent to which the child and caregivers are fixed in their assumptions about the child's gender. This will provide information about whether they are thinking about and talking with the child regarding ways they might adjust if they experience a shift in their gender journey in the future, including in their identity, how they embody their gender, or both. This is a step toward embracing the dynamicity of gender and supporting a child's ability to think into the future, an important skill that will be useful should the TGD child pursue medical interventions after puberty. When a TGD child offers information that suggests flexibility to changes in their gender journey (e.g., "I will just tell my mom, and she can help me," or "I don't know what will happen, but this is good for now"), this is a positive sign because gender journeys are demanding of executive function skills (Strang et al., 2022). However, this does not mean that a TGD child offering information more indicative of rigidity or dismissiveness (e.g., "That is never going to happen") is less prepared to navigate their gender journey. These TGD children may just benefit from additional support in a therapeutic setting. Caregivers should also be integrated into these conversations about thinking into the future as the nature of the caregiver–child relationship will impact a TGD child's willingness to share shifts in their gender journey, should they occur. A TGD child's ability to adjust is largely dependent on their support systems, mostly caregivers; therefore, understanding the extent to which caregivers tolerate the ambiguity of potential shifts in their child's gender journey over time will be important, including asking caregivers how they might respond or what they might do to support their child.

Ability to Advocate

So much of the gender discernment and affirmation process requires advocating for one's gender-related needs and goals—sharing a gender identity with a caregiver, correcting a peer when they use the wrong name or pronouns, or asking caregivers to buy certain clothing items. Some TGD children readily ask for what they need or request specific changes with ease, and some struggle to do so, particularly those who are neurodiverse, those who are temperamentally less inclined to share their inner thoughts with others, and those who have a history of negative responses to their gender (Strang et al., 2018). Advocacy is important to assess both with regard to the child's ability to self-advocate and the family's ability to advocate for their child in the context of family dynamics, cultural considerations, and political climate. For TGD children, the responsibility for advocating for gender-related needs should be on the caregivers. Some caregivers may struggle with advocating for their TGD child because, for example, they may want to avoid being embarrassed, fear unwanted negative attention, worry about losing family or friends, believe their child's gender exploration is temporary, are themselves a member of an oppressed or discriminated-against community, or have general anxiety about advocating. Therefore, asking about a caregiver's experience with advocating for their child (or, if they have not advocated, finding out what the barriers have been) can inform possible areas for intervention. In the current sociopolitical climate, families generally need to advocate for their child's care more than ever before, and they may be considering relocating their family or actively navigating being displaced due to their state's legislation.

Family Environment/Attitudes

Aligned with a socioecological framework, the family environment plays a notable role in a child's adjustment and well-being on their gender journey (Barron & Capous-Desyllas, 2017). One of the most prominent protective factors against mental health challenges for TGD youth is caregiver support (Johns et al., 2018; Katz-Wise et al., 2016, 2022; McLaughlin & Sharp, 2018; Simons et al., 2013). Important aspects of the family environment/attitudes to ask about include the following: (a) who the child's caregivers are and what their relationships are like and (b) what thoughts each caregiver has about gender diversity (more generally, the extent to which they embrace diverse ways of being, connections they have with people or spaces who celebrate gender diversity, and then, specifically, feelings they have about their own child being on a gender journey). It is not uncommon for a caregiver to say they are supportive and lesbian, gay, bisexual, transgender, queer, or questioning (LGBTQ) affirming but struggle with accepting their own child's gender exploration. It is important not to pathologize families' cultural, religious, or spiritual affiliations that shape their perspectives on gender diversity. Taking time to better understand how these overlapping aspects of the family's identities inform their views on their child's gender diversity from a cultural humility lens is time well invested because it has important implications for the child's ability to navigate their gender journey, and ultimately, their well-being.

School Environment/Attitudes

Similar to family environment/attitudes, asking the TGD child and family about the school environment often helps identify points of intervention, given this is where a child spends most of their time outside of their home. Important aspects to assess include the following: (a) what social transition steps the child has taken at school and why or why not; (b) the child's feelings of safety at school; (c) ways LGBTQ+ representation is addressed at school, if at all; (d) teachers' accommodations to using a TGD child's name and pronouns; (e) options related to bathrooms and locker rooms; (f) options for sport participation; and (g) the family's experience with developing a gender support plan (e.g., available on the Gender Spectrum website at https://www.genderspectrum.org/new-page) at school, if any.

Neurodiversity

A sizable proportion of TGD youth are autistic or have other neurodevelopmental differences (e.g., ADHD or learning disorders; Strang, Anthony, et al., 2023; Strang et al., 2018, 2022; Warrier et al., 2020). Sometimes these are already diagnosed at the time of the assessment, and sometimes they are not. Throughout the getting-to-know-you process, it is important to pay attention to qualities that might indicate neurodiversity because neurodevelopmental differences can affect the unfolding of someone's gender journey and gender-related needs. Providers can explore with families whether seeking a comprehensive neuropsychological evaluation has value to them in terms of self-understanding, ruling out other potential clinical explanations (e.g., trauma), and access to resources and accommodations in light of potential marginalization that may come with an autism diagnosis. Neurodiversity-related qualities that may manifest during the getting-to-know-you process include differences in social communication (e.g., challenges with social reciprocity, social motivation, or social awareness), differences in flexibility (e.g., challenges shifting between tasks), focused interests (e.g., getting stuck on a topic or frequently returning to a specific topic), or sensory processing differences (e.g., sensitivity to loud noises, stimming, and hand or whole-body mannerisms). For TGD children who have a neurodiversity-related diagnosis, the assessment process may need to be modified. This can take the following forms: creating an agenda for each session to build in more structure; supporting verbal communication with visuals, when possible, keeping in mind that the child may have needs they are struggling to advocate around; offering more time within and between sessions to accommodate different processing and thinking styles; or making environmental adjustments to increase accessibility (e.g., low lighting and providing fidget toys). If a gender health clinician does not feel adequately trained to support autistic gender diverse children, they are encouraged to seek additional training, in accordance with the World Professional Association for Transgender Health Standards of Care (version 8; Coleman et al., 2022).

HOW TO CONSIDER ASSESSMENT COMPONENTS

As you were reading through the previous section on what to focus on, you might have had the reaction, "Yeah, this all sounds potentially useful. Also, (1) how do I actually assess these different components, and (2) how do I do all of this in a single session?" The short answer is (1) you ask questions, and (2) you do not. The getting-to-know-you process unfolds over time with

TGD children and their families, and there is no possible way to have a solid understanding of all the components of someone's gender experience in a single hour-long session. Aligned with the principle of being family based, during the assessment process, there should be time to ask questions with the child and caregivers together, time with just the child, and time with just the caregivers. The order in which this happens and who conducts which components of the assessment (e.g., care navigator, peer support specialist, social worker, therapist, nurse, psychologist, or primary care provider) should be individualized to each family's circumstances and, in some cases, is influenced by insurance coverage, health care system, and the family's resources. Beyond asking questions, observations of the child's reactions and behaviors to the various assessment activities, the caregivers' way of referring to the child and describing their understanding of the child's gender, and the child–caregiver dynamic can provide helpful information regarding the child's level of comfort in embodying their gender in the presence of others and caregivers' levels of comfort with their child's gender embodiment.

In the following sections, we will outline various methods and tools we have found to be helpful in gathering information about different aspects of a TGD child's gender experience (see Table 8.1). We want to emphasize that these are options, not steadfast rules, and including all of these measures or methods in your assessment process would be a pathologizing practice. Please see Chapter 7 on child and family assessment in the first edition of this book (Berg & Edwards-Leeper, 2018) for a critical review of all the existing measures available, including those that we discourage using in clinical practice. We encourage you to review the options presented in this updated chapter, think about what is feasible in your setting or in your practice based on your approach and training background, and consider how you might adjust your approach to efficiently learn more about your TGD child client to support them holistically as well as in their gender journey. To be clear, an assessment can be conducted with or without the use of assessment tools; a focused clinical interview may be sufficient for adolescents, but our experience tells us that the tools described next are helpful in eliciting information from younger children that might not surface if only using a clinical interview.

Child Self-Report Tools

The best reporter of a TGD child's gender experience is the child. Sometimes, people forget that children are experts on their own experiences because of assumptions that at their developmental stage, children do not have the capacity to understand themselves. Decades of research on cisgender children shows that they are able to identify their gender by age 2 to 3 years (Martin &

Little, 1990; Ruble et al., 2006; Wehren & De Lisi, 1983). Anecdotal evidence suggests that some TGD children begin to identify their gender around the same time. Other work comparing cisgender and transgender children on gender development milestones has found similar patterns in development in TGD children who are supported in their identities (Fast & Olson, 2018; Gülgöz et al., 2019). The child self-report measures described next are best done jointly with the child and, unless modified for a smart device that allows drawing with a stylus, should be given on paper. The measures are also most useful in gaining qualitative information; but because of the very little psychometric work done with these measures, using them to obtain a total score or numerical metric that has corresponding meaning is not useful or appropriate for clinical practice (although can have benefit in the context of research). Our last disclaimer is that, as discussed previously by Berg and Edwards-Leeper (2018), even with concerted efforts to make revisions based on contemporary understandings of gender, these measures are imperfect and have many limitations (Berg et al., 2022). As such, providers must think critically about what information is being gathered with these measures, and they must have open conversations with the TGD child and their families about the limitations of the measures (for information about gender literacy of the provider, see Berg & Edwards-Leeper, 2018).

One of the measures that has been revised, and that we find informative and enjoyable for the child, is the draw-a-person–gender spectrum (DAP-GS; Berg, Becker-Warner, Connor, & Rider, 2019). The clinician asks the child to draw a whole person, then to draw another person who is a different gender from the first person. Open-ended follow-up questions ask about how the child is defining and characterizing the genders of the people they drew, what they know about how bodies change as people grow older, and the extent to which they are applying that knowledge to themself. The activity is best used to assess gender literacy, puberty literacy, gender embodiment, and potential body dysphoria of the child, but it can also be shared with caregivers in a way that elicits their own ideas about gender and puberty. This activity can be extrapolated to have the child draw themselves as a baby, as they are now, as a teenager, as an adult, and as an older adult to explore how children are thinking of themselves at different developmental stages.

There are two additional interview-style measures that have been revised and have some useful questions to ask during the getting-to-know-you process with TGD children. The Gender Identity Interview for Children–Gender Spectrum (GIIC-GS) asks the child about their current gender identity, the degree to which they question their gender identity, and their thinking into the future about gender (Berg, Becker-Warner, Connor, LeClair, et al.,

2019a). The Gender Preference Interview–Gender Spectrum (GPI-GS) asks the child about their interests, friends, feelings about relationships, attractions, thinking into the future about gender, gender embodiment, and both positive and negative emotionality toward their body (Berg, Becker-Warner, Connor, LeClair, et al., 2019b). Although this measure asks questions that seem to be relying on gender stereotypes (e.g., what role a child takes in pretend play, type of toys used in solo play), we have found that including these broader questions helps build rapport and can offer useful information about the child's level of gender literacy (e.g., as a child talks about their interests, they say, "Some of the boys at school don't want me playing football because I'm a girl, but anybody can play anything").

Another useful visual activity is the Gender Development Scale–Child Report (GDS-Child; Strang, Harrop, et al., 2023), which asks the child (around ages 4–10 years) to indicate their sense of their gender identity as well as other gender-related constructs on a graphical line that ranges from girl to boy as well as an option for not a girl or a boy. When children complete this measure, it often offers useful information about gender literacy, puberty literacy, gender embodiment, and body dysphoria (specifically related to genitals). There are also questions about how the child might feel when they grow up and become an adult or parent, which offers useful information about the child's ability to think into the future and, by proxy, their ability to adjust to changes in their gender journey.

Caregiver Report Measures

Given that caregivers often spend the most time with the TGD child, their perspective and observations are important to include. However, caregivers' perspectives must be appropriately contextualized as through their own individual lens of gender diversity and their degree of gender literacy. A caregiver report tool that measures family environment/attitudes is the Parental Attitudes of Gender Expansiveness Scale for Parents (PAGES-P; Reguitti et al., 2022). The PAGES-P also asks caregivers (a) if they advocate on behalf of their child and (b) their general degree of support of their child's gender experience, which offers useful information about the family's ability to adjust to shifts in the child's gender journey and the family's ability to advocate. Although this measure was designed for youth age 12 or older, the questions will likely still be clinically informative for younger children. Regarding school environment/attitudes, measurement options are limited. However, the seven-item School Climate Scale (SCS; Schueler et al., 2014) for caregivers asks about general school climate and can be used to facilitate follow-up questions related to their child's gender experience at school.

Neurodiversity and Mental Health Measures

With the known co-occurrence of autism/neurodiversity and gender diversity (Warrier et al., 2020), screening for aspects of neurodiversity in the getting-to-know-you process is an investment in the TGD child's holistic well-being and will inform a provider's clinical approach with a TGD child in treatment. A number of measures are available publicly and for pay to assess aspects of neurodiversity, and we present a few that have shown clinical utility in our personal practice. The Behavior Rating Inventory of Executive Function (BRIEF; Gioia et al., 2000) is a comprehensive caregiver report of the child's skills in the areas of organization/integration, planning, future thinking, delaying gratification, flexibility, and attention. There are separate forms for caregivers of preschool-aged children (ages 2–5) and older children and adolescents (ages 6–18). The Social Communication Questionnaire (SCQ; Rutter et al., 2003) is a specific autism screening tool for children age 4 or older and is completed by caregivers. Finally, the Behavior Assessment System for Children, Third Edition (BASC-3; Reynolds & Kamphaus, 2015), which has a self-report for children (ages 8–11) and a parent report for preschool-aged children (ages 2–5), school-aged children (ages 6–11), and adolescents (ages 12–21), assesses broad behavioral and emotional challenges as well as adaptive skills. The scales can be combined to offer probability indices for specific clinical presentations, including ones for autism and ADHD. A particular strength of the BASC-3 is that it circumvents the typical limitations of standardized batteries that require selecting a binary gender norm template (e.g., either female or male) by allowing the comparison of children to a combined gender norm template (McAdaragh et al., 2024; Rider, Berg, et al., 2019).

Interactive Tools

Although measures and interview questions can be informative, toys and games tend to be more engaging and tangible for children. Some clinicians have found benefit in using drawings, dolls, toy potato heads, stuffed animals, or sand trays to facilitate discussions about gender identity and embodiment, but no empirically tested and community-informed therapeutic tool has been published for TGD children. The MyGender Dolls™ (MGDs; see https://alphanews.org/u-of-ms-gender-dolls-teach-kids-that-their-gender-identity-is-valid-no-matter-what-parts-they-have/), an innovation developed by authors of this chapter, consists of a set of two-dimensional dolls, sensitive to body size and skin tone, that are accompanied with a range of vinyl gonads, external genitals, hairstyles, clothing, and other accessories that can be layered onto the doll (Berg et al., 2024, 2025;

Parchem et al., 2024). We are currently developing therapeutic exercises and piloting them with TGD children, their caregivers, and clinicians who work with TGD children. The MGDs are rooted in the GALA model (Rider, Vencill, et al., 2019; Spencer, Berg, et al., 2021; Spencer & Vencill, 2017), and they can be used in the context of an assessment (e.g., to gather information on the child's gender and puberty literacy, gender embodiment, or gender dysphoria and euphoria) as well as function as an intervention to provide psychoeducation on gender-related topics.

FUTURE DIRECTIONS FOR MEASUREMENT METHODS

In Table 8.1, you will see that robust or standardized ways of assessing some aspects of a TGD child's gender experience are not currently available. Although the future directions are endless, a few areas for growth include the following: (a) a caregiver report of their child's gender development over time, (b) a child self-report of gender joy/euphoria/contentment, (c) a child and caregiver measure assessing capacity to adjust to shifts in gender identity/embodiment over time, (d) a child self-report of gender-related self-advocacy, (e) a child self-report of their perception of school climate as it relates to their gender experience, (f) a child and caregiver report tool to measure gender literacy, (g) a developmentally appropriate child version of the Gender Minority Stress and Resilience Scale (Hidalgo et al., 2019), and (h) the PAGES-P (Reguitti et al., 2022) of prepubescent children.

Via the National Center for Gender Health, a few authors of this chapter are currently conducting related research called the Gender and Flexible Thinking Project, which has been asking children of all genders what they think about various child self-report and interview-style measures related to gender (Reigada et al., 2024; Schaefer et al., 2024, 2025). Results thus far suggest that children prefer measures with several gender identity response options (especially open-ended ones), and they generally feel positively toward the measures. Children have expressed appreciation for measures that extend beyond binary gender options, although vocabulary differences about gender remain a barrier to using measures scaled down from use with adolescents and adults.

In addition to these advancements in measures and although the MGDs show promise, it may be useful to develop additional interactive tools for learning about a child's gender journey and gender embodiment needs and goals. One example (derived from the clinical practice of a few of this chapter's authors and colleague, Jonathan Poquiz, coauthor of Chapter 3, this volume) is working with the TGD child to make a book about their gender journey, depicting various milestones in their gender experience.

SAMPLE ASSESSMENT PROTOCOL

To attempt to make this content more practically useful for gender health clinicians, we offer a sample protocol for the getting-to-know-you process (Table 8.2) that can be done over time with TGD children and their caregivers. We want to emphasize that this is an example and by no means is the correct or only way to conduct an assessment with TGD children.

CONCLUSION

TGD children and their families have a human right to a high-quality health care experience. The assessment process is a starting point. TGD children have faced a long history of pathologizing approaches when trying to seek support from gender health clinicians. In an effort to recognize this history and do better moving forward, we offered guiding frameworks for the getting-to-know-you process with prepubescent TGD children and their caregivers, clinically useful guidance on what components are important in the assessment process, and how to gather information on these various aspects of a child's gender experience. If there is one message we hope you take from this chapter, it is that TGD children know who they are. TGD children have the capacity to be a captain on the ship that is their gender journey, and our job as gender health clinicians is to provide information and education to the child and their caregivers to help them steer the ship. In a time when the humanity of TGD people is being politicized, the least we can do is offer an affirming and empowering space for children to just be.

TABLE 8.2. Sample Assessment Protocol With Transgender and Gender Diverse Children and Their Caregivers

Visit	Division of time	What occurs?
1. Intake	Meet with the child and caregivers together Offer individual time with caregivers, if desired[a]	Introductions to share names/pronouns Explanation of the clinician's approach to gender care (e.g., following the child's lead, having no agenda for the child's gender journey, and seeing the therapeutic role as supportive to the child and caregivers as they navigate the gender journey) Creation of space for the family to ask questions Psychosocial history Interview with the child and caregivers to discuss the gender journey, gender needs and goals, and existing supports (including school environment)

TABLE 8.2. Sample Assessment Protocol With Transgender and Gender Diverse Children and Their Caregivers (*Continued*)

Visit	Division of time	What occurs?
2. Gender-related measures	Primarily with the child, unless the clinician has remaining questions for caregivers from Visit 1 or the caregivers request individual time	Gather any remaining information leftover from Visit 1 Caregivers complete the PAGES-P, SCS, BRIEF, SCQ, and BASC-3[b] Child completes the DAP-GS, GDS-Child, GIIC-GS, and GPI-GS; may also play with MGDs
3. Feedback	Primarily with the caregivers; children are welcome but should not attend if the caregiver(s) or the clinician has concerns that should be discussed with just adults first	Remind the family of the approach to gender care Reflect back the child's gender journey to confirm information is still accurate Share impressions of the child's adjustment to their gender experience Contextualize the diagnosis of Gender Dysphoria and/or Gender Incongruence (if appropriate or indicated) Engage in goal-setting with the child and caregivers Discuss frequency of visits and expectations of caregiver(s) involvement

Note. BASC-3 = Behavior Assessment System for Children, Third Edition (Reynolds & Kamphaus, 2015); BRIEF = Behavior Rating Inventory of Executive Function (Gioia et al., 2000); DAP-GS = Draw-A-Person-Gender Spectrum (Berg, Becker-Warner, Connor, & Rider, 2019); GDS-Child = Gender Development Scale-Child Report (Strang, Harrop, et al., 2023); GIIC-GS = Gender Identity Interview for Children-Gender Spectrum (Berg, Becker-Warner, Connor, LeClair, et al., 2019a); GPI-GS = Gender Preference Interview-Gender Spectrum (Berg, Becker-Warner, Connor, LeClair, et al., 2019b); MGD = MyGender Doll (Berg et al., 2024, 2025; Parchem et al., 2024); PAGES-P = Parental Attitudes of Gender Expansiveness Scale for Parents (Reguitti et al., 2022); SCQ = Social Communication Questionnaire (Rutter et al., 2003); SCS = School Climate Scale (Schueler et al., 2014).
[a]Being flexible with families is important and creating a plan with families to establish who meets with the provider at which points in the "getting to know you process" allows the assessment to be neurodiverse and trauma informed. [b]Caregivers could complete these measures beforehand if mailed to their home, in the waiting room during the visit, or electronically online before or during the visit.

REFERENCES

American Psychiatric Association. (2022). *Diagnostic and statistical manual of mental disorders* (5th ed., text rev.). https://doi.org/10.1176/appi.books.9780890425787

Barron, C., & Capous-Desyllas, M. (2017). Transgressing the gendered norms in childhood: Understanding transgender children and their families. *Journal of GLBT Family Studies, 13*(5), 407–438. https://doi.org/10.1080/1550428X.2016.1273155

Berg, D., & Edwards-Leeper, L. (2018). Child and family assessment. In C. Keo-Meier & D. Ehrensaft (Eds.), *The gender affirmative model: An interdisciplinary approach to supporting transgender and gender expansive children* (pp. 101–124). American Psychological Association. https://doi.org/10.1037/0000095-007

Berg, D., Rider, G. N., & Reigada, T. (2025, April). *Introducing the MyGender Dolls: A new psychotherapeutic tool for transgender and gender diverse children* [Oral presentation]. Annual Child and Adolescent Mental Health Conference of the Minnesota Association for Children's Mental Health, Duluth, MN, United States.

Berg, D., Tellawi, G., Anderson, S. O., & Nic Rider, G. (2022). Beyond diagnosis: Prepubescent gender expansive children on the margins of clinical measures. *Infant and Child Development, 31*(3), 1–16. https://doi.org/10.1002/icd.2311

Berg, D. R., Becker-Warner, R., Connor, J., LeClair, C., Plessy, K., & Rider, G. N. (2019a). *Gender Identity Interview for Children–Gender Spectrum* [Unpublished]. University of Minnesota.

Berg, D. R., Becker-Warner, R., Connor, J., LeClair, C., Plessy, K., & Rider, G. N. (2019b). *Gender Preference Interview–Gender Spectrum* [Unpublished]. University of Minnesota.

Berg, D. R., Becker-Warner, R., Connor, J., & Rider, G. N. (2019). *Draw-A-Person–Gender Spectrum* [Unpublished]. University of Minnesota.

Berg, D. R., Parchem, B., & Rider, G. N. (2024). *MyGender Dolls clinical use manual*. Eli Coleman Institute for Sexual and Gender Health, University of Minnesota. https://med.umn.edu/sexualhealth/ncgsh/projects/mygender-dolls

Bronfenbrenner, U. (1996). *The ecology of human development: Experiments by nature and design*. Harvard University Press.

Chen, D., Hidalgo, M. A., Leibowitz, S., Leininger, J., Simons, L., Finlayson, C., & Garofalo, R. (2016). Multidisciplinary care for gender-diverse youth: A narrative review and unique model of gender-affirming care. *Transgender Health, 1*(1), 117–123. https://doi.org/10.1089/trgh.2016.0009

Coleman, E., Radix, A. E., Bouman, W. P., Brown, G. R., de Vries, A. L. C., Deutsch, M. B., Ettner, R., Fraser, L., Goodman, M., Green, J., Hancock, A. B., Johnson, T. W., Karasic, D. H., Knudson, G. A., Leibowitz, S. F., Meyer-Bahlburg, H. F. L., Monstrey, S. J., Motmans, J., Nahata, L., . . . Arcelus, J. (2022). Standards of care for the health of transgender and gender diverse people, version 8. *International Journal of Transgender Health, 23*(Suppl. 1), S1–S259. https://doi.org/10.1080/26895269.2022.2100644

Crenshaw, K. (1991). Mapping the margins: Intersectionality, identity politics, and violence against women of color. *Stanford Law Review, 43*(6), 1241–1299. https://doi.org/10.2307/1229039

Fast, A. A., & Olson, K. R. (2018). Gender development in transgender preschool children. *Child Development, 89*(2), 620–637. https://doi.org/10.1111/cdev.12758

Gioia, G. A., Isquith, P. K., Guy, S. C., & Kenworthy, L. (2000). Test review: Behavior Rating Inventory of Executive Function. *Child Neuropsychology, 6*(3), 235–238. https://doi.org/10.1076/chin.6.3.235.3152

Gülgöz, S., Glazier, J. J., Enright, E. A., Alonso, D. J., Durwood, L. J., Fast, A. A., Lowe, R., Ji, C., Heer, J., Martin, C. L., & Olson, K. R. (2019). Similarity in transgender and cisgender children's gender development. *Proceedings of the National Academy of Sciences of the United States of America, 116*(49), 24480–24485. https://doi.org/10.1073/pnas.1909367116

Hastings, J., Bobb, C., Wolfe, M., Zo, A. J., & St. Amand, C. (2021). Medical care for nonbinary youth: Individualized gender care beyond a binary framework. *Pediatric Annals, 50*(9), e384–e390. https://doi.org/10.3928/19382359-20210818-03

Hidalgo, M. A., Ehrensaft, D., Tishelman, A. C., Clark, L. F., Garofalo, R., Rosenthal, S. M., Spack, N. P., & Olson, J. (2013). The gender affirmative model: What we know and what we aim to learn. *Human Development, 56*(5), 285–290. https://doi.org/10.1159/000355235

Hidalgo, M. A., Petras, H., Chen, D., & Chodzen, G. (2019). The gender minority stress and resilience measure: Psychometric validity of an adolescent extension. *Clinical Practice in Pediatric Psychology, 7*(3), 278–290. https://doi.org/10.1037/cpp0000297

Johns, M. M., Beltran, O., Armstrong, H. L., Jayne, P. E., & Barrios, L. C. (2018). Protective factors among transgender and gender variant youth: A systematic review by socioecological level. *The Journal of Primary Prevention, 39*(3), 263–301. https://doi.org/10.1007/s10935-018-0508-9

Katz-Wise, S. L., Gordon, A. R., Sharp, K. J., Johnson, N. P., & Hart, L. M. (2022). Developing parenting guidelines to support transgender and gender diverse children's well-being. *Pediatrics, 150*(3), e2021055347. https://doi.org/10.1542/peds.2021-055347

Katz-Wise, S. L., Rosario, M., & Tsappis, M. (2016). Lesbian, gay, bisexual, and transgender youth and family acceptance. *Pediatric Clinics of North America, 63*(6), 1011–1025. https://doi.org/10.1016/j.pcl.2016.07.005

Kuper, L., Rider, G. N., Brewer, A., Moundas, S., & St. Amand, C. (2022). *Framework for conducting a SOC8-informed "Comprehensive Biopsychosocial Assessment" for Adolescents: Perspectives from TNB2S and adjacent clinicians* [Mini-symposium]. 27th World Professional Association for Transgender Health Scientific Symposium, Montreal, Quebec, Canada.

Langer, S. J. (2019). *Theorizing transgender identity for clinical practice: A new model for understanding gender*. Jessica Kingsley Publishers.

Leibowitz, S., Edwards-Leeper, L., Janssen, A., & De Vries, A. (2016). *How much is too much? Assessments and the affirmative approach to TGNC youth* [Symposium]. 24th World Professional Association for Transgender Health Scientific Symposium, Amsterdam, The Netherlands.

Malpas, J., Glaeser, E., & Giammattei, S. V. (2018). Building resilience in transgender and gender expansive children, families, and communities: A multidimensional family approach. In C. Keo-Meier & D. Ehrensaft (Eds.), *The gender affirmative model: An interdisciplinary approach to supporting transgender and gender expansive children* (pp. 141–156). American Psychological Association. https://doi.org/10.1037/0000095-009

Martin, C. L., & Little, J. K. (1990). The relation of gender understanding to children's sex-typed preferences and gender stereotype. *Child Development, 61*(5), 1427. https://doi.org/10.2307/1130753

McAdaragh, M. O., Parchem, B., Duval, J., Baccam, Z. G., Caso, T. J., Arenella, K., Berg, D. R., & Rider, G. N. (2024). Gender-inclusive clinical screeners: Using CBCLs and YSRs in a clinic-based sample of transgender/gender-diverse youth. *Psychological Assessment, 36*(2), 89–101. https://doi.org/10.1037/pas0001290

McLaughlin, R. J., & Sharp, R. N. (2018). Working with parents and caregivers when conflicts arise. In C. Keo-Meier & D. Ehrensaft (Eds.), *The gender affirmative model: An interdisciplinary approach to supporting transgender and gender expansive children* (pp. 157–172). American Psychological Association. https://doi.org/10.1037/0000095-010

Moore, J. K., Thomas, C. S., van Hall, H. W., Strauss, P., Saunders, L. A., Harry, M., Mahfouda, S., Lawrence, S. J., Zepf, F. D., & Lin, A. (2021). The Perth Gender Picture (PGP): Young people's feedback about acceptability and usefulness of a new pictorial and narrative approach to gender identity assessment and exploration. *International Journal of Transgender Health*, *22*(3), 337–348. https://doi.org/10.1080/26895269.2020.1795960

Nienow, S. (2024). *Seven steps to teaching children body autonomy*. Kite Insights. https://www.rchsd.org/2019/12/seven-steps-to-teaching-children-body-autonomy/

Olson, K. R., Durwood, L., DeMeules, M., & McLaughlin, K. A. (2016). Mental health of transgender children who are supported in their identities. *Pediatrics*, *137*(3), e20153223. https://doi.org/10.1542/peds.2015-3223

Parchem, B., Panetta, E., Poquiz, J., Pournoor, S., Rider, G. N., & Berg, D. R. (2024, September). Centering gender diverse young children: Community feedback on the MyGender Dolls therapeutic tool. In G. N. Rider (chair), *Centering gender diverse young children's voices and experiences in clinical care and research* [Symposium]. World Professional Association for Transgender Health Scientific Symposium, Lisbon, Portugal.

Reguitti, V., Poquiz, J. L., Jackson, K., Coyne, C. A., Hidalgo, M. A., Forbes, C., & Chen, D. (2022). Preliminary factor structure of the Parental Attitudes of Gender Expansiveness Scale for Parents (PAGES-P). *Clinical Practice in Pediatric Psychology*, *10*(1), 1–8. https://doi.org/10.1037/cpp0000384

Reigada, T., Schaefer, C., Jegraj, A., Transforming Families, Rider, G. N., & Berg, D. (2024, September). *"I'm a they/them": Young children's responses to gender identity measures* [Oral presentation]. World Professional Association for Transgender Health Scientific Symposium, Lisbon, Portugal.

Reynolds, C. R., & Kamphaus, R. W. (2015). *Behavior assessment system for children* (3rd ed.). Pearson.

Rider, G. N., Berg, D., Pardo, S. T., Olson-Kennedy, J., Sharp, C., Tran, K. M., Calvetti, S., & Keo-Meier, C. L. (2019). Using the Child Behavior Checklist (CBCL) with transgender/gender nonconforming children and adolescents. *Clinical Practice in Pediatric Psychology*, *7*(3), 291–301. https://doi.org/10.1037/cpp0000296

Rider, G. N., & St. Amand, C. (2022). Youth. In L. Erickson-Schroth (Ed.), *Trans bodies, trans selves: A resource by and for transgender communities* (2nd ed., pp. 530–561). Oxford University Press.

Rider, G. N., Vencill, J. A., Berg, D. R., Becker-Warner, R., Candelario-Pérez, L., & Spencer, K. G. (2019). The Gender Affirmative Lifespan Approach (GALA): A framework for competent clinical care with nonbinary clients. *International Journal of Transgenderism*, *20*(2–3), 275–288. https://doi.org/10.1080/15532739.2018.1485069

Riggs, D. W., Pearce, R., Pfeffer, C. A., Hines, S., White, F., & Ruspini, E. (2019). Transnormativity in the psy disciplines: Constructing pathology in the *Diagnostic and Statistical Manual of Mental Disorders* and *Standards of Care*. *American Psychologist*, *74*(8), 912–924. https://doi.org/10.1037/amp0000545

Ruble, D. N., Martin, C. L., & Berenbaum, S. A. (2006). Gender development. In N. Eisenberg, W. Damon, & R. M. Lerner (Eds.), *Handbook of child psychology: Social, emotional, and personality development* (6th ed., pp. 858–932). John Wiley & Sons.

Rutter, M., Bailey, A., & Lord, C. (2003). *The Social Communication Questionnaire: Manual*. Western Psychological Services.

Schaefer, C., Reigada, T., McAdarach, M., Transforming Families, Blando, N., Jegraj, A., Berg, D., & Rider, G. N. (2024, October). *"They made me feel proud of myself": Gender identity measures among gender diverse 5–8-year-old* [Oral presentation]. American Public Health Association, Minneapolis, MN, United States.

Schaefer, C., Reigada, T., Rider, G. N., Transforming Families MN, Parchem, B., MN Trans Health Education Network, & Berg, D. R. (2025, September). The gender and flexible thinking study: A mixed methods study with children ages 5 to 8. In C. Schaefer (chair), *Fostering gender literacy and centering trans joy in young children: Insights from the GenderFlex Study* [Symposium]. Bi-Annual Conference of the United States Professional Association for Transgender Health, Santa Ana Pueblo, NM, United States.

Schueler, B. E., Capotosto, L., Bahena, S., McIntyre, J., & Gehlbach, H. (2014). Measuring parent perceptions of school climate. *Psychological Assessment, 26*(1), 314–320. https://doi.org/10.1037/a0034830

Silverberg, C. (2013). *What makes a baby*. Seven Stories Press.

Silverberg, C. (2015). *Sex is a funny word: A book about bodies, feelings, and YOU*. Seven Stories Press.

Simon, R. (2020). *The every body book: The LGBTQ+ inclusive guide for kids about sex, gender, bodies, and families*. Jessica Kingsley Publishers.

Simons, L., Schrager, S. M., Clark, L. F., Belzer, M., & Olson, J. (2013). Parental support and mental health among transgender adolescents. *Journal of Adolescent Health, 53*(6), 791–793. https://doi.org/10.1016/j.jadohealth.2013.07.019

Spencer, K. G., Berg, D. R., Bradford, N. J., Vencill, J. A., Tellawi, G., & Rider, G. N. (2021). The gender-affirmative life span approach: A developmental model for clinical work with transgender and gender-diverse children, adolescents, and adults. *Psychotherapy, 58*(1), 37–49. https://doi.org/10.1037/pst0000363

Spencer, K. G., & Vencill, J. A. (2017). Body beyond: A pleasure-based, sex-positive group therapy curriculum for transfeminine adults. *Psychology of Sexual Orientation and Gender Diversity, 4*(4), 392–402. https://doi.org/10.1037/sgd0000248

Srinath, S., Jacob, P., Sharma, E., & Gautam, A. (2019). Clinical practice guidelines for assessment of children and adolescents. *Indian Journal of Psychiatry, 61* (Suppl. 2), 158–175. https://doi.org/10.4103/psychiatry.IndianJPsychiatry_580_18

St. Amand, C., Brewer, A., Giammattei, S. V., Rider, G. N., Sauceda, A., & Kuper, L. (2023). *Conducting an SOC8-informed "comprehensive biopsychosocial assessment" for adolescents in the current politicized environment: Perspectives from TNB2S and adjacent clinicians* [Mini-symposium]. United States Professional Association for Transgender Health Scientific Symposium, Westminster, CO, United States.

Steensma, T. D., McGuire, J. K., Kreukels, B. P. C., Beekman, A. J., & Cohen-Kettenis, P. T. (2013). Factors associated with desistence and persistence of childhood gender dysphoria: A quantitative follow-up study. *Journal of the American Academy of Child and Adolescent Psychiatry, 52*(6), 582–590. https://doi.org/10.1016/j.jaac.2013.03.016

Strang, J. F., Anthony, L. G., Song, A., Lai, M.-C., Knauss, M., Sadikova, E., Graham, E., Zaks, Z., Wimms, H., Willing, L., Call, D., Mancilla, M., Shakin, S., Vilain, E., Kim, D.-Y., Maisashvili, T., Khawaja, A., & Kenworthy, L. (2023). In addition to stigma: Cognitive and autism-related predictors of mental health in transgender adolescents. *Journal of Clinical Child and Adolescent Psychology, 52*(2), 212–229. https://doi.org/10.1080/15374416.2021.1916940

Strang, J. F., Chen, D., Nelson, E., Leibowitz, S. F., Nahata, L., Anthony, L. G., Song, A., Grannis, C., Graham, E., Henise, S., Vilain, E., Sadikova, E., Freeman, A., Pugliese, C., Khawaja, A., Maisashvili, T., Mancilla, M., & Kenworthy, L. (2022). Transgender youth executive functioning: Relationships with anxiety symptoms, autism spectrum disorder, and gender-affirming medical treatment status. *Child Psychiatry & Human Development, 53*(6), 1252–1265. https://doi.org/10.1007/s10578-021-01195-6

Strang, J. F., Harrop, C., Putnam, O., & Yang, J. S. (2023). *Gender Development Scale: A visually supported gender self-report tool for children* [Unpublished scale].

Strang, J. F., Meagher, H., Kenworthy, L., de Vries, A. L. C., Menvielle, E., Leibowitz, S., Janssen, A., Cohen-Kettenis, P., Shumer, D. E., Edwards-Leeper, L., Pleak, R. R., Spack, N., Karasic, D. H., Schreier, H., Balleur, A., Tishelman, A., Ehrensaft, D., Rodnan, L., Kuschner, E. S., . . . Anthony, L. G. (2018). Initial clinical guidelines for co-occurring autism spectrum disorder and gender dysphoria or incongruence in adolescents. *Journal of Clinical Child & Adolescent Psychology, 47*(1), 105–115. https://doi.org/10.1080/15374416.2016.1228462

Temple Newhook, J., Pyne, J., Winters, K., Feder, S., Holmes, C., Tosh, J., Sinnott, M.-L., Jamieson, A., & Pickett, S. (2018). A critical commentary on follow-up studies and "desistance" theories about transgender and gender-nonconforming children. *International Journal of Transgenderism, 19*(2), 212–224. https://doi.org/10.1080/15532739.2018.1456390

Warrier, V., Greenberg, D. M., Weir, E., Buckingham, C., Smith, P., Lai, M.-C., Allison, C., & Baron-Cohen, S. (2020). Elevated rates of autism, other neurodevelopmental and psychiatric diagnoses, and autistic traits in transgender and gender-diverse individuals. *Nature Communications, 11*(1), 3959. https://doi.org/10.1038/s41467-020-17794-1

Wehren, A., & De Lisi, R. (1983). The development of gender understanding: Judgments and explanations. *Child Development, 54*(6), 1568. https://doi.org/10.2307/1129820

World Health Organization. (2019). *International statistical classification of diseases and related health problems* (11th ed.). https://icd.who.int/

9 HELPING FAMILIES MOVE FROM DISTRESS TO ATTUNEMENT WITH A CHILD'S GENDER

DEB COOLHART, JESSIE ROSE COHEN, AND
MOLLY OBER FECHTER-LEGGETT

Although the number of families able to respond to their child's gender diverse identity and/or expressions with acceptance and support or at least tolerance has increased (Malpas, 2011; Ryan et al., 2010; The Trevor Project, 2022), for many families, these responses are accompanied by varying levels of distress. It is common for parents to wrestle with difficult feelings, such as fear for their transgender and gender diverse (TGD) children's safety as well as disappointment, anxiety, embarrassment, blame, confusion, anger, concern, denial, self-blame, and shame (Katz-Wise et al., 2022; Kidd et al., 2024; Lev, 2004; Malpas, 2011). Parents may also experience direct loss, wherein they feel like they are losing their child, or ambiguous loss, wherein the loss is indistinct and confusing (Boss, 1999; Coolhart et al., 2018; Ryan et al., 2010), both of which can lead to a grieving process.

When a family seeks the assistance of a clinician because of distress about their child's gender, it can be a delicate balance to support both child and parents as well as siblings (Abrams et al., 2020; Bhattacharya et al., 2021; Coolhart, 2012; Coolhart & Martin, 2021). The stance of a pediatric gender health clinician is that a TGD child should be helped to live and express gender in ways

https://doi.org/10.1037/0000494-010
Pediatric Gender Health Care: The Gender Affirmative Model Revisited, Second Edition, G. N. Rider, D. Ehrensaft, and C. St. Amand (Editors)

that are most authentic for the child (Hidalgo et al., 2013). Often, gender expressions that are most authentic for the child are not comfortable for the family and, in fact, cause distress for the family. Therefore, clinicians must find ways to support and validate parents' emotional processes, while simultaneously offering accurate information and education creating safety and support for the child to develop gender health. Understanding a parent's view of their goals in raising their child and any belief systems they hold about childrearing can be a helpful point of assessment and connection.

As clinicians work with families in distress, it is important to keep in mind that families are in a process that usually shifts and changes over time (Brown, Porta, et al., 2020). In other words, when families begin therapy struggling with a child's gender, often where they begin emotionally is not where they end up eventually. Although it is assumed in the provision of pediatric gender health care that each parent wants the best for their child, that intent may be undermined by their actual interactions with their TGD child. Thus, the goal of therapy is to help families reach an increased level of attunement to their child. The term *attunement* implies reaching a level of harmony, understanding, and peace with their child's gender self. This moves beyond the idea of tolerating or accepting the presence of gender diversity as though it is a problem that will not go away. Rather, in reaching attunement, families recognize that gender diversity is a normal variation of humanity and the challenges that families face are due to society's inability to embrace these natural variations. Clinicians can help parents explore their own internalized negative feelings about their child being TGD, freeing them to further attune by mirroring back the gender the child knows themself to be rather than the gender others assume or want them to be. The clinician's ability to hold complexity and understand parental fears and concerns while advocating for the child's voice to be heard is a unique challenge of gender care. This chapter aims to provide strategies for creating balance between support for parents and for the TGD child, to address common presentations of family distress as it relates to a child's gender identity and expression, and to discuss pathways for families to achieve a greater level of attunement with their child's true gender self.

STRUCTURING SESSIONS

When families are in distress, oftentimes they are expressing views, thoughts, and feelings that are hurtful to the child. For example, parents may present in therapy with comments like these: "He shouldn't be acting like a girl. It is just wrong! I refuse to see him as a girl," or "She thinks she's a little boy, which is the most ridiculous thing I have ever heard. It's breaking my heart. It's killing me." Pediatric gender health treatment aims to normalize the child's gender and assist parents in helping their child develop self-esteem (Lev, 2004). One role of the clinician is to help parents understand ways in which their communications may be hurtful to their child and encourage them not to share such thoughts and feelings directly with their child. Separate parent sessions can be a way for parents to protect their child from further negative messages, as well as give parents a space to be supported through a process that is sometimes emotionally complicated (Coolhart, 2012; Coolhart & Martin, 2021).

Separate child sessions aim to support the child's true gender self and expression of that self and to build rapport for later joint sessions with parents. The clinician should be transparent with parents that the approach taken in the sessions alone with the child is informed by a gender health perspective, and that the clinician will be honoring the child's wishes in sessions regarding gender. For example, the clinician will be facilitating the child articulating gender in whatever ways feel most congruent for the child, and the clinician will be using whatever name and pronouns the child requests. Parents in distress about their child's gender presentation may struggle with their perception that their child's gender is being "encouraged" by the clinician. If that becomes an issue, clinicians can explain to parents that a nonaffirmative approach may cause harm to the child. If parents are still not comfortable enough, clinicians can first work with parents alone, without meeting with the child, until enough trust is established in the therapeutic process for parents to receive feedback about how to attune to their child's experience.

In this approach, it is important to meet parents where they are while supporting the child's gender health. The last thing we want to do as clinicians is to alienate parents, causing them to discontinue therapy. For example, when parents are not able to tolerate the therapist using the child's chosen name and pronouns, a first step may be to avoid using a name (i.e., use "your child") and to use gender-neutral pronouns (i.e., use "they/them"). This approach holds the parents' struggle while avoiding misgendering the child.

Ultimately, the therapeutic goal is to have joint sessions with the parents and the child to discuss ways in which they will incorporate the child's gender into their family. Although these important interchanges facilitate treatment goals, the child's safety and well-being, along with the establishment of a gender-affirming environment, should be the priority before these conversations occur. With some families, the milieu is safe enough for the child to begin family sessions immediately; other families may need more time, with separate parent and child sessions. When parents have had enough space to process their own positions and vent the hurtful emotions and expressions away from their child, family sessions including the child can begin. The following section discusses strategies for facilitating this work with parents.

IMPROVING GENDER LITERACY: PROVIDING PARENTS WITH ACCURATE GENDER EDUCATION

In parent sessions, it often becomes evident that parents have limited and sometimes inaccurate beliefs about TGD experiences. Sessions with these parents should include providing information and education about gender diversity (Coolhart & Martin, 2021; Lev, 2004; Malpas, 2011; Spencer, Berg, et al., 2021). Many times, the therapist functions as a teacher and a coach, helping parents develop increasingly supportive responses to their child. Although this resembles a directive approach, care should be taken so that parents feel neither proselytized nor chastised. The key is to fully listen to parents' current beliefs and feelings, hold and validate their struggle, and utilize therapeutic timing to gently challenge parents to expand how they think and feel about gender diversity. Clinicians will be ineffective in helping TGD children unless they are able to establish a loving and trusting rapport with parents and imagine the possibility of the parents moving to a place of attunement, valuing their challenges and strengths as parents. In addition to a family's own timeline in understanding and integrating the child's authentic gender identity, the current climate of fear and misinformation can add confusing elements for parents to wade through. Table 9.1 presents common parent misconceptions and responses as well as recommended therapeutic interventions.

PROCESSING PARENTS' LOSS AND FEAR

Parents in distress about their child's gender are often overwhelmed with emotions that are difficult to manage, particularly loss and fear. Two common types of losses that parents of TGD children experience are the loss of hopes and dreams for their child and the perceived loss of one child while another child emerges (Bhattacharya et al., 2021; Brill & Pepper, 2008; Katz-Wise et al., 2022). The first type of loss is often experienced as the loss of gender-related rites of passage. For example, some parents grieve the loss of their dream of seeing their daughter in a wedding dress on her wedding day. The second type of loss is ambiguous loss, defined as a loss that is indistinct and confusing (Boss, 1999). Parents may feel an ambiguous sense of loss knowing they physically still have a child, but the child's psychological existence as a certain gender may be perceived as gone. Further, a parent may be experiencing that much of the child's personality and psychological sense of self are present, but the child's physical presence as a certain gender is gone (Coolhart et al., 2018; Wahlig, 2015). As with any experience of loss, these feelings take time to move through, and parents can be supported in their articulation of these feelings.

TABLE 9.1. Common Misconceptions, Parent Responses, and Recommended Interventions

Common misconceptions	Common parent responses	Recommended interventions
Gender is binary, and there is a right way to be a boy or a girl	• How can my child be a girl when they enjoy so many boy/masculine activities? • How can a person not be a boy or a girl? • If he's a boy, why does he want to paint his nails?	Explore parents' views about gender and sexuality and how they are influenced by social locations such as religion, race and ethnicity, class, migration history, and so on Help parents differentiate identity vs. expression (i.e., a boy can still be a boy and wear nail polish) Gently invite parents to entertain other possible views of gender (Coolhart & Martin, 2021; Szilagyi, 2021), including nonbinary identities and expressions, and offer examples of how parents can respond to their child in more supportive ways
Children are transgender and gender diverse (TGD) because of something the parents did, or the parents could have prevented the child from being TGD	• Was it trauma? • Was it because my child didn't have positive role models of their designated gender? • Did I encourage this? Is this my fault?	Approach parents' concerns and feelings with compassion Acknowledge that parents' feelings are typically rooted in love for the child Advise that gender diversity is rarely caused by stressors (Malpas, 2011); if this happened, it would not be likely to persist Assure parents that nothing they did or did not do could have caused their child to be TGD Help parents navigate others' judgments and practice responses to challenging situations
If one's child is trans, the child will not be normal, safe, happy, loved, successful, and so on	• Will someone harm my child? • What if my child changes their mind after starting a gender transition? • Will my child end up depressed or suicidal? • Will my child make friends? • Will my child be able to find a partner to love them?	Advise parents that TGD presentations are not negative or pathological; rather, they are natural variations of humanity Let parents know that their child exploring their authentic self is a strength Help parents understand that being TGD brings challenges due to dysphoria and societal mistreatment, but TGD people can be resilient, happy, and loved Share that children with supportive parents have better mental health outcomes Discuss with parents that children supported in transition have better mental health outcomes than those who have to wait until later adolescence or adulthood Assure parents that a gender journey is a lifelong process, so people may indeed find themselves with a new sense of their authentic gender as life moves on

Clinicians can also normalize these feelings, letting parents know that many other parents of TGD children have similar feelings. Parents may benefit from meeting other families in support groups, chatting with other parents in online forums, or attending gender conferences, as the topic of grieving frequently arises in these settings. Helping the parents to grieve separately from the child can minimize the responsibility the child may feel for their parents' grief and also give the child space to have a separate set of feelings, especially elation and relief accompanying the freedom to live in their authentic gender.

Fear is also often central in the emotional experience of parents of TGD children and can take different forms, such as fear for the child's safety and well-being, fear of condemnation (Bhattacharya et al., 2021; Brill & Pepper, 2008; Katz-Wise et al., 2022), fear of their child being vilified or denied access to gender health care due to antitrans legislation, or fear of legal consequences of affirming their child's gender. When parents are organized by fear, they are living in the future of what-ifs rather than the present potentials, and they may be prevented from clearly seeing what is in the child's best interest. Thus, therapy should provide space for exploring and processing parents' fears. When parents' anxiety is decreased, they can have more control over their fears and can recognize that their needs are separate from their child's (Malpas, 2011). Clinicians can help parents articulate the fears, the source of those fears, and the level of control they have over their fears being actualized. For example, parents may not have much control over the reactions of extended family members, but they do have control over their disclosure of their child's gender identity, the boundaries they set in their familial and community relationships, their responses to conflicts, and their support of their child through the conflict. Similarly, parents may not have control over antitrans laws that prohibit gender health medical care for their child and criminalize supportive parents, but they may have the ability to connect to virtual and in-person support networks. In some cases, when resources are available, some families may relocate to a safer place or source pediatric gender care from neighboring states. Moving is not a long-term solution, naturally. The overall goal is a parallel level of attunement and acceptance in the larger culture and within families. As clinicians, strengthening family attunement can serve as a powerful salve to the wider challenges.

COACHING PARENTS TO LISTEN TO THEIR CHILD

When parents are struggling to support their child's gender diversity, clinicians can reflect their feelings (e.g., "This experience is very challenging for you"), while communicating to them that the statements they are making about their child's gender can have a negative impact on the child's long-term emotional and physical well-being. Parents are often worried about the discrimination their child will face, which is a valid concern; in these instances, clinicians can make them aware that research suggests parental support to be a major protective factor for youths' mental health. Young adults who experience high parental rejection of their lesbian, gay, bisexual, transgender, queer, or questioning (LGBTQ) identity are more likely to attempt suicide, to report high levels of depression, to use illegal drugs, and to engage in unprotected sex (Ryan et al., 2009; Wittlin et al., 2023). On the other hand, parental acceptance is predictive of higher self-esteem, social support, and better general health status (Ryan et al., 2010), as well as higher grade point averages and greater levels of school belonging (Watson et al., 2016). Research on TGD people specifically corroborates these findings (Grant et al., 2011; James et al., 2016; Travers et al., 2012), confirming that the level of support parents provide to their TGD children has a long-term impact, including the respect of pronouns as particularly important (Brown, Frohard-Dourlent, et al., 2020).

The first step for parents in supporting their child's gender development is to gain an understanding of their child's experience. Clinicians can coach parents to simply listen to what their child is experiencing and how their child feels. According to Ehrensaft (2011), "listening to children and paying attention to what they are telling you about their authentic gender self is the cornerstone of helping them grow healthy and strong" (p. 103). Although this sounds simple and straightforward, it is often difficult for parents to do. Their own emotional processes and misinformation in the larger culture can get in the way of them truly listening to their child. Most of the time, parents' love for their child is at the core of their distress. Parents do not want their child to experience the difficult path that accompanies gender diversity and possible eventual gender transition and, in some cases, parents state that they "know their child best" and are "protecting them." This is in alignment with many cultures, as parents are a guide and protector. The clinician offering gender care needs to translate the mode to help parents understand that the idea is not to relinquish parenting, but that an issue such as core identity requires a broader approach. Clinicians can access this love as the source of distress and use it as a building block for future increased attunement around gender, assuring parents that what their child needs from them the most is for them to really listen. Additionally, the gender affirmative model (Hidalgo et al., 2013; Keo-Meier & Ehrensaft, 2018) offers an understanding of development as a guide rather than an obstacle. "They are too young to know," for example, is asserted when there is a nonconforming gender assertion but rarely when there is one that is expected in the larger culture (e.g., a cisgender girl says she is a princess) or a normal developmental trait is used to discredit a young person's inability to know themselves (e.g., a teen presents with an urgency and at times marked mental health issues when feeling dismissed, and they are in turn considered "unstable" and therefore "unable to know"). According to Lev (2004), parents "need to learn to love their children as they are and not send messages of disappointment" (p. 335). Although parents have little control over their child's gender identity, they do have control over how they respond to their child. Their responses can have a significant effect on their child's self-acceptance, well-being, social–emotional adjustment, and safety (Malpas, 2011). Parents may need to learn to let go of their own dreams for their child, honor the dreams their child has for themself, and create room for new understandings, hopes, and dreams to be created.

In parent–child sessions, clinicians can encourage the child to discuss their feelings and self-perceptions about their gender. For example, the clinician can ask the child when they first felt they were different, if they did, or were aware of their gender, and how it feels when forced to express gender in a way that is uncomfortable for them. During these sessions, parents may still deny or repudiate their child's experiences. The clinician's role, then, is to gently coach the parents to listen in a nonreactive way. For example, a parent might say, "It's just that there was no evidence of this early on. He always fit in with the boys." In these moments, the child might feel hurt. Clinicians can invite parents to take seriously what their child is communicating by asking questions like these: "What if what your child is saying is true? That even though you didn't see it, your child was in pain at that time?" and "What if your child didn't understand that what they were experiencing at the time was gender dysphoria, but that they know it now?"

HELPING PARENTS NAVIGATE ANTITRANS RHETORIC

Since the rise in antitrans legislation, there has also been a rise in conservative voices attacking trans identities. Of particular concern to some parents may be the antitrans rhetoric against allowing access to pediatric gender health medical treatments. This rhetoric often claims that there is not enough research to support making these medical decisions that sometimes have irreversible effects. While it is true that further research on trans physical and mental health is needed, a robust and growing body of research exists to inform best practices. As clinicians, we can become familiar with this research to help parents lean on science in the process of making the best-informed decisions with their children. As a baseline, it is important to be aware of the ample studies that indicate improved mental health, including less suicidality, for youth who desire and receive pediatric gender health medical care compared with youth who desire but cannot access this care (Budge et al., 2013; Cornell University What We Know Project, 2018; Durwood et al., 2017; Green et al., 2022; Lopez et al., 2017; Olson et al., 2016; Reisner et al., 2015; Telfer et al., 2018; Turban et al., 2020).

One of the terms introduced by opponents of pediatric gender health care for trans youth and not recognized by any diagnostic criteria or professional association is *rapid-onset gender dysphoria*, which was coined in 2016 to describe an alleged subset of gender dysphoric youth who have shown no prior indication of gender dysphoria and suddenly and mistakenly believe they are transgender (Ashley, 2020). This term is not a recognized diagnosis within the *Diagnostic and Statistical Manual of Mental Disorders* (*DSM-5-TR*; American Psychiatric Association, 2022) or the *International Statistical Classification of Diseases and Related Health Problems* (*ICD-11*; World Health Organization, 2019); rather, it is a hypothesis of one researcher (Littman, 2018) whose research has been debunked. Users of the term attribute this "rapid onset" to social contagion and exposure to trans internet communities; as stated earlier, opponents of pediatric gender health care use typical development such as a draw to peers and accessing information online in adolescence as "evidence" of illegitimacy rather than a strength (e.g., "I see myself and my experience in this person; that makes sense for me, and I want to know more people with a range of experiences"). One study published in *PLOS One* (Littman, 2018) recruited parents from trans-antagonistic platforms to report on their children's so-called rapid-onset gender dysphoria, giving credit to this phenomenon. The study did not include the perspectives of the transgender youth, who very well may have been going through a gender journey privately, without the knowledge of their parents. The study also did not consider the possibility that the significant variable was actually *rapid-onset parental discovery*, as it is commonly known that youth often know for months to years before communicating to their parents their gender self (Ehrensaft & Jurkiewicz, 2024). *PLOS One* later published a correction to the Littman (2018) article (Littman, 2019), a formal comment (Brandelli Costa, 2019), and an apology to trans communities (Heber, 2019). Restar (2020) also published a methodological critique. However, the 2018 Littman article is still widely cited by opponents of gender health care (Ashley, 2020). Because the parents in the Littman (2018) study sample were recruited from trans-antagonistic platforms, it is likely that these parents were disproportionately unsupportive of their children's identities (i.e., 63.8% of parents in the study reported that teens accused them of being transphobic). The assertion that a later onset or later awareness is considered anything but someone's timing and path leaves no room for the range of feelings and trajectories that exist in TGD children and youth. Ironically, these so-called later reports often coincide with pubertal onset, which is understood as a common point of awareness and, at times, crisis. Research has repeatedly demonstrated that parental support is associated with more positive mental health outcomes, including less suicidality, for trans people compared with those with unsupportive families (Grant et al., 2011; James et al., 2016; Tankersley et al., 2021).

Although some youth begin to identify as TGD after exposure to other trans people, young people tend to describe this experience as related to visibility and representation of trans identities. When youth have had no prior knowledge of the existence of trans people, they often struggle to understand what is happening for them and do not have the language to describe it. Once youth gain access to representation, accurate labeling as trans and nonbinary becomes possible. It is also common for trans youth to have trans and queer friends, in both online and in-person spaces. These relationships are often critical to the development of positive self-understanding, helping youth to accept themselves and share their identities with others (Kuper et al., 2018).

Another strategy used by those who oppose gender health care for youth is to emphasize the experiences of those who stop, shift, or reverse a gender transition (sometimes referred to as *detransition*). Although the number of people who change direction in their gender journey is hard to measure, some literature suggests the rate is 0.3% to 0.6% (McNamara et al., 2022; Rosenthal, 2021). Further, the largest study of transgender experiences to date, with more than 92,000 participants, reported that 94% of people who transition are more satisfied with their life (James et al., 2024). When thinking about those who change direction in their gender journey, it is important to consider that many youths who change direction express gratitude for having had the opportunity to explore their gender identity (Ashley, 2019; MacKinnon et al., 2022; Turban & Keuroghlian, 2018; Turban et al., 2018). Additionally, some youth may transition away from a binary trans identity as female or male to a nonbinary identity, often still appreciating the choices they made with regard to gender health medical treatments. Therefore, regret is not an experience shared by all who cease gender health medical treatments. When people make that choice, many report at least one external driving factor for changing direction in transition, including pressure from family, lack of support, and social stigma (MacKinnon et al., 2025; Turban et al., 2021). Although more long-term studies are needed, subgroups of TGD youth who have detransitioned often reintegrate a TGD identity when no longer a minor or living with parents. This suggests that the choice to transition is not necessarily the problem; societal and family rejection may be the problem.

WORKING WITH SIBLINGS

Parents of TGD children often express concern about the impact of their child's gender presentations on their other children. They may worry that the child's gender diversity will cause siblings distress and confusion. Little research has been done on this topic, although anecdotally, siblings sometimes exhibit less distress regarding their sibling's gender identity or expressions than parents do, perhaps because siblings are less invested in a sibling's outcome than parents. Siblings are also growing up in a different generation than their parents, one with more information about and exposure to diverse expressions of gender and sexuality, which may also contribute to the ease with which many are able to understand and support their TGD sibling. Yet in other families, siblings may experience significant distress about having a TGD sibling, sometimes struggling more than parents (Brill & Pepper, 2008), especially if they live in communities where gender diversity is not supported. Although parents may have fears about telling siblings about their TGD child's expression or identity, it is important that siblings be aware of and become involved in their sibling's gender experience, particularly when they are presenting as their gender outside the home. Siblings may very likely receive questions and hear comments about it from their peers. In fact, it is common for peers to first ask questions of the sibling before asking the gender diverse child directly. Beyond siblings, families will be best equipped if they are able to discuss gender diversity with all immediate family members and decide on the level of privacy the family wants to have, guided by the gender diverse child's needs and desires (i.e., what gets to be known by whom, and what stays within the immediate family).

When siblings struggle, they, like the parents, may be experiencing feelings of loss and grief—for the sister who is no longer a sister, for example. They may have concerns about their friends' or schoolmates' reactions to their sibling's gender expression. They may be teased, bullied, or asked why their brother is wearing a dress or their sister got a buzz cut. They may feel that all the attention in the family, even if it is negative, is being given to the TGD sibling. Clinicians can create space for siblings to express these feelings, sensitizing the parents to their other children's struggles and inviting parents to spend intentional time giving attention to siblings. This not only helps siblings feel valued, but it also may create openings for siblings to grow compassion and understanding for their TGD sibling.

Siblings may have internalized transphobic messages about gender diversity. Clinicians may need to use some of the previously discussed strategies for parents with siblings as well, such as educating them about various gender paths and normalizing gender diversity. When siblings are particularly distressed, they can become the worst enemy of the TGD child, outing them at school or generally harassing or mistreating them. If this occurs, clinicians can work with parents to support the siblings who are struggling while also preventing them from abusing their TGD sibling. Clinicians can work with siblings in transitioning from adversaries to allies.

Although much of the work with siblings may be done in family sessions, it may be helpful for siblings to also have individual sessions, depending on their level of distress. Siblings can discuss their specific concerns and fears, and clinicians can help them develop strategies for dealing with specific situations that may arise. For example, sessions can include role-playing ways to tell a friend about their TGD sibling or respond to a transphobic peer at school. Some siblings may do best with a response set of support and advocacy for their TGD sibling, in the context of a protective and proactive stance, which might include educating peers about gender expansiveness or normalizing their sibling's gender expression. Other siblings may do best with a more noninterventionist approach, such as responding to peers' queries with, "I don't really get it; it's just their thing." Clinicians can help siblings figure out an approach that is a good fit.

COMMUNITY CONNECTIONS

Pediatric gender health clinicians generally recommend that parents and children be connected with other people in the community who share their experiences (Brill & Pepper, 2008; Coolhart, 2012; Lev, 2004; Thornburgh et al., 2020). Malpas (2011) discussed how parents in multifamily groups were able to not only connect with others around shared experiences but also to maintain or restore the bond with their child by having the opportunity to process their experiences in an honest, nonjudgmental space. Although therapy can be helpful for discussing experiences, the benefit of meeting others who are going through, or have successfully navigated, similar situations can be additionally validating. Of course, in-person group settings are not a fit for all children and parents; some may not feel comfortable sharing personal information with multiple people, and some may feel alienated by groups when their experiences differ from dominant narratives. Therefore, parents and children should ultimately decide what feels most helpful.

When families do not live in areas with access to supportive youth and parent groups, they can be referred to reading materials, online resources, and internet-based support groups where they can experience some of the same benefits of mutuality and normalization. Many families may feel as if they are the only ones dealing with gender diversity, so learning about the experiences of others can greatly reduce feelings of isolation (Lev, 2004; Thornburgh et al., 2020). Additionally, families can be made aware of opportunities where they may spend time with other TGD children and their families (e.g., summer camps, conferences, and support groups). Families can also benefit from the wisdom of trans adults and elders (e.g., through writings, at Pride events, and through support groups), learning from their stories of resilience and resistance.

PATHWAYS TO INCREASED ATTUNEMENT

As parents work through their distress, several paths may lead them to an increased level of attunement with their child's gender; clinicians can help parents navigate these paths. Increased attunement can come through the realization that gender diversity is not just a phase but a stable part of their child's experience, and this takes time. Parents in distress sometimes have pathology-oriented ideas about why people develop gender diversity, whereas the child may have a much more naturalistic view of their gender experience, such as believing that nothing caused their gender but rather that it has always just been there. Discussing multiple perspectives can help parents expand their views and feelings about gender diversity, helping them to see that it is not a problem to be fixed but is something that will be with their child potentially for a lifetime—and while their child's journey, identity, and presentation may shift over time, parents can strive to embrace this journey.

Parents also increase attunement by recognizing the presence of gender diversity in their child's history, if it was indeed present. Clinicians can facilitate this process by asking parents what they recall about their child's early gender expressions or assertions. By reflecting on early experiences, parents may bring into focus ways that their child expressed gender diversity early in life, sometimes as early as age 2 or 3 years. Clinicians can also ask the child to share early memories, experiences, and emotions around gender expression and socialization. Children can often recall specific times when they felt different or uncomfortable being forced into a designated gender role. For example, a child who was designated female at birth might remember being forced to wear a dress for their kindergarten graduation and being embarrassed and ashamed at the forced femininity. Similarly, a child who was designated male at birth may recall being punished for playing dress-up with their sisters and being confused about why their sisters did not receive any punishment. Clinicians can help parents listen to and have compassion for the distress and/or dysphoria their child may have been experiencing over time as a result of being blocked from playing with and exploring gender. Conversely, as a child's comfort in their own identity strengthens, the child may be able to celebrate joyous times and family milestones without the memory being solely associated with gender (e.g., "Oh! Remember when we decorated these ornaments? You still love piano and dogs, and maybe we can update your name on those!"). Here the family can increase cohesion when the narrative is not only a before-and-after paradigm.

Finally, witnessing their child's happiness upon being afforded the opportunity to express gender in a way that feels congruent and authentic offers a third pathway for increased parental attunement. Often, as children actualize their internal gender experience more outwardly, they feel better and signs of distress decrease. Clinicians can assist parents in seeing these positive changes by inviting them to discuss their observations of their child's level of happiness before and after the gender diversity was acknowledged and addressed. Clinicians can also invite the child to talk about how it feels to be able to express their gender openly. If parents are not allowing the expression of gender diversity at home or if they limit its expression only to the home, the youth can reflect on how it feels to experience the gender safe space in therapy with no monitoring or limitations. If the child is experiencing gender dysphoria, it can also be helpful for the child to identify triggers as well as ways the dysphoria emotionally affects them. Bearing witness to their child's experience can help parents see that pushing the child toward an incongruent gender role can be harmful to their child and that freedom of gender expression has the opposite effect—it is emotionally beneficial for the child.

AS ATTUNEMENT INCREASES

As levels of distress decrease and attunement increases, parents may be able to slowly tolerate broader discussions of gender identity and expressions. By this time, the clinician will have a clearer sense of the nature of the child's gender experience. For example, the clinician will likely know whether the child simply wants to be able to express so-called masculine or feminine behaviors, whether it is the child's gender identity that needs to be addressed, or both. Accordingly, the clinician can begin to advocate for the child with the parents, helping them find ways to support the child's gender. For example, if the child desires gender transition, the clinician can discuss the idea of transition and what that might look like for the family. Discussions may include parents' feelings of readiness for such a step, the potential for extended family support, the child's safety in the family's community if transition occurs, and support (or lack thereof) in the school environment. Additionally, it should be considered whether the child's personality, sensitivities, and temperament or attributes of introversion versus extroversion would support or create challenges to a transition at this particular time. With preadolescent children, clinicians can also begin to talk about different options for gender health, including social transition, disclosure to people outside the family, and, as the child approaches puberty, puberty blocker use. It is important to note that gender health is not a one-size-fits-all process; each person has their own unique path. Children who are experiencing significant distress and dysphoria in the gender they are living in may move through transition rapidly, whereas children who experience less distress or more gender fluidity may take steps in transition at a slower rate or may only take one step. It is essential to listen to the child, while balancing parents' readiness and concerns, and to make decisions that are in the best interest of the child and family in the larger contexts in which they are embedded (i.e., racial and ethnic or homeland communities, religious community, and residence in a state banning gender health medical care).

Clinicians can explore with parents ways to be supportive of their child's gender self. Some children may want parents to use a chosen name and appropriate pronouns. Clinicians can discuss parents' comfort with shifts and consider situations in which the name and pronouns should be used (e.g., only in the home or everywhere). If the child is concerned more with expression than identity, the clinician can encourage the parents to take steps to support those expressions (e.g., allowing preferred clothing, presentation, and activities) at first in the home and then outside the home if the child desires. The qualification here is that by delivering a message to children that expressions are acceptable at home but not elsewhere, children who are eager to express themselves everywhere may internalize the message that the expressions are still something to be hidden or to be shameful about. If it is necessary to limit such a child's expressions to the home environment, it should be communicated to the child that this limitation is not because something is wrong with the child but because the world still has some learning to do about gender expansiveness (Ehrensaft, 2011, 2016). With that said, it is important to discuss with the parents the child's safety in expressing their gender, particularly outside the home. Drawing on a parent's knowledge of culture and environment regarding legitimate safety concerns can help form a negotiated plan with which all are in agreement. Appropriate boundary and limit setting should be discussed in therapy (Lev, 2004). Malpas (2011) promulgated a both/and stance in which families accept and affirm the child's gender fluidity while still recognizing the limitations of a gender binary society, thus making decisions that both support and protect the child. Conversations should include potential challenges in settings such as school, extended family, places of worship, and other communities in which the family is embedded. As the challenges are identified, potential solutions and options can be discussed before moving forward with an action. Clinicians are essentially coaching parents to move from distress to acceptance, protection, and advocacy for their child. A parent shifts from embarrassment or fear that a neighbor will say something or spread gossip when they see a child expressing their authentic gender to something like this: "That corner store has never been quiet. I'd prefer you changed just to go get the snacks, and you can put your dress back on when you get home. Maybe I overworry, but that is my request."

Shifting into the role of advocacy can be challenging for some parents, and clinicians can support them in this role, either by physically attending meetings at school, for example, or by talking through the role of advocate with parents. When parents are in distress and experiencing fear, this fear can be put into action through advocacy, such as working to create safer places for their child. School is the most common place for needed advocacy, which can be an ongoing process requiring multiple interventions. For example, school administrators may say they will support a child's gender, but a child designated male at birth may be forced to change when they wear a skirt or "girls'" shoes to school, resulting in the child feeling shamed for their gender expression. In these situations, parents can draw upon their parental instincts to protect their child and continue to stand up for them, creating environments in which their child feels valued and free to express a true gender self. Think back to the earlier discussion in this chapter regarding sharing messages with the child about the unfair world: Rather than the cisgenderist messages that suggest the child is damaged because of their diverse gender and/or expression, it is important for the child to know that although people may not understand yet, we're all working to change that (Ehrensaft, 2011, 2016). Parents may also want to talk with the school about completing a gender support plan, and therapists could find sample gender support plans online to assist families in thinking about what steps at school would feel most supportive for the youth.

CASE EXAMPLE: "WE LOVE RISHI, BUT HE IS TOO YOUNG TO KNOW WHAT HE NEEDS"

The following case example is a composite case made up from multiple clients containing common case themes. The case does not represent one or any specific actual client.

Rishi (she/they) is a 6-year-old South Asian (Pakistani and Indian) child living in a suburban community 30 minutes outside of a major metropolitan area with many other families of South Asian descent. Rishi (designated male at birth) began requesting she/they pronouns in preschool (2 years ago) after reading a book about a child who was "all the colors of the rainbow." However, Rishi's parents have continued to use he/him pronouns and refer to Rishi as "our boy" and "our king." Rishi has a 9-year-old sister, Ankita, and both live with their mother and father, Mahvish and Deepak. Both children and Mahvish were born in the United States, and Deepak was born in Goa, India, migrating to the United States for medical school. Mahvish and Deepak practice Islam and are raising the children Muslim. The maternal grandparents live nearby and are integral in raising Rishi and Ankita. The family ascribes to a modern relationship with Islam and attends what would be considered a progressive type of mosque. The family travels once a year to India to see the paternal grandparents.

Mahvish and Deepak are loving and supportive and offer consistent parenting, although they believe Rishi is just a "sensitive boy who wants to be like his older sister." The family was recently invited to a wedding in India, and Rishi has requested to wear a saree. She also expressed that when she enters first grade in a few months, she wants to tell her teacher and peers to use she/her pronouns for her, and she wants to wear more feminine clothing that helps her feel more "like the girl I am." Although Rishi is overall a happy and engaged child, she has been starting to withdraw more and express frustration more openly. This is when the family entered therapy.

Because Rishi asserted her gender identity at age 4 and is now 6 and her parents were not yet able to imagine their child being anything other than a boy, the therapist viewed this as a situation where the parents may benefit from the therapist meeting alone with them as a first point of assessment and intervention. During these sessions, Mahvish and Deepak were clearly feeling the competing tensions of their child's well-being, their own sense of things, the larger community they are very much a part of, and their faith. Despite their more modern participation in their faith, the idea that children grow up to embody their parents' values, which include marriage and family building, was very much ingrained in both parents. Mahvish and Deepak were struggling to imagine a version of these values while simultaneously grieving the lost fantasy version. It evokes fear of being unwelcome in the community—of being "too different," especially because the family already is impacted by structural racism in the larger world. Additionally, the fact that Mahvish is Pakistani and Deepak is Indian brought up old grief about how much effort it took to reassure the families and get their unwavering support for the union. They all joked that at least one was not a practicing Hindu or that would be even more to contend with. Similarly, the idea that parents would have to share Rishi's assertion to the wider family brought with it anxiety. They were loving/supportive and simultaneously uncomfortable/

distressed about the requests Rishi was making. Mahvish and Deepak were worried about Rishi's ability to know herself at a young age, ways she and the family may be ostracized, and possibilities that supporting feminine expression might "encourage" a pathway. The therapist attuned to the parents' emotional process, validated their fears, and also validated the deep love and care they have for their child. The clinician discussed the notion of "two timelines" to include the parents' current feeling that this is acute and the fact that Rishi expressed this for the first time 4 years prior.

As Mahvish and Deepak began to unpack their understandings of gender and their concerns, they acknowledged some cultural lineage that supports gender variance as a legitimate identity, but that this typically happens much later in life after surgery. They expressed openness to supporting Rishi's gender later "if it becomes clear he needs surgery." Prior to this, they wanted Rishi to continue to "live as a boy." At the family's mosque, congregants are separated by gender, and Mahvish expressed worry that they would be ostracized from the community if they support Rishi in a feminine presentation, as Rishi recently asked to wear a hijab. Mahvish discussed already being different as a multiethnic family and worried about calling more attention to Rishi, especially at such a young age. In these conversations, the therapist continued to attend to the parents' emotional process, validated the importance of their community, and held the heaviness of the fear of judgment and loss of community. The therapist also highlighted the parents' potential openness to Rishi's gender diversity in the future, pointing to it as a strength in their potential to open themselves more to Rishi's journey now.

In a session alone with Rishi, the therapist explored Rishi's internal sense of gender. She said, "I am a girl . . . a girl with a penis." Rishi expressed she "wants boobs like Mama. I don't want my body to change to be like Appa." When the therapist assessed Rishi's distress related to not being able to be her full authentic self, Rishi reported feeling sad and that recently the big feelings sometimes get out of control. When asked what helps, Rishi described secretly expressing herself by going into Ankita's room to use her clothes and toys and by using the toilet to urinate while sitting down. The therapist validated how hard it is when we cannot be who we really are and how strong Rishi was for sharing her truth.

When meeting subsequently with Rishi's parents, the therapist reflected their experience of Rishi as a kind and bright child who is also feeling a lot of sadness. Mahvish and Deepak agreed with these observations and seemed visibly sad hearing Rishi's sadness observed by the therapist. The therapist tuned into this emotion and talked about how the parents could help relieve some of Rishi's sadness by finding ways to support her gender. Rishi requested the therapist use she/her pronouns, so the therapist told Mahvish and Deepak that they would be using Rishi's pronouns as an example of support. The therapist also suggested a gender holiday, where the family could go away locally for a weekend, for example, and let Rishi dress how she wants to practice tolerating reactions and see how that feels for Rishi. Support was also discussed as a protective factor against challenges Rishi will face, as a sign of faith that Rishi is telling them something important, and that showing support does not promote any specific pathway. Because of Rishi's age, the therapist assured the parents that there were no current medical decisions to make and that at this time, the only decisions to be made were about supporting social aspects of expression. Both parents were asked to explore their comfort and discomfort with choosing to support Rishi in different ways, such as honoring her name and pronouns, allowing feminine dress, and so on.

As Mahvish and Deepak's attunement increased, family sessions began. The therapist helped the family talk about Rishi's requests, her underlying emotions, and her dysphoria. Although her parents were not ready for Rishi to wear a saree for the wedding because they feared the family's reaction, they were open to Rishi "playing dress-up at home" with whatever she wanted to wear and began to purchase some "girls" clothing for Rishi. Her parents also agreed to practice using she/her pronouns at home and allow Rishi to begin to grow her hair longer. These initial steps toward support helped Rishi feel better, and her parents could see that some of the weight had been lifted off Rishi.

Later sessions helped the family navigate coming out to Mahvish's parents and included them in the therapy process as important caregivers for Rishi. Ankita also attended some sessions; she adjusted quickly to Rishi's authentic gender, stating she always knew Rishi was not really a boy. Her ease seemed to help Mahvish and Deepak see Rishi through a new lens. Parent sessions also continued to assist parents with their emotions, such as Deepak's grief that Rishi does not want to "be like me" and will not be the "man in this family." Cultural and familial values around gender, sons, and patriarchy were discussed to help explore this pain.

Because this family was embedded in many layers of community, all with their own challenges, they chose to pace coming out starting in spaces they perceived to be easier (Mahvish's parents and Rishi's school) and postponing sharing Rishi's truth in other spaces they considered more challenging (their mosque and Deepak's family). Mahvish and Deepak were able to express to Rishi that waiting did not mean there was something wrong with Rishi's gender; rather, the family was on a journey of facing one challenge at a time. Rishi was enjoying her new freedom she had in some places and understood that her parents would eventually help her live authentically in all spaces. Over the course of therapy, the family seemed to shift from thinking that being

TGD was something happening to Rishi to thinking about it as something the family would grow through and navigate together.

CONCLUSION

From the time their child is born, most parents view the gender matching their child's designated sex at birth as a truth and unchangeable. Although TGD identities are becoming more visible in society, society still has a long way to go before TGD people are treated with equality, compassion, and kindness in general. Therefore, out of fear for their child's well-being, it is normal that parents experience distress when their child does not fit into the societal notion of binary gender fixed at birth. This in no way suggests parents do not love their children; yet they may be limited by available tools and resources to understand that with a TGD child, love also means taking action. By supporting parents and families through this challenging time, clinicians have the opportunity to assist families in moving toward greater attunement to their child's gender. Efforts and increases in acceptance and attunement, even when flawed or slow, are shown to have positive impacts on TGD children. Clinicians should embrace the goal of increasing attunement as a goal for the family to develop in their overall health as a family system. By allowing space for parents to experience their challenging emotions while also maintaining a gender health stance, clinicians can coach parents to listen to their child and value their experience. As parents move from distress to attunement, they become better equipped to understand, support, and advocate for their child, ultimately promoting their child's long-term happiness and well-being and overall gender health.

REFERENCES

Abrams, M., Golden, R. L., & Cohen, J. R. (2020). Affirming and inclusive mental health care for transgender and nonbinary young people. In S. K. Kattari, L. Kattari, & B. Holloway (Eds.), *Social work and health care practice with transgender and nonbinary individuals and communities* (pp. 76–88). Routledge. https://doi.org/10.4324/9780429443176-7

American Psychiatric Association. (2022). *Diagnostic and statistical manual of mental disorders* (5th ed., text rev.). https://doi.org/10.1176/appi.books.9780890425787

Ashley, F. (2019). Thinking an ethics of gender exploration: Against delaying transition for transgender and gender creative youth. *Clinical Child Psychology and Psychiatry, 24*(2), 223–236. https://doi.org/10.1177/1359104519836462

Ashley, F. (2020). A critical commentary on 'rapid-onset gender dysphoria.' *The Sociological Review Monographs, 68*(4), 779–799. https://doi.org/10.1177/0038026120934693

Bhattacharya, N., Budge, S. L., Pantalone, D. W., & Katz-Wise, S. L. (2021). Conceptualizing relationships among transgender and gender diverse youth and their caregivers. *Journal of Family Psychology, 35*(5), 595–605. https://doi.org/10.1037/fam0000815

Boss, P. G. (1999). *Ambiguous loss: Learning to live with unresolved grief.* Harvard University Press.

Brandelli Costa, A. (2019). Formal comment on: "Parent reports of adolescents and young adults perceived to show signs of a rapid onset of gender dysphoria." *PLOS One, 14*(3), e0212578. https://doi.org/10.1371/journal.pone.0212578

Brill, S., & Pepper, R. (2008). *The transgender child: A handbook for families and professionals.* Cleis Press.

Brown, C., Frohard-Dourlent, H., Wood, B. A., Saewyc, E., Eisenberg, M. E., & Porta, C. M. (2020). *"It makes such a difference"*: An examination of how LGBTQ youth talk about personal gender pronouns. *Journal of the American Association of Nurse Practitioners, 32*(1), 70–80. https://doi.org/10.1097/JXX.0000000000000217

Brown, C., Porta, C. M., Eisenberg, M. E., McMorris, B. J., & Sieving, R. E. (2020). Family relationships and the health and well-being of transgender and gender-diverse youth: A critical review. *LGBT Health, 7*(8), 407–419. https://doi.org/10.1089/lgbt.2019.0200

Budge, S. L., Adelson, J. L., & Howard, K. A. S. (2013). Anxiety and depression in transgender individuals: The roles of transition status, loss, social support, and coping. *Journal of Consulting and Clinical Psychology, 81*(3), 545–557. https://doi.org/10.1037/a0031774

Coolhart, D. (2012). Supporting transgender youth and their families in therapy: Facing challenges and harnessing strengths. In J. Bigner & J. Wetchler (Eds.), *Handbook of LGBT-affirmative couple and family therapy* (pp. 287–303). Routledge.

Coolhart, D., & Martin, T. K. (2021). Gender affirmative therapy with trans and gender expansive youth: Listening to youth and thoughtfully following their lead. In R. Harvey & M. Murphy's (Eds.), *Handbook of LGBT-affirmative couple and family therapy* (2nd ed., pp. 259–275). Routledge Press.

Coolhart, D., Ritenour, K., & Grodzinski, A. (2018). Experiences of ambiguous loss for parents of transgender male youth: A phenomenological exploration. *Contemporary Family Therapy, 40*(1), 28–41. https://doi.org/10.1007/s10591-017-9426-x

Cornell University What We Know Project. (2018). *What does the scholarly research say about the effect of gender transition on transgender well-being?* What We Know: The Public Policy Research Portal. https://whatweknow.inequality.cornell.edu/topics/lgbt-equality/what-does-the-scholarly-research-say-about-the-well-being-of-transgender-people/

Durwood, L., McLaughlin, K. A., & Olson, K. R. (2017). Mental health and self-worth in socially transitioned transgender youth. *Journal of the American Academy of Child & Adolescent Psychiatry, 56*(2), 116–123.e2. https://doi.org/10.1016/j.jaac.2016.10.016

Ehrensaft, D. (2011). *Gender born, gender made: Raising healthy gender-nonconforming children.* The Experiment.

Ehrensaft, D. (2016). *The gender creative child: Pathways for nurturing and supporting children who live outside gender boxes.* The Experiment.

Ehrensaft, D., & Jurkiewicz, M. (2024). *Gender explained: A new understanding of identity in a gender creative world.* The Experiment.

Grant, J. M., Mottet, L. A., Tanis, J., Harrison, J., Herman, J. L., & Keisling, M. (2011). *Injustice at every turn: A report of the National Transgender Discrimination Survey*. National Center for Transgender Equality and National Gay and Lesbian Task Force. https://www.thetaskforce.org/static_html/downloads/reports/reports/ntds_full.pdf

Green, A. E., DeChants, J. P., Price, M. N., & Davis, C. K. (2022). Association of gender-affirming hormone therapy with depression, thoughts of suicide, and attempted suicide among transgender and nonbinary youth. *Journal of Adolescent Health*, *70*(4), 643–649. https://doi.org/10.1016/j.jadohealth.2021.10.036

Heber, J. (2019, March 19). Correcting the scientific record on gender incongruence—And an apology. *EveryONE Blog*. https://everyone.plos.org/2019/03/19/correcting-the-scientific-record-and-an-apology/

Hidalgo, M. A., Ehrensaft, D., Tishelman, A. C., Clark, L. F., Garofalo, R., Rosenthal, S. M., Spack, N. P., & Olson, J. (2013). The gender affirmative model: What we know and what we aim to learn. *Human Development*, *56*(5), 285–290. https://doi.org/10.1159/000355235

James, S. E., Herman, J. L., Durso, L. E., & Heng-Lehtinen, R. (2024). *Early insights: A report of the 2022 U.S. Transgender Survey*. National Center for Transgender Equality. https://transequality.org/sites/default/files/2024-02/2022%20USTS%20Early%20Insights%20Report_FINAL.pdf

James, S. E., Herman, J. L., Rankin, S., Keisling, M., Mottet, L., & Anafi, M. (2016). *The report of the 2015 U.S. Transgender Survey*. National Center for Transgender Equality. https://transequality.org/sites/default/files/docs/usts/USTS-Full-Report-Dec17.pdf

Katz-Wise, S. L., Galman, S. C., Friedman, L. E., & Kidd, K. M. (2022). Parent/caregiver narratives of challenges related to raising transgender and/or nonbinary youth. *Journal of Family Issues*, *43*(12), 3321–3345. https://doi.org/10.1177/0192513X211044484

Keo-Meier, C., & Ehrensaft, D. (Eds.). (2018). *The gender affirmative model: An interdisciplinary approach to supporting transgender and gender expansive children*. American Psychological Association. https://doi.org/10.1037/0000095-000

Kidd, K. M., Didden, E., Harman, H., Sequeira, G. M., Faeder, M., Inwards-Breland, D. J., Voss, R. V., & Katz-Wise, S. L. (2024). Parents of gender diverse youth: Support sought, received, and still needed. *Journal of Adolescent Health*, *74*(6), 1078–1087. https://doi.org/10.1016/j.jadohealth.2023.08.001

Kuper, L. E., Wright, L., & Mustanski, B. (2018). Gender identity development among transgender and gender nonconforming emerging adults: An intersectional approach. *International Journal of Transgenderism*, *19*(4), 436–455. https://doi.org/10.1080/15532739.2018.1443869

Lev, A. I. (2004). *Transgender emergence: Therapeutic guidelines for working with gender variant people and their families*. Haworth Press.

Littman, L. (2018). Parent reports of adolescents and young adults perceived to show signs of a rapid onset of gender dysphoria. *PLOS One*, *13*(8), e0202330. https://doi.org/10.1371/journal.pone.0202330

Littman, L. (2019). Correction: Parent reports of adolescents and young adults perceived to show signs of a rapid onset of gender dysphoria. *PLOS One*, *14*(3), e0214157. https://doi.org/10.1371/journal.pone.0214157

Lopez, X., Marinkovic, M., Eimicke, T., Rosenthal, S. M., & Olshan, J. S. (2017). Statement on gender-affirmative approach to care from the Pediatric Endocrine Society Special Interest Group on Transgender Health. *Current Opinion in Pediatrics*, *29*(4), 475–480. https://doi.org/10.1097/MOP.0000000000000516

MacKinnon, K. R., Kia, H., Gould, W. A., Ross, L. E., Abramovich, A., Enxuga, G., & Lam, J. S. H. (2025). A typology of pathways to detransition: Considerations for care practice with transgender and gender diverse people who stop or reverse their gender transition. *Psychology of Sexual Orientation and Gender Diversity, 12*(1), 142–153. https://doi.org/10.1037/sgd0000678

MacKinnon, K. R., Kia, H., Salway, T., Ashley, F., Lacombe-Duncan, A., Abramovich, A., Enxuga, G., & Ross, L. E. (2022). Health care experiences of patients discontinuing or reversing prior gender-affirming treatments. *JAMA Network Open, 5*(7), e2224717. https://doi.org/10.1001/jamanetworkopen.2022.24717

Malpas, J. (2011). Between pink and blue: A multi-dimensional family approach to gender nonconforming children and their families. *Family Process, 50*(4), 453–470. https://doi.org/10.1111/j.1545-5300.2011.01371.x

McNamara, M., Lepore, C., Alstott, A., Kamody, R., Kuper, L., Szilagyi, N., Boulware, S., & Olezeski, C. (2022). Scientific misinformation and gender affirming care: Tools for providers on the front lines. *Journal of Adolescent Health, 71*(3), 251–253. https://doi.org/10.1016/j.jadohealth.2022.06.008

Olson, K. R., Durwood, L., DeMeules, M., & McLaughlin, K. A. (2016). Mental health of transgender children who are supported in their identities. *Pediatrics, 137*(3), e20153223. https://doi.org/10.1542/peds.2015-3223

Reisner, S. L., Vetters, R., Leclerc, M., Zaslow, S., Wolfrum, S., Shumer, D., & Mimiaga, M. J. (2015). Mental health of transgender youth in care at an adolescent urban community health center: A matched retrospective cohort study. *Journal of Adolescent Health, 56*(3), 274–279. https://doi.org/10.1016/j.jadohealth.2014.10.264

Restar, A. J. (2020). Methodological critique of Littman's (2018) parental-respondents accounts of "rapid-onset gender dysphoria." *Archives of Sexual Behavior, 49*(1), 61–66. https://doi.org/10.1007/s10508-019-1453-2

Rosenthal, S. M. (2021). Challenges in the care of transgender and gender-diverse youth: An endocrinologist's view. *Nature Reviews Endocrinology, 17*(10), 581–591. https://doi.org/10.1038/s41574-021-00535-9

Ryan, C., Huebner, D., Diaz, R. M., & Sanchez, J. (2009). Family rejection as a predictor of negative health outcomes in white and Latino lesbian, gay, and bisexual young adults. *Pediatrics, 123*(1), 346–352. https://doi.org/10.1542/peds.2007-3524

Ryan, C., Russell, S. T., Huebner, D., Diaz, R., & Sanchez, J. (2010). Family acceptance in adolescence and the health of LGBT young adults. *Journal of Child and Adolescent Psychiatric Nursing, 23*(4), 205–213. https://doi.org/10.1111/j.1744-6171.2010.00246.x

Spencer, K. G., Berg, D. R., Bradford, N. J., Vencill, J. A., Tellawi, G., & Rider, G. N. (2021). The gender-affirmative life span approach: A developmental model for clinical work with transgender and gender-diverse children, adolescents, and adults. *Psychotherapy, 58*(1), 37–49. https://doi.org/10.1037/pst0000363

Szilagyi, N. (2021). Transcending cultural and religious barriers: Working with gender-diverse youth and their families in the pandemic and beyond. *Journal of the American Academy of Child and Adolescent Psychiatry, 60*(10), S85. https://doi.org/10.1016/j.jaac.2021.07.357

Tankersley, A. P., Grafsky, E. L., Dike, J., & Jones, R. T. (2021). Risk and resilience factors for mental health among transgender and gender nonconforming (TGNC) youth: A systematic review. *Clinical Child and Family Psychology Review, 24*(2), 183–206. https://doi.org/10.1007/s10567-021-00344-6

Telfer, M. M., Tollit, M. A., Pace, C. C., & Pang, K. C. (2018). Australian standards of care and treatment guidelines for transgender and gender diverse children and adolescents. *The Medical Journal of Australia, 209*(3), 132–136. https://doi.org/10.5694/mja17.01044

Thornburgh, C., Kidd, K. M., Burnett, J. D., & Sequeira, G. M. (2020). Community-informed peer support for parents of gender-diverse youth. *Pediatrics, 146*(4), e20200571. https://doi.org/10.1542/peds.2020-0571

Travers, R., Bauer, G., Pyne, J., Bradley, K., Gale, L., & Papadimitriou, M. (2012). *Impacts of strong parental support for trans youth: A report prepared for Children's Aid Society of Toronto and Delisle Youth Services*. Trans PULSE. https://transpulseproject.ca/wp-content/uploads/2012/10/Impacts-of-Strong-Parental-Support-for-Trans-Youth-vFINAL.pdf

The Trevor Project. (2022, May). *Behaviors of supportive parents and caregivers for LGBTQ youth*. https://www.thetrevorproject.org/wp-content/uploads/2022/05/May-Research-Brief-Supportive-Caregiver-Behavior.pdf

Turban, J. L., Beckwith, N., Reisner, S. L., & Keuroghlian, A. S. (2020). Association between recalled exposure to gender identity conversion efforts and psychological distress and suicide attempts among transgender adults. *JAMA Psychiatry, 77*(1), 68–76. https://doi.org/10.1001/jamapsychiatry.2019.2285

Turban, J. L., Carswell, J., & Keuroghlian, A. S. (2018). Understanding pediatric patients who discontinue gender-affirming hormonal interventions. *JAMA Pediatrics, 172*(10), 903–904. https://doi.org/10.1001/jamapediatrics.2018.1817

Turban, J. L., & Keuroghlian, A. S. (2018). Dynamic gender presentations: Understanding transition and "de-transition" among transgender youth. *Journal of the American Academy of Child and Adolescent Psychiatry, 57*(7), 451–453. https://doi.org/10.1016/j.jaac.2018.03.016

Turban, J. L., Loo, S. S., Almazan, A. N., & Keuroghlian, A. S. (2021). Factors leading to "detransition" among transgender and gender diverse people in the United States: A mixed-methods analysis. *LGBT Health, 8*(4), 273–280. https://doi.org/10.1089/lgbt.2020.0437

Wahlig, J. L. (2015). Losing the child they thought they had: Therapeutic suggestions for an ambiguous loss perspective with parents of a transgender child. *Journal of GLBT Family Studies, 11*(4), 305–326. https://doi.org/10.1080/1550428X.2014.945676

Watson, R. J., Barnett, M. A., & Russell, S. T. (2016). Parent support matters for the educational success of sexual minorities. *Journal of GLBT Family Studies, 12*(2), 188–202. https://doi.org/10.1080/1550428X.2015.1028694

Wittlin, N. M., Kuper, L. E., & Olson, K. R. (2023). Mental health of transgender and gender diverse youth. *Annual Review of Clinical Psychology, 19*, 207–232. https://doi.org/10.1146/annurev-clinpsy-072220-020326

World Health Organization. (2019). *International statistical classification of diseases and related health problems* (11th ed.). https://icd.who.int/

10 NETWORKS OF CARE FOR TRANSGENDER AND GENDER DIVERSE YOUTH

CATELYN G. DEVLIN AND KAYDEN J. SCHUMACHER

Building and maintaining a network of professionals trained to support transgender and gender diverse (TGD) children, ranging from but not limited to teachers, school counselors, coaches, health care providers, spiritual leaders, cultural elders, social workers, and legal experts, is essential to TGD children's healthy development. Through an ecological framework, mental health providers play a key role in assessing the needs of and guiding clients and families in cultivating care networks to build their external and internal resilience factors and well-being. Providers also play a critical role in educating families and network members on evidence-based pediatric gender health care practices amidst growing misinformation and antitrans policies.

This chapter will discuss creating, building, and maintaining a well-informed, prudent, and committed network of professionals for TGD children, utilizing Urie Bronfenbrenner's (1979) ecological model of human development. The chapter will delve further into various areas of concentration and discuss the professionals to include in the network. Following the breakdown of each sector, the chapter will end by piecing together vital components within Bronfenbrenner's ecological model toward effecting change and advocating for TGD children.

https://doi.org/10.1037/0000494-011
Pediatric Gender Health Care: The Gender Affirmative Model Revisited, Second Edition, G. N. Rider, D. Ehrensaft, and C. St. Amand (Editors)

THEORETICAL FRAMEWORK: BRONFENBRENNER'S ECOLOGICAL MODEL

Bronfenbrenner's (1979) ecological systems theory (BEST) continues as a foundational perspective for mental health providers in understanding their young clients' worlds and experiences, identifying possible sources of harm and stress, and, more importantly, identifying possible solutions and sources of resilience within different arenas of a client's environment.

Functionally, BEST traditionally centers on the client as the targeted focal point encompassed by five standardized systems that grow larger in scope the further away they are from the client (Bronfenbrenner, 1979). While mental health providers may initially orient their focus around a client's *microsystem* (e.g., the client's innermost world and most immediate setting, such as a client's home or classroom environment, relationship with their parents, or relationship with their own chronic illness), the client's *mesosystem* (e.g., the relationships between two or more immediate settings or microsystems, like the dynamic between a client's home and school), *exosystem* (e.g., a client's relationship with their school or faith community), *macrosystem* (e.g., the client's experience of the laws that mandate their school attendance), and *chronosystem* (e.g., the client's shift in technology use from last year to the current assessment), all have equal bearing in the client's mental health and development (Bronfenbrenner, 1979, 2005). Like other systems theories, BEST emphasizes some key points:

- *Nothing happens in a vacuum*: If an event or change affects one system, often there is a ripple effect extending out in all directions to impact other systems (Crawford, 2020).
- There is limitless potential for *reciprocal interplay*, or mutual influence between individuals and their environments, within and between systems, regardless of size or scope, allowing small systems to impact larger systems (Bronfenbrenner, 1994).
- Because of the diversity of and interplay between systems, *equifinality* means multiple strategies can be utilized to achieve client goals. This endlessly creative approach can help identify clients' potential stressors, supports, risks, and opportunities (Crawford, 2020).

Within BEST, systems develop a *homeostasis* or steady state when systems can move and interact with each other in ways that are balanced and functional. A healthy system can be described as having *goodness of fit* between the client's needs and the environment's ability to sustainably meet those needs (Germain, 1973). Providers should help clients assess available *assets* within systems that can positively contribute to the child's development, well-being, and ability to adapt in healthy ways. Assets can be any type of resource available to the client, including their social support system (micro- and mesosystems) or laws and policies that can be leveraged to protect the client (macrosystems). Assets like supportive friends and relatives, therapy for the TGD child and their caregivers, participation in lesbian, gay, bisexual, transgender, queer, or questioning (LGBTQ+) communities and faith communities, and a comprehensive network of care providers can mitigate some of the stress and barriers common to TGD children and their families (see Spencer et al., 2019).

If there is a lack of fit between the client and their systems, available resources and resilience can be used to help the client and/or their systems *adapt* to create a better fit. Maladaptive exchanges can occur as systems find a better fit with one another, and sometimes those maladaptive behaviors can become part of the homeostasis. Homeostasis is generally self-perpetuating with multiple systems working to maintain it; subsequently, a homeostasis can be difficult to change. When events or changes disrupt the homeostasis, systems work to return to the former homeostasis or create a new one (Hearn, 1958, as cited in Staub-Bernasconi, 2009). For example, when a child shares that they are TGD, the child's ecological system may be temporarily disrupted as everyone adjusts to new ways of supporting the child, but eventually the child's ecological system adapts to the child being TGD and the child's gender blends into the background, much like how their gender existed when the child was assumed to be cisgender. During a crisis, such as pediatric gender health care bans, homeostasis is an important trauma-informed consideration to assess and support the child and their family.

BEST centers the child as the active agent in their development, juxtaposed against formidable and institutional structures like law, policies, and culture (Bronfenbrenner, 1979). BEST was developed in part as a response to a lack of fit between the lived experiences of diverse children and the contemporary child development theories and positivist methodologies that regularly used samples of White children from families with higher socioeconomic status to establish what was considered developmentally appropriate and what was considered other (see Bronfenbrenner, 2005; Spencer & Swanson, 2013). Rather than helping clients adapt to an inappropriate standard, mental health providers can help clients adapt to the stress of not meeting society's standards while actively working to change the standard—not only for their clients but for their own ethical and empirical mental health practice.

Phenomenological Variant of Ecological Systems Theory and Black Feminist Thought

In light of the disproportionate violence that Black trans women, trans women of color, and Black families face within the child welfare, juvenile justice, and criminal justice systems, it is recommended that providers seek out culturally specific and justice-informed resilience resources as part of their ecological assessments and therapeutic services for clients. Further, while Black feminist thought is by and for Black women and Black families, many of the practices may be helpful to non-Black TGD children and their families due to White supremacy's enforcement of cisheteronormativity and the cultural adaptations families may make when losing cisgender privilege through trans identity disclosure (see Collins, 2008; Spencer & Swanson, 2013; Spencer et al., 2019). Two models recommended include the phenomenological variant of ecological systems theory (PVEST; Spencer, 1995, 2006) and Black feminist thought.

Margaret Beale Spencer's (1995, 2006) PVEST focuses on the client's perception of themself, their networks of support, and their lived experiences across intersecting cultures and structural systems. Through PVEST, a client's identity development is fostered through the client's own meaning-making of their perception and experience of their microsystem, mesosystem, exosystem, macrosystem, and chronosystem. This client-centered approach considers positionality in how the model is being applied, reflecting how the client sees the structure and systems of support as opposed to how the practitioner sees it for the client, which can be especially important for cisgender practitioners. In this way, PVEST supports client empowerment with the support of the mental health practitioner and can be especially helpful for TGD children working to understand their relationship to gender and how they navigate the world, how others interpret them, and how they interpret themselves. As an ecological approach, PVEST helps youth hold multiple ecosystems at once to process how their experience of their gender, race, ethnicity, socioeconomic status, religion, abilities, and other characteristics interact with one another within themselves and how their environment interacts with those intersecting attributes. As part of their healthy child development, the insights the child arrives at in examining and making meaning of their multiple systems is invaluable. PVEST's emphasis on "reality in context and truth acknowledging" (Spencer et al., 2019, p. 103) is key in helping youth understand and give weight and validity to their own experiences and the experiences of others, including when others' experiences and perspectives are dramatically different than the youth's own experiences. Spencer et al.'s (2019) PVEST can be used as an advanced, critical, and more culturally humble form of BEST due to its use of intersectionality as an analytical tool to explore and understand diverse identities within individuals and its emphasis on child development, identity formation, meaning-making, and the balancing of ecological risks and assets "decreas[ing] overall vulnerability . . . [and] reclaiming a threatened future" (p. 106).

An important aspect of Black feminist epistemology is the reverence given to the wisdom gained by lived experience (Collins, 2008). Trusting one's lived experience is seen as a key part of wisdom and survival, and a dialectical, call-and-response approach of holding two seemingly contradictory thoughts as both valid is an important part of finding integrity, self-definition, and agency within oneself and navigating relationships with others in a way that respects their lived experiences. This meaning-making, trust of experience, and dialectical respect of diverse opinions contributes to self-definition, a key aspect of identity development for children and adolescents and an essential part of liberation within Black feminist thought (Collins, 2008; Velez & Spencer, 2018). Applied to TGD clients, PVEST and Black feminist thought provide opportunities to assess internalized oppression and dialogue between how the world defines them and how they define themselves. With ecological theories like BEST and PVEST originating in attachment theory, the caregivers of trans youth helping youth co-regulate during times of distress, affirming their experiences and emotions, and supporting youth as they navigate a challenging world also fit well within attachment and Black youth development frameworks (Stern et al., 2022).

Overall, PVEST's focus on a child's identity development and its associated behavioral outcomes is a key feature of Black feminist thought and Patricia Hill Collins's (2008) power of self-definition and "lived experience as a criterion of meaning" (p. 275). PVEST can be used as one of a mental health provider's "strategies for neutralizing intersectionality effects and maximizing resiliency outcomes" (Spencer et al., 2019, p. 104; also see Spencer & Swanson, 2013). Although PVEST fits well within Black feminist thought and is tailored to be a more culturally competent approach for Black clients, PVEST is recommended for practitioners working with youth from any background as a theoretical framework and practice tool based on the centrality of youth identity development in light of their experiences of discrimination tied to their experience of their gender (Velez & Spencer, 2018). Because of the disproportionate impact on Black TGD people and families, these practices are being highlighted and elevated to speak to evidence-based solutions tailored to Black clients and their families when they are otherwise often neglected by mainstream psychology and publication (Goldenberg et al., 2019).

BUILDING AND PROTECTING NETWORK PARTNERS: SYSTEMS-WIDE CONSIDERATIONS

Supporting TGD children and their families requires a coordinated, systems-level approach. Each institution that intersects with the child's life—legal, educational, medical, mental health, professional, and spiritual—can either help or hinder access to affirming care. The following sections outline system- and partner-specific considerations for building and protecting a supportive network of care, with attention to the ethical, practical, and collaborative strategies mental health providers can implement across settings.

Legal System

Within their role assessing and treating the client's mental health in the midst of antitrans government attacks, mental health providers should ask caregivers of TGD children if they have an attorney to address potential legal challenges related to caring for their TGD child. If caregivers do not have an attorney, mental health providers can direct them to local LGBTQ+ organizations or the Lambda Legal Help Desk. Mental health providers can work with lawyers to help families access and create resources such as a *safe folder*[1] (a collection of essential documents, affirmations, and plans), establish a relocation plan, and identify contacts for out-of-state support in anticipation of restricted local care (Trans Youth Family Allies, 2025). Tools such as a card that includes name (legal and nonlegal), pronouns, contact numbers and addresses of relevant people and organizations associated with their care, and potentially notable personal information like their social security number, may also help safeguard rights and access to care for children involved in protective services. A card like this could help support the young person if in a time of crisis and/or when navigating multiple systems that ask many questions they may not have answers to.

Despite the fears clients and families may have in creating a documentation trail via gender marker changes, it is critical for clients to have government documentation that reflects who they are, their name, and, to a certain extent, their current appearance (Advocates for Trans Equality, 2024a; Lambda Legal, 2024). Mental health providers play an important role in ensuring youth have access to resources to help them change their gender markers, often led by local LGBTQ+ organizations or legal clinics, and in helping clients process their experience of the gender marker update. If clients are unable to update their name and gender marker legally, mental health providers can advocate to the clients' network of care partners to use the clients' chosen name and

[1]An example of a safe folder list, along with information on its use and storage, can be located in Appendix 10.1.

pronouns to the fullest extent possible. Although some providers may say they are required to use certain names for legal purposes, mental health providers can work with partners to identify creative workarounds to minimize the harmful effects of dysphoric names and gender markers, and they can work with clients on treatment approaches to minimize client distress from seemingly unavoidable or accidental misgendering moments.

Mental health providers play a vital role in the ongoing legal fight for trans rights by intervening before rules and laws are passed. These professionals are ethically obligated to resolve conflicts between what is in the client's best interests and well-being, human rights, and fights for justice and what is legally binding (Coleman et al., 2022). Advocacy is an important way mental health providers can resolve the conflicts between their ethical obligations and the laws, regulations, and other governing authorities that attempt to ban pediatric gender health care and force providers to discriminate against LGBTQ+ clients in treatment options (American Psychological Association [APA], 2024a, 2024b; Toth, 2023a, 2023b). Providers should see the APA (2017) *Ethical Principles of Psychologists and Code of Conduct* (APA Ethics Code; particularly Standard 1.02, Conflicts Between Ethics and Law, Regulations, or Other Governing Legal Authority; and Standard 3.01, Unfair Discrimination), the American Counseling Association (ACA; 2014) *Code of Ethics* (Section A.7.a: Advocacy), the American School Counselor Association (ASCA; 2022) *Ethical Standards for School Counselors*, and the National Association of Social Workers (NASW; 2021) *Code of Ethics* (Standard 6, Social Workers' Ethical Responsibilities to the Broader Society).

Mental health providers working with TGD children should also ensure their malpractice insurance is up to date, and they should stay connected with resources on any changes to malpractice or health care insurance related to pediatric gender health care (Georges et al., 2024; Senate Finance Committee–Majority Staff, 2024). Professional organizations often have resources on malpractice or health care insurance changes and can provide opportunities to advocate for trans-inclusive insurance policies (Advocates for Trans Equality, 2024b). Consult with your local, state, and national APA, ACA, ASCA, or NASW chapters.

Educational System

The traditional school system is not inherently designed to cater to the unique needs of TGD children (Cohen et al., 2023; Horton, 2023; Watters, 2015). Taking a proactive stance in establishing a support system within the educational microsystem involves ongoing training and professional development, ideally led and created by TGD individuals and organizations (Coleman et al., 2022). This approach aligns with Bronfenbrenner's (1979) concept of the mesosystem, emphasizing the interconnectedness between the educational environment and the TGD community (Guy-Evans, 2023). Educational professionals often benefit from training programs offered by LGBTQ+ organizations (Russell et al., 2021; Soyei, 2019), regardless of the school type, emphasizing the critical role of engagement with the LGBTQ+ community and organizations within the mesosystem. Training for teachers, counselors, and psychologists may be provided by a local LGBTQ+ nonprofit organization, illustrating the interconnectedness of the microsystem and the mesosystem. This training may incorporate approaches for normalizing gender diversity in school, including acknowledging pronouns, implementing gender-neutral facilities, modeling gender-neutral uniform or dress code options, discussing First Amendment freedom of expression protections TGD youth have, and describing privacy protections under the Family Educational Rights and Privacy Act (FERPA; 1974) that prohibit disclosing sexual orientation, gender identity, and expression (SOGIE) status or medical records without caregiver consent (Advocates for Trans Equality, 2024c; American Civil Liberties Union, 2024; U.S. Department of Health and Human Services, 2024).

After educational professionals receive initial training on basic vocabulary and common issues faced by TGD children, it is crucial for them to acknowledge the diversity among children, recognizing individual differences within the microsystem, and for training to continue throughout the school year. Each child possesses unique needs that require tailored approaches to suit the educational environment effectively. Once educational professionals are initially educated on one aspect of a child's identity, they should recognize the intersections and crossroads of a child's larger positionality and approach such a positionality with humility and aim for understanding.

Throughout these processes, specific educational professionals, such as a school counselor, school psychologist, teacher, or, ideally, TGD educator, can serve as a focal point for a TGD child. By acting as a point person and a bridge to other providers, this professional becomes a valuable part of the network of care providers, ensuring ongoing support for the child's needs and facilitating effective communication of needs and interventions to other necessary stakeholders. Simultaneously, it offers a safety point for the child in moments of stress, such as when a bullying incident has just occurred. A prominent example of such a point person is a school nurse in a public school setting, bridging the gap between the educational microsystem and the medical microsystem in supporting TGD children in a school environment with various educational professionals and a medical environment made up of a child's general practitioner, gender clinic, or even psychiatrist. Possessing confidential, student-specific information under FERPA, the school nurse can use this information to link in necessary stakeholders and approach the student's needs in an informed and equitable way. However, navigating the complexities of disclosing confidential information while ensuring protection and intervention in cases of harm can be challenging, which is why collaboration and open honest communication among trusted stakeholders is essential in supporting TGD kids.

Medical System

In the United States, 26 states have banned best practices for pediatric gender health care as of November 2024, representing 47% of the total population and 49% of children younger than age 18 (Children's Bureau, 2024; Movement Advancement Project, 2024;[2] U.S. Census Bureau, 2022). However, these 26 states also represent 53% of all U.S. children living in poverty and 60% of all Black children in the United States (Children's Bureau, 2024). Residing in a state with banned care results in unequal expenses in accessing care: A report by the Campaign for Southern Equality found that traveling to a safe state for regular doctor's appointments costs approximately $300 to $900 per trip in airfare or gas and mileage, lodging and meals, and child care expenses (Chinn et al., 2024). Loose estimates indicate that moving to a safer state costs $1,000 to $12,000 in initial relocation expenses, which is beyond many clients' capacity (Declan, 2025; DePillis, 2024). Relocating one's family to escape pediatric gender health care bans or routinely traveling out of state for regular care is financially unfeasible for many; yet 47% of transgender adults report having considered relocating due to anti-LGBTQ+ state legislation (James et al., 2024). Some organizations such as the Campaign for Southern Equality and Elevate Access provide cash and in-kind assistance for families traveling out of state for care. However, there has been significant service interruption due to high demand and dwindling resources for similar cash and in-kind travel assistance programs for abortion access in 2023 and 2024, demonstrating the difficulty of sustaining interstate in-person care access (Goldhill, 2024).

Bans on medically necessary health care have had a chilling effect on providers, driving many providers out of state and creating a disproportionate decrease in the pipeline of new medical doctors' applications for residencies in states with bans (Melhado, 2023; Orgera & Grover, 2024). The enforcement of these bans has seen doctors and hospitals sued and investigated, even before the bans take legal effect (*Abbott v. Doe,* 2024; Texas Attorney General, 2024).

---

[2]The Movement Advancement Project (MAP) website (https://www.lgbtmap.org) is an important tool for families, detailing state-by-state comparisons on sociopolitical climates and legal protections. MAP's up-to-date resources can assist families considering travel or relocation plans.

Antitrans discrimination is already associated with avoiding preventive and emergency medical care, and bans are likely to complicate that avoidance for vulnerable families (see Reisner et al., 2014). With research showing a statistically significant increase in suicide attempts among TGD young people ages 13 to 17 within 12 months following legislation enactment, mental health providers should work with local LGBTQ+ organizations and medical providers to protect medical care by practicing network safety and privacy best practices and helping families access safe medical care for TGD youth (Austin et al., 2022; Lee et al., 2024). Refer to Chapter 2 of this volume for more specific information on medical interventions included in pediatric gender health care.

Mental Health System

Building a network of mental health care advocates for TGD children requires professionals spanning a range of specialties to be involved, each playing critical roles. This interdisciplinary team ideally needs to comprise mental health professionals such as social workers, therapists, counselors, psychologists, and psychiatrists. Additionally, the team may include family doctors, gender clinic doctors, nurses, and various specialists, among others. A robust team can harness the collaborative and collective efforts of professionals' contributions and expertise. Given the structural and institutional barriers inherent in the larger system, as well as the wide range of mental health issues faced by TGD children, assembling a comprehensive team becomes imperative (K. R. Olson et al., 2016; Rafferty et al., 2018). Kristina R. Olson and colleagues (2016) found that when TGD children have access to mental health supports when needed and the ability to socially transition, they have "developmentally normative levels of depression and anxiety" (p. 5). Infrastructure-related considerations, such as inconsistent insurance coverage, limited numbers of trained pediatric gender care providers, financial constraints, geographical accessibility, legislative protocols, and specialty services, further compound the complexity of gaining access to mental health care for TGD children (Gridley et al., 2016). Moreover, intersecting cultural factors like religion and language add considerations that often are inadequately addressed (Yun et al., 2019). TGD youth who seek mental health care without the support of their parents face additional challenges in consenting to and affording mental health care.

Despite the need for mental health support for TGD children, legislative bans on pediatric gender health care have profound mental health effects on TGD children and their families (Abreu, Sostre, Gonzalez, Lockett, & Matsuno, 2022; Abreu, Sostre, Gonzalez, Lockett, Matsuno, & Mosley, 2022; Kidd et al., 2021; Novotney, 2023). These bans cultivate an atmosphere of fear and uncertainty, leading to heightened stress, anxiety, and feelings of isolation among affected individuals, not to mention a heightening of internalized transphobia. Anticipated attacks on pediatric gender mental health care exacerbate these challenges, jeopardizing the availability and quality of care for TGD children. Efforts to restrict or prohibit pediatric gender health care treatments not only compromise the autonomy and well-being of these individuals but also perpetuate harmful stigmatization and discrimination. Consequently, without access to pediatric gender health care, the number of TGD young people facing deleterious mental health effects from erasure and an outlaw of care will likely increase drastically. Fears for their child's present and future mental health, along with fears regarding access to medically necessary health care, are a waking nightmare for thousands of parents of TGD youth in the United States (Herman et al., 2022). Mental health providers can raise awareness of the need for accessible mental health care for TGD youth and their families as part of psychoeducation and advocacy. Through collaborative efforts, including the engagement of diverse professionals, the enhancement of infrastructural support, and the implementation of comprehensive privacy protections, stakeholders can work collaboratively to promote and protect access to pediatric gender health care.

Institutional and Professional Collaboration

The impact of legislative bans on pediatric gender health care extends beyond the realm of clinical practice and into the academic and educational domain (Mousavian et al., 2024). These bans often result in a chilling effect on research and publication, stifling academic inquiry into the mental health needs and experiences of TGD children and impeding the advancement of knowledge and understanding in this critical area (McNamara et al., 2023, 2024). Restricting access to research opportunities and clinical experiences with TGD populations undermines the training and expertise of future professionals (Shipman & Martin, 2019). Without the ability to study and work openly with TGD clients, professionals are deprived of learning experiences essential to their competence and efficacy in providing care.

Professional organizations also have a vital role in this network. By releasing clear, simple, easily accessible, and widely publicized best practices, ethical guides, and approaches grounded in cultural humility, these organizations can maximize the safety of clients and professionals alike (APA, 2015; Marshall et al., 2022). Professional organizations can drive the dissemination of best practices across various sectors of the mental health field, including clinical practice, research, education, and policy development. Collaborative efforts among these organizations can foster a culture of inclusivity and support, ensuring that TGD children receive the care and advocacy they deserve.

Institutional collaboration between universities and professional organizations can also advance research, education, and advocacy initiatives, contributing to the advancement of knowledge and services for TGD children.

Spiritual Life

A TGD child's spiritual life can be a fulcrum to their well-being. The involvement of spiritual professionals including clergy (e.g., imam, priest, pastor, elder, or rabbi), counselors, and community leaders can considerably impact a TGD child's ecosystem (Bockting & Cesaretti, 2001; Chan, 2017; Paige, 2022; Rubano, 2016). Spiritual professionals can play an essential role in producing TGD inclusive spaces (Paige, 2022; Rubano, 2016). This involves developing spiritual outlets and gatherings that incorporate and promote understanding and acceptance of diverse gender identities and expressions (Rubano, 2016). By including inclusive language and curriculum materials within spiritual spaces, spiritual leaders contribute to a positive and affirming environment for TGD children and their families. Additionally, they can offer counseling and support to TGD children and their families, creating a sense of belonging within their spiritual communities (Chan, 2017), which can go a long way in combating religious trauma often experienced by TGD individuals.

Within different religions and denominations exist some branches that are encouraging and affirming; caregivers may need to explore options within their faith traditions to locate supportive religious services. Family Acceptance Project (2025) and the Human Rights Campaign (2025) provide lists of affirming faith resources within any major religious tradition. The PFLAG website (https://pflag.org) lists several summer camps across the United States that provide opportunities for spiritual growth and development within a supportive community. Mental health providers can help children and caregivers identify affirming spiritual resources, including by providing resources on affirming spiritual traditions, encouraging caregivers and clients to expect clarity from faith organizations on whether the organization fully affirms the child's gender identity, and helping caregivers know that certain phrases associated with SOGIE change efforts (e.g., conversion therapy, reparative therapy, and sexual identity therapy) may be harmful and should be avoided to minimize the harm associated with SOGIE change efforts and rejecting behaviors (Haldeman, 2024; Ryan, 2021; Turban et al., 2020). Mental health providers can also help children and families evaluate the positive impact spiritual resources may have in a way that is tailored to each child and family. The APA (2021) prohibits psychologists from practicing SOGIE change efforts, and mental health providers should not make referrals to spiritual resources that may expose the family to harmful conversion therapy practices.

Using Bronfenbrenner's (1979) ecological model, within the mesosystem, the alliance between spiritual leaders, medical professionals, and mental health experts becomes crucial. For TGD children, navigating their identity often involves a multidimensional approach incorporating numerous identities all coalescing. Spiritual leaders can work together with health care professionals in supplying resources and support that tackle both the spiritual and medical aspects of a child's journey. By engaging in communication and understanding between these systems, spiritual professionals contribute to a mesosystem that acknowledges and accommodates the diverse needs of TGD children.

CASE EXAMPLE

A Black, nonbinary youth,[3] age 9, is exhibiting symptoms of depression, experiencing gender dysphoria, and desiring puberty blockers. The youth lives in Texas with two married caregivers and two siblings in a middle-class family in the suburbs. One caregiver is a school teacher who is worried about a child abuse/neglect investigation if they pursue pediatric gender health care from an out-of-state provider, knowing that they would be placed on unpaid administrative leave if a child abuse investigation is opened against them. The caregiver is a Black adult and is concerned about how anti-Black discrimination in the child welfare system increases their risk of being reported, being investigated, and having a child abuse allegation unreasonably substantiated. In addition to their fears for their TGD child and their parental rights over their child, they are concerned about how a child abuse investigation may impact their other children, their career as an educator, their income, and their ability to pay their mortgage and other expenses. The other caregiver demonstrates hesitancy to affirm the child's TGD identity.

The mental health provider meets with the TGD youth and their family to complete an EcoMap[4] to assess present and potential assets and sources of support, along with present and potential sources of stress. The provider uses a PVEST framework and centers the EcoMap's microsystem on the TGD youth (the client). In private sessions, the provider asks the client about different parts of their identities and how the client sees themself. The provider also asks

---

[3]This case study example is fictionalized and does not include any real-life identifying information that connects to a real client or their confidentiality.
[4]See Figure 10A.1 in Appendix 10.2 for a description and example of an EcoMap.

the client about their environment, including sources of stress and support, how their environment impacts the client's experience of themself, and how their environment affects the client's behavior and outcomes. During sessions, the provider and the client explore the client's perception of the feedback the client receives from their environment and the client's potential responses, the client's experiences of inequity related to their identities, the coping strategies the client has used before and strategies the client may use moving forward when experiencing and resisting oppressive feedback in their environments, and the agency the client can have in their responses to their environment, their self-perception, and their present and future outcomes and goals. The provider supports the client in the meaning-making of their own experiences, their perception of their environment, and their self-definition both within and regardless of their environment (A. B. Olson et al., 2023; Spencer et al., 2019; Velez & Spencer, 2018). The provider also practices their own mindfulness regarding their position of power in supporting rather than leading the client and the biases they have in delivering an intersectional modality.

Additionally, the provider meets privately with the child's caregivers to add to the client's EcoMap by exploring sources of stress and support for the child and family from the caregiver's perspective. This conversation can illuminate other service providers that would be important for the child's network of care providers, and the provider can discuss stressors and sources of support for the caregivers as individuals. The provider practices truth acknowledging with the caregivers and support their agency in their own experience of the child's life and their environment at-large. Ideally, in the first meeting when an EcoMap is initiated, the mental health provider will also discuss and provide resources to the caregiver regarding the following:

- a legal help desk or list of vetted attorneys, where the caregivers can review how to keep the youth and family safe as they pursue medically necessary care for their child, including concerns over potential child abuse investigations impacting their employment and the risks of pursuing medical care outside of the state;
- a list of in-person and online support groups of other parents of TGD children and youth;
- a list of medical professionals with whom caregivers could consult on medically necessary pediatric gender health care for their child;
- a list of organizations providing in-kind and cash assistance to travel out of state to access medically necessary pediatric gender health care

(e.g., emergency cash assistance grants from the Campaign for Southern Equality and travel support from Elevated Access);

- a safe folder containing a list of needed items along with resources, including templates for medical records privacy request letters, guides for parents on TGD children's rights at school and with the child welfare system, and cards youth can carry with them at school detailing their rights and how to respond to child abuse investigation attempts made when the child is at school; and
- a list of affirming spiritual resources representing diverse religious and racial identities (for more information, see the faith resources information shared by the Texas Foster Youth Connections, n.d.).

The mental health provider can help the client and caregivers assemble a network of care providers and provide education on medically necessary pediatric gender mental health care that professionals or other adults may need, as the provider is able. The provider can initiate care team meetings and speak directly with other care providers, with the consent of the caregivers, to ensure the child has a network of committed, prudent, technologically and legally secure, and well-trained professionals to support the TGD youth and their family as the child grows and develops with resilience and authenticity.

CONCLUSION

According to Bronfenbrenner's (1979) ecological model, multiple systems interact to influence a child's development: the microsystem, mesosystem, exosystem, macrosystem, and chronosystem. In building a network of care advocates within mental health for TGD children, professionals are called upon to play diverse and critical roles across these systems. This multidisciplinary team often comprises mental health professionals such as social workers, therapists, counselors, psychologists, and psychiatrists, but it can also encompass family doctors, gender clinic doctors, nurses, and other specialists. These professionals each contribute their expertise in various ways to tailor treatment and ongoing support to TGD children. This chapter highlights the requirement of a potentially far-reaching and unique team in order to meet the care needs of TGD children. The pressures of navigating structural and institutional barriers and addressing the wide range of issues TGD children face necessitate a diverse and specialized team. Infrastructural elements such as insurance coverage, health care systems, financial considerations, geographic access to care, legislative frameworks, specialty, and mores add another layer of complexity because children cannot seek care independently. These elements align with the exosystem in Bronfenbrenner's model, influencing the child's immediate environment indirectly but significantly.

As such, creating a network of care professionals for TGD children requires a multifaceted approach that includes mental health professionals, family doctors, gender clinic doctors, nurses, and other specialists. This network must navigate complex infrastructural elements and address the significant challenges posed by legislative bans and anticipated attacks on pediatric gender health care. By leveraging the strengths and opportunities held by network partners, including individual providers and institutional assets, mental health providers can build a comprehensive and inclusive support system that empowers and advocates for the holistic well-being of TGD children. By integrating Bronfenbrenner's ecological model with intersectional tools and frameworks, this network can effectively address the diverse and nuanced needs of TGD children, ensuring their development within a supportive and affirming environment.

APPENDIX 10.1: CREATING A SAFE FOLDER

Once a caregiver suspects their child might be transgender, it is recommended they assemble a safe folder of important documentation that provides corroborated evidence of their child's gender journey and their family's stability and caregiving practices. Trans Youth Family Allies (2025) recommends having two safe folders, one at home and another in a secure location away from the home (e.g., a safety deposit box), with both files being updated regularly.

SAFE FOLDER: LIST, STORAGE, AND USES

Based on resources from Trans Youth Family Allies (2025), a safe folder should include the following:

- a letter from the child's medical health care provider affirming the child's gender identity based on their professional assessment
- a letter from the child's mental health care provider affirming the child's gender identity and the stability of their family based on their professional assessment
- letters from any other medical or mental health care providers affirming the child's gender identity

- copies of letters submitted to health care providers prohibiting the disclosure of medical records without caregivers' permission
- letters from family members, friends, teachers, clergy, coaches, or other adults who know the child and child's family and can speak to the child's gender expression and caregivers' parenting abilities (Trans Youth Family Allies recommends that letters include how long the person has known the child and family, along with the person's current contact information, and that families have at least three of these letters written by adults connected to the family.)
- photographs or videos of the child or artwork and writing created by the child where the child expresses their gender identity (Having documentation from various points in the child's life can be helpful to demonstrate the child's sense of their gender.)
- legal documents such as birth certificates, government identification, and name change documentation if applicable
- Know Your Rights guides for transgender and gender diverse youth and their caregivers, including their rights at school, with medical providers, with child welfare professionals, and in other settings
- contact information for legal help desks (e.g., Lambda Legal or the American Civil Liberties Union) and mental health helplines (e.g., Trans Lifeline and The Trevor Project)

If available, caregivers can also include home studies documenting the family's stability. Templates for these documents can be found at Trans Youth Family Allies (2025) and at local LGBTQ+ organizations. These organizations have most up-to-date resources tailored to specific geopolitical communities, and they may also include sample documents tailored to the caregivers' geopolitical and legal systems.

APPENDIX 10.2: EcoMapping

Figure 10A.1 depicts potential interconnections for a hypothetical 9-year-old transgender young person. The arrows indicate the various systems and their connection with this young person. The double-sided arrows indicate the relationship goes both ways. The dashed arrows indicate areas where there may be some tension or lack of support for trans-affirmative care for this young person. The gray circle indicates individuals within this youth's microsystem that may impact the larger mesosystem and macrosystem.

FIGURE 10A.1. EcoMap Example

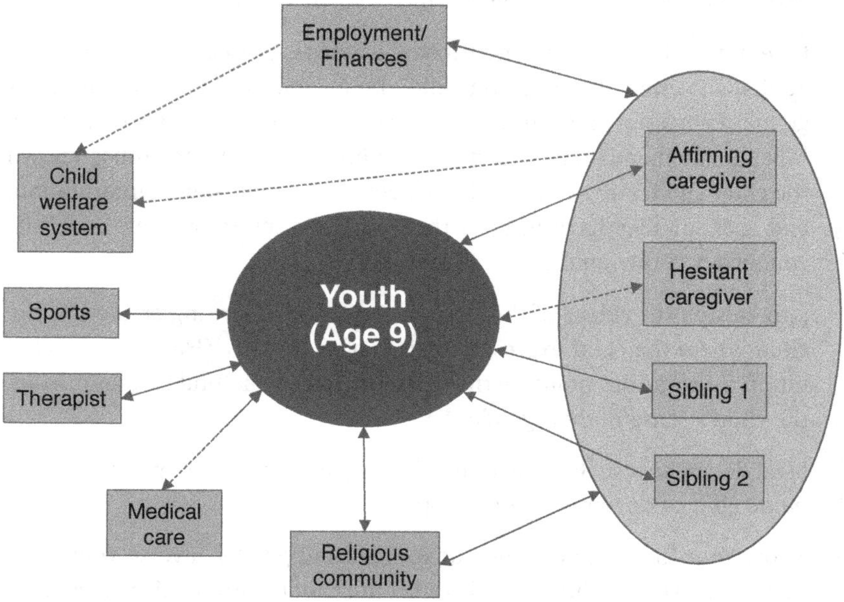

REFERENCES

Abbott v. Doe, 691 S.W.3d 55 (2024).

Abreu, R. L., Sostre, J. P., Gonzalez, K. A., Lockett, G. M., & Matsuno, E. (2022). "*I am afraid for those kids who might find death preferable*": Parental figures' reactions and coping strategies to bans on gender-affirming care for transgender and gender diverse youth. *Psychology of Sexual Orientation and Gender Diversity*, *9*(4), 500–510. https://doi.org/10.1037/sgd0000495

Abreu, R. L., Sostre, J. P., Gonzalez, K. A., Lockett, G. M., Matsuno, E., & Mosley, D. V. (2022). Impact of gender-affirming care bans on transgender and gender diverse youth: Parental figures' perspective. *Journal of Family Psychology*, *36*(5), 643–652. https://doi.org/10.1037/fam0000987

Advocates for Trans Equality. (2024a). *ID documents center*. https://transequality.org/documents

Advocates for Trans Equality. (2024b). *Know your rights: Schools*. https://transequality.org/resources/know-your-rights-schools

Advocates for Trans Equality. (2024c). *Medical organizational statements*. https://transhealthproject.org/resources/medical-organization-statements/

American Civil Liberties Union. (2024). *Know your rights: Students' rights*. https://www.aclu.org/know-your-rights/students-rights#lgbtq-student-rights

American Counseling Association. (2014). *Code of ethics*. https://www.counseling.org/docs/default-source/default-document-library/ethics/2014-aca-code-of-ethics.pdf

American Psychological Association. (2015). Guidelines for psychological practice with transgender and gender nonconforming people. *American Psychologist, 70*(9), 832–864. https://doi.org/10.1037/a0039906

American Psychological Association. (2017). *Ethical principles of psychologists and code of conduct* (2002, amended effective June 1, 2010, and January 1, 2017). https://www.apa.org/ethics/code/

American Psychological Association. (2021). *APA resolution on gender identity change efforts*. https://www.apa.org/about/policy/resolution-gender-identity-change-efforts.pdf

American Psychological Association. (2024a). *APA policy statement on affirming evidence-based inclusive care for transgender, gender diverse, and nonbinary individuals, addressing misinformation, and the role of psychological practice and science.* https://www.apa.org/about/policy/transgender-nonbinary-inclusive-care.pdf

American Psychological Association. (2024b). *Criminalizing gender affirmative care with minors: Suggested discussion points with resources to oppose transgender exclusion bills.* https://www.apa.org/topics/lgbtq/gender-affirmative-care

American School Counselor Association. (2022). *ASCA ethical standards for school counselors*. https://www.schoolcounselor.org/getmedia/44f30280-ffe8-4b41-9ad8-f15909c3d164/EthicalStandards2022.pdf

Austin, A., Craig, S. L., D'Souza, S., & McInroy, L. B. (2022). Suicidality among transgender youth: Elucidating the role of interpersonal risk factors. *Journal of Interpersonal Violence, 37*(5–6), NP2696–NP2718. https://doi.org/10.1177/0886260520915554

Bockting, W. O., & Cesaretti, C. (2001). Spirituality, transgender identity, and coming out. *Journal of Sex Education and Therapy, 26*(4), 291–300. https://doi.org/10.1080/01614576.2001.11074435

Bronfenbrenner, U. (1979). *The ecology of human development: Experiments by nature and design*. Harvard University Press.

Bronfenbrenner, U. (1994). Ecological models of human development. In T. N. Postlethwaite & T. Husen (Eds.), *International encyclopaedia of education* (2nd ed., Vol. 3, pp. 37–43). Elsevier.

Bronfenbrenner, U. (Ed.). (2005). *Making human beings human: Bioecological perspectives on human development*. Sage.

Chan, C. D. (2017). A critical analysis of systemic influences on spiritual development for LGBTQ+ youth. *Journal of Child and Adolescent Counseling, 3*(3), 146–163. https://doi.org/10.1080/23727810.2017.1341795

Children's Bureau. (2024). *Child welfare outcomes report data: Child population data.* https://cwoutcomes.acf.hhs.gov/cwodatasite/population/index

Chinn, E., Polaski, A., & Hartheimer, H. (2024). *How far? The extreme travel burden of bans on medically necessary care for transgender youth*. Campaign for Southern Equality. https://southernequality.org/howfar/

Cohen, S. S., Duarte, B. J., & Ross, J. (2023). Finding home in a hopeless place: Schools as sites of heteronormativity. *Equity & Excellence in Education, 56*(1–2), 100–113. https://doi.org/10.1080/10665684.2022.2158394

Coleman, E., Radix, A. E., Bouman, W. P., Brown, G. R., de Vries, A. L. C., Deutsch, M. B., Ettner, R., Fraser, L., Goodman, M., Green, J., Hancock, A. B., Johnson, T. W., Karasic, D. H., Knudson, G. A., Leibowitz, S. F., Meyer-Bahlburg, H. F. L., Monstrey, S. J., Motmans, J., Nahata, L., . . . Arcelus, J. (2022). Standards of care for the health of transgender and gender diverse people, version 8. *International*

Journal of Transgender Heath, 23(Suppl. 1), S1–S259. https://doi.org/10.1080/26895269.2022.2100644

Collins, P. H. (2008). *Black feminist thought: Knowledge, consciousness, and the politics of empowerment* (3rd ed.). Routledge.

Crawford, M. (2020). Ecological systems theory: Exploring the development of the theoretical framework as conceived by Bronfenbrenner. *Journal of Public Health Issues and Practices Volume, 4*(2), 170–175. https://doi.org/10.33790/jphip1100170

Declan, L. (2025, July 16). *The price of protection: LGBTQ+ families and the cost of moving*. News Is Out. https://newsisout.com/2025/06/the-price-of-protection-lgbtq-families-and-the-cost-of-moving/32454/

DePillis, L. (2024, July 11). For L.G.B.T.Q. people, moving to friendlier states comes with a cost. *The New York Times*. https://www.nytimes.com/2024/07/11/business/economy/lgbtq-moving-cost.html

Family Acceptance Project. (2025). *Faith-based resources*. https://lgbtqfamilyacceptance.org/faith-based-resources/

Family Educational Rights and Privacy Act of 1974, 20 U.S.C. § 1232g (1974). https://www.law.cornell.edu/uscode/text/20/1232g

Georges, E., Brown, E. C. B., & Cohen, R. S. (2024). Prohibition of gender-affirming care as a form of child maltreatment: Reframing the discussion. *Pediatrics, 153*(1), e2023064292. https://doi.org/10.1542/peds.2023-064292

Germain, C. B. (1973). An ecological perspective in casework practice. *Social Casework, 54*(6), 323–330. https://doi.org/10.1177/104438947305400601

Goldenberg, T., Jadwin-Cakmak, L., Popoff, E., Reisner, S. L., Campbell, B. A., & Harper, G. W. (2019). Stigma, gender affirmation, and primary healthcare use among Black transgender youth. *Journal of Adolescent Health, 65*(4), 483–490. https://doi.org/10.1016/j.jadohealth.2019.04.029

Goldhill, O. (2024, January 23). *Abortion funds run short of money as demand soars and donations fall*. STAT. https://www.statnews.com/2024/01/23/abortion-fund-warning-demand-up-donations-down/

Gridley, S. J., Crouch, J. M., Evans, Y., Eng, W., Antoon, E., Lyapustina, M., Schimmel-Bristow, A., Woodward, J., Dundon, K., Schaff, R., McCarty, C., Ahrens, K., & Breland, D. J. (2016). Youth and caregiver perspectives on barriers to gender-affirming health care for transgender youth. *Journal of Adolescent Health, 59*(3), 254–261. https://doi.org/10.1016/j.jadohealth.2016.03.017

Guy-Evans, O. (2023). *Bronfenbrenner's ecological systems theory*. Simply Psychology. https://www.simplypsychology.org/bronfenbrenner.html

Haldeman, D. C. (2024). A counteroffensive against conversion therapy in the culture wars. *Cognitive and Behavioral Practice, 31*(1), 10–14. https://doi.org/10.1016/j.cbpra.2023.10.001

Hearn, G. (1958). *Theory building in social work*. University of Toronto Press.

Herman, J. L., Flores, A. R., & O'Neill, K. K. (2022). *How many adults and youth identify as transgender in the United States?* The Williams Institute. https://williamsinstitute.law.ucla.edu/publications/trans-adults-united-states

Horton, C. (2023). Institutional cisnormativity and educational injustice: Trans children's experiences in primary and early secondary education in the UK. *British Journal of Educational Psychology, 93*(1), 73–90. https://doi.org/10.1111/bjep.12540

Human Rights Campaign. (2025). *Faith resources*. https://www.hrc.org/resources/faith-resources

James, S. E., Herman, J. L., Durso, L. E., & Heng-Lehtinen, R. (2024). *Early insights: A report of the 2022 U.S. Transgender Survey*. National Center for Transgender Equality. https://transequality.org/sites/default/files/2024-02/2022%20USTS%20Early%20Insights%20Report_FINAL.pdf

Kidd, K. M., Sequeira, G. M., Paglisotti, T., Katz-Wise, S. L., Kazmerski, T. M., Hillier, A., Miller, E., & Dowshen, N. (2021). "This could mean death for my child": Parent perspectives on laws banning gender-affirming care for transgender adolescents. *Journal of Adolescent Health, 68*(6), 1082–1088. https://doi.org/10.1016/j.jadohealth.2020.09.010

Lambda Legal. (2024). *Know your rights: Identity documents*. https://lambdalegal.org/trans-id-guidance-faq/

Lee, W. Y., Hobbs, J. N., Hobaica, S., DeChants, J. P., Price, M. N., & Nath, R. (2024). State-level anti-transgender laws increase past-year suicide attempts among transgender and non-binary young people in the USA. *Nature Human Behaviour, 8*(11), 2096–2106. https://doi.org/10.1038/s41562-024-01979-5

Marshall, Z., Kaposy, C., Brunger, F., & Welch, V. (2022). Trans research ethics: Challenges and recommendations for change. *Bulletin of Applied Transgender Studies, 1*(3–4), 187–210. https://doi.org/10.57814/2rv3-kf42

McNamara, M., Barondeau, J., & Brown, J. (2024). Mental health, climate change, and bodily autonomy: An analysis of adolescent health policy in the post-pandemic climate. *Pediatric Clinics of North America, 71*(4), 729–744. https://doi.org/10.1016/j.pcl.2024.05.004

McNamara, M., Sequeira, G. M., Hughes, L., Goepferd, A. K., & Kidd, K. (2023). Bans on gender-affirming healthcare: The adolescent medicine provider's dilemma. *Journal of Adolescent Health, 73*(3), 406–409. https://doi.org/10.1016/j.jadohealth.2023.05.029

Melhado, W. (2023, July 17). "Unbearable": Doctors treating trans kids are leaving Texas, exacerbating adolescent care crisis. *The Texas Tribune*. https://www.texastribune.org/2023/07/17/texas-gender-affirming-care-doctors-hospitals/

Mousavian, M., Ranganathan, K., Keuroghlian, A. S., Park, Y. S., & Kumar, A. (2024). What are the barriers to health professionals' training on gender-affirming care from patients' and clinicians' perspectives? *Social Science & Medicine, 351*, 116983. https://doi.org/10.1016/j.socscimed.2024.116983

Movement Advancement Project. (2024). *Bans on best practice medical care for transgender youth*. https://www.mapresearch.org/equality-maps/healthcare/youth_medical_care_bans

National Association of Social Workers. (2021). *Code of ethics*. https://www.socialworkers.org/About/Ethics/Code-of-Ethics/Code-of-Ethics-English

Novotney, A. (2023, June 29). *'The young people feel it in their bones': A look at the mental health impact of antitrans legislation*. https://www.apa.org/topics/lgbtq/mental-health-anti-transgender-legislation

Olson, A. B., Ozaki, C. C., & Johnston-Guerrero, M. P. (2023). Recentering the individual in context using the phenomenological variant of ecological systems theory: Applications for higher education. *New Directions for Higher Education, 2023*(204), 83–92. https://doi.org/10.1002/he.20486

Olson, K. R., Durwood, L., DeMeules, M., & McLaughlin, K. A. (2016). Mental health of transgender children who are supported in their identities. *Pediatrics, 137*(3), e20153223. https://doi.org/10.1542/peds.2015-3223

Orgera, K., & Grover, A. (2024). *States with abortion bans see continued decrease in U.S. MD senior residency applicants*. Association of American Medical Colleges. https://doi.org/10.15766/rai_dnhob2ma

Paige, C. (2022). Transgender-affirming spiritual care: A bibliographic essay. *Theological Librarianship, 15*(1), 1–13. https://serials.atla.com/theolib/article/view/2944/4020

Rafferty, J., Committee on Psychosocial Aspects of Child and Family Health; Committee on Adolescence; Section on Lesbian, Gay, Bisexual, and Transgender Health and Wellness, Yogman, M., Baum, R., Gambon, T. B., Lavin, A., Mattson, G., Wissow, L. S., Breuner, C., Alderman, E. M., Grubb, L. K., Powers, M. E., Upadhya, K., Wallace, S. B., Hunt, L., Gearhart, A. T., Harris, C., Lowe, K. M., Rodgers, C. T., & Sherer, I. M. (2018). Ensuring comprehensive care and support for transgender and gender-diverse children and adolescents. *Pediatrics, 142*(4), e20182162. https://doi.org/10.1542/peds.2018-2162

Reisner, S. L., White, J. M., Dunham, E. E., Heflin, K., Begenyi, J., Cahill, S., & The Project Voice Team. (2014). *Discrimination and health in Massachusetts: A statewide survey of transgender and gender nonconforming adults*. The Fenway Institute, Fenway Health. https://fenwayhealth.org/wp-content/uploads/The-Fenway-Institute-MTPC-Project-VOICE-Report-July-2014.pdf

Rubano, C. (2016). Where do the mermaids stand? Toward a "gender-creative" pastoral sensibility. *Pastoral Psychology, 65*(6), 821–834. https://doi.org/10.1007/s11089-015-0680-2

Russell, S. T., Bishop, M. D., Saba, V. C., James, I., & Ioverno, S. (2021). Promoting school safety for LGBTQ and all students. *Policy Insights From the Behavioral and Brain Sciences, 8*(2), 160–166. https://doi.org/10.1177/23727322211031938

Ryan, C. (2021). *Helping diverse families learn to support their LGBTQ children to prevent health and mental health risks and promote well-being*. San Francisco State University Family Acceptance Project. https://familyproject.sfsu.edu/publications

Senate Finance Committee–Majority Staff. (2024, April 16). *How state attorneys general target transgender youth and adults by weaponizing the Medicaid program and their health oversight authority* (Staff Report). United States Senate. https://www.finance.senate.gov/imo/media/doc/senate_finance_committee_majority_staff_report_how_state_attorneys_general_target_transgender_youth_and_adults_by_weaponizing_the_medicaid_program_and_their_health_oversight_authority.pdf

Shipman, D., & Martin, T. (2019). Clinical and supervisory considerations for transgender therapists: Implications for working with clients. *Journal of Marital and Family Therapy, 45*(1), 92–105. https://doi.org/10.1111/jmft.12300

Soyei, S. (2019, March 29). *The importance of LGBT+ inclusive primary schools*. Equaliteach. https://equaliteach.co.uk/importance-lgbt-inclusive-primary-schools/

Spencer, M. B. (1995). Old issues and new theorizing about African American youth: A phenomenological variant of ecological systems theory. In R. L. Taylor (Ed.), *African-American youth: Their social and economic status in the United States* (pp. 37–69). Praeger.

Spencer, M. B. (2006). Phenomenology and ecological systems theory: Development of diverse groups. In R. M. Lerner & W. Damon (Eds.), *Handbook of child psychology:*

Theoretical models of human development (6th ed., pp. 829–893). John Wiley & Sons.

Spencer, M. B., Lodato, B. N., Spencer, C., Rich, L., Graziul, C., & English-Clarke, T. (2019). Innovating resilience promotion: Integrating cultural practices, social ecologies and development-sensitive conceptual strategies for advancing child well-being. *Advances in Child Development and Behavior, 57*, 101–148. https://doi.org/10.1016/bs.acdb.2019.05.005

Spencer, M. B., & Swanson, D. P. (2013). Opportunities and challenges to the development of healthy children and youth living in diverse communities. *Development and Psychopathology, 25*(4 Pt. 2), 1551–1566. https://doi.org/10.1017/S095457941300076X

Staub-Bernasconi, S. (2009). Social work as a discipline and profession. In V. Leskošek (Ed.), *Theories and methods of social work: Exploring different perspectives*. University of Ljubljana Faculty of Social Work.

Stern, J. A., Barbarin, O., & Cassidy, J. (2022). Working toward anti-racist perspectives in attachment theory, research, and practice. *Attachment & Human Development, 24*(3), 392–422. https://doi.org/10.1080/14616734.2021.1976933

Texas Attorney General. (2024, November 8). *Attorney General Ken Paxton sues another Dallas doctor for prescribing illegal "gender transition" drugs to more than a dozen Texas minors* [Press release]. https://www.texasattorneygeneral.gov/news/releases/attorney-general-ken-paxton-sues-another-dallas-doctor-prescribing-illegal-gender-transition-drugs-0

Texas Foster Youth Connections. (n.d.). *Affirming faith resources & organizations*. https://texasfosteryouthconnections.squarespace.com/lgbtq-youth-practice-guide/faith-resources

Toth, S. (2023a). *H.B. No. 41: Relating to professional liability insurance coverage for and prohibitions on the provision to certain children of procedures and treatments for gender transitioning, gender reassignment, or gender dysphoria* (88th Leg., Reg. Sess.). Texas Legislature Online. https://capitol.texas.gov/BillLookup/History.aspx?LegSess=88R&Bill=HB41

Toth, S. (2023b). *H.B. No. 1752: Relating to liability for the provision to certain children of procedures and treatments for gender transitioning, gender reassignment, or gender dysphoria; providing a civil penalty* (88th Leg., Reg. Sess.). Texas Legislature Online. https://capitol.texas.gov/BillLookup/History.aspx?LegSess=88R&Bill=HB1752

Trans Youth Family Allies. (2025). *Resources: Create a safe folder*. http://imatyfa.org/safe-folder.html

Turban, J. L., Beckwith, N., Reisner, S. L., & Keuroghlian, A. S. (2020). Association between recalled exposure to gender identity conversion efforts and psychological distress and suicide attempts among transgender adults. *JAMA Psychiatry, 77*(1), 68–76. https://doi.org/10.1001/jamapsychiatry.2019.2285

U.S. Census Bureau. (2022). *ACS demographic and housing estimates: American Community Survey, ACS 1-year estimates data profiles, Table DP05*. https://data.census.gov/table/ACSDP1Y2022.DP05?g=010XX00US$0400000&moe=false

U.S. Department of Health and Human Services. (2024, April 26). HIPAA privacy rule to support reproductive health care privacy (Final Rule, 89 FR 32976). *Federal Register*. https://www.federalregister.gov/d/2024-08503/p-560

Velez, G., & Spencer, M. B. (2018). Phenomenology and intersectionality: Using PVEST as a frame for adolescent identity formation amid intersecting ecological systems of inequality. *New Directions for Child and Adolescent Development, 2018*(161), 75–90. https://doi.org/10.1002/cad.20247

Watters, A. (2015, April 25). *The invented history of 'the factory model of education.'* https://hackeducation.com/2015/04/25/factory-model

Yun, K., Jenicek, G., & Gerdes, M. (2019). Overcoming language barriers in mental and behavioral health care for children and adolescents—Policies and priorities. *JAMA Pediatrics, 173*(6), 511–512. https://doi.org/10.1001/jamapediatrics.2019.0400

11 TRANSGENDER YOUTH MEDICAL CARE BANS

Legislation, Psychological Impacts, and Advocacy

SARA A. MAR, CLAIRE COYNE, JESSICA M. BERNACKI, AND KELLAN BAKER

Published literature documents that one's external environment, including political climate, community attitudes, and laws and policies, has a significant influence on mental health (Price & Hollinsaid, 2022). This is particularly true for marginalized populations, such as transgender and gender diverse (TGD) youth, who face structural stigma and discrimination in their daily lives. Over the past several years, TGD youth have been the subject of increasingly hostile political rhetoric and the target of antitransgender laws in health care, schools, bathrooms, and athletics. Research shows that such increasing hostility, discrimination, and exacerbation of structural stigma is associated with worsening behavioral health symptomatology (Leventhal et al., 2018). In fact, recent research has found that antitransgender laws significantly increase the risk of suicide attempts among TGD youth (Lee et al., 2024).

Supporting TGD youth across all areas of life can mitigate the negative mental health impacts of structural stigma. Pediatric gender health care can play an essential role in helping TGD youth explore their gender identity so they can live as their authentic selves. This individualized and evidence-based model of care recognizes that gender identity can develop over time and is not pathological (Hidalgo et al., 2013). In the current political and

https://doi.org/10.1037/0000494-012
Pediatric Gender Health Care: The Gender Affirmative Model Revisited, Second Edition, G. N. Rider, D. Ehrensaft, and C. St. Amand (Editors)

legislative climate, behavioral health providers have a critical role to play as both clinical professionals and advocates to ensure TGD youth can access the health care and social supports they need.

THE LEGISLATIVE LANDSCAPE

Transgender medical care, also known as *gender health care*, has increasingly been a target of politically motivated attacks from state and federal lawmakers over the last several years. The rapid rise in antitransgender legislation has been fueled by the rampant spread of mis- and disinformation about the realities of what gender health care entails for patients, families, and health care providers. While the most recent discourse in the public sphere has been concentrated around restricting access to health care for TGD youth, there is an ever-growing list of bills across the country that target the well-being and participation of transgender young people in other areas of public life, including in schools and on sports teams. The overwhelming flood of antitransgender discourse and policies in all aspects of public life is exacerbating discrimination and stigmatization against transgender people, with especially acute effects on TGD youth.

As of July 2025, 28 U.S. states have enacted laws or policies to ban medically necessary care for TGD youth (Dawson & Kates, 2025). In general, these laws prohibit all TGD individuals younger than the legal age of majority—even with the support of their families—from accessing best practice, evidence-based medical care, including puberty-delaying medications and hormone therapy. Additionally, these laws subject health care providers to professional, civil, and/or criminal penalties for providing this care and, in some cases, for simply referring a TGD youth to another clinician.

In June 2025, the U.S. Supreme Court issued a ruling in the case *United States v. Skrmetti*, in which the majority found that Tennessee's ban on medical care for transgender minors does not discriminate on the basis of sex and therefore satisfies a minimal rational standard of judicial review. Although the ruling allows Tennessee's ban to remain in effect, the decision does not affect the legality of this care in states that have not enacted bans. Importantly, the ruling did not address whether transgender people are a "suspect class" (i.e., a group that has historically suffered from discrimination), which typically warrants higher standards of judicial review. Because the U.S. Supreme Court decided that Tennessee's law discriminated on the basis of age and medical diagnosis, not sex, the case also does not directly impact other civil rights protections for transgender people. Furthermore, the decision does not foreclose legal challenges to bans in other states, meaning that other tools remain available to continue challenging the constitutionality of these health care bans.

Although several states have attempted to ban mental health services for TGD youth, most enacted versions of these bills allow access to behavioral health care thanks to advocacy efforts from grassroots organizations, parents, and clinicians during the legislative process. However, it should be noted that state and federal lawmakers have repeatedly pathologized TGD young people in bill texts, in hearings, and in mainstream media. For example, the Arkansas General Assembly wrote that "individuals struggling with distress at identifying with their biological sex often have already experienced psychopathology, which indicates these individuals should be encouraged to seek mental health services to address comorbidities and underlying causes of their distress" (Lundstrum, 2021, p. 2, lines 7–11). Policymakers have also spewed hateful rhetoric in public hearings and the media, such as a Florida Representative calling transgender people demons and comparing them to mutants during a Florida House of Representatives Commerce Committee (2023) hearing. This rhetoric in the public sphere is directly affecting the health of transgender people, particularly youth. A survey from The Trevor Project (2023) found that 86% of transgender and nonbinary youth say that the recent debates around antitransgender bills have negatively impacted their mental health in the past year.

Antitransgender policy rhetoric and persistent misinformation about the mental well-being of TGD youth has resulted in both outright medical care bans and onerous requirements that would significantly restrict access to care for transgender young people. In Ohio, for example, proposed regulations would have required patients to receive prespecified mental health counseling and evaluation for at least 6 months, which would violate existing standards of care and would funnel patients into an already overstretched behavioral health workforce while creating unnecessary and dangerous delays in accessing medical care (Ohio Department of Health, 2024). Furthermore, a standardized requirement incorrectly assumes that every person's mental health needs are the same and creates an inefficient (rather than individualized) model of care. Lastly, this onerous requirement goes against decades of clinical practice and scientific evidence (Huit et al., 2024; see also Coyne et al., 2023), which demonstrate that a range of clinical professionals, including psychologists, social workers, family medicine physicians, and nurse practitioners, are capable of correctly and competently conducting thorough assessments for the diagnosis and treatment of gender dysphoria and gender incongruence.

Transgender health care is not the only subject of attack by state lawmakers. TGD youth face other infringements on their freedom to show up as their authentic selves, particularly in school. For example, several states promote or have laws that require school staff to out a transgender young person to their family, regardless of whether this may put the child in danger of abuse, neglect, homelessness, or other detrimental outcomes. Other states are passing censorship laws that prohibit school curricula on lesbian, gay, bisexual, transgender, queer, or questioning (LGBTQ+) history, gender identity, and sexuality (Movement Advancement Project [MAP], 2026). These laws targeting education prevent LGBTQ+ youth from seeing themselves represented in the world and are harmful to all youth who benefit from learning about the diversity of experiences and identities. Lastly, legislators have forcefully pursued legislation to ban transgender youth from using the bathroom or participating on sports teams that match their gender identity (Arrayales & Redfield, 2026; MAP, 2026), which further perpetuates discrimination, worsens health disparities, and deprives transgender young people of the mental health benefits of peer support and feelings of belonging.

These state attacks on transgender people have been exacerbated by a hostile federal administration. Since January 2025, the Trump administration has issued numerous executive orders targeting TGD people, including those that seek to stop TGD people from receiving passports with an accurate gender marker; censoring LGBTQ+ curriculum materials; withholding federal funding from institutions that provide medical care to TGD youth; removing mention of LGBTQ+ people from government websites; defunding research on LGBTQ+ communities; and banning TGD youth, particularly trans girls, from playing on the sports team that matches their gender identity (Dawson & Kates, 2025; LGBTQ+ Bar, 2025). As federal agencies attempt to implement the Trump administration's executive orders, legal groups are challenging them in court to prevent further harm and marginalization of LGBTQ+ people, families, and communities.

PSYCHOLOGICAL IMPACTS

Compared to their cisgender and sexual minoritized peers, TGD youth experience disproportionately high rates of emotional distress, including a two- to three-fold increase in risk for anxiety disorders, depression, and suicidal ideation (Reisner et al., 2015). Significant disparities exist in suicide attempts based on gender identity, with transmasculine (50.8%), nonbinary (41.8%), and transfeminine (29.9%) adolescents reporting substantially higher rates of past attempts than their female (17.6%) and male (9.8%) cisgender peers (Toomey et al., 2018). Consistent with the gender minority stress and resilience model (GMSR; Hendricks & Testa, 2012), these mental health disparities are attributable to chronic, stigma-related stressors (e.g., gender-based discrimination) experienced by TGD youth due to their gender identity

(Hatzenbuehler & Pachankis, 2016). Within the GMSR model, gender identity–specific risk factors, including distal stress factors (e.g., gender-based discrimination, peer and family rejection, victimization, and nonaffirmation) and proximal stress factors (e.g., internalized transphobia, negative expectations for the future, and identity concealment), contribute to negative physical and mental health outcomes. For TGD youth, this disproportionate accumulation of exposure to stress compared to their cisgender peers increases their vulnerability to negative health outcomes (Hatzenbuehler & Pachankis, 2016).

Developmental context also impacts exposure to gender minority stressors and access to the supports that would mitigate negative health effects. During childhood and adolescence, family members shape youths' felt level of comfort expressing and sharing their gender identity, the degree to which they can make affirming social changes (e.g., pronouns, chosen name, and clothing), and their ability to access supportive resources, including health care. In contrast to adults, TGD youth are not able to access health care independently and require caregiver support and consent.

To account for these unique developmental considerations, Toomey (2021) proposed an adapted gender minority stress model for TGD youth that includes experiencing gender dysphoria as both a proximal stressor (i.e., when the distress is associated with incongruence between one's gender identity and physical anatomy) and a distal stressor (i.e., when the distress is due to nonaffirmation of gender identity by others in social contexts). The model also adds access to gender health care as a resilience factor that moderates the impact of all forms of gender minority stress on mental health and well-being. This developmentally informed model highlights clear targets for clinical intervention—reduce exposure to nonaffirmation and facilitate access to appropriate health care—that are aligned with the goals of gender health care.

Pediatric gender health care is the predominant approach to addressing the health care needs of TGD youth (Coyne et al., 2023; Keo-Meier & Ehrensaft, 2018). Gender health care is collaborative and individualized. It may include support for social changes (e.g., name, pronouns) that allow youth to present publicly as their authentic self, as well as medical interventions (e.g., pubertal suppression, hormone therapy, and, rarely, surgery) to reduce gender dysphoria following the onset of puberty. Health care providers working with TGD youth prioritize healthy psychosocial development and recognize that there is not a single "right way" to explore psychosocial or medical interventions (Hastings et al., 2021; Hidalgo et al., 2013). Gender health care is interdisciplinary and can include evidence-based mental health care to address the range of psychosocial and structural factors that contribute to mental health disparities for TGD youth (Huit et al., 2024).

A significant body of research suggests that both individualized social interventions and medical care can improve psychosocial outcomes for TGD youth (Durwood et al., 2024; Huit et al., 2024; Olson et al., 2024; Russell et al., 2018; Wittlin et al., 2023, 2025). When prepubertal children are socially supported in their gender, they report developmentally normative levels of depression and minimally elevated anxiety compared with age-matched peers and their cisgender siblings (Olson et al., 2016). Among prepubertal children who were socially supported in their gender identity, the overwhelming majority (94%) continue to identify with their transgender identity 5 years later (Olson et al., 2022). Social supports in settings outside the home are equally as important as familial support for the psychological well-being of TGD youth. Negative school environments can have detrimental effects on the mental health of TGD youth, who often experience more bullying and are more likely than their cisgender peers to skip school because of feeling unsafe (McQuillan et al., 2024). However, when youth have access to resources that acknowledge and support their identity, such as gay–straight alliances, supportive educators, and LGBTQ+-inclusive curricula, that access reduces their likelihood of skipping school or being victimized by their peers (Greytak et al., 2013). Furthermore, when TGD youth can participate in extracurricular activities, such as team sports, they are significantly less likely to experience depression and suicidal ideation (LaRocca et al., 2022). Sports participation plays a role in improving self-esteem, boosting self-confidence, and feeling connected to one's community (Goldberg, 2021), while also being important for physical health, including improving cardiovascular health and bone mineral density (Barrera et al., 2022). It is therefore critical that TGD youth have similar access as their cisgender peers to developmentally appropriate extracurricular activities.

In regard to medical interventions, longitudinal and cross-sectional studies suggest pubertal suppression is associated with improved (Costa et al., 2015; de Vries et al., 2011; van der Miesen et al., 2020) or stable (Carmichael et al., 2021) psychosocial functioning. Similarly, prospective studies have found that pediatric gender health hormone therapy is associated with improvements in depression, anxiety, body dissatisfaction, suicidality, life satisfaction, and overall well-being (Achille et al., 2020; Allen et al., 2019; Chen et al., 2023; Kuper et al., 2020).

Before current antitransgender legislation, TGD youth reported poorer health outcomes compared to their cisgender peers (Rider et al., 2018) and faced significant barriers to accessing health care, including a limited number of pediatric multidisciplinary gender specialty clinics with culturally competent pediatric gender health care providers (Gridley et al., 2016). Further restricting access to health care through legislative bans increases mental health distress, including suicidality, depression, and anxiety (Abreu et al., 2022; Redfield et al., 2023), and exacerbates existing health disparities between TGD and cisgender youth. From studies encompassing a wide range of minoritized and stigmatized individuals (e.g., transgender youth and youth of color), evidence is clear that structural stigma, including discriminatory laws, a hostile political climate, and community-wide attitudes, impact the mental and physical health of stigmatized youth (Chodzen et al., 2019; Lee et al., 2024; Price & Hollinsaid, 2022). At the community level, stigmatized youth (e.g., transgender youth) living in areas with high levels of structural stigma (e.g., laws banning access to medical care) are more likely to experience interpersonal discrimination and bullying, which in turn can lead to poor mental health outcomes (Price & Hollinsaid, 2022).

In a novel study of structural transphobia in the United States, researchers found that TGD adults living in states with higher levels of transphobic laws, policies, and attitudes reported higher levels of psychological distress, suicidal ideation, and suicidal behavior compared with TGD adults living in states with lower levels of state-level transphobia (Price et al., 2024). Similarly, a mixed-method study of TGD youth found adverse effects of legislation aiming to restrict access to public spaces and pediatric gender health care on mental health and well-being via both direct and indirect pathways (Dhanani & Totton, 2023). Legislation banning access to gender health care leaves TGD youth without interventions to alleviate psychological distress associated with gender dysphoria. Youth who are not in states with legislative restrictions, but who are exposed to news stories related to transphobic legislation and perceive that individuals in their social network are supportive of this legislation, report increased rumination, mental and physical health symptoms, and fear of disclosing their gender identity. Parents of TGD youth are also concerned about the impact of proposed legislation on their children's mental health, the restriction of their rights as parents, and the risk of increased stigma, violence, and discrimination (Abreu et al., 2021, 2022; Kidd et al., 2021).

Behavioral health providers play an important role in supporting the mental well-being of TGD youth. Within the framework of the GMSR model, providers should assess the degree to which antitransgender legislation and rhetoric are impacting their client's psychological well-being.

PROVIDER RECOMMENDATIONS

Behavioral health providers can support TGD youth in several critical ways. Approaches include providing direct clinical services, helping families understand the legal landscape, and serving as advocates within and outside their institutions.

Mental Health Support

There are established best practices for providing behavioral health care for TGD youth (Huit et al., 2024). By nature of their training, child psychologists have many of the necessary skills to provide family-focused support for TGD youth (Oransky et al., 2019). The gender affirmative model (Hidalgo et al., 2013), as well as the best practice guidelines for family-based gender behavioral health care (Buckloh et al., 2022; Malpas et al., 2022), is a valuable framework for reference. A recent policy statement by the American Psychological Association (APA; 2024) highlights the importance of psychological practice in evidence-based care for TGD individuals. The World Professional Association for Transgender Health (WPATH) Standards of Care for the Health of Transgender and Gender Diverse People, version 8 (SOC8; Coleman et al., 2022) provides "clinical guidance to health care providers to assist TGD people in accessing safe and effective pathways to achieving lasting personal comfort with their gendered selves" (p. S3). SOC8 has multiple relevant chapters, including on adolescents, children, and mental health. Interdisciplinary assessment is a required part of documentation for pediatric gender health medical care, and increasing access to knowledgeable providers is a great need. Given this, knowledge about evidence-based care is indicated for all pediatric behavioral health providers (Oransky et al., 2019).

Many TGD youth and their families present not only for support with gender exploration and affirmation but also for coping with minority stress and related symptomatology as a result of living in the current sociopolitical climate (Barbee et al., 2022). Evidence-based treatments exist for depression and anxiety, and there are proposed adaptations for TGD youth that consider the impact of minority stress and protective factors such as parental affirmation (Coyne et al., 2020). Providers should be familiar with pertinent local, state, and national legislation to keep families informed of policy developments that may affect their child at school or in other areas of public life.[1] Mental health support may include direct conversations with youth and caregivers about stressors associated with legislation and concerns about potential changes in access to care. Providers can also help young people and their families make decisions about when and how they share their gender identity, highlighting how gender identity can be private without communicating potentially stigmatizing messages related to keeping gender

[1]The MAP is a free online resource (https://www.lgbtmap.org/equality-maps) that tracks LGBTQ-related legislation in all 50 U.S. states plus Washington, DC.

identity a secret. Youth, particularly those who socially transition at a young age or change schools after social transition, may choose not to disclose their gender identity in school settings. Decisions about disclosure, including disclosure in the context of public advocacy or on social media, should take into account the young person's wishes. It is important for youth and caregivers to understand that information about their transgender identity is information that cannot be unshared.

Providers should also be familiar with legislation as it pertains to youth participation in extracurricular activities, such as sex-segregated sports.[2] Youth benefit physically, socially, and emotionally from engagement in extracurricular activities (Barrera et al., 2022; Clark & Kosciw, 2022; Eime et al., 2013); yet they may be reluctant to participate or, depending on the state, may be legally barred from participating (Dechants et al., 2024). Providers can support youth interested in engaging in sex-segregated sports by exploring the legal and personal factors that may influence their decision to play. Families may benefit from communicating directly with school or sports organization staff about support provided to transgender youth who are seeking opportunities to participate in sports.

Providers should also familiarize themselves with community resources that may help TGD youth beyond just medical and mental health supports (e.g., peer support groups, mutual aid, legal resources, and intergenerational gatherings and mentoring). There are local and regional organizations that provide supportive spaces and programming that can complement services provided in a gender specialty clinic. Community-based providers can support their clients by familiarizing themselves with the treatment model of the local gender program. The additional interaction of community- and clinic-based behavioral health providers through peer consultation, regional consultation groups, and clinician, school, and community training can build the capacity of local providers to serve the increasing needs of TGD youth and their families (Coyne et al., 2023).

Responding to Concerns About Legislation

National professional organizations for medical and mental health providers recognize that legislation preventing access to pediatric gender health

[2]See the MAP website (https://www.lgbtmap.org/equality-maps/youth/sports_participation_bans) for a map of U.S. states with bans on TGD youth participation in sports.

care services endangers the mental and physical well-being of TGD youth (APA, 2024; Barbee et al., 2022), and they have issued policy statements opposing these legislative efforts and reaffirming support for gender health care (American Medical Association, 2021; American Psychiatric Association, 2020; Rafferty et al., 2018). Behavioral health providers can assist TGD youth impacted by these barriers not only with the mental health support already discussed but also through adjunctive support and advocacy efforts.[3,4]

One way behavioral health providers can assist TGD youth pursuing gender health care is by providing supportive documentation. For example, providers may confirm a diagnosis of gender dysphoria or gender incongruence, and they may document a history of gender exploration and social transition steps that support the gender history that may culminate in requests for pediatric gender medical care. Some TGD youth may require formal statements of support to access medical care. At the state level, the criteria vary for changing a gender marker on birth certificates and state-issued identification. Many states do not require a letter from a health care provider or court order to change gender markers on birth certificates or state-issued identification. In some states, individuals can change their gender marker on state-issued identification with a letter from a health care provider or a court order, but they may not be able to change the gender marker on their birth certificate at all or without proof of specific surgery. Some states (e.g., Texas, Florida) will not allow individuals to change their gender marker on either their birth certificate or driver's license (MAP, 2026). Because these policies vary from state to state, it is important for providers to be familiar with the laws that apply to the regions where they practice.[5] For youth who reside in states without access to pediatric gender health care, families may seek recommendations from their behavioral health provider. Thus, it is valuable for behavioral health providers to be familiar with reputable care centers. For families who do not have the means to travel (even

[3]Erin in the Morning (https://www.erininthemorning.com/) posts frequent updates on antitrans legislation and provides fact checks on pieces of mis- and disinformation in the media.

[4]State LGBTQ organizations play a central role in advocacy and monitoring policy changes in their state. Visit the Equality Federation website (https://www.equalityfederation.org/).

[5]The Trans Lifeline ID Change Library (https://translifeline.org/resources/id-change-library/) has information on name and gender change processes for identification documents at the county, state, and federal levels.

locally) to seek medical consultation, behavioral health providers should be able to share resources to help youth and families navigate the supports available to them. This can include sharing the names of nonmedical organizations that offer financial assistance for medical care costs, in-person or virtual peer and family support groups, and legal aid organizations, among others.[6] It should be noted that some states have laws against "aiding and abetting" TGD youth from accessing medical care. Providers should consult their specific state law to understand the scope of resource sharing that is allowed under the law.

In some situations, TGD youth may be unable to access or be at risk of losing access to care, given legislative developments. Behavioral health providers can serve as liaisons for families, referring youth to alternative solutions for addressing embodiment goals (e.g., voice therapy and oral contraceptive pills for TGD adolescents who lose access to testosterone). Familiarity with such alternatives is a means to mitigate complications from untreated gender dysphoria. In response to distress associated with the sociopolitical context, clinicians can adopt mental health promotion strategies from evidence-based interventions such as Psychological First Aid (PFA; Brymer et al., 2006) and the Family Acceptance Project family support model (Ryan et al., 2023) to help TGD youth and their families. The core components of PFA are to promote adaptive coping by enhancing safety, emotional comfort, and connection to social support, as well as a sense of self and community efficacy and hope (Hobfoll et al., 2007). These strategies have been adapted as culturally responsive interventions to alleviate distress, promote resilience, and prevent mental health crises due to political events and policy changes impacting other communities of stigmatized youth (e.g., refugee and immigrant youth; Ford-Paz et al., 2020). Clinicians who are not TGD themselves should partner with adult TGD people to create PFA through intergenerational mentoring. In this way, children and parents can learn from TGD adults who can pass along learned resilience strategies.

Behavioral health providers are encouraged to discuss the impact of gender minority stress in sessions with clients, validating their distress and

---

[6]Some national organizations to be familiar with include the Campaign for Southern Equality (https://southernequality.org/tyep/) for medical care access; PFLAG (https://pflag.org/) for families; the Transgender Law Center (https://transgenderlawcenter.org/get-help/) and GLAD (https://www.glad.org/know-your-rights/glad-answers/) for legal support; and The Trevor Project suicide hotline (https://www.thetrevorproject.org/get-help/).

helping youth and their families create plans and strategies for coping with the uncertainty and preparing for such restrictions if they were to arise (Abreu et al., 2021; Williams & Medlock, 2017). Effective planning may include gathering documents for a safe folder (e.g., including documents regarding history of medical and mental health care, legal name or gender marker changes, and school-based gender plans; see Chapter 10, this volume) and creating and identifying safe community spaces (Bockting et al., 2020).

Role of Providers in Advocacy

Behavioral health providers can support TGD youth through advocacy efforts in institutional and political settings. Kuper et al. (2022) outlined why behavioral health providers are in an ideal position to be advocates, and they described how doing so aligns with the ethical principle of beneficence outlined by the APA (2017) *Ethical Principles of Psychologists and Code of Conduct*. Through this advocacy, behavioral health providers can dispel the myths and misinformation perpetuated about pediatric gender health care and promote the science behind the mental health benefits associated with access to this care. An "action item menu" created by Kuper et al. (2022) suggests additional spaces for advocacy with families, professionally, organizationally, in the community, in the media, and politically.

Family advocacy can include sharing knowledge of community resources with families and caregivers to advocate for their child's access to care. This may include providing information about legal rights, health care privacy laws, and district policies. For families who choose to become involved with advocacy efforts, behavioral health providers can help discuss the risks of such engagement and explore how a youth's thoughts about being engaged in such advocacy may change over time as they age (Kuper et al., 2022).

Professional advocacy may include (a) using pronouns in signature lines and introductions; (b) engaging in equity, diversity, and inclusion committees in the provider's local, state, or national associations; and (c) providing training to colleagues and peers. For behavioral health providers working in health care organizations, reviewing existing inclusive and affirming policies and practices, or encouraging the development of new policies, is an organizational-level intervention. As key stakeholders, members of the TGD community should be involved in developing policies and procedures, and there should be ways for community members to provide ongoing feedback (e.g., a community advisory board). In the community, providers can network with local affirming spaces and attend community events. Awareness of locally based affirming community organizations and spaces is useful when connecting TGD youth and families with community support.

Advocacy can also occur outside a provider's professional institution. Interviews with media outlets[7] are a mechanism to disseminate the mental health benefits that TGD youth experience from access to gender health care and to dispel misinformation.[8] Media and advocacy training is advised for providers who engage in these interviews, and organizations often have communication policies and media relations departments to assist with preparation and vetting media requests. Another outlet for external communications is with local, state, or federal decision-makers. Health care professionals can share their expertise in meetings with policymakers, or they can provide written or oral testimony on proposed laws and regulations. Lastly, responding to action alerts shared by professional organizations and voting in elections at all levels of government are other ways for providers to engage in advocacy.

POLICY RECOMMENDATIONS

Advocating for laws and policies that advance the health and well-being of TGD youth is critical in reducing the structural stigma that this population faces. These opportunities exist in local, state, and federal legislative and regulatory processes, as well as through internal institutional policies and in submitting amicus curiae briefs or other expert materials in court cases. Mental health clinicians can participate in advocacy opportunities through their professional organizations on the local, state, and national levels as well as through direct educational engagement with policymakers at multiple levels of government. Regardless of where and how policy is made, it must always be

---

[7]Media training for health care professionals may be offered by their institution's communications or public relations department. Professional associations (e.g., the American Academy of Pediatrics and the APA) may offer media training as well.

[8]Resources on high-level rebuttals to common pieces of misinformation about pediatric gender health care include a 2022 published piece by Dr. Meredithe McNamara and colleagues (https://doi.org/10.1016/j.jadohealth.2022.06.008) and a 2023 guide authored by Greenesmith for Political Research Associates (https://politicalresearch.org/sites/default/files/2023-01/Anti-LGBTQ%20Organizing%20201_0.pdf).

driven by sound science and credible evidence. As noted earlier, the evidence supports the current standard of care for TGD youth. One notable example of this evidence is a 1,000-plus page report commissioned from medical experts by the Utah State Legislature (Lafleur et al., 2025). The findings of this report corroborate the positions of every major medical association in the United States, which all continue to endorse the standard of care and oppose health care bans. Unfortunately, the findings of this report have not yet been acted on by the legislature, and the state's care ban persists.

Several states have made steps toward ensuring TGD young people can access the medical care they need, such as by shoring up protections for clinicians who provide this care to prevent these health care professionals from facing penalties, subpoenas, or other investigations from states with care bans (MAP, 2026). Additionally, states should invest in research to identify gaps in health care access and the impact of medical care bans on the well-being of transgender youth. The results of these studies should be translated for public audiences and used to inform and generate new policies that will improve the health of transgender young people.

Telemedicine continues to be a critical method of delivering necessary medical care to marginalized populations. For TGD youth, particularly those in rural areas, telemedicine can reduce no-show rates and improve access to and continuity of care (DeGuzman et al., 2024). Policymakers should continue to explore and expand telemedicine options, particularly as families with TGD youth navigate a patchwork of state bans and seek care across state lines. Initiatives like PSYPACT (https://www.psypact.gov), which facilitates telemental health services across state borders, should continue to be expanded so youth can access the mental health care they need. Furthermore, telemedicine flexibilities during the COVID-19 pandemic and corresponding public health emergency improved access to overall health care services for transgender adolescents (Lucas et al., 2023). These flexibilities included allowing clinicians to conduct visits with patients via virtual platforms across state lines and write prescriptions after virtual appointments. Investment in proactive telemedicine policies is crucial for TGD youth to continue accessing care, particularly in a quickly changing political landscape.

Outside of health care, there are many opportunities to advance policies that improve social support structures. Passing antibullying policies can significantly improve school climate, particularly for LGBTQ youth, and create a safer social and learning environment (Kull et al., 2016). Often such policies are passed at the local level, including by individual school boards. School nondiscrimination laws are another avenue to help

TGD youth feel safe and accepted at school by ensuring they can access facilities (e.g., bathrooms and locker rooms), clubs, and sports teams that align with their gender identity. State-level antidiscrimination policies are also critical, including policies that protect TGD youth in the child welfare system from discrimination on the basis of their sexual orientation or gender identity.

Lastly, organizations and institutions must work toward making their internal policies as inclusive and affirming as possible. As previously mentioned, it is best practice for intake forms to include spaces for individuals to share their chosen name and pronouns. Organizations should also establish processes and systems to include TGD people in their work. This can look like systematically diversifying hiring practices, having TGD voices on advisory boards, or paying TGD people to lead workplace and professional development opportunities. Shoring up organizations to be more inclusive and affirming can create safer spaces for TGD people to access resources and support without fear of discrimination or harassment. We summarize considerations for providers working with TGD youth in Figure 11.1 to assist in identifying ways to support youth in their practices.

CONCLUSION

The current sociopolitical climate threatens the mental health and well-being of TGD youth. Antitransgender laws in health care, sports, and schools have created an environment that is exposing TGD young people to increasing stigma, violence, harassment, and discrimination. For many TGD youth, access to gender health care is medically necessary to alleviate their gender dysphoria and live as their authentic selves. Reputable professional medical organizations have established evidence-based best practices for this care, including the role of behavioral health providers. Mental health professionals can offer a range of supportive services to TGD youth, including offering a safe space for the young person to explore their gender identity, sharing resources with patients and families, and providing supportive documentation of gender dysphoria. Furthermore, behavioral health providers are important advocates, given their research and clinical expertise. Dispelling misinformation, providing expert testimony on proposed laws, and pushing for more inclusive organizational policies can all make a difference in creating a safer environment for TGD youth to live and thrive.

FIGURE 11.1. Case Study/Decision Tree–Transgender Youth Medical Care Bans: Legislation, Psychological Impacts, and Advocacy

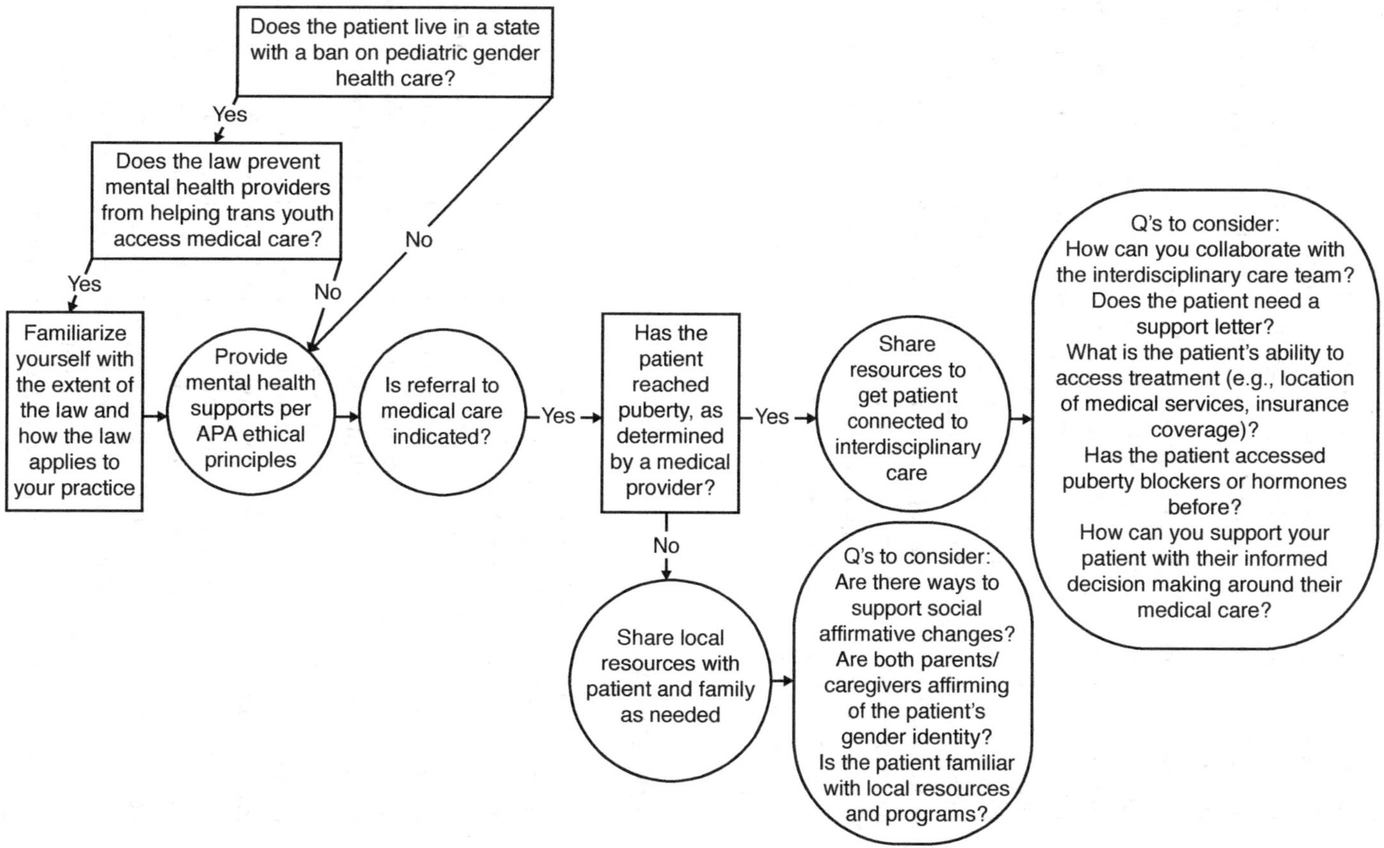

Note. APA = American Psychological Association.

REFERENCES

Abreu, R. L., Gonzalez, K. A., Capielo Rosario, C., Lindley, L., & Lockett, G. M. (2021). "What American dream is this?": The effect of Trump's presidency on immigrant Latinx transgender people. *Journal of Counseling Psychology, 68*(6), 657–669. https://doi.org/10.1037/cou0000541

Abreu, R. L., Sostre, J. P., Gonzalez, K. A., Lockett, G. M., & Matsuno, E. (2022). "I am afraid for those kids who might find death preferable": Parental figures' reactions and coping strategies to bans on gender affirming care for transgender and gender diverse youth. *Psychology of Sexual Orientation and Gender Diversity, 9*(4), 500–510. https://doi.org/10.1037/sgd0000495

Achille, C., Taggart, T., Eaton, N. R., Osipoff, J., Tafuri, K., Lane, A., & Wilson, T. A. (2020). Longitudinal impact of gender-affirming endocrine intervention on the mental health and well-being of transgender youths: Preliminary results. *International Journal of Pediatric Endocrinology, 2020*(1), 8. https://doi.org/10.1186/s13633-020-00078-2

Allen, L. R., Watson, L. B., Egan, A. M., & Moser, C. N. (2019). Well-being and suicidality among transgender youth after gender-affirming hormones. *Clinical Practice in Pediatric Psychology, 7*(3), 302–311. https://doi.org/10.1037/cpp0000288

American Medical Association. (2021). *AMA reinforces opposition to restrictions on transgender medical care*. https://www.ama-assn.org/press-center/press-releases/ama-reinforces-opposition-restrictions-transgender-medical-care

American Psychiatric Association. (2020). *Position statement on treatment of transgender (trans) and gender diverse youth*. https://www.psychiatry.org/File%20Library/About-APA/Organization-Documents-Policies/Policies/Position-Transgender-Gender-Diverse-Youth.pdf

American Psychological Association. (2017). *Ethical principles of psychologists and code of conduct* (2002, amended effective June 1, 2010, and January 1, 2017). https://www.apa.org/ethics/code/

American Psychological Association. (2024). *APA policy statement on affirming evidence-based inclusive care for transgender, gender diverse, and nonbinary individuals, addressing misinformation, and the role of psychological practice and science*. https://www.apa.org/about/policy/transgender-nonbinary-inclusive-care

Arrayales, J., & Redfield, E. (2026, January). *The impact of 2025 state anti-transgender legislation on youth*. Williams Institute, UCLA School of Law. https://williamsinstitute.law.ucla.edu/wp-content/uploads/2025-Anti-Trans-Legislation-Jan-2026.pdf

Barbee, H., Deal, C., & Gonzales, G. (2022). Antitransgender legislation—A public health concern for transgender youth. *JAMA Pediatrics, 176*(2), 125–126. https://doi.org/10.1001/jamapediatrics.2021.4483

Barrera, E., Millington, K., & Kremen, J. (2022). The medical implications of banning transgender youth from sport participation. *JAMA Pediatrics, 176*(3), 223–224. https://doi.org/10.1001/jamapediatrics.2021.4597

Bockting, W., Barucco, R., LeBlanc, A., Singh, A., Mellman, W., Dolezal, C., & Ehrhardt, A. (2020). Sociopolitical change and transgender people's perceptions of vulnerability and resilience. *Sexuality Research and Social Policy, 17*(1), 162–174. https://doi.org/10.1007/s13178-019-00381-5

Brymer, M., Jacobs, A., Layne, C., Pynoos, R., Ruzek, J., Steinberg, A., Vernberg, E., Watson, P., National Child Traumatic Stress Network, & National Center for PTSD. (2006). *Psychological first aid: Field operations guide* (2nd ed.). NCTSN & NCPTSD.

Buckloh, L. M., Poquiz, J. L., Alioto, A., Moyer, D. N., & Axelrad, M. E. (2022). Best practices in working with parents and caregivers of transgender and gender diverse youth. *Clinical Practice in Pediatric Psychology, 10*(3), 325–335. https://doi.org/10.1037/cpp0000442

Carmichael, P., Butler, G., Masic, U., Cole, T. J., De Stavola, B. L., Davidson, S., Skageberg, E. M., Khadr, S., & Viner, R. M. (2021). Short-term outcomes of pubertal suppression in a selected cohort of 12 to 15 year old young people with persistent gender dysphoria in the UK. *PLOS One, 16*(2), e0243894. https://doi.org/10.1371/journal.pone.0243894

Chen, D., Berona, J., Chan, Y.-M., Ehrensaft, D., Garofalo, R., Hidalgo, M. A., Rosenthal, S. M., Tishelman, A. C., & Olson-Kennedy, J. (2023). Psychosocial functioning in transgender youth after 2 years of hormones. *New England Journal of Medicine, 388*(3), 240–250. https://doi.org/10.1056/NEJMoa2206297

Chodzen, G., Hidalgo, M. A., Chen, D., & Garofalo, R. (2019). Minority stress factors associated with depression and anxiety among transgender and gender-nonconforming youth. *Journal of Adolescent Health, 64*(4), 467–471. https://doi.org/10.1016/j.jadohealth.2018.07.006

Clark, C. M., & Kosciw, J. G. (2022). Engaged or excluded: LGBTQ youth's participation in school sports and their relationship to psychological well-being. *Psychology in the Schools, 59*(1), 95–114. https://doi.org/10.1002/pits.22500

Coleman, E., Radix, A. E., Bouman, W. P., Brown, G. R., de Vries, A. L. C., Deutsch, M. B., Ettner, R., Fraser, L., Goodman, M., Green, J., Hancock, A. B., Johnson, T. W., Karasic, D. H., Knudson, G. A., Leibowitz, S. F., Meyer-Bahlburg, H. F. L., Monstrey, S. J., Motmans, J., Nahata, L., . . . Arcelus, J. (2022). Standards of care for the health of transgender and gender diverse people, version 8. *International Journal of Transgender Health, 23*(Suppl. 1), S1–S259. https://doi.org/10.1080/26895269.2022.2100644

Costa, R., Dunsford, M., Skagerberg, E., Holt, V., Carmichael, P., & Colizzi, M. (2015). Psychological support, puberty suppression, and psychosocial functioning in adolescents with gender dysphoria. *The Journal of Sexual Medicine, 12*(11), 2206–2214. https://doi.org/10.1111/jsm.13034

Coyne, C. A., Poquiz, J. L., Janssen, A., & Chen, D. (2020). Evidence-based psychological practice for transgender and non-binary youth: defining the need, framework for treatment adaptation, and future directions. *Evidence-Based Practice in Child and Adolescent Mental Health, 5*(3), 340–353. https://doi.org/10.1080/23794925.2020.1765433

Coyne, C. A., Yuodsnukis, B. T., & Chen, D. (2023). Gender dysphoria: Optimizing healthcare for transgender and gender diverse youth with a multidisciplinary approach. *Neuropsychiatric Disease and Treatment, 19*, 479–493. https://doi.org/10.2147/ndt.S359979

Dawson, L., & Kates, J. (2025). *Policy tracker: Youth access to gender affirming care and state policy restrictions*. KFF. https://www.kff.org/other/dashboard/gender-affirming-care-policy-tracker/

DeChants, J. P., Green, A. E., Price, M. N., & Davis, C. K. (2024). "I get treated poorly in regular school—Why add to it?": Transgender girls' experiences choosing to play or not play sports. *Transgender Health, 9*(1), 61–67. https://doi.org/10.1089/trgh.2022.0066

DeGuzman, P. B., Lyons, G. R., Azar, F. N., Kimble, A., Huang, G., Rheuban, K., & Gray, S. H. (2024). Impact of telemedicine on access to care for rural transgender and gender-diverse youth. *The Journal of Pediatrics, 267,* 113911. https://doi.org/10.1016/j.jpeds.2024.113911

de Vries, A. L., Steensma, T. D., Doreleijers, T. A., & Cohen-Kettenis, P. T. (2011). Puberty suppression in adolescents with gender identity disorder: A prospective follow-up study. *Journal of Sexual Medicine, 8*(8), 2276–2283. https://doi.org/10.1111/j.1743-6109.2010.01943.x

Dhanani, L. Y., & Totton, R. R. (2023). Have you heard the news? The effects of exposure to news about recent transgender legislation on transgender youth and young adults. *Sexuality Research and Social Policy, 20,* 1345–1359. https://doi.org/10.1007/s13178-023-00810-6

Durwood, L., Gallagher, N. M., Sifre, R., & Olson, K. R. (2024). A study of parent-reported internalizing symptoms in transgender youths before and after childhood social transitions. *Clinical Psychological Science, 12*(5), 984–996. https://doi.org/10.1177/21677026231208086

Eime, R. M., Young, J. A., Harvey, J. T., Charity, M. J., & Payne, W. R. (2013). A systematic review of the psychological and social benefits of participation in sport for children and adolescents: Informing development of a conceptual model of health through sport. *International Journal of Behavioral Nutrition and Physical Activity, 10*(1), 98. https://doi.org/10.1186/1479-5868-10-98

Florida House of Representatives Commerce Committee. (2023). *Hearing on the Safety in Private Spaces Act.* https://www.flsenate.gov/Laws/Statutes/2023/0553.865

Ford-Paz, R. E., Santiago, C. D., Coyne, C. A., Rivera, C., Guo, S., Rusch, D., St. Jean, N., Hilado, A., & Cicchetti, C. (2020). You're not alone: A public health response to immigrant/refugee distress in the current sociopolitical context. *Psychological Services, 17*(S1), 128–138. https://doi.org/10.1037/ser0000381

Goldberg, S. K. (2021). *Fair play: The importance of sports participation for transgender youth.* The Center for American Progress. https://www.americanprogress.org/article/fair-play/

Greenesmith, H. (2023, January). *Combating antitransgender discrimination.* Political Research Associates. https://politicalresearch.org/sites/default/files/2023-01/Anti-LGBTQ%20Organizing%20201_0.pdf

Greytak, E. A., Kosciw, J. G., & Boesen, M. J. (2013). Putting the "T" in "resource": The benefits of LGBT-related school resources for transgender youth. *Journal of LGBT Youth, 10*(1–2), 45–63. https://doi.org/10.1080/19361653.2012.718522

Gridley, S. J., Crouch, J. M., Evans, Y., Eng, W., Antoon, E., Lyapustina, M., Schimmel-Bristow, A., Woodward, J., Dundon, K., Schaff, R., McCarty, C., Ahrens, K., & Breland, D. J. (2016). Youth and caregiver perspectives on barriers to gender-affirming health care for transgender youth. *Journal of Adolescent Health, 59*(3), 254–261. https://doi.org/10.1016/j.jadohealth.2016.03.017

Hastings, J., Bobb, C., Wolfe, M., Amaro Jimenez, Z., & Amand, C. S. (2021). Medical care for nonbinary youth: Individualized gender care beyond a binary framework. *Pediatric Annals, 50*(9), e384–e390. https://doi.org/10.3928/19382359-20210818-03

Hatzenbuehler, M. L., & Pachankis, J. E. (2016). Stigma and minority stress as social determinants of health among lesbian, gay, bisexual, and transgender youth: Research evidence and clinical implications. *Pediatric Clinics of North America, 63*(6), 985–997. https://doi.org/10.1016/j.pcl.2016.07.003

Hendricks, M. L., & Testa, R. J. (2012). A conceptual framework for clinical work with transgender and gender nonconforming clients: An adaptation of the minority stress model. *Professional Psychology: Research and Practice, 43*(5), 460–467. https://doi.org/10.1037/a0029597

Hidalgo, M. A., Ehrensaft, D., Tishelman, A. C., Clark, L. F., Garofalo, R., Rosenthal, S. M., Spack, N. P., & Olson, J. (2013). The gender affirmative model: What we know and what we aim to learn. *Human Development, 56*(5), 285–290. https://doi.org/10.1159/000355235

Hobfoll, S. E., Watson, P., Bell, C. C., Bryant, R. A., Brymer, M. J., Friedman, M. J., Friedman, M., Gersons, B. P. R., de Jong, J. T. V. M., Layne, C. M., Maguen, S., Neria, Y., Norwood, A. E., Pynoos, R. S., Reissman, D., Ruzek, J. I., Shalev, A. Y., Solomon, Z., Steinberg, A. M., & Ursano, R. J. (2007). Five essential elements of immediate and mid-term mass trauma intervention: Empirical evidence. *Psychiatry, 70*(4), 283–315. https://doi.org/10.1521/psyc.2007.70.4.283

Huit, T. Z., Coyne, C., & Chen, D. (2024). State of the science: Gender-affirming care for transgender and gender diverse youth. *Behavior Therapy, 55*(6), 1335–1347. https://doi.org/10.1016/j.beth.2024.02.010

Keo-Meier, C., & Ehrensaft, D. (Eds.). (2018). *The gender affirmative model: An interdisciplinary approach to supporting transgender and gender expansive children.* American Psychological Association. https://doi.org/10.1037/0000095-000

Kidd, K. M., Sequeira, G. M., Paglisotti, T., Katz-Wise, S. L., Kazmerski, T. M., Hillier, A., Miller, E., & Dowshen, N. (2021). "This could mean death for my child": Parent perspectives on laws banning gender-affirming care for transgender adolescents. *Journal of Adolescent Health, 68*(6), 1082–1088. https://doi.org/10.1016/j.jadohealth.2020.09.010

Kull, R. M., Greytak, E. A., Kosciw, J. G., & Villenas, C. (2016). Effectiveness of school district antibullying policies in improving LGBT youths' school climate. *Psychology of Sexual Orientation and Gender Diversity, 3*(4), 407–415. https://doi.org/10.1037/sgd0000196

Kuper, L. E., Cooper, M. B., & Mooney, M. A. (2022). Supporting and advocating for transgender and gender diverse youth and their families within the sociopolitical context of widespread discriminatory legislation and policies. *Clinical Practice in Pediatric Psychology, 10*(3), 336–345. https://doi.org/10.1037/cpp0000456

Kuper, L. E., Stewart, S., Preston, S., Lau, M., & Lopez, X. (2020). Body dissatisfaction and mental health outcomes of youth on gender-affirming hormone therapy. *Pediatrics, 145*(4), e20193006. https://doi.org/10.1542/peds.2019-3006

Lafleur, J., Heath, L., Gonzales, V., Luloh, M., Henkels, R., Vadipour, A., Nguyen, D., Liang, X., Haines, T., & Knippenberg, K. (2025). *Gender-affirming medical treatments for pediatric patients with gender dysphoria.* https://doi.org/10.13140/RG.2.2.17321.04963

LaRocca, D., James, K. A., Rosenberg, S., Ma, M., & Brooks-Russell, A. (2022). Team sports participation, depression, and suicidal ideation in lesbian, gay, bisexual, transgender, and questioning adolescents. *Psychology in the Schools, 60*(4), 902–911. https://doi.org/10.1002/pits.22792

Lee, W. Y., Hobbs, J. N., Hobaica, S., DeChants, J. P., Price, M. N., & Nath, R. (2024). State-level antitransgender laws increase past-year suicide attempts among transgender and non-binary young people in the USA. *Nature Human Behavior, 8*(11), 2096–2106. https://doi.org/10.1038/s41562-024-01979-5

Leventhal, A. M., Cho, J., Andrabi, N., & Barrington-Trimis, J. (2018). Association of reported concern about increasing societal discrimination with adverse behavioral health outcomes in late adolescence. *JAMA Pediatrics, 172*(10), 924–933. https://doi.org/10.1001/jamapediatrics.2018.2022

LGBTQ+ Bar. (2025). *Trump anti-LGBTQ+ executive order litigation tracker*. https://lgbtqbar.org/programs/trump-executive-order-tracker/

Lucas, R., Kahn, N., Bocek, K., Tordoff, D. M., Karrington, B., Richardson, L. P., & Sequeira, G. M. (2023). Telemedicine utilization among transgender and gender-diverse adolescents before and after the COVID-19 pandemic. *Telemedicine and E-Health, 29*(9), 1304–1311. https://doi.org/10.1089/tmj.2022.0382

Lundstrum, R. (2021). *H.B. No. 1570: To create the Arkansas Save Adolescents From Experimentation (SAFE) Act* (93rd Gen. Assemb., Reg. Sess.). Arkansas Legislature. https://www.arkleg.state.ar.us/Bills/Detail?id=HB1570&ddBienniumSession=2021%2F2021R

Malpas, J., Pellicane, M. J., & Glaeser, E. (2022). Family-based interventions with transgender and gender expansive youth: Systematic review and best practice recommendations. *Transgender Health, 7*(1), 7–29. https://doi.org/10.1089/trgh.2020.0165

McNamara, M., Lepore, C., Alstott, A., Kamody, R., Kuper, L., Szilagyi, N., Boulware, S., & Olezeski, C. (2022). Scientific misinformation and gender affirming care: Tools for providers on the front lines. *Journal of Adolescent Health, 71*(3), 251–253. https://doi.org/10.1016/j.jadohealth.2022.06.008

McQuillan, M. T., Cimpian, J. R., Lebovitz, B. A., & Gill, E. K. (2024). Transgender adolescent school climate, mental health, and adult social support. *JAMA Pediatrics, 178*(10), 1082–1084. https://doi.org/10.1001/jamapediatrics.2024.3079

Movement Advancement Project. (2026). *LGBTQ equality program: LGBTQ equality maps*. Retrieved April 3, 2026, from https://www.mapresearch.org/equality/

Ohio Department of Health. (2024). *Gender transition quality care* [Unfiled draft]. https://dbh.ohio.gov/static/AboutUs/RulesandRegulations/DraftRules/5122-26-19-Final_01052024.pdf

Olson, K. R., Durwood, L., DeMeules, M., & McLaughlin, K. A. (2016). Mental health of transgender children who are supported in their identities. *Pediatrics, 137*(3), e20153223. https://doi.org/10.1542/peds.2015-3223

Olson, K. R., Durwood, L., Horton, R., Gallagher, N. M., & Devor, A. (2022). Gender identity 5 years after social transition. *Pediatrics, 150*(2), e2021056082. https://doi.org/10.1542/peds.2021-056082

Olson, K. R., Raber, G. F., & Gallagher, N. M. (2024). Levels of satisfaction and regret with gender-affirming medical care in adolescence. *JAMA Pediatrics, 178*(12), 1354–1361. https://doi.org/10.1001/jamapediatrics.2024.4527

Oransky, M., Burke, E. Z., & Steever, J. (2019). Building professional competency: Training psychologists in gender affirmative care. *Clinical Practice in Pediatric Psychology, 7*(3), 322–333. https://doi.org/10.1037/cpp0000292

Price, M. A., & Hollinsaid, N. L. (2022). Future directions in mental health treatment with stigmatized youth. *Journal of Clinical Child and Adolescent Psychology, 51*(5), 810–825. https://doi.org/10.1080/15374416.2022.2109652

Price, M. A., Hollinsaid, N. L., McKetta, S., Mellen, E. J., & Rakhilin, M. (2024). Structural transphobia is associated with psychological distress and suicidality in a large national sample of transgender adults. *Social Psychiatry and Psychiatric Epidemiology, 59*(2), 285–294. https://doi.org/10.1007/s00127-023-02482-4

Rafferty, J., Committee on Psychosocial Aspects of Child and Family Health; Committee on Adolescence; Section on Lesbian, Gay, Bisexual, and Transgender Health and Wellness, Yogman, M., Baum, R., Gambon, T. B., Lavin, A., Mattson, G., Wissow, L. S., Breuner, C., Alderman, E. M., Grubb, L. K., Powers, M. E., Upadhya, K., Wallace, S. B., Hunt, L., Gearhart, A. T., Harris, C., Lowe, K. M., Rodgers, C. T., & Sherer, I. M.

(2018). Ensuring comprehensive care and support for transgender and gender-diverse children and adolescents. *Pediatrics, 142*(4), e20182162. https://doi.org/10.1542/peds.2018-2162

Redfield, E., Conron, K. J., Tentindo, W., & Browning, E. (2023). *Prohibiting gender-affirming medical care for youth*. UCLA School of Law Williams Institute. https://williamsinstitute.law.ucla.edu/publications/bans-trans-youth-health-care/

Reisner, S. L., Vetters, R., Leclerc, M., Zaslow, S., Wolfrum, S., Shumer, D., & Mimiaga, M. J. (2015). Mental health of transgender youth in care at an adolescent urban community health center: A matched retrospective cohort study. *Journal of Adolescent Health, 56*(3), 274–279. https://doi.org/10.1016/j.jadohealth.2014.10.264

Rider, G. N., McMorris, B. J., Gower, A. L., Coleman, E., & Eisenberg, M. E. (2018). Health and care utilization of transgender and gender nonconforming youth: A population-based study. *Pediatrics, 141*(3), e20171683. https://doi.org/10.1542/peds.2017-1683

Russell, S. T., Pollitt, A. M., Li, G., & Grossman, A. H. (2018). Chosen name use is linked to reduced depressive symptoms, suicidal ideation, and suicidal behavior among transgender youth. *Journal of Adolescent Health, 63*(4), 503–505. https://doi.org/10.1016/j.jadohealth.2018.02.003

Ryan, C., Barba, A., & Cohen, J. A. (2023). Family-based psychosocial care for transgender and gender-diverse children and youth. *Child and Adolescent Psychiatric Clinics of North America, 32*(4), 775–788. https://doi.org/10.1016/j.chc.2023.03.002

Toomey, R. B. (2021). Advancing research on minority stress and resilience in trans children and adolescents in the 21st century. *Child Development Perspectives, 15*(2), 96–102. https://doi.org/10.1111/cdep.12405

Toomey, R. B., Syvertsen, A. K., & Shramko, M. (2018). Transgender adolescent suicide behavior. *Pediatrics, 142*(4), e20174218. https://doi.org/10.1542/peds.2017-4218

The Trevor Project. (2023, January 19). *New poll emphasizes negative impacts of anti-LGBTQ policies on LGBTQ youth*. https://www.thetrevorproject.org/blog/new-poll-emphasizes-negative-impacts-of-anti-lgbtq-policies-on-lgbtq-youth/

United States v. Skrmetti, 605 U.S. 495 (2025). https://www.supremecourt.gov/opinions/24pdf/23-477_2cp3.pdf

van der Miesen, A. I. R., Steensma, T. D., de Vries, A. L. C., Bos, H., & Popma, A. (2020). Psychological functioning in transgender adolescents before and after gender-affirmative care compared with cisgender general population peers. *Journal of Adolescent Health, 66*(6), 699–704. https://doi.org/10.1016/j.jadohealth.2019.12.018

Williams, D. R., & Medlock, M. M. (2017). Health effects of dramatic societal events—Ramifications of the recent presidential election. *New England Journal of Medicine, 376*(23), 2295–2299. https://doi.org/10.1056/NEJMms1702111

Wittlin, N. M., Gallagher, N. M., Atwood, S., & Olson, K. R. (2025). Mental health during medical transition in a US and Canadian sample of early socially transitioned transgender youth. *Journal of Adolescent Health*, 76(2), 228–237. https://doi.org/10.1016/j.jadohealth.2024.10.023

Wittlin, N. M., Kuper, L. E., & Olson, K. R. (2023). Mental health of transgender and gender diverse youth. *Annual Review of Clinical Psychology, 19*(1), 207–232. https://doi.org/10.1146/annurev-clinpsy-072220-020326

12 ETHICAL PRACTICE IN THE CARE OF TRANSGENDER AND GENDER DIVERSE CHILDREN

DREW B. A. CLARK

This chapter begins with an overview of concepts relevant to ethical health care practice with transgender and gender diverse (TGD) children and their families. Next is an introduction to five approaches to ethical reasoning, with an in-depth exploration of narrative ethics. The final section focuses on external factors that constrain the ability of health care providers to uphold their values. Throughout the chapter, we follow the story of Milo (she), her parents, Rebecca (she) and Trent (he), and her counselor, Janine (she).

INTRODUCTION TO ETHICAL PRACTICE

In our daily lives, we make many choices based on our core beliefs about what is right. These deeply held beliefs can be called *personal values*. When we "do good," "choose the right path," or "act according to our conscience," we are living our values. Personal values form our sense of morality and are foundational to how we live our lives, including the vocations we pursue. For example, the values of service and care can be enacted through careers in health care. The clients (i.e., patients and other recipients of care) and

https://doi.org/10.1037/0000494-013
Pediatric Gender Health Care: The Gender Affirmative Model Revisited, Second Edition, G. N. Rider, D. Ehrensaft, and C. St. Amand (Editors)

families with whom we work live their lives and make decisions based on their personal values, which may be similar to or different from our own.

Health Care Ethics

Ethics is a structured approach to determining what is good or right or just, based on shared values (Chaddha & Agrawal, 2023). As health care providers, those shared values may be explicated in our *codes of ethics* or implicitly understood as part of health care practice. Mental health care providers should abide by the American Psychological Association (APA; 2017) *Ethical Principles of Psychologists and Code of Conduct*, along with ethics codes of other professional organizations such as the American Medical Association (AMA; 2016), the American Nurses Association (ANA; 2015), the Canadian Medical Association (CMA; 2004), the Canadian Nurses Association (CNA; 2017), or the National Association of Social Workers (NASW; 2021). Commonly held *health care values* include care, equity, fidelity (i.e., placing the interests of our clients above our own), humility (i.e., acknowledging our limitations and being willing to learn from others), justice, and respect. Clients and families are not bound by health care values or codes of ethics; however, as health care providers, we are held to ethical standards by our professional bodies to promote fair treatment of those in our care.

Milo's Gender Journey

Before we move on to ways we may approach ethical reasoning in practice, let us consider a scenario that could arise in the care of TGD children and their families.[1]

Milo (she/her) is 9 years old, designated male at birth, and has been determined by her pediatrician to be in Tanner stage 2 of pubertal development. When Rebecca (mother) has talked with Milo about changes that will happen in puberty, Milo has become very upset. She does not want to grow facial hair or have her voice deepen. She is also worried that she will grow to be 6′4″, like her father. Milo has been asking her mother for help to go through "girl puberty" instead of "boy puberty." Milo's parents are divorced, and she lives with Rebecca. Milo sees Trent (father) one weekend each month. Milo has not talked with Trent about her gender, her use of she pronouns, or her concerns about puberty, as she is worried about his response. Rebecca has agreed to take Milo to a counselor who specializes in gender health care. Rebecca has

[1]The clinical example provided in this chapter is fictional.

also recently learned about a gender clinic at a nearby hospital in the midwestern U.S. state where Milo, Rebecca, and Trent all reside.

We will revisit Milo's story throughout this chapter.

Ethical Practice in Health Care

Ethical practice in health care involves upholding health care values in our decisions, actions, and relationships (ANA, 2015; CNA, 2017). There are ethical dimensions to everything we do in our health care practices. *Everyday ethics* describes how we strive each day, in every interaction, to do what is right (CNA, 2017). In doing this, we practice our ethical duty of *fidelity*, placing the interests of our clients above our own (i.e., in the context of fiduciary relationships; Lo, 2013).

"What should I do?" When you are asking this question of yourself in the context of clinical practice, you may be encountering an *ethical dilemma*. Ethical dilemmas include situations when values come into conflict, creating uncertainty about the right course of action (Post & Blustein, 2015). For example, the values of respect and care may come into tension when respect for a person's autonomy to make their own decisions comes into conflict with providing health care that, in your professional opinion, is in their best interests. An ethical dilemma occurs when you genuinely do not know the right thing to do because any course of action will result in a transgression of one or more health care values.

Janine's Ethical Dilemma

Let us continue with Milo's story.

Milo discusses her need to prevent voice deepening, facial hair growth, and "turning into a boy" with her new counselor, Janine. Janine provides a developmentally appropriate explanation of the process of puberty and treatments used for pubertal suppression that pause unwanted bodily changes, to which Milo responds with great relief. Milo is feeling optimistic about starting puberty blockers and understands, at a developmentally appropriate level, how they work. After a few sessions, Milo decides she wants to tell Trent, who shares medical decision-making authority with Rebecca, about her need for puberty blockers. Rebecca tells Janine she is confident Trent will be receptive, but that he may need some time to wrap his mind around the idea. Milo talks with Trent and reports to Janine, "It did not go well." Rebecca shares with Janine that Trent called her and said, "Milo is confused. I will not allow her to take drugs to stop puberty. If you take Milo to that gender clinic without my permission, I will petition the court for full custody." Milo overheard Trent and Rebecca's conversation and is devastated by Trent's response. Milo asks Janine if there is any way she can secretly get puberty blockers. She asks Janine whether Trent could really take her away from her mother, saying, "He can't do that, right? My mom is the only one who understands me. I hardly know my dad." At Rebecca's request, Janine had already drafted a letter of support for pubertal suppression to accompany the referral Milo's pediatrician will be sending to the local gender clinic. Now Janine is uncertain whether to send the letter.

Janine is in the midst of an ethical dilemma. She is uncertain whether to support Milo's referral for puberty blockers at this time. She is bound to uphold fidelity, putting Milo's interests first. However, Janine is no longer sure what is in Milo's best interests because it appears that Milo will face harm in her familial situation if the referral moves forward, but Milo will not have her gender health care needs met if the referral is not made.

Ethics and the Law

It is important to distinguish ethics from the law. The law addresses particular aspects of human behavior that are allowed or disallowed within a particular jurisdiction, whereas ethical thinking can be applied to all decisions, interactions, and actions of human beings. Based on our personal values, we may agree with some laws but not others. Many laws are enacted to support ethical practice in health care (e.g., privacy laws), but others may go against health care values when applied in certain contexts. Health care professionals and their professional organizations can play pivotal roles in helping governments align laws with ethical health care practices (AMA, 2024; APA, n.d.; Canadian Psychiatric Association, n.d.; World Professional Association for Transgender Health, n.d.).

This chapter focuses on resolving ethical dilemmas in clinical practice. Health care is delivered within systems that can constrain the ability of health care providers to provide care that aligns with their values (Bernhardt et al., 2021; Jameton, 1984). This includes health care systems that do not provide accessible services to all people, as well as legal systems that interfere with the ability of health care providers and their clients to make evidence-based decisions about their health care. The existence of such constraints does not constitute an ethical dilemma (i.e., all people should have access to health care), but these constraints can be relevant to our practices and may shape both ethical dilemmas and possibilities for resolving them. Therefore, in this chapter, we will address how these constraints affect us and our ability to engage in ethical practice.

Ethical and Legal Issues in Milo's Care

In Milo's situation, ethical and legal issues are intertwined.

Janine is uncertain what is in Milo's best interests because there are potential risks of harm from supporting a referral for pubertal suppression, including relational conflict with Trent and potential constraints on the support Rebecca will be allowed to provide in the future. Janine is also well aware of the potential harms from not proceeding with the pubertal suppression referral, including distress from pubertal changes and harm to the therapeutic relationship between Janine and Milo.

Legal issues that affect this scenario include that Rebecca and Trent share medical decision-making authority and that Trent could petition the court for sole medical decision-making authority or sole custody if Rebecca were to go forth unilaterally with a visit to a gender clinic. If laws are proposed or in place that restrict access to gender-affirming medical interventions for minors, this could further complicate the situation. The sociopolitical climate, as well as the particular judge assigned to the case, might also impact whether the court would rule in favor of Rebecca or Trent if petitions for sole medical decision-making authority or sole custody were pursued.

Key Ethical and Legal Concepts

Ethics in pediatric health care provides structured approaches for determining an appropriate course of action when values come into conflict and there is uncertainty or disagreement about how to proceed in caring for a child or family. Concepts important to define when talking about pediatric ethics in the care of TGD children include capacity, authority, consent, best interests, human rights, and bias.

Capacity in health care is the ability of a person to make a decision about a particular health care intervention, including consenting to or refusing treatment (Cummings & Mercurio, 2010; Harrison et al., 2004). Higher-magnitude decisions with more significant consequences (e.g., refusing life-saving treatment) require a higher level of capacity than lower-magnitude decisions with less significant implications (e.g., initiating hormonal contraceptives; Cummings & Mercurio, 2010; Harrison et al., 2004). The health care provider treating the client is responsible for providing the person with information about the intervention and ensuring that the person is capable of providing consent or assent (i.e., permission; Canadian Medical Protective Association [CMPA], 2022). Capacity to consent to a health care intervention is evaluated based on four criteria: the client's ability to (1) understand information about the intervention (e.g., how the intervention and alternatives work; the benefits, risks, and alternatives), (2) appreciate the information in terms of their own life (e.g., anticipated challenges that may arise), (3) reason about intervention options (e.g., what options best support their gender embodiment goals), and (4) communicate a well-reasoned choice aligned with their values (e.g., why this choice is right for them; Lo, 2013; Palmer & Harmell, 2016; Ruhe et al., 2015). For more on these four criteria, also see Appendix 12.1 (Clark & Virani, 2024). For example, a person could demonstrate capacity by receiving accurate information about hormone therapy from their doctor; demonstrating that they understand that information by considering what it would be like for them to take hormone therapy; reflecting on whether hormone therapy is the best option for them; and communicating to the doctor a choice that initiating hormone therapy aligns with their value of authenticity and is the best option for their gender embodiment at this time.

This standard process for evaluating capacity in health care decision-making supports well-thought-out decisions. Concerns are sometimes raised about the capacity of minor youth to consent to health care interventions. However, research confirms that minor youth can demonstrate capacity to consent to health care interventions, including gender embodiment care (Clark & Virani, 2021; Grootens-Wiegers et al., 2017; Weithorn & Campbell, 1982). The issue of impulsivity is also raised with respect to youth decision-making. All humans are susceptible to impulsivity, depending on the circumstances surrounding a decision. *Hot decisions* refer to those made quickly and under pressure (e.g., impulsively deciding to steal a candy bar from a convenience store), whereas *cold decisions* are those made over time, with guidance and thoughtful reasoning (e.g., deciding to proceed with a medical intervention after discussing it with a health care provider). The capacity evaluation process in health care supports cold decisions that are in the client's best interests (Ravindranath et al., 2024).

In a health care decision-making context, *authority* describes the legal ability to give permission for a health care intervention or to refuse an intervention (Clark & Virani, 2021). The term authority is used here in the interest of clarity to denote a person's legal standing to make health care decisions; however, this concept may be described elsewhere using other terms, such as *legal capacity* (i.e., age of majority combined with decisional capacity). For example, in the United States, people must be 18 years of age before they have the legal authority to give consent for most health care services (depending on the state, there may be exceptions for some forms of health care; Goodlander & Berg, 2011). In Canada, legislation in most provinces and territories is not based on an arbitrary, stipulated age of consent but rather on the capacity of a minor to consent to a specific health care intervention (Coughlin, 2018). This approach supports youth autonomy and self-determination in exercising legal authority over their own health care decisions.

Consent in health care is the act of giving permission for a health care intervention. This is a legal and ethical act, with three specific requirements: (a) The person giving consent must have capacity to make this health care decision; (b) the treating health care provider must ensure the person is informed of the nature, purpose, benefits, and risks of the intervention and available alternatives; and (c) consent must be given voluntarily, without duress or coercion (CMPA, 2024). *Assent* is another form of agreement, given by a client when they lack either capacity or legal authority to consent to an intervention (Harrison et al., 2004; Unguru, 2011). For example, a child may not have developed the capacity to make a specific health care decision, in which case their proxy decision-maker, usually a parent or guardian, makes the decision and provides consent or refusal on the child's behalf. Although the child may not have full capacity to provide consent, assent indicates they have been informed about the proposed intervention at a developmentally appropriate level, and they agree to the intervention. The assent process supports children in developing decision-making capacity and ensures their views are considered and supported where possible. Alternatively, a 16-year-old may have capacity to consent to care but be legally prohibited from doing so because of a law about the age of consent in the jurisdiction where they are accessing care. In this situation, a proxy decision-maker would be asked to provide consent, and the youth would be asked to assent. Depending on the jurisdiction and relevant legal orders (e.g., custody agreement), either one or all parents or guardians would be required to provide consent to a medical intervention when a child lacks the capacity and/or authority to provide their own consent (Coleman et al., 2022).

Best interests is an important concept in pediatric health care ethics, as this is a common standard for making decisions on behalf of those who cannot make decisions for themselves (Kopelman, 2007). Interests of particular relevance to gender health include autonomy, health, identity, life, protection from neglect, self-expression, and sense of self (Clark & Virani, 2021; Malek, 2009). Health care providers act in the best interest of clients as part of their duty of fidelity. Proxy decision-makers are also expected to make decisions that promote the overall well-being of the child, although people may be in disagreement about actions or interventions that are in the best interests of a child in a given situation (Kopelman, 2007). When health care providers believe a proxy decision-maker is not acting in the best interests of a child (e.g., not providing the minimum standard of care, or circumstances of medical neglect), they may seek intervention through child protective services or the courts, for example, to give legal authority for medical decision-making to another party to prevent serious harm to the child (Diekema, 2011; Kopelman, 2007).

Human rights are rights held by (or owed to) individuals because of their innate worth as human beings (United Nations [UN], 1948). These rights include the right to the highest attainable standard of health, nondiscrimination, access to health services, privacy, dignity, and life (Office of the United Nations High Commissioner for Human Rights [OHCHR], 2008). Human rights are paired with responsibilities; so when one person has rights, others have responsibilities to uphold them. Even though children may be limited in capacity to make certain decisions, they are inherent human rights holders. Parents, guardians, and others (e.g., health care providers and teachers) are obligated to uphold children's human rights. Sometimes the term *parental rights* is used in a manner that is inconsistent with the concept of human rights (e.g., a parental right to control a child's gender would violate the inherent human rights of the child; Ashley, 2024). Parents and guardians have the responsibility and also the legal authority to make decisions in their children's best interests (provided the parents and guardians themselves have the capacity to do so). However, this legal authority is not absolute, as the state and/or government has the authority to intervene when parents and guardians are unable or unwilling to uphold the rights of their children (e.g., medical neglect in violation of a child's right to the highest attainable standard of health; Goodlander & Berg, 2011). When parental rights are discussed in the context of TGD children, it is typically the idea of parental authority to make decisions on behalf of children that is being invoked. Although this authority is broad in scope and extent, it has limits when the well-being of a child is endangered (Diekema, 2011; Kopelman, 2007).

Finally, it is important to consider how *bias* can affect ethical decision making in the realm of gender embodiment care for TGD children. When implicit or explicit biases are enacted in ways that cause inequity and injustice for TGD people, this is ethically problematic (Clark, 2021). Endocisnormativity (i.e., assuming only expected binary male/female sex characteristics and cisgender experiences are normal) can negatively affect care for TGD children (Hastings et al., 2021). Endocisnormative biases can manifest in the form of erroneous assumptions that being cisgender is preferable to being transgender or that being TGD is reflective of mental illness. Another misconception affecting the care of TGD people concerns the nature and magnitude of decisions about gender embodiment care (e.g., pubertal suppression, hormone therapy) relative to decisions about other forms of health care (e.g., refusing life-saving treatment, initiating hormonal contraceptives, and choosing which antidepressant to trial). TGD people can be problematically expected to demonstrate higher levels of capacity for gender embodiment interventions than people consenting to comparable forms of health care, based on biases about gender and gender embodiment care. In accordance with procedural justice (i.e., fair process), TGD people should not be expected to demonstrate higher levels of capacity or be subjected to more stringent requirements for consent to health care than people attempting to access similar forms of health care.

Milo's Best Interests

We do not know whether Milo has capacity to consent to pubertal suppression treatment, as she has not had the opportunity to meet with a health care provider to receive the information necessary to provide informed consent for this treatment. However, as she understands the purpose and effects of the treatment, Milo could likely, at a minimum, give assent. Milo resides in the United States, where authority to consent to health care rests with Rebecca and Trent, because Milo is younger than age 18 and her parents are joint medical decision-makers according to their custody agreement. Janine and Rebecca have agreed that a referral to the gender clinic to discuss pubertal suppression treatment is in Milo's best interests, but Trent disagrees with this. To better understand Trent's position and whether biases are affecting his understanding of Milo's best interests, more information is needed.

Milo asks Janine to talk with Trent. Rebecca thinks this might be helpful. Trent and Janine talk by phone, and she invites him to discuss his understandings and concerns. Trent shares misinformation about gender embodiment care, and puberty suppression treatment in particular, which aligns with endocisnormative misinformation messages currently circulating online. Janine listens and validates Trent's concern for his child's well-being. Trent is not interested in discussing scientific evidence with Janine during the appointment but does provide an email address so she can send resources to him. He ends the conversation by saying he will not change his mind about withholding consent for Milo to access puberty blockers. In her next appointment, Milo asks Janine if she has sent her letter of support to the gender clinic yet.

APPROACHES TO ETHICAL REASONING IN GENDER HEALTH CARE

In an ideal health care world, there would be no ethical dilemmas. We would easily be able to do what is right by acting in alignment with our personal and health care values. In the real world, conflicts and tensions emerge among health care values, and it is our ethical obligation to thoughtfully navigate such situations. We do this through ethical reasoning, taking a structured approach to determining the right way forward in the face of ethical uncertainty (Chaddha & Agrawal, 2023). *Procedural justice,* following consistent processes in resolving ethical dilemmas, can help reduce bias, promote equity, and develop support for a resolution. When an ethical dilemma arises, we want to engage in good processes to gather information, apply established approaches to ethical reasoning, and develop resolutions well aligned with health care values and what is important to those at the center of the ethical dilemma.

We all have biases, make assumptions, and are limited by our own positionalities and experiences. Collaborative ethical practice is a way to promote procedural justice and reduce bias in ethical reasoning. When we encounter ethical dilemmas, we should engage with *humility,* acknowledging our limitations and being willing to learn from others (Chochinov, 2010). Humility can be upheld through listening to those central to the ethical dilemma, asking questions, expanding our understandings, and being open to different ways of knowing. Humility helps us be open to understanding a person's unique needs and circumstances and to appreciate that what works for one person may not work for another. Collaborative ethical practice may take place within interdisciplinary teams, in consultation with professional bodies, and alongside clients and families.

To support ethical reasoning, it is crucial to collect information to ensure we have a reasonably complete understanding of the issues involved. Key information may take the form of empirical research evidence, medical indications, the preferences and values of clients and families, and the sociopolitical context in which the dilemma is playing out (Faissner et al., 2024; Frader, 1992; Jonsen et al., 2015). Some ethical dilemmas need to be resolved quickly (e.g., emergency situations), which can limit the amount of information obtained; however, often there is time to gather information and perspectives and to facilitate a robust collaborative process to resolve ethical dilemmas.

Approaches to Ethical Analysis

There are many approaches to ethical analysis that can support ethical practice in all areas of health care, including the care of TGD children. A principles-based approach, analyzing the four principles of biomedical ethics (i.e., autonomy, beneficence, nonmaleficence, and justice), is a colonial, western approach dominant within U.S. and Canadian health care systems. Balanced application of the four principles can be helpful in resolving many ethical dilemmas (Beauchamp & Childress, 2013). However, the principles-based approaches have been critiqued for paying insufficient attention to context (i.e., the relational, social, and political realities of clients and families), which has the potential to compromise fair treatment, particularly of members of equity-deserving groups (Huxtable, 2013; Marway & Widdows, 2015; Ray, 2021). Four additional approaches to ethical analysis, which attend specifically to relationship, rights, intersectionality, and narratives, are briefly described next.

Relational ethics helps us center themes such as embodiment, engagement, environment, and mutual respect in ethical analysis (Bergum, 2013; Moore et al., 2014). The theme of embodiment is particularly relevant within the gender affirmative model, as supporting mind–body connection is aligned with freely and comfortably living in one's gender (Bergum, 2013). *Rights-based ethics* is grounded in fundamental rights that are codified in international human rights documents, such as the Convention on the Rights of the Child (Beracochea et al., 2010; Melia, 2014; Peel, 2005; UN, 1989, 2007). Specific rights central to gender embodiment care include the rights to preserve identity, be afforded freedom of expression, have views given weight in accordance with maturity, and have access to the highest attainable standard of health. *Intersectional bioethics* centers context, specifically intersectional oppression and the impacts this has on health care access, health care experiences, and health outcomes (Brünig et al., 2024; Grzanka et al., 2016; Wilson et al., 2019). *Narrative ethics* focuses on developing ethical resolutions that make sense within the story of the client, accounting for the characters, events, and outside influences that have shaped the story up to the point of the dilemma to help determine the best possible path forward (Brody & Clark, 2014; Montello, 2014). The most appropriate approach or approaches to analyzing an ethical dilemma should be selected based on the nature and context of the dilemma.

Narrative Ethics

In this section, we explore narrative ethics in greater depth to demonstrate its applicability in gender embodiment care for TGD children. Narrative ethics focuses on stories, and in this context, the stories that intersect with health and health care (Baldwin, 2015; Brody & Clark, 2014; Montello, 2014). When encountering an ethical dilemma, narratives provide rich information that can guide us to an ethical resolution. We focus on the *characters* present in the story, the *voices* telling the story (as well as the voices not heard), and the *plot* of the story (Montello, 2014). We look for ruptures in the plotline, which cause the story to take unexpected turns (Montello, 2014). These ruptures can help us understand how values have come into conflict and shaped the ethical dilemma.

In addition to the three elements of character, voice, and plot, narrative ethics calls on us to analyze the story temporally and contextually—looking backward, side to side, and forward (Lindemann, 2014). We look backward to understand the past that has brought the characters to this point in the story. We look side to side to understand the contextual influences (e.g., access to health care, antitrans legislation) on the story (Lindemann, 2014). Lastly, we draw on character, voice, plot, and contextual information in looking forward to reach a *resolution* that will bring consonance to a dissonant story (Montello, 2014). The resolution in narrative ethics is that which makes sense as the best next step in the main character's (i.e., client's) story.

Narrative Ethics and Gender Journeys

The field of gender health, shaped by the gender affirmative model, focuses on opportunities for children to live in genders that feel most real and/or comfortable (Hidalgo et al., 2013). This goal is well aligned with that of narrative ethics, through which we seek a resolution to a dilemma that makes sense in the story of the client, sometimes referred to as the *gender journey*. Through exploring narratives, we can come alongside a child, learning the story of who they are and who they are becoming. This process facilitates openness to the many possible directions a person's life may take, as we work toward the best next plot points during the brief time that we intersect with a child's gender journey. The resolution should be a next step forward on their pathway to gender health. The process of reaching the resolution can help people make sense of their own medical and gender journeys.

As health care providers, we are aware of the lifelong health implications of adverse childhood events (ACEs) and gender minority stress (Feil et al., 2023; Hendricks & Testa, 2012; Reisner et al., 2015; Testa et al., 2017). We see higher burdens of disease, mental health concerns, and, more recently, long COVID among TGD populations (Cohen & van der Meulen Rodgers, 2023; Eisenberg et al., 2017; Scheim et al., 2024). These findings intersect with social determinants of health, including less access to education, employment, housing, and health care on a population level (Clark et al., 2018; Glick et al., 2020; Gonzales & Henning-Smith, 2017; Gonzales et al., 2024). As we explore narratives with TGD children, we may uncover ACEs and other factors causing gender minority stress. Understanding how these events have unfolded and how external forces have affected a child's gender journey can provide important information for ethical resolutions that can promote better health outcomes over the lifespan.

In today's sociopolitical climate, we are often trying to support children to live in their genders as comfortably as possible under circumstances that are not ideal, including the colonial imposition of a sex and gender binary and legal restrictions on access to gender embodiment care (Costello, 2020; Hughes et al., 2021; Kraschel et al., 2022). Negative messages about TGD experiences and communities are pervasive, from playgrounds to political advertisements. As we explore a child's narrative, we may uncover instances or patterns of invalidation of gender-related experiences. Narrative ethics can support resolutions to ethical dilemmas that address past and ongoing harms. Our responsibility as health care providers is to look for clues about what has shaped a child's gender journey to this point, so we may discern what steps should be taken to enhance gender health moving forward, within the context of a complex lived reality.

Narrative ethics involves deep listening to discern what is important to a person (Montello, 2014). As such, resolving an ethical dilemma through narrative ethical analysis could be understood as a supportive intervention unto itself. The experience of being truly heard, being seen for who you are, and having your needs centered can be a powerful experience. This can become part of a child's narrative moving forward. Narrative ethics can also support understanding that we can take the next step on a journey while leaving doors open for the future. The resolution can provide a plot point a person can draw upon in the face of future challenges. The narrative ethical analysis process can provide a roadmap for making well-thought-out decisions about best next steps on a person's journey, within the context of their overall well-being, relationships, and environment.

Milo's Gender Journey: A Narrative Ethical Analysis

Ethical dilemma: Should Janine submit a letter in support of the referral Milo's pediatrician is making to the gender clinic regarding pubertal suppression?

Characters: Milo (she) is 9 years old and the main character in this narrative. Rebecca (she) is Milo's mother, and Trent (he) is Milo's father. Janine (she) is Milo's counselor and has expertise in the field of pediatric gender health.

Voice: While all of the characters' voices are heard, it is Janine's voice that is most dominant in the telling of the story. Janine has shared key quotes from Milo and Trent and summarized her communications with all three family members. The story is presented through her lens as a counselor who has a duty of fidelity to Milo.

Plot: Some of the important plot points in this story include Milo asking Rebecca for help to go through "girl puberty"; Milo engaging with Janine for counseling; Milo talking with Trent about her gender health needs; Trent rejecting Milo's requests; Trent threatening Rebecca that he will petition the family court for full custody if she takes Milo to the gender clinic; Trent sharing with Janine his objections to pubertal suppression grounded in misinformation; and Milo reiterating to Janine her need to go through "girl puberty" and have support from Rebecca. The most significant rupture in the plot of Milo's story is Trent's rejection of her request for support to access pubertal suppression. This has resulted in distress for Milo and Rebecca as well as in an ethical dilemma for Janine, who is uncertain how to best support Milo in the face of multiple potential harms.

Resolution: In deliberating about her ethical dilemma, Janine focuses on the needs that Milo, the main character in the narrative, has clearly and consistently voiced—to access pubertal suppression and live primarily in Rebecca's supportive home. Janine reflects on Milo's distress around Trent's reaction to their conversation about her gender health and Milo's fear of being removed from Rebecca's custody. Janine is concerned over this point of dissonance about the potential negative effects on Milo if she feels unsupported by Janine and if she is unable to access pubertal suppression. Janine decides the best next step will be for her to send the letter of support for Milo's pubertal suppression referral to the gender clinic. This will convey to Milo that Janine understands the importance and urgency of her need for pubertal suppression and is actively supporting her.

Before Janine submits the letter, she talks with Rebecca, who asks if Janine will meet with her and Trent together. In the meeting, Janine tells Rebecca and Trent that in her professional opinion, Milo's best interests would be served by a referral to the gender clinic to discuss pubertal suppression. Janine explains that a referral is being made by Milo's pediatrician and that there will be a wait time of 2 to 4 months for an initial appointment with a medical provider at the gender clinic. Trent says he is relieved, as he thought the process would move much faster based on things he had read online. He says he read the material Janine emailed to him and discussed some of it with his doctor. Janine answers questions from Rebecca and Trent about pubertal suppression and the many possible ways Milo's gender journey might unfold.

At the end of the session, Janine shares that she will be sending a letter of support to accompany the referral to the gender clinic and asks if either parent has any questions or perspectives that they would like her to include in the letter. Rebecca and Trent agree that they want to support Milo's well-being, but they have some reservations about pubertal suppression. They would both like to speak with an experienced medical provider to learn more about the benefits and risks of pubertal suppression. Janine documents this information, submits the letter, and lets Milo know that she has sent her letter of support to the gender clinic.

TAKING ACTION: NAVIGATING CONSTRAINTS ON ETHICAL PRACTICE

The reality of practicing gender embodiment care in today's sociopolitical context is that health care providers' ability to deliver high-quality, timely, evidence-based services may be constrained. When we know the right thing to do (i.e., there is no ethical dilemma) but are prevented from doing so due to internal or external factors (e.g., restrictions on the provision of gender embodiment care), we may experience moral distress (Bernhardt et al., 2021; Gzesh et al., 2024; Jameton, 1984; Mabel et al., 2022). The manner in which we navigate constraints is important for our own well-being, for the health of our clients, and for the future of gender embodiment care. This section focuses on moral distress and strategies that could be applied in ethically navigating constraints on practice.

Moral Distress

Moral distress is a form of psychological distress experienced by health care providers when we are unable to act in alignment with our values (Bernhardt et al., 2021; Jameton, 1984). Moral distress can lead to burnout and people leaving health care practice (Dzeng & Wachter, 2020; Fernandez-Parsons et al., 2013; Sriharan et al., 2021). Moral distress is often connected to constrained agency, when we are prevented from doing what we believe is right by internal or external constraints (Silverman et al., 2021). It is important for the well-being of ourselves and our clients that we find ways to sustain ourselves in practice in the face of such constraints. Understanding the nature of the constraints and ways to address them can be important in responding to moral distress. When faced with limited options, as we work within systems that may include relational, resource-related, political, or legal constraints on our agency, we still must find the best pathways forward for our clients and ourselves.

Janine's Moral Distress

Although the ethical dilemma with Milo, Rebecca, and Trent has been resolved, Janine is experiencing moral distress. She sees other TGD children in her practice who do not have access to adequate social and health care supports. She has had colleagues and family members criticize her decision to support TGD children in her clinical practice. She recognizes that her moral distress is resulting in sleep disturbance and leading her to consider finding another career path. Janine reflects on her personal value of service that she has always described as calling her to the counseling profession. She thinks about her duties of care, fidelity, respect, and her intention to support greater health equity through her practice. As she reflects on the strength of her clients, Janine recognizes the privilege she holds as a cisgender woman and decides to engage with greater humility to learn from TGD communities about ways she can be of service in increasingly challenging sociopolitical times.

Strategies for Navigating System Constraints

Ethical practice is not neutral practice. Ethics calls on us to address inequities and injustice through connecting values to action. When structural factors constrain possibilities for optimal gender health, the stage is set for gender minority stress to have negative effects on a person's well-being across the lifespan. The following are strategies we can employ to proactively and responsively address constraints within systems of care to improve the gender health of our clients both individually and on a population level.

- **Evidence-based practice:** We can ensure our practices are evidence based, aligned with valid research evidence and practice standards. We can support policymakers and colleagues to access evidence-based information on gender and gender embodiment care.
- **Collaborative practice:** We can practice evidence-based care collaboratively and support one another when we encounter system constraints (e.g., policy changes) or other barriers (e.g., antitrans legislation) to ethical practice.
- **Education:** We can proactively and responsively provide accurate information about gender embodiment care. This may include addressing misinformation and drawing on our professional status as trusted health professionals to educate others about evidence-based practice and research findings (Lepore et al., 2022; McNamara et al., 2022).
- **Advocacy:** We can engage in advocacy to change unjust systems that constrain our ability to meet client needs. Advocacy may occur within small or large health care systems (e.g., policy, programming) and governments (e.g., funding allocation, laws).

Acting Outside Systems That Constrain Us

In addition to addressing constraints from within systems, there are many possibilities to act outside the systems that constrain us to create change.

The following four concepts describe possibilities for creating change by acting outside of roles that are typically expected of health care providers.

- **Direct action:** When services to meet the needs of TGD children do not exist or are inadequate, it may be possible to fill these gaps through volunteering to provide services (e.g., name change paperwork).
- **Conscientious objection:** When health care providers decide not to provide a service that is legally allowed due to their sincerely held belief that it is not right, this is called *conscientious objection* (Jonsen et al., 2015). Conscientious or moral objection is generally legally protected, with some limitations (Dickens & Cook, 2000).
- **Conscientious provision of care:** A lesser recognized moral concept is *conscientious provision of care*, which involves a health care provider acting outside of law or policy in providing care that aligns with their values or professional duties to clients (Matthews, 2024). Conscientious provision of care can carry significant risks for the health care provider (e.g., loss of licensure, lawsuits, or incarceration) and clients (e.g., loss of access to care) if it directly violates legislation (Lepore et al., 2022).
- **Community-building:** As long as health care for TGD people is politicized, system constraints will continue to pose challenges to health care providers' ability to provide evidence-based care. TGD and cisgender health care providers can find strength in working alongside TGD communities, drawing on the wisdom of TGD elders who have built the communities we serve today. We have not arrived by accident at this place, where evidence-based gender embodiment care has been developed for TGD people. It is the work of TGD elders that has brought us forward, and we can collectively work to ensure ongoing access to evidence-based and ethical care.

Taking Action

Janine decides to take action first by working within her health care system. She clearly articulates how her practices are evidence based and aligned with the current World Professional Association for Transgender Health Standards of Care.[2] She creates accessible summary resources and feels prepared to answer questions from colleagues, administrators, parents, and others about her practice. Janine then reaches out to other health care providers working with TGD children to form a collaborative practice group. They meet monthly to share experiences, offer support, and review new research. Working with

[2]See Coleman et al. (2022) for the latest standards.

another member from her collaborative practice group, Janine develops education resources and provides workshops for members of her health care organization that focus on accurate information about TGD children and gender embodiment care. The workshops include discussion of strategies for identifying and addressing misinformation. After these foundational steps, Janine successfully engages in advocacy to expand services for TGD children within her health care organization.

Janine is heartened by the progress made within her organization, but she and her colleagues are overwhelmed by referrals and unable to see new clients in a timely manner. Many children are well supported in their lives (e.g., strong parent/family support, counseling) but are looking for an experienced health care provider to complete an assessment for pubertal suppression or complete documentation for a legal name change. As a result of the constraints within her health care organization, Janine decides to engage in direct action and community-building to address some of these needs. She connects with TGD community members who are starting a low-barrier legal and medical clinic and offers her services free of charge one day per month.

Through these actions, Janine is able to enact her personal value of service and to uphold health care values of care, equity, fidelity, humility, justice, and respect. Taking action helps alleviate Janine's moral distress, as she identifies and better understands specific system constraints and works to actively expand access to care. These practices can be described as everyday ethics, as Janine aligns her clinical practice and volunteerism with health care values and the needs of her clients.

CONCLUSION

Ethical practice necessitates upholding health care values in clinical practice, including engaging with humility and maintaining fidelity to our clients' best interests. We encounter ethical dilemmas when we are genuinely uncertain about the best pathway forward. There are many tools available to us to support structured reasoning to resolve ethical dilemmas. Narrative ethics can be particularly applicable in working with TGD children and their families, allowing us to come alongside our clients, better understand their gender journeys, and work together to choose the best next step. It is important to recognize that health care and legal systems may impose constraints on our practices, and this can lead to moral distress. We can take action, both within and outside the systems that constrain us, by upholding values, engaging in ethical practice, and addressing system constraints in order to support TGD children to live comfortably in their genders, experience holistic well-being, and follow their passions and dreams with support of their loved ones.

APPENDIX 12.1: EVALUATING DECISION-MAKING CAPACITY FOR GENDER EMBODIMENT HEALTH CARE INTERVENTIONS

This practice tool provides guidance for healthcare providers supporting informed decision-making about gender embodiment healthcare interventions.

- Patients providing consent for any healthcare intervention must be informed, capable of making the decision, and acting voluntarily (without coercion).
- Healthcare providers should ensure patients have received the information necessary to make an informed decision (e.g., nature, purpose, benefits, risks, alternatives), as well as opportunities to have their questions answered.
- Healthcare providers should support patients with emerging capacity (e.g., youth) in developing their understanding, appreciation, reasoning, and communication throughout the care planning process.

Healthcare decision-making capacity is evaluated by the treating healthcare provider based on four components:

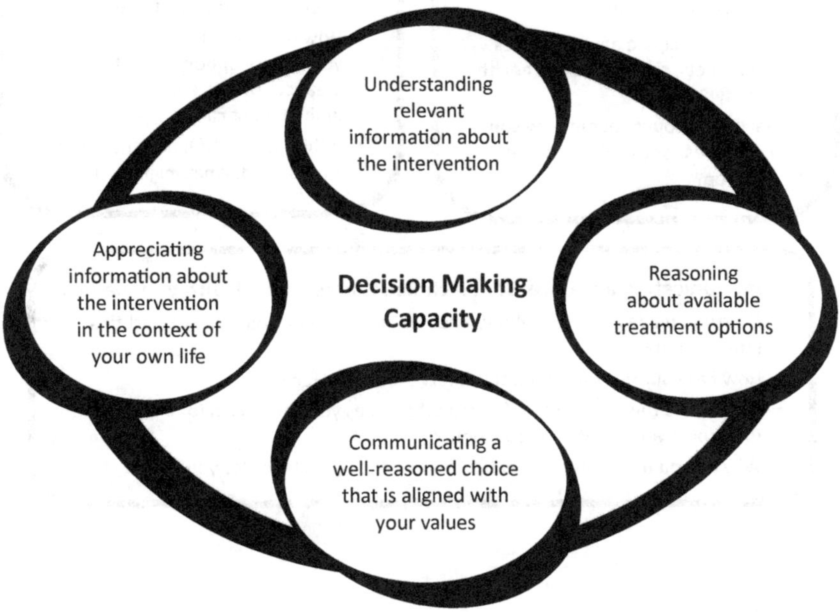

The following questions can support evaluation of decision-making capacity for gender embodiment healthcare interventions:

Understanding relevant information about the treatment

- Can you describe how the treatment works?
- What do you anticipate the main benefits of this treatment would be for you?
- Are you aware of possible risks?
- Are there any precautions you know you should take?

Appreciating information about the treatment in the context of your own life

- What specific changes or effects are you hoping for?
- Are there changes or effects that you prefer to avoid?
- Do you anticipate any challenges (e.g., safety, support, sexual health, fertility)?
- Have you thought about how you will address any challenges that come up?

Reasoning about available treatment options

- How would this intervention support your gender embodiment goals?
- Have you considered any alternatives to this intervention?
- How might this intervention affect your future options (e.g., family creation, other gender embodiment care)?
- If this intervention does not work as expected, what might you do?

Communicating a well-reasoned choice that is aligned with your values

- Have you made a decision about whether or when you would like to start this intervention?
- How has your thinking about this intervention evolved?
- How would this intervention fit with other steps you have taken (or plan to take) to support your gender embodiment?
- Why do you think this intervention may be the right choice for you?

Note. Adapted from *Evaluating Decision Making Capacity for Gender Embodiment Healthcare Interventions*, by D. B. A. Clark and A. Virani, 2024, Provincial Health Services Authority Ethics Service and the University of British Columbia (https://www.transcarebc.ca/sites/default/files/2024-11/EvaluatingDecision-makingCapacity.pdf).

REFERENCES

American Medical Association. (2016). *Code of medical ethics*. https://code-medical-ethics.ama-assn.org/

American Medical Association. (2024). *Health care advocacy*. https://www.ama-assn.org/advocacy

American Nurses Association. (2015). *Code of ethics for nurses with interpretive statements*. https://www.nursingworld.org/practice-policy/nursing-excellence/ethics/code-of-ethics-for-nurses/

American Psychological Association. (n.d.). *Advocacy*. https://www.apaservices.org/advocacy

American Psychological Association. (2017). *Ethical principles of psychologists and code of conduct* (2002, amended effective June 1, 2010, and January 1, 2017). https://www.apa.org/ethics/code/

Ashley, F. (2024). Parental rights over transgender youth: Furthering a pressing and substantial objective? *Alberta Law Review*, *62*(1), 87–120. https://doi.org/10.29173/alr2797

Baldwin, C. (2015). Narrative ethics for narrative care. *Journal of Aging Studies*, *34*, 183–189. https://doi.org/10.1016/j.jaging.2015.02.014

Beauchamp, T. L., & Childress, J. F. (2013). *Principles of biomedical ethics* (7th ed.). Oxford University Press.

Beracochea, E., Weinstein, C., & Evans, D. (2010). *Rights-based approaches to public health*. Springer.

Bergum, V. (2013). Relational ethics for health care. In J. L. Storch, P. Rodney, & R. Starzomski (Eds.), *Toward a moral horizon: Nursing ethics for leadership and practice* (2nd ed., pp. 127–142). Pearson.

Bernhardt, C., Forgetta, S., & Sualp, K. (2021). Violations of health as a human right and moral distress: Considerations for social work practice and education. *Journal of Human Rights and Social Work*, *6*(1), 91–96. https://doi.org/10.1007/s41134-020-00150-0

Brody, H., & Clark, M. (2014). Narrative ethics: A narrative. *Hastings Center Report*, *44*(1 Suppl.), S7–S11. https://doi.org/10.1002/hast.261

Brünig, L., Kahrass, H., & Salloch, S. (2024). The concept of intersectionality in bioethics: A systematic review. *BMC Medical Ethics*, *25*(1), 64. https://doi.org/10.1186/s12910-024-01057-5

Canadian Medical Association. (2004). *CMA code of ethics*. https://www.cma.ca/En/Pages/code-of-ethics.aspx

Canadian Medical Protective Association. (2022). *Informed consent: Helping patients make informed decisions*. https://www.cmpa-acpm.ca/en/education-events/good-practices/physician-patient/informed-consent

Canadian Medical Protective Association. (2024). *Consent: A guide for Canadian physicians*. https://www.cmpa-acpm.ca/en/advice-publications/handbooks/consent-a-guide-for-canadian-physicians#intro

Canadian Nurses Association. (2017). *Code of ethics for registered nurses*. https://www.cna-aiic.ca/en/nursing/regulated-nursing-in-canada/nursing-ethics

Canadian Psychiatric Association. (n.d.). *What do we advocate for?* https://www.cpa-apc.org/news-policy-advocacy/advocacy-policy/what-do-we-advocate-for/

Chaddha, R., & Agrawal, G. (2023). Ethics and morality. *Indian Journal of Orthopaedics*, *57*(11), 1707–1713. https://doi.org/10.1007/s43465-023-01004-3

Chochinov, H. M. (2010). Humility and the practice of medicine: Tasting humble pie. *Canadian Medical Association Journal, 182*(11), 1217–1218. https://doi.org/10.1503/cmaj.100874

Clark, D. B. A. (2021). Narratives of regret: Resisting cisnormative and bionormative biases in fertility and family creation counseling for transgender youth. *International Journal of Feminist Approaches to Bioethics, 14*(2), 157–179. https://doi.org/10.3138/ijfab-14.2.09

Clark, D. B. A., Veale, J. F., Greyson, D., & Saewyc, E. (2018). Primary care access and foregone care: A survey of transgender adolescents and young adults. *Family Practice, 35*(3), 302–306. https://doi.org/10.1093/fampra/cmx112

Clark, D. B. A., & Virani, A. (2021). "This wasn't a split-second decision": An empirical ethical analysis of transgender youth capacity, rights, and authority to consent to hormone therapy. *Journal of Bioethical Inquiry, 18*(1), 151–164. https://doi.org/10.1007/s11673-020-10086-9

Clark, D. B. A., & Virani, A. (2024). *Evaluating decision-making capacity for gender-affirming medical interventions* (2nd ed.). Provincial Health Services Authority Ethics Service. https://www.transcarebc.ca/sites/default/files/2024-11/EvaluatingDecision-makingCapacity.pdf

Cohen, J., & van der Meulen Rodgers, Y. (2023). An intersectional analysis of long COVID prevalence. *International Journal for Equity in Health, 22*(1), 261. https://doi.org/10.1186/s12939-023-02072-5

Coleman, E., Radix, A. E., Bouman, W. P., Brown, G. R., de Vries, A. L. C., Deutsch, M. B., Ettner, R., Fraser, L., Goodman, M., Green, J., Hancock, A. B., Johnson, T. W., Karasic, D. H., Knudson, G. A., Leibowitz, S. F., Meyer-Bahlburg, H. F. L., Monstrey, S. J., Motmans, J., Nahata, L., . . . Arcelus, J. (2022). Standards of care for the health of transgender and gender diverse people, version 8. *International Journal of Transgender Health, 23*(Suppl. 1), S1–S259. https://doi.org/10.1080/26895269.2022.2100644

Costello, C. G. (2020). Beyond binary sex and gender ideology. In N. Boero & K. Mason (Eds.), *The Oxford handbook of the sociology of body and embodiment* (pp. 199–220). Oxford University Press. https://doi.org/10.1093/oxfordhb/9780190842475.013.14

Coughlin, K. W. (2018). Medical decision-making in paediatrics: Infancy to adolescence. *Paediatrics & Child Health, 23*(2), 138–146. https://doi.org/10.1093/pch/pxx127

Cummings, C. L., & Mercurio, M. R. (2010). Ethics for the pediatrician: Autonomy, beneficence, and rights. *Pediatrics in Review, 31*(6), 252–255. https://doi.org/10.1542/pir.31.6.252

Dickens, B. M., & Cook, R. J. (2000). The scope and limits of conscientious objection. *International Journal of Gynecology & Obstetrics, 71*(1), 71–77. https://doi.org/10.1016/S0020-7292(00)00330-1

Diekema, D. S. (2011). Revisiting the best interest standard: Uses and misuses. *The Journal of Clinical Ethics, 22*(2), 128–133. https://doi.org/10.1086/jce201122204

Dzeng, E., & Wachter, R. M. (2020). Ethics in conflict: Moral distress as a root cause of burnout. *Journal of General Internal Medicine, 35*(2), 409–411. https://doi.org/10.1007/s11606-019-05505-6

Eisenberg, M. E., Gower, A. L., McMorris, B. J., Rider, G. N., Shea, G., & Coleman, E. (2017). Risk and protective factors in the lives of transgender/gender nonconforming adolescents. *Journal of Adolescent Health*, *61*(4), 521–526. https://doi.org/10.1016/j.jadohealth.2017.04.014

Faissner, M., Brünig, L., Gaillard, A. S., Jieman, A. T., Gather, J., & Hempeler, C. (2024). Intersectionality as a tool for clinical ethics consultation in mental healthcare. *Philosophy, Ethics, and Humanities in Medicine*, *19*(1), 6. https://doi.org/10.1186/s13010-024-00156-w

Feil, K., Riedl, D., Böttcher, B., Fuchs, M., Kapelari, K., Gräßer, S., Toth, B., & Lampe, A. (2023). Higher prevalence of adverse childhood experiences in transgender than in cisgender individuals: Results from a single-center observational study. *Journal of Clinical Medicine*, *12*(13), 4501. https://doi.org/10.3390/jcm12134501

Fernandez-Parsons, R., Rodriguez, L., & Goyal, D. (2013). Moral distress in emergency nurses. *Journal of Emergency Nursing*, *39*(6), 547–552. https://doi.org/10.1016/j.jen.2012.12.009

Frader, J. E. (1992). Political and interpersonal aspects of ethics consultation. *Theoretical Medicine*, *13*(1), 31–44. https://doi.org/10.1007/BF00489218

Glick, J. L., Lopez, A., Pollock, M., & Theall, K. P. (2020). Housing insecurity and intersecting social determinants of health among transgender people in the USA: A targeted ethnography. *International Journal of Transgender Health*, *21*(3), 337–349. https://www.tandfonline.com/doi/abs/10.1080/26895269.2020.1780661

Gonzales, G., & Henning-Smith, C. (2017). Barriers to care among transgender and gender nonconforming adults. *The Milbank Quarterly*, *95*(4), 726–748. https://doi.org/10.1111/1468-0009.12297

Gonzales, G., Wilder, J., & Tran, N. (2024). Disparities in mental health and the social determinants of health among privately insured transgender patients in the United States. *European Journal of Public Health*, *34*(Suppl. 3), ckae144.064. https://doi.org/10.1093/eurpub/ckae144.064

Goodlander, E. C., & Berg, J. W. (2011). Pediatric decision-making: Adolescent patients. In D. S. Diekema, M. R. Mercurio, & M. B. Adam (Eds.), *Clinical ethics in pediatrics: A case-based textbook* (pp. 7–13). Cambridge University Press. https://doi.org/10.1017/cbo9780511740336.003

Grootens-Wiegers, P., Hein, I. M., van den Broek, J. M., & de Vries, M. C. (2017). Medical decision-making in children and adolescents: Developmental and neuroscientific aspects. *BMC Pediatrics*, *17*(1), 120. https://doi.org/10.1186/s12887-017-0869-x

Grzanka, P. R., Brian, J. D., & Shim, J. K. (2016). My bioethics will be intersectional or it will be [bleep]. *The American Journal of Bioethics*, *16*(4), 27–29. https://doi.org/10.1080/15265161.2016.1145289

Gzesh, A. S., Prince, D., Jelinek, S. K., Hillier, A., Kattari, S. K., Shelton, J., & Paceley, M. S. (2024). "Death threats and despair": A conceptual model delineating moral distress experienced by pediatric gender-affirming care providers. *Social Sciences & Humanities Open*, *9*, 100867. https://doi.org/10.1016/j.ssaho.2024.100867

Harrison, C., Canadian Paediatric Society, & Bioethics Committee. (2004). Treatment decisions regarding infants, children and adolescents. *Paediatrics & Child Health*, *9*(2), 99–103. https://doi.org/10.1093/pch/9.2.99

Hastings, J., Bobb, C., Wolfe, M., Amaro Jimenez, Z., & St. Amand, C. (2021). Medical care for nonbinary youth: Individualized gender care beyond a binary framework. *Pediatric Annals*, *50*(9), e384–e390. https://doi.org/10.3928/19382359-20210818-03

Hendricks, M. L., & Testa, R. J. (2012). A conceptual framework for clinical work with transgender and gender nonconforming clients: An adaptation of the minority stress model. *Professional Psychology: Research and Practice, 43*(5), 460–467. https://doi.org/10.1037/a0029597

Hidalgo, M. A., Ehrensaft, D., Tishelman, A. C., Clark, L. F., Garofalo, R., Rosenthal, S. M., Spack, N. P., & Olson, J. (2013). The gender affirmative model: What we know and what we aim to learn. *Human Development, 56*(5), 285–290. https://doi.org/10.1159/000355235

Hughes, L. D., Kidd, K. M., Gamarel, K. E., Operario, D., & Dowshen, N. (2021). "These laws will be devastating": Provider perspectives on legislation banning gender-affirming care for transgender adolescents. *Journal of Adolescent Health, 69*(6), 976–982. https://doi.org/10.1016/j.jadohealth.2021.08.020

Huxtable, R. (2013). For and against the four principles of biomedical ethics. *Clinical Ethics, 8*(2–3), 39–43. https://doi.org/10.1177/1477750913486245

Jameton, A. (1984). *Nursing practice: The ethical issues*. Prentice-Hall.

Jonsen, A. R., Siegler, M., & Winslade, W. J. (Eds.). (2015). *Clinical ethics: A practical approach to ethical decisions in clinical medicine* (8th ed.). McGraw-Hill Education.

Kopelman, L. M. (2007). The best interests standard for incompetent or incapacitated persons of all ages. *The Journal of Law, Medicine & Ethics, 35*(1), 187–196. https://doi.org/10.1111/j.1748-720X.2007.00123.x

Kraschel, K. L., Chen, A., Turban, J. L., & Cohen, I. G. (2022). Legislation restricting gender-affirming care for transgender youth: Politics eclipse healthcare. *Cell Reports Medicine, 3*(8), 100719. https://doi.org/10.1016/j.xcrm.2022.100719

Lepore, C., Alstott, A., & McNamara, M. (2022). Scientific misinformation is criminalizing the standard of care for transgender youth. *JAMA Pediatrics, 176*(10), 965–966. https://doi.org/10.1001/jamapediatrics.2022.2959

Lindemann, H. (2014). When stories go wrong. *Hastings Center Report, 44*(1 Suppl.), S28–S31. https://doi.org/10.1002/hast.266

Lo, B. (2013). *Resolving ethical dilemmas: A guide for clinicians* (5th ed.). Lippincott Williams & Wilkins.

Mabel, H., Morley, G., Jensen, V. K., Sankary, L. R., Wimbiscus, M., Cartaya, J., & Rome, E. S. (2022). Clinician and ethicist perspectives: Understanding moral distress in gender-affirming care for pediatric patients. *The Journal of Pediatrics, 240*, 265–271. https://doi.org/10.1016/j.jpeds.2021.10.059

Malek, J. (2009). What really is in a child's best interest? Toward a more precise picture of the interests of children. *The Journal of Clinical Ethics, 20*(2), 175–182. https://doi.org/10.1086/jce200920212

Marway, H., & Widdows, H. (2015). Philosophical feminist bioethics: Past, present, and future. *Cambridge Quarterly of Healthcare Ethics, 24*(2), 165–174. https://doi.org/10.1017/s0963180114000474

Matthews, R. (2024). The moral asymmetry of conscientious provision and conscientious refusal: Insights from oppression and allyship. *International Journal of Feminist Approaches to Bioethics, 17*(1), 49–72. https://doi.org/10.3138/ijfab-2023-0005

McNamara, M., Lepore, C., Alstott, A., Kamody, R., Kuper, L., Szilagyi, N., Boulware, S., & Olezeski, C. (2022). Scientific misinformation and gender affirming care: Tools for providers on the front lines. *Journal of Adolescent Health, 71*(3), 251–253. https://doi.org/10.1016/j.jadohealth.2022.06.008

Melia, K. (Ed.). (2014). Rights-based ethics. In *Ethics for nursing and healthcare practice* (pp. 109–122). Sage. https://doi.org/10.4135/9781526435903.n8

Montello, M. (2014). Narrative ethics. *Hastings Center Report*, *44*(1 Suppl.), S2–S6. https://doi.org/10.1002/hast.260

Moore, J., Engel, J., & Prentice, D. (2014). Relational ethics in everyday practice. *Canadian Oncology Nursing Journal*, *24*(1), 31–34. https://doi.org/10.5737/1181912x2413134

National Association of Social Workers. (2021). *Code of ethics*. https://www.socialworkers.org/About/Ethics/Code-of-Ethics/Code-of-Ethics-English

Office of the United Nations High Commissioner for Human Rights. (2008). *The right to health: Fact sheet no. 31*. http://www.ohchr.org/Documents/Publications/Factsheet31.pdf

Palmer, B. W., & Harmell, A. L. (2016). Assessment of healthcare decision-making capacity. *Archives of Clinical Neuropsychology*, *31*(6), 530–540. https://doi.org/10.1093/arclin/acw051

Peel, M. (2005). Human rights and medical ethics. *Journal of the Royal Society of Medicine*, *98*(4), 171–173. https://doi.org/10.1177/014107680509800412

Post, L. F., & Blustein, J. (Eds.). (2015). Ethical foundations of clinical practice. In *Handbook for health care ethics committees* (2nd ed., pp. 3–16). Johns Hopkins University Press.

Ravindranath, O., Perica, M. I., Parr, A. C., Ojha, A., McKeon, S. D., Montano, G., Ullendorff, N., Luna, B., & Edmiston, E. K. (2024). Adolescent neurocognitive development and decision-making abilities regarding gender-affirming care. *Developmental Cognitive Neuroscience*, *67*, 101351. https://doi.org/10.1016/j.dcn.2024.101351

Ray, K. S. (2021). It's time for a Black bioethics. *The American Journal of Bioethics*, *21*(2), 38–40. https://doi.org/10.1080/15265161.2020.1861381

Reisner, S. L., Greytak, E. A., Parsons, J. T., & Ybarra, M. L. (2015). Gender minority social stress in adolescence: Disparities in adolescent bullying and substance use by gender identity. *The Journal of Sex Research*, *52*(3), 243–256. https://doi.org/10.1080/00224499.2014.886321

Ruhe, K. M., Wangmo, T., Badarau, D. O., Elger, B. S., & Niggli, F. (2015). Decision-making capacity of children and adolescents—Suggestions for advancing the concept's implementation in pediatric healthcare. *European Journal of Pediatrics*, *174*(6), 775–782. https://doi.org/10.1007/s00431-014-2462-8

Scheim, A. I., Rich, A. J., Zubizarreta, D., Malik, M., Baker, K. E., Restar, A. J., van der Merwe, L. A., Wang, J., Beebe, B., Ridgeway, K., Baral, S. D., Poteat, T., & Reisner, S. L. (2024). Health status of transgender people globally: A systematic review of research on disease burden and correlates. *PLOS One*, *19*(3), e0299373. https://doi.org/10.1371/journal.pone.0299373

Silverman, H. J., Kheirbek, R. E., Moscou-Jackson, G., & Day, J. (2021). Moral distress in nurses caring for patients with Covid-19. *Nursing Ethics*, *28*(7–8), 1137–1164. https://doi.org/10.1177/09697330211003217

Sriharan, A., West, K. J., Almost, J., & Hamza, A. (2021). COVID-19-related occupational burnout and moral distress among nurses: A rapid scoping review. *Nursing Leadership*, *34*(1), 7–19. https://doi.org/10.12927/cjnl.2021.26459

Testa, R. J., Michaels, M. S., Bliss, W., Rogers, M. L., Balsam, K. F., & Joiner, T. (2017). Suicidal ideation in transgender people: Gender minority stress and interpersonal theory factors. *Journal of Abnormal Psychology, 126*(1), 125–136. https://doi.org/10.1037/abn0000234

Unguru, D. S. (2011). Pediatric decision-making: Informed consent, parental permission, and child assent. In D. S. Diekema, M. R. Mercurio, & M. B. Adam (Eds.), *Clinical ethics in pediatrics: A case-based textbook* (pp. 1–6). Cambridge University Press. https://doi.org/10.1017/cbo9780511740336.002

United Nations. (1948). *Universal declaration of human rights*. https://www.un.org/en/about-us/universal-declaration-of-human-rights

United Nations. (1989). *Convention on the rights of the child*. https://www.ohchr.org/en/professionalinterest/pages/crc.aspx

United Nations. (2007). *United Nations declaration on the rights of Indigenous peoples*. https://www.un.org/development/desa/indigenouspeoples/wp-content/uploads/sites/19/2018/11/UNDRIP_E_web.pdf

Weithorn, L. A., & Campbell, S. B. (1982). The competency of children and adolescents to make informed treatment decisions. *Child Development, 53*(6), 1589–1598. https://doi.org/10.2307/1130087

Wilson, Y., White, A., Jefferson, A., & Danis, M. (2019). Intersectionality in clinical medicine: The need for a conceptual framework. *American Journal of Bioethics, 19*(2), 8–19. https://doi.org/10.1080/15265161.2018.1557275

World Professional Association for Transgender Health. (n.d.). *WPATH/USPATH public statements*. https://www.wpath.org/policies

CONCLUSION

Where Do We Go From Here?

DIANE EHRENSAFT, COLT ST. AMAND, AND G. NIC RIDER

All of us are put in boxes by our family, by our religion, by our society, our moment in history, even our own bodies. Some people have the courage to break free.

—Geena Rocero, *Horse Barbie*

In 2018, the first edition of this book (*The Gender Affirmative Model: An Interdisciplinary Approach to Supporting Transgender and Gender Expansive Children*; Keo-Meier & Ehrensaft, 2018) was published in the midst of the first Trump administration. We wrote at that time: "We presently live under a federal administration that appears to be intent on dismantling some of the important gains made for transgender people of all ages" (Keo-Meier & Ehrensaft, 2018, p. 209). We could never have known how prescient that sentiment would be for the future as well. Seven years later, as we finish the closing lines of the revised edition of this volume (now retitled *Pediatric Gender Health Care: The Gender Affirmative Model Revisited*), we have entered the second iteration of a Trump administration, whose members are more intent and vocal than ever in

https://doi.org/10.1037/0000494-014
Pediatric Gender Health Care: The Gender Affirmative Model Revisited, Second Edition, G. N. Rider, D. Ehrensaft, and C. St. Amand (Editors)

eliminating pediatric gender care and attacking transgender and gender diverse (TGD) people from every angle—from bathroom access to participation in sports, to pediatric gender health care, to transgender people's participation in the military, to books children can read in the library, to topics they can learn in the classroom, and to privacy they can have at school.

Indeed, we write this conclusion as three professionals in the United States at a moment in history where an administration that has taken over is pledging to put a stop to gender affirmative care for minors. Hopefully, the chapters in this volume will demonstrate how harmful this would be if it were to come to fruition for the children, for their families, for the TGD community, and for society at large. As authors and editors, our greatest hope is that when readers arrive at our closing chapter, our collective group of providers, researchers, and advocates, coming from diverse genders ourselves, in their wisdom, have been able to dispel myths and replace them with the principles, the tenets, the science, the practice, and the ethics of client-centered care for TGD children and their families. We also hope that our documentation of the efficacy of pediatric gender health care and the means for implementing it will spur us all to action. Our ongoing work is to stretch beyond the boxes we have been put in, recognizing the importance of keeping going in our work and pouring every effort into putting a stop to blockades to the multidimensional care we all provide, a blockade that would put a whole generation of children at risk, not to mention their families and the communities surrounding them.

As we scan the 8 years from the publication of the first edition of *The Gender Affirmative Model* (Keo-Meier & Ehrensaft, 2018) to the completion of this edition, we have come to realize how much more we have learned and how much more the youth have to teach us about the best and essential means for promoting gender health, defined as the opportunity for every child and adult to live in the gender authentic to them scaffolded by acceptance and shielded from aspersion. Despite rumors to the contrary, research abounds, pediatric gender health programs are expanding across the globe, and more scientific data and research observations fortify knowledge many of us, certainly the authors of this volume, have held for many years: The opportunity for children to be listened to and supported as they consolidate their gender selves promotes physical, psychological, social, and spiritual well-being. Efforts to squelch those opportunities put children at increased risk for stress, psychological challenges, and adverse physical and mental health outcomes.

As more time has passed to implement the gender affirmative model in the field of gender health, we also recognize with cultural humility that our framework is a living growing organism that will evolve over time in the context of scientific discovery and historical changes:

> Gender stress, gender distress, gender dysphoria, and gender resilience have been woven together to create the fabric of the myriad banners of gender exploration and gender consolidation under which we do our work as gender affirmative mental health professionals. Yet any good professional will carry with them a healthy dosage of agnosticism—we know what we know but we also know that what we know today may not prove to be true tomorrow, or was clearer to us than it ought to have been. (Keo-Meier & Ehrensaft, 2018, p. 209)

With that said, what do we need to learn as we move forward and establish where to go from here?

HAVE WE CROSSED A GENDER THRESHOLD?

The term *liminal* derives from the Latin word *threshold*. *Liminal space* is defined as the actual space or time in which you shift from one phase to another. Historical examples of liminal space include when people first learned that the earth was round rather than flat; when scribes were replaced with printing presses; when industrial machines reduced the need for manual labor; when computers replaced typewriters; and most recently, when artificial intelligence (AI) appears to be overtaking the human brain. What all these historical examples have in common is the fear by so many people that civilization was now about to go to hell in a handbasket—until they adjusted to the change (Ehrensaft & Jurkiewicz, 2024).

And the change was never at rapid speed. It was established in the third century that the earth was round, but it took until the 15th century for people to commonly accept it. In the 15th century, after the printing of the *Gutenberg Bible*, it was argued that the printing press would never last and that handwritten paper manuscripts were morally superior to mechanically produced documents. It took more than a few centuries to overcome that sentiment. During the Industrial Revolution, the Luddites made their mark in the early 19th century as a group of English workers who attacked factories and destroyed machinery as a means of protest against the destruction of the cottage textile industry in which cloth was made by hand. To this day, we still have Luddites, now defined as a person who is opposed to technological change.

So, let us review. In the 21st century, it is now commonly accepted that the earth is round; very few people opt for a handwritten text over a mass-produced book or prefer a manual typewriter over a computer to write a document.

People have accepted an automated society. AI—the jury's out on that one, but it seems like only a few are fleeing from ChatGPT, Copilot, or Claude.

Now, throw gender into the mix. In Western culture, gender in all its combinations and permutations is replacing gender in two boxes with its rigid rules and regulations—albeit that in other cultures and other historical times, gender outside boxes is nothing new. Are we caught in a liminal space, or have we already crossed the threshold with no turning back? History will tell, but in learning from the past and clarifying the present, as we project into the future, all signs point in the direction of a gender evolution that is now crystallizing into a more radical gender revolution. The revolution is led by the children—the next generation—with the adults sometimes chasing behind. We appear to have a revolution that makes some people so anxious that they lose their capacity for learning, reflection, and compassion. Given time, people learn, regain their footing, and absorb new information, and change prevails. Historically, here is where the gender affirmative model finds itself—carried forward and advanced in the era of a new zeitgeist of gender.

THE 21ST CENTURY ZEITGEIST OF GENDER

When four pediatric gender clinics expanded to more than 60 within a decade in the United States, it was apparent that something was afoot. Throw a dart at a date in history, and you will discover a zeitgeist: the spirit of the age, the invisible force or agent dominating the characteristic of a given era in world history. It would not be far-fetched to assert that gender has become a central component of the Western zeitgeist as the 21st century has rolled out. For example, hardly a day goes by without reference to a gender-related issue across all media outlets.

This new zeitgeist of gender is faced with challenges from those who work desperately to turn the clock back to something more knowable and predictable where boys would be boys and girls would be girls, and never the twain shall cross. When groups of us first got together to co-construct a gender affirmative model of care for children of all genders, we never imagined that we would end up being accused of being wizards or rubber stampers: wizards who have the power to turn boys into girls and girls into boys; or rubber stampers who need only to hear one sentence coming from the mouth of a youth to give them a green light to legally change their name and gender markers and receive medical interventions for their gender—whether puberty suppression, gender-affirming hormones that replace testosterone for estrogen or estrogen for testosterone, or even surgeries. We can say with assurance that unlike Cinderella's fairy godmother who could turn a pumpkin into a carriage, no provider possesses a magic wand that can transform boys into girls or girls into boys or into some other iteration of gender. The only person who holds that power is the child themself as they consolidate their gender self. As for being rubber stampers, regretfully, we cannot say with the same assurance that no provider has ever rubber-stamped a youth's gender requests without first taking a deep dive to listen, understand, and get that youth's gender in focus, with a goal of setting up a positive gender health plan. For those providers, we hope the information in this book will reflect the new zeitgeist of gender and provide a comprehensive guidebook for the gender affirmative model in all its iterations—in our offices, in the community, and in society at large.

WHAT HAVE WE LEARNED, AND WHAT IS YET TO KNOW?

To say that we finish this volume with no unanswered questions would be to turn our backs on the beauty and significance of never-ending evaluative endeavors. In the first edition of this book (Keo-Meier & Ehrensaft, 2018), we wrapped up with questions still to be explored:

1. How exactly does gender unfold in a young child so that some children follow a pathway that aligns their designated sex with their self-defined gender, while others carve a path in which their self-defined gender is not concordant with sex designated at birth?
2. If gender is a state of mind rather than a physiological state, would it not be better to assume no gender at all until a child has the capacity to exercise that mind and communicate to others what their mind tells them about their own gender?
3. Should young children be allowed or encouraged to socially transition from one gender to another, or does it risk locking them into a fixed gender identity prematurely?
4. Why does a child have to change their name to authenticate their gender; why can't Susie just be a person's name rather than a girl's name, and why does someone have to grow breasts to claim their female self?
5. What is gender anyway? Who says so? What responsibility do we have for shaping that conversation and challenging our own protocols that may inadvertently endorse outmoded binary modes of gender identity and expression?

We feel confident that each of these questions has been addressed in one form or another throughout the chapters of this book, from our exploration of gender development to our understanding of the importance of social transitions for gender and overall well-being; to the ability of a young child, when listened to and supported, to articulate the gender they know themself to be; to the importance of facilitating that supportive function in parents; and to the critical need to explore our own implicit or explicit biases if we are to support children in their gender development and identity formation.

So, what are our questions for the future, questions that anyone having read this volume might want to take up under their own banner of investigation? They are not exhaustive at all, but here is a sampling:

1. We cannot time travel into the future, but as more children have grown up receiving the benefits of affirming gender care as it has evolved in the 21st century, we can begin to ask: What is the life experience of these children as they reach age 30, 40, 50, and beyond? Do they continue to evolve into different gender selves, or do they remain consistent with their childhood iteration?

2. Again, looking into the future, if children entered puberty and received puberty blockers and/or gender-affirming hormones before age 18, how have those interventions served them over the course of their lives?

3. We have identified social transition as a nonmedical gender-affirming possibility for TGD children, but do we have more work to do breaking down social transition into its many components and identifying separate groups of children, groups that might be differentiated by the means in which they execute that transition and the meaning underlying those means? For example, a child may in no way change their gender expressions or choose a new name but benefit from a gender marker change, whereas another child cannot feel fully comfortable in their gender until they do a full sweep of gender presentation, name and pronoun change, disclosure to others, and legal name and gender marker changes. To date, we often use the assessment *complete/partial/no* social transition. Years of clinical observation are teaching us that this approach provides only a very rough cut and does not totally get its finger on the pulse of the various pathways a child travels to live most confidently and comfortably in their gender.

4. A report released by Hilary Cass (2024) to the U.K. National Health Service, known as the Cass review, purported to have provided a comprehensive review of pediatric gender care and proffering recommendations for care in stark opposition to the wisdom shared by the gender experts throughout the chapters of our book. Soon after, the U.S. Department

of Health and Human Services (2025) produced its own 400-plus page report, relying heavily on the Cass review, to make its own recommendations for shutting down pediatric gender health programs in our country. In the face of assertions found in these reports that research on pediatric gender care meeting the scientific standards of reliability and validity is nonexistent, what do we need to do to (a) demonstrate that this is not a true statement, and (b) push against outmoded and restrictive definitions of so-called scientific research and the measures we use to evaluate research? How can we help others understand that research on human beings in the context of their social environments must be measured by other standards than archaic ones that insist, for example, that only with a randomized control group and ideally a double-blind study can we accept the findings of research on treatment effectiveness, a research protocol that would be unthinkable if it meant denying children the care they need?

5. In the context of the adverse political climate in which we finish the final pages of this book, what are our clinical and ethical obligations to ensure pediatric gender care is in the best interests of children and protects them from harm even when we find such care is legally barred by government entities, both in our own country and around the globe?

A PEDIATRIC GENDER HEALTH SPECIALIST'S WORK IS NEVER DONE

In the 21st century zeitgeist of gender, we are aware that when it comes to the efficacy of pediatric gender health care, the train has left the station, there is no turning back, and this way of conceptualizing and actualizing the gender health of all children, meaning a framework that is inherently gender affirming, is here to stay. Yet there are those who will attempt to throw logs across the way to stop us in our tracks and prevent us from moving forward in the care of TGD children. Logs are movable, and although it may take heavy lifting, removing those logs or preventing them from being heaved onto the tracks in the first place is simply one thing to add to the tasks of our interdisciplinary, community-embedded model of care. We hope we have provided sufficient evidence that in this moment of history the gender affirmative model continues to be the optimal practice modality for ensuring the gender health of all our TGD children and youth. Again, let us remind ourselves that people are throwing those logs on the tracks not because the train must be stopped before it kills someone, but because the form of treatment we have presented in the pages of this book is ascendant and powerful, making many people, perhaps we could call them "gender Luddites," anxious.

But just as each child's gender is an interweaving of nature, nurture, and culture, over time, so too is the evolution of our framework of care. As the social milieu changes, as science uncovers more of nature and nurture's interwoven contributions to gender development, and as our own gender literacy expands and grows, we must leave room for alterations in pediatric gender care to meet the evolving tapestries of gender. Let the work never be done.

REFERENCES

Cass, H. (2024, December). *Independent review of gender identity services for children and young people: Final report.* https://cass.independent-review.uk/home/publications/final-report/

Ehrensaft, D., & Jurkiewicz, M. (2024). *Gender explained: A new understanding of identity in a gender creative world.* The Experiment.

Keo-Meier, C., & Ehrensaft, D. (Eds.). (2018). *The gender affirmative model: An interdisciplinary approach to supporting transgender and gender expansive children.* American Psychological Association. https://doi.org/10.1037/0000095-000

U.S. Department of Health and Human Services. (2025, May 1). *Treatment for pediatric gender dysphoria: Review of evidence and best practices.* https://opa.hhs.gov/gender-dysphoria-report

Index

A

B

C

D

H

I

J

K

L

M

N

O

P

R

S

About the Editors

G. Nic Rider, PhD, LP, (they/them), is an associate professor and licensed psychologist at the Eli Coleman Institute for Sexual and Gender Health and director of the National Center for Gender Health, which are both housed within the University of Minnesota Medical School. They received a doctorate in counseling psychology from Howard University in Washington, DC. Their research broadly focuses on improving health care for and exploring resilience among marginalized communities, with a focus on sexual and gender diverse people of color. They often focus on social and structural factors impacting the lived experiences and well-being of historically excluded communities, emphasizing community strengths, resilience, and advocacy. Dr. Rider's clinical training includes psychotherapy and assessment experiences in a university counseling center, as well as hospital, private practice, community clinic, residential treatment, and juvenile justice settings. Their professional interests include intersectionality, culturally responsive care, health equity, pleasure, systems change, and social justice advocacy. They serve as president of American Psychological Association Division 44 (The Society for the Psychology of Sexual Orientation and Gender Diversity), on the board of directors for The Society for the Scientific Study of Sexuality, and on the World Association for Sexual Health Advisory Committee. They are also a coauthor of the World Professional Association for Transgender Health's (WPATH) Standards of Care for the Health of Transgender and Gender Diverse People, version 8 (SOC8), and a certified mentor and faculty member at the WPATH Gender Education Institute.

Diane Ehrensaft, PhD, (she/her), is a developmental and clinical psychologist, adjunct professor of pediatrics at University of California San Francisco (UCSF), and director of mental health at the Child and Adolescent Gender Center, UCSF Benioff Children's Hospital. She specializes in research, writing, clinical work, training, consultation, expert witness testimony related to gender diverse children and youth, publishing and lecturing nationally and internationally on gender diversity, gender development, and the role of assisted reproductive technology in family building. Dr. Ehrensaft has served as co-investigator in a four-site National Institutes of Health grant, studying the effects of puberty blockers and gender-affirming hormones in gender diverse and transgender youth; and as principal investigator in a companion four-site grant, The Gender Journey Project, studying the psychological experiences of prepubertal gender diverse children. She is a coauthor of the World Professional Association for Transgender Health's (WPATH) Standards of Care for the Health of Transgender and Gender Diverse People, version 8 (SOC8) and a faculty member of the WPATH Gender Education Institute. Dr. Ehrensaft is a founder of Mind the Gap, a Child and Adolescent Gender Center community consortium of mental health pediatric gender health providers in the San Francisco Bay Area and beyond.

Colt St. Amand, PhD, MD, (he/they), is a child and family clinical psychologist, board-certified family medicine physician, and founder and medical director of Riverside Family Medicine. He was born and raised in Texas, where he survived 13 years of Catholic schooling and then completed his undergraduate studies at Rice University, PhD at the University of Houston, Interprofessional LGBT Health Fellowship at the Michael E. DeBakey Veterans Affairs Medical Center, and MD at the University of Texas Medical Branch. He is proud to be an openly transgender-queer two-spirit man who transitioned in the early 2000s. After completing his family medicine residency at the Mayo Clinic, Dr. Colt knew he could not safely practice taking care of transgender young people in his home state of Texas, so he moved to New York to complete the Department of Health AIDS Institute Advanced Transgender Clinical Scholars Fellowship and is now practicing psychology and medicine in upstate New York at Riverside Family Medicine, the first known fully trans-led and trans-run clinic in the United States. Dr. Colt is an internationally recognized expert in research, clinical practice, consultation, and teaching in the field of gender health care, known most for work with youth and the intersection of mental health and medical treatment. Since 2011, he has published over 40 peer-reviewed research articles in the fields of gender health and sexual health. He served as a Transgender Health ECHO faculty member on the Northwest Portland Area Indian Health Board. Dr. Colt is a coauthor of the World Professional Association for Transgender Health's (WPATH) Standards of Care for the Health of Transgender and Gender Diverse People, version 8 (SOC8) and a mental health and medical certification mentor at the WPATH Gender Education Institute. To learn more, visit The Gender Doctor (https://www.thegenderdoctor.com) or Riverside Family Medicine (https://www.riversidedpc.com/).